D0845361

YOU KNOW MY STEEZ: AN ETHNOGRAPHIC AND SOCIOLINGUISTIC STUDY OF STYLESHIFTING IN A BLACK AMERICAN SPEECH COMMUNITY

YOU KNOW MY STEEZ: AN ETHNOGRAPHIC AND SOCIOLINGUISTIC STUDY OF STYLESHIFTING IN A BLACK AMERICAN SPEECH COMMUNITY

H. SAMY ALIM

University of California, Los Angeles

Publication of the
American Dialect Society

•

Number 89

•

Published by Duke University Press
for the American Dialect Society

Annual Supplement to American Speech

PUBLICATION OF THE AMERICAN DIALECT SOCIETY

RONALD R. BUTTERS, Editor, *Duke University*
CHARLES E. CARSON, Managing Editor, *Duke University*

Number 89

ISBN: 0-8223-6608-8

Library of Congress Cataloging-in-Publication Data

Alim, H. Samy
You know my steez : an ethnographic and sociolinguistic study of styleshifting in a Black American speech community / H. Samy Alim
p. cm. — (Publication of the American Dialect Society ; no. 89)
Includes bibliographical references
ISBN 0-8223-6608-8 (alk. paper)
1. African American teenagers—Language—Case studies. 2. English language—Spoken English—United States—Case studies. 3. English language—Social aspects—United States—Case studies. 4. English language—Variation—United States—Case studies. 5. African Americans—Languages—Case studies. 6. Black English—California—Case studies. 7. Americanisms—California—Case studies. I. Title. II. Series.

PE3102.N44A44 2004
427'.973'08996073–dc22 2004028246

British Library Cataloguing-in-Publication Data available

The genius of Black people is that you ain't seen rap coming. We keep reinventing ourselves through our expressions. The reality is the different styles that young people invent are an attempt to mark their own particular environments with the style they are accustomed to. And style is an attempt to put your stamp on your existence.... Black people keep inventing and reinventing, asserting and re-asserting so that we can mark our own existence through the prism of style and give some sense to the weightiness of our existence.

—Michael Eric Dyson, June 25, 2000,
in Mount Olive Baptist Church, Fort Lauderdale, Florida

CONTENTS

FOREWORD

You Know My Steez is an exceptional analysis of urban language in use, which builds upon empirical studies of subordinated groups throughout the world. I know Haven High very well, having helped citizens of Sunnyside realize their dream of creating a high-quality college preparatory high school within their urban community: a community that—at the time—did not have a local public high school. H. Samy Alim's ethnosensitivity in this nonwhite community and others (e.g., West Philadelphia) is unsurpassed and displayed with understated elegance throughout this marvelous work. Before Alim ever considered turning the full power of his intellect upon the educational plight of students in America for whom standard English is not native, he was destined for either medical school or a promising career in journalism. These two seemingly divergent paths represent Alim's desire to "help people," a commitment that he has turned to the tools of social science to fulfill. Viewing language as culture and discourse as power, Alim builds upon traditional sociolinguistic studies by turning a more critical lens to the study of speech style. His effort to expose unequal power relations as they are manifested in the minutest syllables of our speech bears fruit in this volume. Alim is emphatic about his quest for linguistic and educational justice for students who are culturally marginalized. He writes with the precision of a disinterested diagnostician, but he never conceals his steadfast desire to devote his social science talents toward the betterment of humankind.

Readers who are familiar with the demographics of urban public school districts in America will recognize many parallels to communities around the world where people who look different, and sound different, from members of the dominant cultures fare less well than do privileged people who are native speakers of the dominant standard dialects. Alim is mindful of the international relevance of this groundbreaking study, which can be recalibrated to support other communities that truly seek to advance what he calls LINGUISTIC EQUANIMITY. As he writes in the preface, "It is my intention to globalize the 'African American question,' so as not to provincialize the complexity of the social, political, economic, and educational issues that impact this community.... The centrality of Black American issues to larger practical and theoretical questions should be evident in this work." Writing with both global consciousness and alliterative lyricism, he points out that the situation in Black America is "deeply and intricately connected to the situation of oppressed peoples worldwide—from West Philly to West Africa to the West Bank."

It has been my pleasure to witness many of Alim's sophisticated intellectual accomplishments, of which *You Know My Steez* represents a formidable milestone. Alim's insights will serve the novice and the cynical veteran of polemical debates that saturate the linguistic literature pertaining to Black Language; that is, its birth, its linguistic structure, and its legal and educational relevance. Students at Haven High were trained by Alim to become young ethnographers, or as he writes, Hiphopographers. He did so as a participant observer in the classical tradition of a teacher/ethnographer/linguistic researcher. As a teacher and resident of the Sunnyside community, Alim was able to collect a vast amount of speech data, only some of which is analyzed in this volume, but all of which helped him gain a better appreciation for the nuances of the way Black people speak their thoughts. Those who are new to studies of Black Language will note that Alim controls his passion for the communities he loves by deftly giving voice to "real talk" among Hip Hop enthusiasts who are pragmatic about their need to survive "in a White man's world." Further, as most readers will realize, Alim's writing style is a remarkable display of styleshifting, navigating between the most technical sociolinguistic and anthropological terminology and the slickest, most streetwise Hip Hop Nation Language. This is not purely an aesthetic choice, but a political one.

Established scholars should note that Alim skillfully builds his analyses in layers that pay explicit tribute to his expansive network of mentors, all of whom study language in anthropological, dialectological, educational, historical, legal, linguistic, philosophical, and sociological detail. As such, the potential audience for this work is vast and highly interdisciplinary. There is a technical, scientific matter of great empirical concern that I dare not neglect: namely, Alim's careful characterization of styleshifting among his high-school students. The methodological rigor evident in this study—through the synergistic use of ethnographic techniques, quantitative sociolinguistic variation, and discourse analysis—was necessary in order to develop the larger theoretical conceptualization of styleshifting as a "dialogic, coconstructed, and continually-developing project." While Alim relentlessly analyzes the sociolinguistic variable, he also goes beyond the variable by adhering to a unified view of language that considers both structure and use. Throughout his work, Alim urges us to view speech style as consisting of both sociolinguistic and interactional dimensions, an approach that is beautifully exemplified in this text.

Those who are unfamiliar with urban Black Language in America will come to learn what members of the Hip Hop Nation have known for many years: namely, that men and women of words still yearn for the peaceful resolution of racial conflicts throughout the world, and it is in the hallowed spirit of that tradition that I am honored to commend *You Know My Steez* with utmost enthusiasm.

JOHN BAUGH
Stanford University
October 12, 2004

PREFACE: REAL TALK

> Have you not heard that words kill as fast as bullets?
>
> —The Rzarector, "Twelve Jewelz," *The Pick, The Sickle, and the Shovel*, 1997

> As history constantly teaches us, discourse is not simply that which translates struggles or systems of domination, but it is the thing for which and by which there is struggle; discourse is the power which is to be seized.
>
> —Michel Foucault, "The Order of Discourse," *Language and Politics*, 1984, 110

ARMING LINGUISTICALLY PROFILED AND MARGINALIZED STUDENTS WITH THE SILENT WEAPONS NEEDED FOR QUIET, DISCURSIVE WARS

Peace to Killarmy, who dropped a bomb album on us in 1997, *Silent Weapons for Quiet Wars*. Like the rest of the The Mighty Wu-Tang Clan, they wreckognize that the tongue is a double-edged sword and repeatedly hurl the Rza's question at the Hip Hop Nation: "Have you not heard that words kill as fast as bullets?" Influenced heavily by the Five Percent Nation of Islam (see Spady, Lee, and Alim 1999), which sees the connection between discourse, power, and knowledge ('knowing the ledge') at least as clearly as Foucault, they view language as a weapon to be used in discursive combat—and most folks ain't even knowin that it's a war goin on. That's Real Talk. The contemporary Black notion of REAL TALK is similar to what generations of Black Americans have been referring to as STRAIGHT TALK. Real Talk is like the Hip Hop Nation Language version of an evolving metalinguistic discourse on language and authenticity in the Black community. In other words, in a speech community where there's a whole lotta TALK ABOUT TALK, Real Talk captures both the discourse on "keepin it real" and "talkin straight." In chapter 4 of this book, I describe the process of engaging in Real Talk like this: "Not only is you expressin yoself freely (as in 'straight talk'), but you allegedly speakin the truth as you see it, understand it, and know it to be. In addition, you stand ready to defend Real Talk" (86). I stand ready to defend this work, cuz it ain't nuttin but Real Talk up in here. So, like the big homie Dr. Dre said on that classic *Chronic* joint, "peep out the manuscript."

As contemporary societies are becoming increasingly more diverse, as national and group boundaries are simultaneously being reified and dismantled through war, gentrification, displacement, transnational movements, globalization, and terrorism, and as indigenous people in the mineral-rich regions of the earth continue to resist neocolonial occupation and straight-up land grabbin tactics, those concerned with linguistic and educational policy and practice have had to face a new and increasingly complex array of issues and problems. In current times, scholars and activists are arguing and agitating for Mother-Tongue Education in "post-Apartheid" South Africa (Alexander 2004), reviving old debates about the unifying and divisive impact of a Modern Standard Arabic across the Arabic-speaking world, particularly on the formation of a "Palestinian national identity" (Khalidi 1997), developing new ways to revive and nurture indigenous languages in schooling (Hinton 2003), and uncovering and documenting new ways that American (and global) institutions continue to maintain inequality in housing, labor, education, and other markets, particularly through "linguistic profiling," discrimination based SOLELY on speech and writing, or as Baugh (2003, 155) describes it, "the auditory equivalent of visual 'racial profiling.'"

In these critical times, how can one avoid feeling the weight of history? This book is being published in the year of the 25th anniversary of "the Black English case" (*Martin Luther King Junior Elementary School Children v. Ann Arbor School District Board*, 1979) in Federal Court on behalf of 15 Black, economically deprived children residing in a low-income housing project on Green Road in Ann Arbor, Michigan; and during the year that scholars of all disciplines are re-examining the successes and failures of 50 years of court-ordered desegregation since *Brown v. Board of Education* (1954). I am also fully aware that American educational systems continue to struggle with ways to develop language and literacy skills in culturally and linguistically diverse populations. Given the timely nature of this publication and the primary subtheme for this year's American Educational Research Association annual meeting (a special focus on *Brown*), this work focuses on the linguistic consequences of the largest involuntary transatlantic movement in human history, the African slave trade. Such large-scale terror and upheaval created myriad social, political, and economic crises for Africans, along with the transformation and transfiguration of cultural and linguistic practices. I open up this work with international struggles for language and literacy rights. It is my intention to globalize the "African American question," so as not to provincialize the complexity of the social, political, economic, and educational issues that impact this community, and to emphasize the point that scholarship on Black Americans should not be ghettoized in the academy as doing, as some academics have been known to mutter, "just Black stuff." In fact, the centrality of Black American issues to larger practical and theoretical questions should be evident in this work. As readers will see, the situation in Black America is deeply and intricately connected to the situation of oppressed peoples worldwide—from West Philly to West Africa to the West Bank. It is in the spirit of brotherhood and nationhood that this book is written.

Turning directly to language and education, researchers have been earnestly, at least in the last four decades, attempting to address the linguistic and literacy issues involving Black Americans. I want to first take a look at what the fields of sociolinguistics and literacy studies have contributed to the language and literacy development of Black Americans and then call for a critical, interdisciplinary dialogue between sociolinguists, literacy scholars, and education scholars, more generally. Sociolinguists and literacy scholars, while utilizing varying methodologies and working within multiple theoretical frameworks, have been working toward the same essential goal—improving the educational welfare of all students, particularly those who are linguistically profiled and marginalized. I will conclude with a call for a more critical approach to the language and literacy education of these students by presenting a brief case study of one sociolinguistic approach toward developing a critical pedagogy on language attitudes. The "Linguistic Profiling Curriculum" represents a new, consciousness-raising effort to establish critical language awareness in the American context (see chapter 9 as well for a more thorough discussion).

Before I discuss the relevant issues, I'd like to begin with a personal anecdote that provides some perspective on where I see the intersection of sociolinguistics and education. In reflecting upon the writing of this book—as a "sociolinguist," or a "linguistic anthropologist," or a "anthroPOLITICAL souljah," considering our collective contributions to education—I thought it important to say that it was years of teaching and directing a literacy program in the classrooms of Southwest Philadelphia's Turner Middle School that led me to sociolinguistics in the first place. I am not writing as a sociolinguist with educational concerns. I'm writing first and foremost as a concerned educator. As an undergraduate, I entered the language and literacy battlefield in the THICK of the Oakland "Ebonics controversy," which eerily revisited much of the same racial and cultural stereotype madness raised by the "Black English case" in Ann Arbor nearly two decades before it. While the media and public discourse stayed busy attacking Black Language (BL), and Black people, for so-called "deficiencies," I was one among a generation of young Hip Hop Headz who spent hours crafting my linguistic skillz and pushin the boundaries of the English language in RHYME CIPHAS and FREESTYLES. Wasn't no way in the world you could get me to see BL as deficient!

I knew that being in the communities and classrooms where BL was spoken—what educators like to call "the trenches"—was the best way to develop language pedagogy for speakers of BL. I wanted to put the full scope of our knowledge "to work for the people," as one of my professors always used to say, and become "equally knowledgeable in sociolinguistic theory and methodology and educational policy and practice" (as I wrote in my personal statement for graduate school). The need for dialogue was even more pressing for me since I attended universities where education schools and linguistics departments—as in many institutions—were right across the street from each other but could not have been further apart. Despite the strange comments that would sometimes emerge from members of both "camps" (linguists were sometimes perceived as intellectual snobs who were afraid of getting their hands dirty in the complex world of classrooms, while educationalists were sometimes perceived as "advocates," not intellectuals, whose research was either "too teachery" or "too touchy-feely"), the works of Black language and literacy scholars like Arnetha Ball, John Baugh, Vivian Gadsden, Sonja Lanehart, Carol Lee, Jabari Mahiri, Angela Rickford, John Rickford, Geneva Smitherman, Orlando Taylor, and others demonstrated the willingness of scholars to collaborate across disciplines. Lanehart's (2004) most recent work exemplifies the willingness of sociolinguists to become more involved in education research as she urges the field to put aside old debates about the historical origins of BL and focus more of its energy on the urgent, pressing educational needs of today's classrooms.

In recent years, through professional activities in sociolinguistic and educational circles, I have collaborated with language and literacy scholars (some of them mentioned above) in an effort to bring sociolinguistic issues to the forefront of our discussions of language education at the annual meetings of the American Educational Research Association (AERA) and, at the same time, bring educational issues to the forefront of our discussions of language diversity at the annual meetings of the Linguistic Society of America and American Dialect Society. This year at AERA we continued this dialogue with our annual panel, "African American Language, Literacy, and Liberation," with this year's focus being, "Confronting Linguistic Discrimination in Schools and Society." As this piece is written in the spirit of brotherhood and nationhood, it is also written in the spirit of encouraging intellectual dialogue across disciplines. The time is ripe for developing a critical interdisciplinary dialogue between language and literacy scholars.

RESPECT DA DIALECT: SOCIOLINGUISTIC APPROACHES TO LANGUAGE AND LITERACY DEVELOPMENT

Unlike generative linguistics (Chomsky 1957, 1965), which abstracts language away from the social contexts within which it is spoken by viewing language essentially as a nonsocial, decontextualized, idealized competence, sociolinguistics places a heavy emphasis on context in a collective effort to uncover who can say what to whom, how and where they can say it, and in what language, dialect, or style they can say it. In other words, sociolinguists view language as more than a psycholinguistic human faculty; language in interaction is seen as central to human activity and as the most salient way to construct and display our social identities (with emphasis on race, class, sexuality, gender, and other social constructions). In recent years, the sociolinguistic view of language has been influenced strongly by the perspective of the related field of linguistic anthropology, which views language as a cultural resource and speaking as cultural practice. While much of American sociolinguistic scholarship (see Labov 1966, 1972a, for example) presents language largely as a mirror of social realities created elsewhere, linguistic anthropologists emphasize the notion that communicative practices are constitutive of the culture of everyday life (see Duranti 1997, 2001, and 2004 for a thorough overview). Despite early efforts to unify sociolinguistic and generative approaches to the study of language (particularly by sociolinguist William Labov), and sociolinguistic and anthropological approaches to language use (most notably by John Gumperz and Dell Hymes; see their coedited 1964 collection), sociolinguistics continues to become more narrowly defined as the quantitative study of language variation and change (although recent literature in the area of STYLE is encouraging integrative, interdisciplinary approaches; see Eckert and Rickford 2001).

Some sociolinguists have been concerned with educational issues and the educational implications of language research for quite some time. Some have even been vocal advocates in times of educational "crises" for students who speak languages other than the dominating norm. Before launching into the studies that address Black American language and literacy development, it is important to note that linguists have been heavily involved in the vast array of language issues in schools, from early attempts to utilize linguistic knowledge to teach reading (Fries 1963), to producing research in support of bilingual education and policy, which has come under increasingly vehement attacks in the last decade, not surprisingly coinciding with the dramatic rise of the Latino population in many areas of the United States (Crawford 1992; Stanford Working Group 1993; Krashen 1996; Zentella 1997; Valdés 2001), to supporting bidialectal programs for native Hawaiians and speakers of "Hawaiian Creole English" (Ah Nee Benham and Heck 1998), to calls for the support and development of academic language and biliteracy in social contexts (Hornberger 1989; Villalva 2003), to providing evidence, legal testimonies, and policy recommendations in the recent and not-so-recent "firestorms" surrounding BL in schools (Smitherman 1981, 2000b; Baugh 1998, 2000a; Rickford and Rickford 2000).

Since the Oakland "Ebonics controversy" of December 1996, John Rickford has continually revised and made available to the public (http://www.stanford.edu/~rickford) his synthesis of sociolinguistic approaches to "working with vernacular varieties of English in schools" (see Rickford 2000). Answering the question that was on the mind of nearly every concerned teacher of Black American students, "How might the vernacular of Black American children be taken into account in efforts to help them do better in schools?" his most recent work (Rickford 2003) outlines four major sociolinguistic efforts toward this end: (1) the linguistically informed approach, (2) contrastive analysis, (3) dialect readers, and (4) dialect awareness programs (see also Green 2002).

The "linguistically informed approach" is primarily characterized by William Labov's work on "reading failure," from his early explorations of the topic (1967) to his current, ongoing, and expansive research agenda to develop "Individualized Reading Programs" (IRPs) (Labov 2001; Labov and Baker 2003) in elementary schools in Philadelphia and California (with Bettina Baker, John and Angela Rickford, John Baugh, and others). Labov begins with one basic and fundamental premise: teachers should distinguish between mistakes in reading and differences in pronunciation. For instance, if a Black American child reads, "I missed my chance" as "I miss my chance," teachers should not view this as a decoding error, but rather, as an utterance that is consistent with the pronunciation patterns of BL. It is not clear whether or not reading teachers are, in fact, failing Black American students for these types of "errors." Nor is it clear how such awareness on the part of teachers will help develop a more responsive reading pedagogy, particularly in areas of comprehension (see Angela Rickford 1999). However, a thorough analysis of the kinds of decoding errors that Black American students DO make and efforts to produce IRPs can only be helpful. If current findings are any indication, we now know more about Black American children's decoding skills than we have in the past, and that is certainly promising.

The "contrastive analysis" approach focuses on making the differences between "standard English" and BL explicit. Rickford reports that this approach has been used successfully by Taylor (1989) in Chicago, by Parker and Crist (1995) in Tennessee and Chicago, and by Harris-Wright (1999) in DeKalb County, Georgia. A vivid example of the potential success of this approach in the teaching of "standard English" writing skills is noted in the work of Taylor, who showed that students taught by this method showed a 91.7% decrease in their use of third-person singular *-s* absence (a well-studied feature of BL), while those taught by more traditional means showed only an 11% decrease. Contrastive analysis, along with other second-language acquisition methodology, has also been used in Noma LeMoine's comprehensive Academic English Mastery Program in the Los Angeles Unified School District, which serves over 50 schools, thousands of teachers, and tens of thousands of students (LeMoine and Hollie 2004).

"Dialect readers" is an approach that introduces reading in the local language of the students and then later makes the switch to "standard English." This approach has been successful internationally but has been received with heated debate here in the United States. Despite research demonstrating that the well-known "Bridge program" (Simpkins and Simpkins 1981) advanced the reading abilities of Black American students, who achieved 6.2 months of reading gain in a 4-month period, the publishers of the program discontinued the product due to community outrage against the use of BL in schooling.

The final approach is the "dialect awareness" approach spearheaded by Walt Wolfram and his colleagues at North Carolina State University (Wolfram, Adger, and Christian 1998). In short, dialect awareness programs seek to infuse the fundamental principles of linguistic variation into school curricula. The programs get students excited about the inherent variability of language and meet standards proposed by the National Council of Teachers of English and the International Reading Association (1996, 3) that students should "develop an understanding of and respect for diversity in language use, patterns, and dialects across cultures, ethnic groups, geographic regions, and social roles." One of the most exciting aspects of the programs is that they encourage students to become ethnographers and collect their own speech data from their local communities. Although the programs have not yet been tried and tested over extended periods of time (most dialect awareness programs are of a very short duration), this approach is viewed positively by teachers who are interested in developing language and other skills (e.g., data analysis, oral history projects) and can be one potential way to reduce dialect discrimination in schools and society.

DISRUPTING THE "NATURAL" SOCIOLINGUISTIC ORDER OF THINGS: THE NEW LITERACY STUDIES AND CRITICAL LANGUAGE AWARENESS

The sociolinguistic approaches described above have one fundamental similarity with the New Literacy Studies (see Hull and Schultz 2002)—both groups of scholars are ultimately working to provide evidence to disprove the notion that the language and literacy practices of students of linguistically marginalized groups are by any means "deficient." Labov (1972b, 212–13) made this statement early on:

> The view of the black speech community which we obtain from our work in the ghetto areas is precisely the opposite from that reported by Deutsch or by Bereiter and Engelmann. We see a child bathed in verbal stimulation from morning to night. We see many speech events which depend upon the competitive exhibition of verbal skills—sounding, singing, toasts, rifting, louding—a whole range of activities in which the individual gains status through his use of language.... We see no connection between verbal skill in the speech events characteristic of the street culture and success in the schoolroom.

Many scholars have utilized another sociolinguistic framework, the ethnography of communication, to drive home the main message that students on the margins of school success often possess "different, not deficient" language and literacy practices in their home communities. This "mismatch," they argue, is one of the causes of the school's failure to reach these pupils. Most notable in this area is Heath's (1983) classic, decadelong study of how families from Black and White working-class communities socialize their children into different "ways with words," or varying language and literacy practices, some of which are closer to school norms than others. Subsequent scholars have taken on research agendas that aim to "bridge" the out-of-school language and literacy practices of Black American students with classroom practice (Lee 1993; Ball 2000; Foster 2001; Dyson 2003), while others have examined the inventive and innovative language and literacy events of Black American youth involved in Hip Hop Culture (Alim 2003a, 2004b), spoken word poetry (Fisher 2003), and other verbal activities (Mahiri and Sablo 1996; Richardson 2003).

The New Literacy Studies (NLS), as exemplified by the work of Gee (1996) and Street (1993), position themselves at the crossroads of sociolinguistics, linguistic anthropology, and critical linguistics. Like linguistic anthropologists, the NLS view literacy—in fact, LITERACIES—as situated within the social and cultural practices that are constitutive of everyday life (Hull and Schultz 2002). Exploring what Ball and Freedman (forthcoming) refer to as "new literacies for new times," the NLS pull away from the noncritical American sociolinguistic tradition by drawing from contemporary social and cultural theorists, such as Bakhtin, Bourdieu, Derrida,

Foucault, Heidegger, and Gramsci, among others, and are thus more closely aligned with the British tradition of Critical Language Awareness (Fairclough 1995; Wodak 1995). Critical Language Awareness views educational institutions as designed to teach citizens about the current sociolinguistic order of things without challenging that order, which is based largely on the ideology of the dominating group and their desire to maintain social control. This view of education interrogates the dominating discourse on language and literacy and centralizes, as in the NLS, the examination and interconnectedness of identities, ideologies, and the hierarchical nature of power relations between groups in a given society. One of the major goals of my own research in this area has been "to make the invisible visible" by examining the well-meaning ways in which educators attempt to silence BL in White public space by inculcating speakers of heterogeneous language varieties into what are, at their core, White ways of speaking and seeing the word/world, that is, the norms of White, middle-class, heterosexist males (Alim 2004c; discussed at length in chapter 9 of this book).

While American sociolinguistic research has certainly been helpful in providing detailed descriptions of language variation and change, as Lippi-Green (1997) points out, this is where it stops. I argue that, by viewing the role of language in society through a noncritical lens, the tradition can actually be harming linguistically profiled and marginalized students. Most American suggestions for a pedagogy on language attitudes and awareness tend to discuss linguistic stigmatization in terms of INDIVIDUAL prejudices, rather than a discrimination that is part and parcel of the SOCIOSTRUCTURAL FABRIC OF SOCIETY and serves the needs of those who currently benefit the most from what is portrayed as the "natural" sociolinguistic order of things. Fairclough (1989, 7–8) argues that the job of sociolinguists should be to do more than ask, "What language varieties are stigmatized?" Rather, we should be asking, "How—in terms of the development of social relationships to power—was the existing sociolinguistic order brought into being? How is it sustained? And how might it be changed to the advantage of those who are dominated by it?"

Currently, through the work being conducted by the Linguistic Profiling Project at Stanford University (Purnell, Idsardi, and Baugh 1999; Baugh 2000b, 2003), we are attempting to apply the findings of our studies on language-based discrimination to educational practice. Toward this end, we are working with bilingual and bidialectal Black American, Arab American, Chicano, and Pacific Islander youth in a diverse working-class city in northern California to develop a Freireian critical pedagogy (Freire 1970) on language that aims to educate linguistically profiled and marginalized students about how language is used and, importantly, how language can be used against them (Alim 2004a). Questions that are central to the project are: How can language be used to maintain, reinforce, and perpetuate existing power relations? Conversely, how can language be used to resist, redefine, and possibly reverse these relations? This approach might be viewed as controversial or confrontational by the American sociolinguistic establishment, but only if it has an incentive to maintain the current sociolinguistic order. Rather than being controversial and confrontational, we are engaging in the process of "consciousness-raising" (as in the Women's Liberation movement, the LGBT movement, and the Black and Chicano Liberation struggles), that is, the process of actively becoming aware of one's own position in the world and, importantly, what to do about it. By learning about the full scope of their language use (through conducting ethnographic and sociolinguistic analyses of their own communicative behavior) and how language can actually be used against them (through linguistic profiling and other means; see Bertrand and Mullainathan 2003), students become more conscious of their communicative behavior and more conscious of ways by which they can transform the conditions under which they live. Here, we are moving far beyond the traditional approaches which bear the slogans "respect for diversity," "certain language varieties are appropriate in certain situations and not others," and "all languages are equal," which continually default in the elevation of the "standard language" over all other varieties. Or as Geneva Smitherman (1977, 77) once wrote, playing on the Orwellian notion of inequality, they give students the message that "all languages are equal, but some are more equal than others."

As we continue our critical interdisciplinary dialogue on education on the anniversaries of "the Black English case" and *Brown v. Board of Education* and well into the future, rather than HARMING linguistically profiled and marginalized students with a pedagogy that fronts like it's all good, our goal should be ARMING them with the silent weapons needed for the quiet, discursive wars that are waged daily against their language and person. It's time for a critical language awareness pedagogy in the United States. In the classic words of my Bay Area Brotha JT the Bigga Figga, "that's real talk right there."

H. SAMY ALIM
Cairo, Egypt
October 6, 2004

SHOUT OUTS

Bismillah Al-Rahman Al-Rahim. In the Name of Allah, the Beneficent, the Merciful... Yo, first and foremost, All Props and Praises due to the Most High. One Love. You have been with me every step of the way, and the blessings are too many to count (as the Muslims say, "God is in the blessing business!"). Thank You for the most valuable gift anyone could ever ask for—a loving, caring, nurturing mother and father, who raised me UP right, taught me how to DO right, and, of course, raised me up to ACK right. :-) I can never thank Allah enough for the many sacrifices that you have made to better the lives of your three sons (Wiss wa Willo, you know I appreciate your support). Thanks to both of you for stressing the value of education and for always pushin me to do my best. I know I have been thousands of miles away from you for years in pursuit of this thang, but believe me, the wisdom you have imparted to me since day one has been like a constant soundtrack to my life—and will undoubtedly continue to be. I can hear you now, "Hesham, remember Allah and He will remember you." Nuthin but love for you, Minky and Tex. Nuthin but love. *Ana bahibukum uktar min entum taarafu. Wa Insha'Allah, hargaalukum wa hab'a maakum wa kulina maa baad. Entum wahashtoony kiteer gidden.*

Alright, y'all, time to give a madd shout out to all the Sunnysidaz mobbin through them Sunnyside streetz. Yo, without y'all, none of this would even be possible. Forreal. Your hard work, willingness to put up with my endless questions and demands, and love for learning was like the BIGGEST inspiration. Please believe it! Y'all truly some thorough Brothas and Sistas—and Hiphopography ain't gon NEVER be the same! You've taught me more about Black Language and Life than any textbook ever could, you feel me? That's Real Talk. Your insights have been invaluable. I know it's real out there, so keep yo heads up and keep rollin, you know what I'm sayin? Y'all got it on lock, and you make this Brotha right here HELLA proud. Love y'all. Amira. Bilal. Careem. Kijana. Shahira. Cici. JoJo. Timbaland. C-dogg. Tre. Taje. Shakim. The Twins. Vik. Maaan, ALLAYALL! Y'all know who y'all is. Keep the Hip Hop scholarship goin. You the next generation and like DMX say, y'all "got a story to tell." Thanks for everything, but especially the memories. You're why I do what I do. Plain and simple. Simple and plain. Much love to all the Brothas at "The Right Price," who not only hooked me up with tight fades for the last four years (and still do every time I'm back in the hood), but who kept it real with a Brotha on the regular. Maaan, that shop is therapy in so many ways. The laughter, the language, the love. Gon miss y'all. Like Jiggaman say, you know the "streets is watchin." Even though the one-time be around all the time, y'all can't be faded. And, of course, big ups to all of the Stanfordians who were down to help me out and gave up their precious time to be a part of this project—no questions asked. Your help was critical to this project, and I am indebted to you always.

You know I couldn'ta did this ishhh without madd people helpin me along the way. I'd be writin for days if I thanked everyone. Yo, like how I say in the book about STYLE bein a coconstructed project, this book has TRULY been a coconstructed project in every sense of the word. You know I gotta give props to the gang at Duke University Press, *American Speech*, and the American Dialect Society. I'd particularly like to thank Ron Butters and Charles Carson, who read this manuscript very closely. I learned a lot under your watchful eyes. We DID THE DAMN THANG from California to Carolina to Cairo. On the move. Thank you for helping me say what I wanna say, and for givin me the freedom to say it. But most of all, thanks for your sincere commitment to making this the best book that it could possibly be.

There are several Black scholars who have invested in me personally and intellectually and, without them, it ain't no tellin where I would be today, you know. I'm standin on the shouldas of souljas, man. No doubt. Big, BIG ups to Brother James G. Spady, who has been there since the Penn days. Maaan, you be STEADY puttin other people first, man. That kind of commitment to the development of so many young scholars is unparalleled. I can't thank you enough for all of the many, MANY supercritical discussions over the years—I'm sure you'll see the fruits of them buried deep in this project and in my future work. Let's keep bangin, Brother! We got a LOT of work to do. To allayall, look out for *Tha Cipha: Hip Hop*

Culture and Consciousness droppin from the Black History Museum crew—big ups to Samir Meghelli and Charles G. Lee for puttin it down.

To the Sista sent from Heaven above—Docta G a.k.a. Geneva Smitherman. From the moment I sent you my undergrad thesis, you been steady on the case. How can I thank you for all of your intellectual insights, advice, care, and love? Your pages and pages of written feedback on this project, and nearly every one of my pieces, have been invaluable. Your accessibility and open lines of communication from e-mail, phone, fax, telegraph—shoot, ANY path—have been crucial in more ways than you even know. And, of course, you the one who got me into this baaad-ass writin style—from you, I learned that our choice of language is a political act, a way of decolonizing the mind, a direct means of working toward linguistic emancipation. Thanks for flyin out to see a Brotha on his big day, Big Sis. It wouldn't have been right without G in the house. Fa sho!

To the BLBs—the Black Language Brothas—John Baugh and John Rickford, who, like Spady and Smitherman, have made incredible intellectual contributions to the study of Black Language and Life. Even if you blind, it should be clear as day that their work on stylistic variation has influenced me TREMENDOUSLY. It's all up in it. Y'all be some baaaddDDD Brothas! Baugh, man, what can a Brotha say? You have been so much more than an advisor to me. I mean, from day one, you've always looked out for me and been my number one supporter. Thanks, Bro, for all the many conversations, gems of wisdom, love, and overall personal investment. I know I'm a "labor-intensive" mutha, but you don't know how invaluable this experience has been for me, from the research projects (the Oakland Project to Linguistic Profiling) to the one-on-one meetings, and yeah, man, to the hours spent sweatin it out on the r-ball courts. I came to Stanford to work with you—and I am so glad that I made the right decision. Thanks for everything. To John Rickford, who supervised my Linguistics Masters and offered his help every step of the way, I learned so much from you through your courses and conversations. You, too, have been an excellent supporter, and your high level of criticality and productivity is, for me, a model to be emulated. Thanks for all of the support, Bruddaman, and for pushin me to do some high quality ishhh. And, yo, Arnetha Ball—the Sista who has been central to my Stanford experience—thank you so much for all of the opportunities, from TAing those courses with you, to conducting research in the field, to the conferences together, and for the HOOK-UPS on so many levels. I was fortunate that you came to Stanford when you did. Thanks.

I'd also like to give a madd shout out to the one, the only, Ray McDermott, whose hundreds of hours of meetings with me have helped expand my mental membranes in new and exciting ways. For over a year, you were willing to meet with me on this project, man, and other work, or even just to chat, and the new direction I have taken as a result is all up in the conceptualization of speech style that you see here. I know you make it your duty to meet regularly with students, but your commitment to my intellectual development cannot be overstated (the whole foray into conversation analysis, ethnomethodology, linguistic anthro, and so on). I hope you know by now how much you have influenced me. Thanks, too, for making Stanford—which can sometimes be dull as hell (I ain't gon lie)—a lil more bearable. O-KAY! (Had to throw one in there for you.) Also, to Penny Eckert, who taught those linguistic variation and style seminars that were so helpful in my methodological and theoretical training. Thanks for literally opening up your office to me and the others and taking the time to make sure we dealt with every issue thoroughly. Your criticality was refreshing, and I thank you for being a down-ass Jersey girl. Thanks also to Bill Labov, Ira Harkavy, Farah Griffin, Christina Bratt Paulston, Robin Kelley, Shirley Brice Heath, Paul Kiparsky, Peter Sells, Kenji Hakuta, Amado Padilla, Michael Kamil, Sonja Lanehart, Mary Bucholtz, Arthur Spears, Carolyn Adger, Dalia Rodriguez, Lisa Green, Marcyliena Morgan, Alessandro Duranti, Ron Butters, Walt Wolfram, Sonia Sanchez, Amiri Baraka, Jabari Mahiri, Anthony Antonio, Joy Williamson, Na'ilah Nasir, Ana Celia Zentella, George Yancy, Harry Elam (thanks for chairing, and thanks, too, to your brother, Guru, for spittin dat legendary line: "You know my steez"), Elena Becks, Kim Fowler and the Committee on Black Performing Arts (whose work in Sunnyside and their ongoing support during *The BAQ* days were crucial), and Ramzi Salti (the best Arabic teacher—well, best teacher PERIOD—that I have ever had; you don't know what you've reconnected me to. *Elf, ELF shukran, ya akhi. Rabinnah yakhaleek*).

BIG shout out to all of my peeps, homies, and close friends who worked with me late into the weeeeee hours of the morning and to the next day. To Blizz, who has been workin and walkin with me for years, thanks for all of the fond memories. We started this thing together and ended it together—like we were both on the same mission. And we did it! Don't it feel good? And, yo, this a special shout out to a Sista name Dee, who I was lucky enough to meet in my final year of grad school. Ahhh, the memories will last a lifetime. Thanks for listening to me talk through my stuff and for reading my work with such great interest and attention to detail. A lot of the time, I would write with you in mind, and your encouragement was always there, "Go Alim!" Most of all, like the Golden Girls sing, "Thank you for being a frieeeend." The Weity lives. Yeahhhh. And, yo, as if these shout outs wasn't long enough, I need to holla at Hernan Diaz, William Perez (Willis), Ali Borjian (*Ehlan wa sehlan*), Albert Lozano, Jennifer Tackman, Michales Michaelides, Jason Raley, Beth Scarloss, Harley Neumann, Kareem Ghanem, Kerry Enright Villalva, Keiko Inoue, Matt Thibeault, Andre Smith, Jonathan Brown (Jubwa), Lonnie Barkus (Lonnie Love), my Palestinian and Jordanian brothers Imad (and family, Omar, Malaak, Malik, Manaar, and Lina), Abdullah, Fadi, Ibrahim, and mis amigos at Med Wraps and Kan Zeman (Best Middle Eastern food in the Bay Area, and even better company), César, Gabino (and, of course, Mela, Nathaly, and niño), Malik, Rafael, David, Curioso, Joanie, and mis carnales at the best French cafe with a Mexican twist, Cafe Brioche, Brother JT the Bigga Figga (thanks for the Real Talk sessions; you're an inspiration to me on so many levels), Brother Mark, Brother Brian, Brother Joe, Brother Min Chris, and all the Brothers, and all the other folks who was there for me.

Lastly, I'd like to acknowledge the Spencer Foundation for making all of this possible. The generous support provided by the Spencer Dissertation Fellowship enabled me to set aside the necessary time to hannel mah bizNASS (think Ludacris), and the Fall and Spring Forums have been a great source of support. Shout out to the Spencer cohort, whom I've gotten to know and exchange ideas with over the past year or so. Collabos are already in the works. Thanks, in particular, to Maisha Fisher and Luis Urrieta Jr., who have already provided incredible support and read through drafts of my most recent work. The future looks bright—let's do it.

Alright, y'all, that's it. One Love. Thanks to everyone and to those that I know I missed. But before I go, a final shout to all speakers of Black Language, particularly to the Hip Hop Headz who have realized that Language IS the revolution. Like Sista Sonia say, "Resist. Resist. Resist." And then recreate the conditions under which we live. Yeahhh, this Language Thang ain't no joke. Ice Cube speaks to the power of the Language in recognizing our past and facing our future: "Four hundred years ago, when black slaves were brought to America, Africans who spoke the same language were separated from each other. What we're seeing today, with this insane campaign to intimidate Rappers and Rap music, is just another form of separating people that speak a common language." Understanding the link between Language and Nationhood is pivotal to our survival. This young generation is the best that's ever been produced. Peep Amira, a young 17-year-old Sista, as she speaks to the power of Language in uniting the Hip Hop Nation: "The East Coast and West Coast vocabulary is interchanging now, like people from the South are saying, 'Wassup, pimpin?' 'pop yo collar,' and they C-Walkin and stuff now, when that's a primarily West Coast thing and it originated HERE. I mean, they're gettin rid of the whole rivalry thing and adoptin each other's language and stuff." Scholars, we gotta play catch up. If the goal of language scholars is to ultimately uncover what it means to be human, to gain insight into humanity and the complex relationships between language, life, and liberation, we must consider the use of language to not only construct our WORLDS but also to construct our very BEINGS. To paraphrase Brother Mos Def, linguistics is our hammer—let's bang the world into shape and let it fall—HUH!

P.E.A.C.E.
not war...

1. INTRODUCTION: YOU KNOW MY STEEZ

My style be wilder than a kamikaze pilot
Don't try it, I'm about to start more than a friggin' riot
Style's unsurpassable...
For I be speakin from my parables and carry you beyond
The mic's either a magic wand
Or it gets tragic like the havoc of a nuclear bomb...
Phat beats, they play on
Want dope rhymes, put me on
Word is bond...
You know my steez

—Guru, "You Know My Steez," 1998

My style's incognito
I'm sharper than a razor blade dressed up in a black tuxedo
Word to Reggie Noble, and to Shaq
Forget Schwarzenegger, I'll be back
You know my steelo...
You know my style, you know my steelo.
You know my style, you know my steelo

—E. Sermon, "My Style, My Steelo," 1994

It's necessary, we styles in Burburry
And our walk is mean in them Frankie B. jeans bwoy
Its necessary, we stays in Burburry
And a Mark Jacob bag and a H-Tod shoe (Whoooooo!)

—Foxy Brown, "Stylin," 2002

I mean, for like, to be cool, to be labeled Hip Hop and like in that category, you have to, for BOYS, it's like the whole sag thing. You can't have your pants all the way up here like Alonzo! [laughter] ... He has his pants way up here with the belt and he's like ... like how Bilal and Careem have their pants right now, like HERE, SAGGIN a little is cool, but you're labeled like a square if you have

> your pants like here [high on your waist] and they're tight... like Alonzo's, he's a square cuz his pants too high! Usually, if you wear a belt, you're not supposed to see the belt, and you're supposed to have your shirt OVER the belt, and [laughter] that's just the Hip Hop style.... Hip Hop language is just, like, the way we talk to each other. How we talk normally, that's Hip Hop.
>
> —Amira, 17-year-old Sunnyside Sista

THIS PROJECT IS an ethnographic and sociolinguistic study of styleshifting in a Black American speech community. Before describing the research, I'd like to introduce some of the terms in the title. I use the term *Black American* for two main reasons. First, as Goodwin (1990) noted in Philadelphia approximately three decades ago (she collected her data in the 1970s), ethnographic observations in this suburb indicate that community members use the term *Black* far more often than *African American* to describe people ("Nah, she talkin about that 'Black girl' over there"), events ("I'm puttin together the 'Black fashion show' this year"), and institutions ("The 'Black church' don't be knowin WHAT'S goin on with these young kids out here"). The phrase *Black American* as a whole, however, is not ethnographically derived, since hardly any community members (except some Caribbean and African members) refer to "African Americans" as "Black Americans." I chose to use *Black American* instead of just *Black* to indicate that the context of the study was in the United States, as opposed to the United Kingdom, Nigeria, Guyana, Egypt, or any other place where Blacks be. While I understand that *Black* is often used to invoke unity and strength within the African Diaspora, I use *Black American* to consciously disambiguate "Blackness," that is, to recognize the multiplicity of ethnicities within Black peoples.

My ethnographic research on the Hip Hop Nation Speech Community shows that this community places an extraordinary emphasis on the creativity and distinctiveness of one's style. Style. Steelo. Steez. The fact that there are at least three different lexical items to describe the concept of style in Hip Hop Nation Language (HHNL) underscores its importance to the community. Oftentimes, when sociolinguists be talkin about style, they ain't talkin about the same ishhh that the quotes above is talkin about, you know what I mean? (see Irvine 2001). When rapper Guru spits, "My style be wilder than a kamikaze pilot," he's engaging in the highly descriptive Black American practice of boasting (Kochman 1981), which is found throughout Hip Hop (Rickford and Rickford 2000; Alim 2004e). Guru let it be known that his style is "unsurpassable" cuz he known for spittin "dope rhymes." Hip Hoppers spend so much time talkin about style that some MCs dedicate entire songs to describin they style. In one collabo effort by Erick Sermon, Redman, and Shaq, heads remember how Erick Sermon (known for his humor) made us all laugh when he described his style as "sharper than a razor blade dressed up in a black tuxedo" and Redman (known for his humor and rawness) rhymed "my styles act wild like Jurassic Park after dark!" There are countless examples of this in Hip Hop texts.

From Redman's line, we know that rappers also talk about the importance of having a range of styles in addition to your main, distinct rhyming style. I mean, cats be flippin and flexin madd styles. On any given day, you might could hear a MC say, "Yo, I got styles for days." Flippin styles refers to a MC's ability to lyrical styleshift, like how Eve flipped into that Caribbean dance hall style on "Eve of Destruction" and smashed on MCs in two different styles. And y'all remember when Jiggaman flipped into that crazy-fast style he useta flex years ago when he was a youngen rappin wit Big Jaz on "Nigga What? Nigga Who?" and Big Jaz claimed the fast-paced rhyme style that young bucks be doin today when he spit it machine-gun style, "Nigga, yo style no style, my style hostile!" Originality, creativity, and versatility are all necessary components in forming one's style(s). As Wu-Tang Clan MC Raekwon once told me,

> Style, you know what I mean, you just gotta be original. You gotta be able to say things, you know, automatically that people don't normally say. You gotta design your own flow, you know what I mean? Because it's so many people out there with different type of flows, but if you make your own flow up, that makes you more original and makes you one of the more outstanding MCs. [Alim 2001, 29]

It's this shared understanding of style within the HHN that caused rapper Craig Mack to tell all other MCs, "get off my tip and stop jockin my style," in what was one of the biggest Hip Hop hits of 1997.

As we can also see from Sista Amira's quotation above, some members of the community believe that there is a Hip Hop style, or styles, of dress. In the passage above, she talkin about how dudes would usually dress wit they pants saggin, shirt out, and all that. That's the more street-affiliated brotha, you know. It's some Hip Hop styles that encourage the most expensive name brands available. In Foxy Brown's "Stylin," she say it's "necessary" that "we styles in Burburry" and runs down a list of brand name fashion designers. Even within recognizable styles of dress and rap, the individual members of the HHN appreciate an aesthetic that is HIGHLY stylized—you can't just be like everybody else; you gotta add your own flava to it, you know.

Importantly for this study, style can also refer to a way of talkin. If you notice in all of the lyrics, there are distinct Black Language (BL) features, such as invariant *be* ("my style be wilder" and "For I be speakin"), copula absence ("my style hostile"), and durative verbal *-s* ("we styles" and "we stays"; notice how *styles* is used as a verb here). Amira makes the connection between HHNL and the everyday language of her local Sunnyside speech community: "Hip Hop language is just, like, the way we talk to each other. How we talk normally, that's Hip Hop." A key phrase in Amira's comment is "to each other," cuz it reminds us that language is inherently interactive, as can be said of speech style. For instance, yeah, we know Guru's style's "unsurpassable" and that it can create the "havoc of a nuclear bomb," but what's important here is that he tells the audience repeatedly, "You KNOW my steez." Yo, a style ain't a style if it ain't RECOGNIZABLE. Plain and simple. This is a key point in that it relays the message that style is a coconstructed phenomenon. It's gotta be a audience for style to even be relevant. Erick Sermon and Redman kick the same message: "You KNOW my style, you KNOW my steelo." This element of recognizability, as we'll see, is important not only for the way MCs drop rhymes, but also for the way we talk and interact in everyday conversation.

Steez, in particular, though, has a broader application that means something closer to 'a mode of being in one's everydayness'. Yo steez not only refers to how you talk or how you walk, but more generally, it's how you do yo thang, how you let it hang—how you let it swang. It's what others come to expect from you, cuz that's just who you BE. By being heavily involved in the lives of the Sunnyside youth, I have attempted not only to capture they speech style, but they STEEZ, who they BEES.

ARRIVING AT THE FIELD

The research for this project grows out of approximately two years of fieldwork as a teacher-researcher and examines the language and linguistic practices of students at Haven High, an ethnically and linguistically diverse high school (multilingual and multilectal: 70% African American, 25% Latino, and 5% Indian American and Pacific Islander). Haven High was designed as an alternative for the residents of the community of Sunnyside, which, like many low-income communities in the United States, regularly experiences a 65% high-school dropout rate (that ishhh just ain't right). Believe it or not, Haven High the first high school that Sunnyside done seen in two decades.

The community demographics are in a state of flux as the silent and sweeping forces of gentrification—which is displacing Black communities across the nation—continue to take their toll on the current residents of this small city of 20,000. What was once a predominantly Black city several decades ago has now become a predominantly Latino (Mexican majority) city, with various ethnically diverse residents (South Asians, Pacific Islanders, and a few Whites). An additional year and a half of insights were gained beyond the teaching experience, as I made weekly visits to the community and became a regular participant in Sunnyside's most (in)famous barbershop, The Right Price. I have been making weekly visits to Sunnyside for nearly four years now and have developed cherished friendships along the way—plus kept up a BAAAD high bald fade!

Prior to my entering Haven High in Sunnyside, I had served as director and lead instructor for a language and literacy program at Turner Middle School in Southwest Philadelphia. The program, Da Bomb Squad Comprehensive Literacy Development Program, utilized the cultural-linguistic practices of contemporary Hip Hop Culture to motivate, assist, and develop students' abilities in obtaining oral, written, and computer literacy, among other skills (see Alim 2001 for a more detailed description). Da Bomb Squad story begins with my study of BL in educational contexts. I had come to a gross realization that while academia had engaged in the serious study of the language of Black Americans for quite some time (well over three decades), those studies yielded small benefits for the speakers of BL, while yielding huge gains for the so-called "experts." I felt that it was time that scholars, educators, and linguists put this research to work for the communities and the youth, who had long been studied but were still struggling academically. It was my belief that decades of accumulated linguistic knowledge ought to be combined with a new and creative pedagogy in order to reverse the educational failure of our urban schools—that is, the failure of schools to properly educate Black students. One main question embodied the central theme of my thinking: How can we, as a community of educators, linguists, and scholars, utilize the cultural-linguistic practices and experiences of Black students as the impetus for creative and effective educational practice?

In the process of producing a student-run magazine (*Da Bomb!*), students engaged in a wide range of literacy activities: hiphopological grammar lessons (using popular Hip Hop lyrics to study grammar via contrastive analysis), oral interviews with peers and members of the Hip Hop community in Philly, polling the student body about favorite topics in Hip Hop Culture, writing raps and poems, comparative analysis and message analysis of Hip Hop song lyrics, and written autobiographies and biographies of their favorite Hip Hop artists.

Many students were not motivated to learn in school. As is often the case, CURRICULUM WAS DISCONNECTED FROM COMMUNITY AND CULTURE. But I knew that Hip Hop Culture had a firm grasp on most Black students. Why not take what the students are already experts at and make them experts in other arenas? This was the driving force behind Da Bomb Squad Comprehensive Literacy Development Program and, I would say, the main reason for our success.

After three years of directing the program, I matriculated into Stanford University's School of Education. I first entered Haven High as a research assistant for a larger research project on literacy learners in the United States and South Africa that worked mainly with middle-school students (Ball and Alim 2002). This project provided invaluable research experience, served as an entrée into the school, and helped me to develop my first impressions of the language and literacy practices of students at Haven High.

At the conclusion of that project, I took on the role of teacher-researcher and developed Language and Communication, a course that used Hip Hop Culture to teach sociolinguistics and ethnography of communication theory and methods. While I was teaching students these theories and methods, I was also talking with students, interviewing them about their own language and communication behavior, and observing their language and literacy practices. My experience at Turner Middle School in Philadelphia made me aware of the fact that middle-school students are capable of far more than we think. Following the work of Heath (1983) and Wolfram, Adger, and Christian (1998), I began teaching the major theoretical approaches to sociolinguistics (variation theory) and the ethnography of communication to a class of seventh and eighth graders. The idea was to steep them in theory and then train them to become field researchers, eventually collecting their own speech data. I used Hip Hop Culture in various ways: (1) reading and critiquing interviews in Hip Hop publications in order to review interview techniques, (2) reading interviews that I conducted with famous Hip Hop artists (like Juvenile and dead prez) and analyzing them within Hymes's theoretical framework (the ethnography of speaking), (3) analyzing Hip Hop interview transcripts in order to learn about variation theory, and (4) reading Hip Hop publications in order to analyze different styles of writing (how and when BL was used).

Teaching in both Philly and Sunnyside provided me with hands-on classroom experience, which was critical in shaping my thinking on language and literacy issues. My early work in Sunnyside led directly to this present study. One moment, in particular, had a lasting impact on me and heavily impacted the work I would later do at Haven High. The following excerpt from my fieldnotes occurred shortly after my transition from a research assistant on the United States and South African literacy learners project to a teacher-researcher teaching Language and Communication. After teaching the ethnography of speaking, I had just introduced a language project in which students would conduct an ethnography of speaking of their own communicative behavior. During a break between classes, I found a quiet corner and excitedly wrote the following fieldnotes:

> Maaan, today was off tha hook. At the 7th grade class, I explained the "Language in My Life" project to the students and went over it in detail—they asked questions and gave examples and I made sure they knew what the assignment was. That went well. After that, we discussed the [local newspaper] article about my class [The students had just found out that I was also teaching a course at Stanford entitled "The Language of Hip Hop Culture."]. Brandy [a teacher] had made them read it for homework the other night. They asked me so many questions about my class it was amazing. They asked "How many students?" "What do you do with the lyrics?" "Do you freestyle in class?" "Do Alim freestyle?" They all had questions about studying the language of Hip Hop Culture. Great enthusiasm.
>
> At the end of the discussion, I come to find out that there are several freestylers in the class and that it's normal for people to freestyle during lunchtime and after school. Jamil said Pasha be freestylin at lunchtime. Turns out that Pasha older brother (18 or 19) might be signing a record deal with Sean T, a famous Sunnyside producer. Wow! And she knew JT the Bigga Figga and so did Jamil. Rah and some others said they could freestyle, too. Elisa said her dad raps in both English and Spanish (he Puerto Rican/her mom is Black). And Maisha's dad was freestylin all weekend outside their garage sale to draw customers in. She said this man sat out front all day to watch her dad till her mom made him leave. Ha. Ha. Ha. There's so much rappin and rap activity goin on in the school/community! Amazing.

Then at break time, I was talkin to the 7th and 8th graders and they was totally informal with me. It was nuthin but Real Talk out there. Straight up. BL is the dominant mode immediately beyond the walls of the classroom. They have a real comfort level with me. . . .

Now after reading the article, Luqman went home and wrote this bomb rap out on his computer and brought it in to class. He ran and showed it to me and we spent some time lookin at it. Boy is tiiiight!!! Serious poet rhymer "like Talib Kweli and Mos Def," he said. He was so proud to show it to me. I have a copy in my pocket right now. Woah, the kids are totally into rappin—and it's cool that they feel they can let me in on this. Luqman walked me to my car and he spit a freestyle on the way out. I spit back and we were vibin for a minute. Straight freestyle raps.

There must be many kids in that school who can rap good, and I know they love Hip Hop. More later. Now, I gotta do the 8th grade class.

What I learned from the students (how attentive they were to language, style, even sociolinguistic features, and the role of Hip Hop Culture in their lives) really gave me the idea of teaching a high school course called "Hiphopography: The ethnography of Hip Hop Culture and communication" as a way to make a real contribution to the school and the students' experience, and to gain access to speech data across various contexts. My students—all ninth and eleventh graders—were charged with becoming ethnographers of their own contemporary culture (see chapter 9). The students were trained in ethnographic field methods (such as participant observation and interviewing) with the aim of helping them to document their own language and culture. It was through teaching this course that I developed close relationships with the students and gained nearly unfettered access to their speech behavior across various contexts and situations.

Access to this type of speech data in this way is rare in sociolinguistic studies. However, more and more researchers are advocating ethnographically informed studies of speech style. In addition, recent sociolinguistic research on style has attempted to analyze style using tight experimental designs, controlling for as many factors in the speech situation as possible. Whereas some researchers may prefer one approach over the other, I believe that both approaches are not only mutually beneficial, but when used in tandem, can enhance our conceptualization of speech style.

MAJOR ISSUES

Chapters 2 and 3 deal largely with methodological and theoretical issues in the study of speech style. In chapter 2, "Designing Sociolinguistic Research on Speech Style," the first section discusses the contributions of social psychology, linguistic anthropology, and sociolinguistics to our theoretical understanding of style. The rest of the chapter deals heavily with the details of designing sociolinguistic research on style and the experimental design used in this study. It is here that I introduce the notions of SOCIOLINGUISTIC STYLE and INTERACTIONAL STYLE, as well as my methodological contribution, the SEMISTRUCTURED CONVERSATION. The selection of participants and variables is also described.

Chapter 3, "How the Other Half Speaks: Ethnosensitivity and the Shifting Roles of the Researcher," attempts to deal with "how the other half speaks." By this, I mean that sociolinguistics has often focused, rather narrowly I believe, on the speech of the RESEARCHED, while ignoring the speech of the RESEARCHER (almost as a rule). Since my view of speech style is that style is coconstructed through conversation and located in and through interaction, this chapter suggests advancements in sociolinguistic methodology in order to achieve a fuller description of speech style. By examining my role as a researcher, as well as my own styleshifting in the field, I revisit the concept of ETHNOSENSITIVITY in ethnographic research in order to begin to view styleshifting as cultural practice, which is consistent with the view of linguistic anthropology. Here, I look at discourse strategies such as the use of FALSETTO and SUCK-TEETH, as well as interactive modes such as BATTLIN MODE and my own SELF-CONSCIOUS LINGUISTIC ADJUSTMENTS.

In chapter 4, "'This Is Corporate America Takin Over': Schooling, Survival, and the Sociohistorical Context of Life in the Occupied Territories," I place my students—all Black American youth (referred to as "the Sunnysidaz")—in historical, social, political, economic, and educational context. Ethnographic description of Sunnyside is combined with historical research to give the reader a "Sunnysidaz-eye-view" of the community. In this chapter, I present the language of my students—in-group, peer Black street speech in a community setting. In chapters 5–8, I analyze the language used in conversational STREET SESSIONS (and other settings) as I discuss styleshifting based on race, gender, Hip Hop cultural knowledge, and interactional style. The Sunnysidaz' stories, which describe the sociohistorical context of life in the "occupied territories," are moving narratives in which a group of youth is trying to come to terms with its powerlessness. Importantly, this chapter makes the connection between language and life, allowing the reader to get a sense of the dynamic social worlds in which these students live and the language they use to talk about it. Ethnographic field data consists of fieldnotes, observations, and audio- and videotaped STREET SESSIONS.

Chapters 5–8 provide a much closer analysis of the sociolinguistic styles of Sunnyside youth. In chapter 5, "We Some BaaaddDDD Styleshifters: The Copula in Stylistic Variation," I introduce the first BL variable that will undergo quantitative analysis, the copula. Beginning with a general description of the feature and why it is the "showcase" variable in BL ("the controversial copula"), I dive right into an analysis of COPULA ABSENCE in the speech of Black male and female Hip Hoppers from the Sunnyside speech community. I consider the effects of race, gender, and Hip Hop cultural knowledge on speech style, showing the overall pattern for 32 SEMISTRUCTURED CONVERSATIONS (16 with Black interlocutors and 16 with White interlocutors). All three identity characteristics are reported as significant indicators of styleshifting for this variable. Finer levels of analysis reveal individual variability within the group and some surprising results that were obscured by the larger-level analysis. Racialized and gendered styleshifts are considered—this is the first study to separate the effects of race, gender, and cultural knowledge on speech style. Finally, an internal linguistic analysis of copula absence sheds light on the historical origins of this feature in BL, and of BL in general.

While chapter 5 deals with syntactic constructions, chapter 6 focuses on phonological variation by examining third-person singular *-s*, possessive *-s*, and plural *-s* absence in BL. Again, the effects of race, gender, and Hip Hop cultural knowledge are considered, to the extent possible, in the styleshifting of the Sunnysidaz. An interesting pattern emerges for third-person singular *-s* absence that MIRRORS the pattern for copula absence, with differences on the level of individual variation.

In chapter 7, I begin with an outline of another salient feature of BL, invariant *be*. After a brief description of the feature as it is used by the Sunnysidaz in the community context, I analyze this feature to see if it is stylistically sensitive based on race, gender, and Hip Hop cultural knowledge. Data is also compared to Black peer in-group usage. I find that race is a significant indicator of stylistic shifts in the use of this variable. Further, I describe a new use of invariant *be* that I am calling the BL EQUATIVE COPULA construction. Data from the field and from other sources (namely Hip Hop lyrics) are used to outline the linguistic and social constraints for this never-before-described equative copula, which is apparently used ONLY in all-Black settings. This reanalysis of invariant *be*, along with our analysis of the copula, can be used to argue for an integrative theory of language change that considers both passive and active processes, with identity and ideology taking more prominent roles in determining our conception of language variation and change than in previous models.

Chapter 8 considers an empirical study of interactional style. Theory development in the area of accommodation has focused on the impact of the general characteristics of speakers, general levels of linguistic variables, and specific levels of linguistic variables. Those who have mentioned interaction have not analyzed any data to show the importance of interaction in style. This chapter presents an analysis of specific linguistic features AND discourse strategies in interaction to determine what the Sunnysidaz are responding to in their speech style. I will begin to show interactional data and analysis of conversation as a way to get beyond "DO race and gender matter?" to "HOW and WHEN do race and gender matter?" One particular discourse strategy, the use of the emphatic agreement *O-kay!*, will be highlighted in relation to this theoretical development.

Chapter 8 takes us beyond examining sociolinguistic accommodation based on specific sociolinguistic variables and starts us on an increasingly complex mode of analysis that explores the work that speakers do in order to coconstruct style and meaning. While varying levels of copula absence may correlate with the identity characteristics of interlocutors (as I show in chapter 5), we have no way of telling HOW that is accomplished unless we examine deeply and thoroughly the structure of the talk that is produced. It is my belief that an approach to style that integrates sociolinguistic variation, interactional analysis, and ethnographic fieldwork will get us much farther down the road in understanding how and when speakers shift their styles. The central question for analysts still remains: How and WHEN do THESE INTERLOCUTORS, INTERACTING in THESE WAYS, COCONSTRUCT speech styles on THESE OCCASIONS?

The final chapter, "The Gentrification of Speech and Speakers: Black Language in White Public Space," discusses issues of language, racism, and power in American institutions, particularly schools. I show how even well-intentioned teachers are enacting Whiteness in their pedagogical praxis and subscribing to a hidden ideology of linguistic supremacy within a system of daily cultural combat. One of the major goals of my research in this area has been "to make the invisible visible" by examining the ways in which well-meaning educators attempt to silence Black Language in White public space by inculcating speakers of heterogeneous language varieties into what are, at their core, White ways of speaking and seeing the word/world, that is, the norms of White, middle-class, heterosexist males. So, by the end of the book, we have come full circle, focusing our efforts once again on the pressing educational issues, cuz like that Chi-Town brotha Common say so soulfully, "The shit be real."

2. DESIGNING SOCIOLINGUISTIC RESEARCH ON SPEECH STYLE

While the concept of stylistic variation (intraspeaker constraints, i.e., the way an individual speaker's speech varies across contexts and situations) is central to sociolinguistics, theory on stylistic variation has developed primarily from three disciplinary perspectives: sociolinguistics, linguistic anthropology, and social psychology (see Eckert and Rickford 2001). The development of a sociolinguistic theory of stylistic variation begins with Labov's (1966, 1972b) isolation of contextual styles, a unidimensional approach focusing on "attention paid to speech" as the main factor influencing speaker style. In the linguistic tradition, Labov was working during a period when most linguists ignored stylistic variation. Furthermore, they considered the techniques of linguistics inadequate to handle stylistic variation although they knew it was occurring. Labov's aim was to develop a methodology sufficient to measure the extent of regularity in stylistic variation—variationist studies were given new life. The sociolinguistic studies of Wolfram (1969) and Fasold (1972) also increased our knowledge of African American speech in this tradition.

Shortly after, speech accommodation theory was being developed by social psychologist Howard Giles and his associates (Giles 1973, 1984; Giles and Powesland 1975) to account for, albeit impressionistically (as noted in Trudgill 1981), the observation that speakers often converged toward one another to show social approval and diverged to show social disapproval. Around the same time, Hymes (1964, 1972) was working to develop the ethnography of speaking, an anthropological approach to the systematic observation and analysis of speech within a given speech situation. In contrast to early sociolinguistic and social psychological approaches, Hymes's theory was a multidimensional one that considered factors such as the setting, participants, act sequence, ends, key, instrumentalities, norms, and genres.

Work on stylistic variation developed into the next decade with sociolinguists (e.g., Baugh 1979, 1983; Hindle 1979; Rickford 1979; Coupland 1980) focusing on the addressee as a factor influencing style. Bell's (1984) influential work on "audience design" theorized the audience (including auditors and overhearers) as the central factor in stylistic variation, with "referee design" (where the reference group is not present) as an additional component. During the same year, Coupland (1984) presented the speech of a travel assistant in Cardiff, Wales, alongside the speech of her clients in what Trudgill (1986, 5) referred to as an "excellent example of the benefits of quantification in the study of accommodation." Figure 2.1 shows that the travel assistant's use of the variable (t) correlates with the speech of her clients based on socioeconomic class.

Developing a theory of "acts of identity" to explain stylistic variation in several Caribbean communities in Belize Le Page and Tabouret-Keller's (1985) framework was one of the earliest to consider both the extent and the limit to which speakers can modify their speech style. Relative to other frameworks, they gave the speaker the greatest sense of agency by claiming that speakers can modify their language to match the language of a group with which they wish to identify if provided: (1) they can identify the desirable

FIGURE 2.1
Variable (t): Comparison of Clients' Use and Assistant's Use (from Coupland 1984)

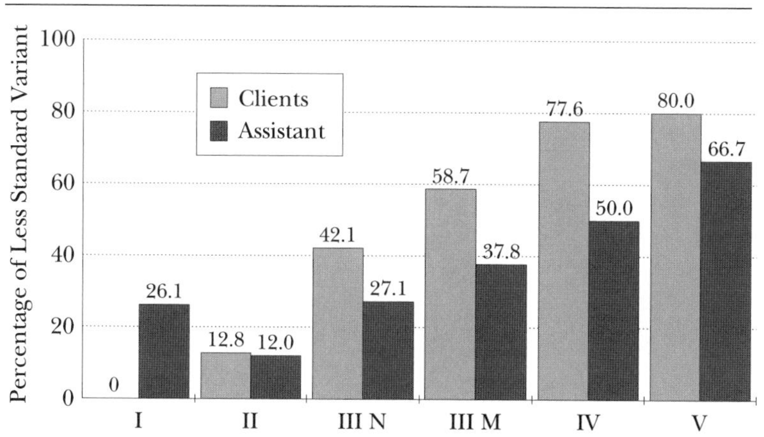

group, (2) they have both adequate access to that group and the ability to analyze their behavior (i.e., their speech patterns), (3) they have a strong enough motivation to "join" the group, and this motivation is either reinforced or rejected by the group, and (4) they have the ability to modify their own behavior.

Anthropological research on stylistic variation continued to develop with the original ethnographic work of Gal (1979), in which she examined the styleshifting AND codeswitching of bilingual speakers of Hungarian and German in Austria. Analyzing the styleshifts within languages and the codeswitches between languages, Gal investigated these micro behaviors in order to help develop a macro theory of language shift. Other anthropological approaches included cross-cultural ethnographic research in Black and White communities in the United States (Heath 1983), in terms of formality and status (Irvine 1979, 1985), and genre and poetics (Bauman 1977).

The current state-of-the-art research on style seeks to combine sociolinguistic and anthropological approaches. A shift toward a theoretical focus on speaker agency, and the revisiting of Bakhtin's (1981) dialogic perspective, has led to some great insights. Coupland (2001), taking quantitative sociolinguistics thoroughly to task, focuses almost exclusively on speaker agency in regard to identity construction as the predominating factor in stylistic variation (though see Rickford 2001 for a response). Bell (2001) has produced research that examines the language of the interviewer and interviewee and now sees "audience" and "referee" design as "concurrent, pervasive processes," an indication of the growing emphasis on examining what speakers DO with the stylistic resources available to them. Other work in this area also pays attention to speaker agency and style as a resource for constructing identities (Bucholtz 1996; Eckert 2000; Alim 2002) by focusing attention on linguistic variation as social practice (Eckert 2001).

Complementary to these approaches, a developing area of research that has contributed to our knowledge of style in language use has considered the role that speakers' language ideologies can have in style choice (Gal and Irvine 1995; Irvine 2001). By defining style as "distinctiveness," Irvine foregrounds the role of community language ideology and identity, reaffirming that styles are cultural projects (always in progress and process) created by many people working together. As research on language ideology is showing (Schieffelin, Woolard, and Kroskrity 1998; Kroskrity 2000), the attention that is increasingly being paid to the role of identity and ideology in language style and choice is leading researchers to develop a theoretical view of style that considers both language and context in reflexive terms. This study advances this current trend by viewing styleshifting as cultural practice, that is, as coconstructed behavior that draws upon community-based, historically rooted language practices and ideologies at the same time as it organizes future practices, ideologies and talk.

STYLE IN SOCIOLINGUISTICS—SOCIOLINGUISTIC STYLE AND INTERACTIONAL STYLE

In the following chapters, we'll see and feel the living language of this Black American speech community as we walk through the streets of Sunnyside. In chapter 3, we witness my own speech in relation to the students' speech, and I argue for a theoretical approach to styleshifting that integrates both sociolinguistic and discursive features and strategies as they are employed and manipulated in interaction. In chapter 4, we get a real sense of what the students' speech sound like when they just talkin amongst themselves—the peer, in-group talk. We gon get real deep wit the experimental research design created expressly for the study of speech style. What we tryina show is how and when speakers shift styles based on a combined analytic approach that views styleshifting as the observed frequencies of variable linguistic features, as well as the discursive and strategic construction of interactional styles.

This point is important in terms of how sociolinguists conceptualize Black Language (BL). In using the term *BL*, *Language* is capitalized to denote both language STRUCTURE and language USE. Viewing Language in this way allows us to conceptualize BL as a distinct set of structural features and communicative norms and practices. For instance, as we've seen above, BL has a habitual verb structure not found in any other variety of English ("I be speakin"). In addition to unique syntactic constructions, BL also exhibits variation in several features, such as the copula ("Jay-Z rhymin wit a crazy flow"), third-person singular *-s* ("Eve rap real hard sometimes"), and possessive *-s* ("I'm feelin Epiphany album; it's hot"). (These three features make up the focus of this study and are explained in detail later.)

Of course, any language is more than a checklist of features. Discursive strategies such as SUCK-TEETH and FALSETTO, for example, can be used in conversation. Further, turn-taking rules in conversation may demonstrate the learning of communicative norms for speakers of BL. Our view of BL also sees linguistic practices and cultural modes of discourse, such as CALL AND RESPONSE, RAPPIN, SIGNIFYIN, and so on, as well as more structured speech events such as PLAYIN THE DOZENS and RHYMIN IN THE CIPHER, as integral to any description of the language variety and the many styles flexed by its speakers. While we are advocating a holistic view of BL, much of the analysis in this study focuses on sociolinguistic variables, and more research needs to be done regarding interactional strategies. This is a beginning.

FIGURE 2.2
Speech Style Broken Down into Sociolinguistic Style and Interactional Style

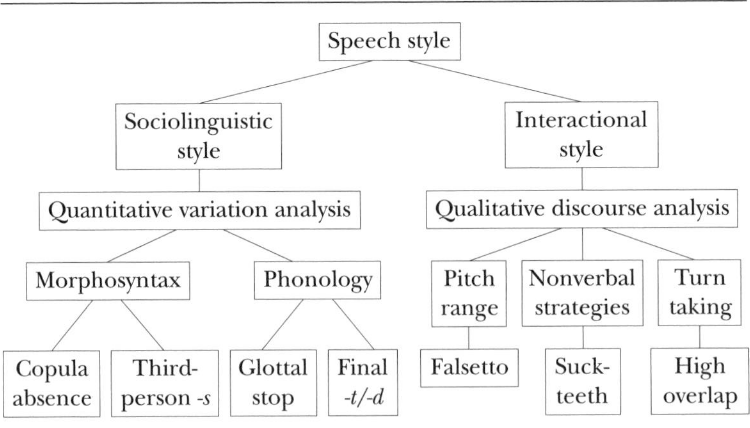

The two broad categories of STRUCTURE and USE lend themselves to two broad categories of speech style that I'm callin SOCIOLINGUISTIC STYLE (based on variation analysis) and INTERACTIONAL STYLE (based on discourse analysis of talk in interaction). Figure 2.2 illustrates some of the ways that speech style might be studied. A study of sociolinguistic style using quantitative variationist analysis may examine the frequency and distribution of several morphosyntactic variables, such as the copula, in addition to several phonological variables, such as word-final *-t/-d.* A study of interactional style may not be concerned so much with sociolinguistic variables, but might focus instead on the use and meaning of FALSETTO and SUCK-TEETH in context or the organizational structure of turn-taking in conversation, for example.

THE SEMISTRUCTURED CONVERSATION (SSC): INTRODUCING A NEW METHODOLOGICAL SPEECH EVENT

Traditionally, sociolinguistic studies of style have relied on the SOCIOLINGUISTIC INTERVIEW to gather speech data from the community. This methodology was developed by Labov (1966) in a conception of style, where "contextual styles" shift up and down a continuum of (in)formality based solely on "attention paid to speech." Labov's aim was to develop a methodology sufficient to measure the extent of regularity in stylistic variation according to various contexts.

Labov studied a number of linguistic variables as they appeared in five different contextual styles (1972b, 79–85; listed in order of increasing formality):

CONTEXT A: Casual speech
CONTEXT B: The Interview situation (careful speech)
CONTEXT C: Reading style
CONTEXT D: Word lists
CONTEXT D': Minimal pairs (i.e., words that have a single differentiating element, e.g., "*r*ap" and "*t*ap")

Labov believed that speakers paid little or no attention to their own speech when engaged in casual speech and increasingly more attention to speech as they moved down the list. His work revealed that, indeed, most speakers used more "nonstandard" or stigmatized forms in their casual speech and that these forms decreased in the same person's speech as they engaged in more formal situations. Importantly, Labov's isolation of contextual styles demonstrated that stylistic variation is context-based and follows a certain amount of regularity. However, Labov was aware that the results he obtained might have been artifacts of the procedure, and several scholars have since built upon his unidimensional approach to variation.

Baugh (1979, 1983) turned to SITUATIONAL STYLES, rather than CONTEXTUAL STYLES, and developed a grid for the analysis of speech in four different situational contexts (see figure 2.3). Two key factors came into play: (1) whether or not the speakers were familiar with each other, and (2) whether or not the speakers were members of the Black Street Culture.

FIGURE 2.3
Baugh's (1983, 25–26) Speech Event Subdivisions

Familiar (frequent contact)	Unfamiliar (occasional contact)	
TYPE 1: Familiar Exchange Depicts speech events that have familiar participants, all of whom are natives of the Black vernacular culture. They also share long-term relationships, which tend to be close-knit and self-supporting.	TYPE 2: Intracommunity Contact Represents speech events where participants are not well acquainted but are members of the Black vernacular culture.	Members of Black Street Culture
TYPE 3: Intercommunity Exchange Indicates speech events where participants are well acquainted but Black street speech is not shared; solidarity may or may not exist between any two or more individuals.	TYPE 4: Outsider Contact Corresponds to speech events where participants are not familiar nor is Black street speech common to all.	Outsiders to Black Street Culture

Unlike most other researchers of style, Baugh was the interviewer for all of his data. Since he was ethnographically positioned in the field as a lifeguard and (for the last two years) a resident of the community, he was able to enlist what he calls "the waiting strategy," in which he simply waited until the topic of language came up before introducing the "researcher-side" of his identity. His dual role in the community was invaluable to collecting the speech data over a period of several years. This type of access, and the lack of time constraints on his data collection (a rare occurrence in sociolinguistics), led him to abandon the SOCIOLINGUISTIC INTERVIEW for an approach that was more rooted in the cultural perspective of his "consultants." He turned to questions about the contributions that Blacks have made to American music, the teaching of Black music and Black history in the schooling experience of the interviewee, the state of race relations between Blacks and Whites, and so on.

Baugh's early research on style is foundational to the current strand of research that centers styleshifting around AUDIENCE DESIGN (Bell 1984). While the ethnographic component was critical to Baugh's research, current research on style has relied less on ethnographic methods and more upon controlled experimentation. Rickford and McNair-Knox (1994) built upon both of these works and attempted to arrive at a more controlled, experimental set-up to test the impact of addressee and topic on speaker style. In brief, the same Black female, Foxy Boston, was interviewed by two interviewers (one Black female and one White female) to determine the effect of addressee characteristics, in this case, race. This study has launched other studies in this direction, where empirical and highly controlled experimental designs have taken center stage (see below). While Rickford and McNair-Knox clearly showed that the characteristics of the addressee impacted speaker style, they were not able to separate the effects of race and familiarity, since Foxy Boston was already familiar with the Black interviewer. Work by Bell and Johnson (1997) and Bell (2001) has further tightened the experimental controls in such a way as to be able to isolate ethnicity and gender.

While the Labovian sociolinguistic interview is still being used by sociolinguistic researchers, many have moved beyond that procedure and created methodology that tackles new conceptions of style. For this research, where I conceptualize style as both sociolinguistic and interactional, I have developed what I am calling the SEMISTRUCTURED CONVERSATION (SSC). The use of the SSC allows us to examine the speech of both interlocutors in a speech event that more closely resembles natural conversation. It is important to note that an INTERVIEW is a particular type of speech event where one speaker does most of the talking. This is not to say that interviewers don't talk at all, but it's expected that the interviewer will be asking the questions while the interviewee will be providing the answers. In fact, it's not uncommon for a speaker's first question, upon being asked to participate in an interview, to be, "Okay, what do you wanna know?"

In this study, interlocutors were invited not to participate in an INTERVIEW, but rather, to engage in a CONVERSATION, a conversation that did NOT include the researcher. All participants were given the same handout with a list of questions and topics to review before beginning the conversations. I reminded them of two important points: "(1) You are encouraged to share your opinions on these topics, and (2) This is not an interview, and even though y'all don't know each other, let's get to know each other by having a free-flowing, natural conversation." Now, while the "set-up" nature of an SSC can never really be a natural conversation, sometimes it come pretty damn close! For example, the following extended snippet of one SSC epitomizes the characteristics of natural, free-flowing conversation (this dialogic exchange will be analyzed later in the chapter). We join the conversation where C talkin about how some people want musicians to shove positive messages down people throats:

C: . . . like, people don't wanna get stuff shoved down their throat . . .
B: Yeah . . .
C: You know, you gotta come and like welcome them, or make them more buy into a positive message. Like sometimes people ask me about like Gospel music like . . .

B: Yeah...
C: ...like, you know, "Don't you listen to Gospel?" And I'm like, "Weeell, kinda, sorta, but..." Like, I always say like, "It's the music."
B: Yeah...
C: You know, I love God and I'm a Christian...
B: Huh...
C: ...so like, I love hearing, you know, positive messages, but like, if the music's wack, it's just hard...
B: Yeah, it's hard...
C: ...it's just really hard for me to get into it...
B: [laughter]
C: So, like, I only like Christian acts that have original music...
B: Yeah...
C: ...and I think that's what you can't do...
B: I don't like when they...
C: ...you can't sacrifice the music...
B: Maaan...
C: ...for saying, "Oh, Jesus, Jesus, Jesus!" Like, at least—don't like...
B: I hate, I hate...
C: [shuddering] Uuuughhhh!
B: I hate groups that copy the same beat off a rapper...
C: And just...
B: ...switch the words around...
C: YESSSS!
B: And God...
C: Dude!
B: Maaan, I hate that!
C: Dude!
B: I hate that!
C: Dude!
B: So much!
C: I hate that so much! Like there's this one rapper...
B: [shuddering] Uuuuuughhhh!
C: ...and he took the beat for, "Every other city we gooo...," and I'm like, "How you gon make a Christian song outta that?!"
B: [laughter]
C: [laughter] How are you gonna like take a song about hoes, and just, [African American falsetto] I mean, and put in Jesus?!
B: That's what really upsets me...

C: But like, I'm like, one, that's not creative. You lazy!

B: [laughter]

C: And two, [African American falsetto] don't talk—that's what you listening to?!

B: [laughter] You try to talk about this, and make people think that you it...

C: [laughter]

B: I mean, be true to yo—maaan...

C: I mean, right, right, just like, be true to—I don't know...

B: Maaan, that's crazy, man...

C: ...take a chance to like be original and creative and don't copy...

B: Yeah, what do you feel about sampling then?

C: Oooooh, oh boy, boy, oh, oh boy, oh boy, oh boy... I like, okay, I really like Puffy...

B: Yeah...

C: ...because he's a self-made man...

B: Yeah...

C: ...and I can't, I can't front on that. I can't front on like a young, Black man being a millionaire by the time, before he was thirty...

B: Mm-hmm...

C: ...and NOT coming from like money. Like he wasn't rich; he's from Harlem...

B: Yeah...

C: He went to college, you know. He was a real ambitious, young man, so I really support him because people don't give him credit...

B: Yeah...

C: ...for like, what he's done...

B: Like, that's smart...

C: ...but sampling had its moment...

B: [laughter]

C: ...and you can't do that anymore...

B: No [laughter]...

C: Like, and I think HE killed it...

B: Yep... [laughter]

C: [laughter] Like he could've stretched it out maybe a little bit longer, but he just got really greedy...

B: Yeah...

C: ...you know, and was like, "I'ma..."—you know, I just think that's the problem with...

B: He overdid it...

C: . . . music, is people get greedy . . .
B: Yep . . .
C: . . . and they overdo certain formulas . . .
B: Master P . . .
C: Yeah, yeah, you overdo certain formulas, man. Now, they gon overdo little kids.
B: Overdo it . . .
C: They gon like have a gazillion little kid rappers, because it sells . . .
B: Lil Romeo, Lil Bow Wow, Lil Sammy, Lil . . .
C: Yeahhhh, Lil J . . .
B: Yeah [laughter] . . .
C: Everybody, and it's like . . .
B: Even the little boy groups, too . . .
C: Yeaaahhh! And it's kinda like . . .
B: B2K and Lil, I don't know . . .
C: I mean, sometimes, I'm just wondering, or sometimes, do you ever think like they think we're stupid as consumers, or like—cause people still buy it. They wouldn't do it unless people buy it, you know what I'm saying?
B: That's true . . .
C: Like do you ever get upset?
B: I get upset ALL the time. It's like, it's crazy, how they, I don't know—it almost make me feel like we stupid. They think we're stupid; we don't know what they doing!
C: [laughter]
B: In reality, we two steps ahead of you! We KNOW what you bout to plan!
C: [laughter] Yeahhh!
B: And when Lil Bow Wow come out, OF COURSE, somebody else's gonna come out with a Lil Romeo. Who WOULDN'T?!
C: [laughter]
B: If they see Lil Bow Wow doing it, and somebody making his lyrics, who wouldn't?

It's clear from several features of the dialogue—the frequent back-channeling, the rapid turn-taking, the frequency of excited laughter, the overlap and completion of one another's sentences, the pitch, tempo, and so on—that this dialogue is amenable to conversation analysis. We will return to this type of dialogue in later chapters, but for now, it provides a sufficient example of what an

SSC can look like, at its best (see appendix A for a complete SSC). In fact, a team of discourse analysts at Stanford University could not agree on who was the interviewer or the interviewee. Of course, in such a design, those terms are irrelevant, but this demonstrates the potential of the natural and free-flowing nature of SSCs and the use of this speech event as a methodological advancement in the study of style, sociolinguistic variation, conversation analysis, and other forms of discourse analysis.

Another important aspect of the SSC is that the researcher can manipulate the topic of discussion to some degree. In my case, we gon see in the next section on research design, all conversations were on the general topic of Hip Hop Culture, with questions like:

1. What kinds of music do you listen to, and how often do you listen to them?
2. Do you remember your very FIRST Hip Hop experience (when you first heard or saw it and what it was like)? What did you think when you heard it?
3. How often do you listen to Hip Hop music now?
4. Are people into Hip Hop music WHERE YOU ARE FROM? Where do you hear or see Hip Hop in your local area?
5. Do you know anyone that does Hip Hop or anyone that raps or makes music (just for fun or professionally)? Do you know any rappers in your area/school? Are they any good?
6. Do you watch any HIP HOP VIDEOS? Which ones are your favorites right now? Do you agree with people who say that Hip Hop videos are too violent? What about Hip Hop movies? Do you know of any?
7. Who is your FAVORITE HIP HOP ARTIST, and why? Who is your favorite artist out of any type of music? What makes them your favorite?
8. What makes a really good artist, to you? What 3 or 4 qualities do they have to have?
9. AS A MAN/WOMAN, do you think you view Hip Hop differently than the opposite sex? How are men and women rappers different? How do they get treated differently?
10. Do you think what rappers talk about has an IMPACT ON KIDS? Does it have an impact on you personally? Why or why not?

11. Should HOMOSEXUALITY have a place in Hip Hop? Do you think the rap community will ever accept a "gay rapper"? Why or why not?
12. What about WHITE ARTISTS in Hip Hop? Or OTHER RACES in Hip Hop? Is Hip Hop Black music? What does it mean to say that something is "BLACK MUSIC"?

To summarize the above discussion, figure 2.4 illustrates the relationship between the SSC and other speech events, namely the sociolinguistic interview and natural, spontaneous conversation. From figure 2.4 we see that SSCs provide several advantages over the sociolinguistic interview to the researcher of an integrated approach to style, including the full participation of both interlocutors. While SSCs cannot occur spontaneously, they may, as we have seen, achieve a high level of spontaneous interaction. The advantage offered by SSCs over natural, spontaneous conversations is that the researcher can use ethnographic insights to preselect a topic that speakers find interesting in their daily lives, providing for an increased possibility of animated discourse. After all, as I'm sure many of us have experienced on the job, in class, or even with some friends, not all natural, spontaneous conversations are INTERESTING. Seriously, though, the SSC allows us to control for topics in ways that are almost impossible in natural, spontaneous conversations.

There are two final points to remember. The first is that the SSC constitutes a new methodological speech event that was birthed out of a theoretical desire to develop an integrated approach to the study of speech style, one that examines both the sociolinguistic and interactional dimensions of styleshifting and that is situated between sociolinguistic and linguistic anthropological methodology. The second point, which cannot be overemphasized, is that the researcher is not a participant in the SSCs. The SSCs occur between two nonsociolinguists brought together expressly for the purpose of conversation. While my own speech is analyzed in chapter 3, it is for the methodological purpose of considering "how the other half speaks"—that is, to analyze the speech of the researcher AND the researched, something that has been missing in sociolinguistics. In the analysis of the 32 SSCs, however, that ain't me talkin. I took myself out, thereby removing the methodological

FIGURE 2.4
The Relationship between Three Speech Events

Increasing informality in speech style ↓

SOCIOLINGUISTIC INTERVIEW Highly structured event that is clearly an interview Interviewer encouraged to do very little talking, but also to elicit as much speech as possible Generally follows a question-answer format Nonethnographically preselected topics chosen by the interviewer Includes reading passages and word lists Used primarily by sociolinguists
SEMISTRUCTURED CONVERSATION Designed and explained as a conversation No interviewer/ee; interlocutors are encouraged to share opinions in a free-flowing conversation Intentionally doesn't follow question-answer format Preselected topics based on ethnographic insights No reading passages or word lists New method for the study of style (cross-disciplinary)
NATURAL, SPONTANEOUS CONVERSATION Least structured event Occurs spontaneously between interlocutors without prompting or "set-up" Structure does not depend on question-answer format, but many end up being so No preselected topics No reading passages or word lists In natural settings Used by anthropologists and ethnographers

Decreasing methodological constraints on speech style ↓

influence that a sociolinguist would surely have on the conversations. So, in the analysis of variation in the copula, third-person singular *-s*, and other features in chapters 5–8, my speech style and sociolinguistic knowledge are not factors. In the SSCs, as we will see, both the speech of the Sunnysidaz and the speech of the Stanfordians is available for analysis.

RESEARCH DESIGN

The research design for this study is obviously influenced heavily by previous research designs (Baugh 1979, 1983; Rickford and McNair-Knox 1994; Bell 2001) and seeks to build upon them. Baugh's research on styleshifting in the Black street speech community was one of the few studies rooted in an ethnographic approach. In the present study, I, too, had a dual role in the community and was a participant on many levels. I not only lived in the community during this research, but I taught at the local high school and middle school for nearly two years. Further, I gathered many ethnographic notes and impressions by visiting the neighborhood barbershop once a week for three years (and, like I said, kept my fade TIGHT while doin it!). All of this allowed me to develop genuine, sustained relationships with the community, as I was seen as an integral member. This relationship building allowed me to gain deep insights into the communicative behavior and norms of the speech community.

While I have collected hundreds of audio- and videotaped conversations and interviews in multiple ethnographic contexts, I also sought to develop a rigorous research model designed expressly to determine the effects of identity characteristics on speaker style. Since I was teaching a course on Hip Hop Culture and since my experiences at the school confirmed the centrality of Hip Hop Culture to my students' identities, that topic was a natural one. In fact, many of the questions/topics discussed were ones that I knew the students had discussed either in or out of class. This ensured that the conversations would be interesting to the speakers because they already held opinions on the issues. Generally speaking, Hip Hop Culture was also a good topic of discussion due to the major airplay it's been getting for the past several years on television stations as diverse as BET, MTV, CNN, ESPN, and even C-SPAN. Colleges and universities are now discussing Hip Hop regularly and offering courses; the music is used to market every product from Pepsi to Lexus to Gap; I mean, damn near everybody and they mama done heard of Hip Hop and the various controversies that surround the music and culture, you know what I'm saying? Even folks that don't know a lot about it, got strong opinions, preconceptions and questions.

These SSCs occurred in an original research design that, although arrived at independently, is similar to Bell's (2001) design, but with some added dimensions. For the purposes of this discussion, the interlocutors in the study will be referred to as "Sunnysidaz" and "Stanfordians." Figure 2.5 identifies the characteristics of participating interlocutors. The grid shows that there are only two types of Sunnysidaz in the sample, Black Male Hip Hoppers and Black Female Hip Hoppers. It also shows that the Stanfordians vary based on race, gender and Hip Hop cultural knowledge. Within these three factor groups, there are two factors each, allowing for eight different types of Stanfordians ($2^3 = 8$ possible combinations). So, each type of Sunnysida speaks to eight different Stanfordians, making for 16 SSC types as shown in figure 2.6. So, the total corpus for this portion of the study consists of 4 Sunnysidaz—2 Black Male Hip Hoppers and 2 Black Female Hip Hoppers—and 8 Stanfordians for a total of 32 conversations. (4 Sunnysidaz × 8 Stanfordians = 32 conversations). The 32 conversations averaged 40 minutes per interview for a total of approximately 1,280 minutes of talk, or over 21 hours. All transcripts were transcribed verbatim, resulting in approximately 1,300 pages. In addition to these 32 conversations, I have recorded the Sunnysidaz' peer, in-group talk, which will serve as an additional point of comparison.

FIGURE 2.5
Interlocutor Characteristics of Sunnysidaz and Stanfordians

		Stanfordians		
		Race	*Gender*	*Hip Hop*
Sunnysidaz	Black male Hip Hopper	Black/ White	Male/ Female	Hip Hop/ No Hip Hop
	Black female Hip Hopper	Black/ White	Male/ Female	Hip Hop/ No Hip Hop

FIGURE 2.6
Sixteen Semistructured Conversation Types: Total of 32 Conversations

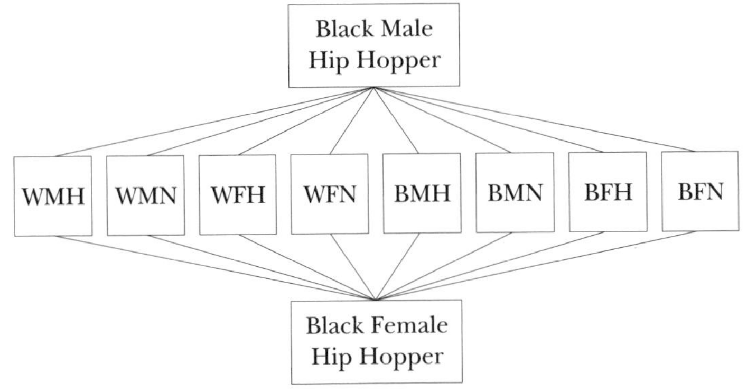

SELECTION OF INTERLOCUTORS

The selection of interlocutors was carried out under necessarily tight experimental controls. The four Sunnysidaz—Amira, Bilal, Careem, and Kijana—were all volunteers from my Hip Hop class at Haven High and speakers of BL. All were 17-year-old Black Americans who grew up in the same working-class Sunnyside hood described in detail in chapter 4. Avid listeners of Hip Hop and R&B music, they all listen to music from two to four hours a day (including radio, music videos, headphones in class, in the car, on the Internet, or at home). Bilal and Careem are not "blood brothers," but they "brothas from a different mutha," as they like to say. On any given day, you might catch Bilal and Careem mobbin through the hood wit the latest joints from Three-X-Krazy, Jay-Z, Beanie Sigel, or 50 Cent on blast. (I can hear that BANGIN 50 Cent joint tearin up the streets right now.) They actually live in the same crib, as Bilal lost his mother and father at an early age. Amira and Kijana are best friends and hang out almost daily, whether they studyin at school, at the local neighborhood dance club for teenagers, or braidin each other hair. And you know they gon have that new Busta Rhymes or DMX jawn on, too, or maybe a lil Alicia Keys and India.Arie to smooth things out (for Amira's sake). All four spend a LOT of time together both in and out of school. In fact, they were selected because they constituted a relatively tight-knit, peer-group speech community. The Sunnysidaz were aware that the Stanfordians were from the elite, private university of Stanford and, given the tremendous economic disparities between Stanford and Sunnyside, were of the same "rich" perceived class.

The selection of the Stanfordians was based on the following criteria:

1. All were chosen from the Stanford University community.
2. Each was around the same age (approximately from mid-20s to 30 years old).
3. All were informed that the Sunnysidaz were from Sunnyside, an area where you are warned NOT to go when you come to Stanford.
4. All had some experience working with Black teens, especially in schools. This was important in order to avoid any kind of cultural "shock" that could occur, given the high degree of residential segregation in the United States.
5. All had a command of "standard English," as most Stanfordians do.

In addition, the following controls were in force:

1. All of the interlocutors were strangers to each other, so familiarity based on contact was under control.
2. All interlocutors were told to come as they normally dress; nothing formal, nothing too flashy, just casual.
3. The use of the SSCs controlled for topic, as much as possible.
4. All SSCs occurred in the same setting (Haven High), with 16 conversations occurring per weekend. The conversations took place two weeks apart.
5. None of the interlocutors were trained in sociolinguistic methodology. This was done to avoid any possible sociolinguistic bias or researcher motivation.

Given the uncertainty involved in dealing with 17-year-old Sunnysidaz and them hectic-schedule-havin Stanfordians, this type of experimental design is difficult to carry out. However, if we are to increase our understanding of style in any appreciable way, we need more studies with tight experimental controls based on ethnographic insights. My categories were arrived at through a combination of two things—careful study of the literature on style in the Black American community and the ethnographic insights that I developed from extensive immersion in Sunnyside. As I reveal in chapter 3, Hip Hop Culture was THE central cultural force in the lives of the students. Racial and ethnic tensions, particularly between the long-standing yet dwindling Black population and the newly gentrifying White population, are a source of constant comment in this community. And within Hip Hop Culture, race and gender issues are battled with tenacity. Questions listed earlier as used to prompt conversation are commonly discussed among the Sunnysidaz. So, race, gender, and familiarity with Hip Hop Culture all were likely candidates as indicators of styleshifts, as the ethnographic context revealed.

In chapters 5–7, I present, interpret, and discuss quantitative variation results using GOLDVARB 2001. The results show that all three factors are significant indicators of styleshifting, and more detailed analysis shows the interaction of these factors as speakers shift through the stylistic spectrum. I will be addressing questions such as: How does one's speech style differ when speaking to a Black, female non–Hip Hopper versus a White, male Hip Hopper? What accounts for the change in style? What is important here—specific linguistic features or discourse-level phenomena? DOES race really matter? What about gender and cultural familiarity? More importantly, HOW and WHEN do these factors matter? What are the roles of identity, ideology, and consciousness?

The final section on the analysis of sociolinguistic style will compare the speakers' language use in the 32 conversations with their peer, in-group talk.

THE SOCIOLINGUISTIC VARIABLES

Following well-known studies of styleshifting in Black American Speech Communities (Labov et al. 1968; Baugh 1979, 1983; Rickford and McNair-Knox 1994), I originally selected five sociolinguistic variables for this study, all of which distinguish BL from other varieties of contemporary American English:

1. Copula absence: "They Ø tryina act like us, but they Ø white" [Careem]; "This coat Ø hecka big" [Kijana]
2. Third-person singular *-s* absence: "however he seeØ fit" [Amira]; "it's the way he flowØ" [Careem]
3. Invariant *be*: "They BE givin MONEY if they run out of candy!" [Amira]; "Dumb-asses BE settin they whole basket of candy out like ain't nobody gon take that junk" [Bilal]
4. Possessive *-s* absence: "That's his uncleØ car" [Kijana]; "You shoulda seen the look on my grandmamaØ face!" [Bilal]
5. Plural *-s* absence: "We gon sell a million copyØ" [rapper Lil Troy]

Each of the features will be analyzed as they appear in the 32 conversations. In the final section, peer, in-group talk will serve as a point of comparison—a BL baseline, if you will—to the 32 SSCs.

In a variation analysis, sociolinguists report the actual occurrences of a variant against the total number of cases in which that variant might have occurred, barring any "don't count" cases (see Labov 1972a, 72, for what he terms the "accountability principle"). By "don't count" cases, I mean that you cannot include cases where the variant cannot ever occur among the total number of cases. The best way to get a sense of how variationists work with speech data is to look at a sample transcript. The following transcript is annotated to show how I marked the occurrence of three of the features. Since the copula can either be absent, contracted, or full, we used three notations: [ca] = copula absent, [cc] = copula contracted, and [cf] = copula full. Third-person singular *-s* and possessive *-s* can only be absent or present, so we used the following notation: [3a] = third-person singular *-s* absent, [3p] = third-person singular *-s* present, [pa] = possessive *-s* absent, [pp] = possessive *-s* present. Finally, since invariant *be* does not, by nature, vary, we simply bolded its occurrences, and "don't count" cases are marked by a capital [DC] (so [cDC] = copula don't count).

Below we enter the conversation where two brothas are talkin about various rappers like Outkast, Biggie, Jay-Z, and Juvenile:

C: . . . Like, do you like rappers from the South, or do you, do you even like Outkast?
K: Um, Outkast is [cf] cool to me, but it just, I like how you were saying like, they [ca] different. That's [cDC] what get [3a] me, like . . .
C: Yeah . . .
K: . . . the way they come out, they [ca] different, but I don't know, some of they songs is [cf] cool, but then it's [cDC] like some that I don't really care for, but . . .
C: Do you think they [ca] kinda over yo head a lil bit . . .
K: Yeah . . .
C: . . . just like, "I don't get that . . ."
K: . . . yeah, like, sometimes they be rappin rhymes, like I don't get it. Like, they be cool, but I'm [cDC] like . . .
C: [laughter] . . .
K: . . . what they talking about?
C: [laughter] . . .
K: It's [cDC] like I was down, we was just in Atlanta, like a couple weeks ago . . .
C: Forreal?
K: Yeah, and I picked up a CD from down there; it was like, they songs is [cf] like . . . different. You could tell the difference, and it's [cDC] like, they . . .
C: [laughter] . . .
K: . . . they, they songs is [cf] more like dance-oriented, like you would hear that in the club. Like, the songs from down there, you'd hear that in the club or whatnot . . .
C: Right, right . . .
K: . . . and . . .
C: . . . but you're [cc] more about beats than lyrics, right—cuz like I look at Jay-Z—Jay Z's [cc] a lyricist . . .
K: Yeah . . .
C: . . . cuz I remember from the git-go when I heard him rap with like Biggie, I was like, "He's [cc] just as good as Biggie," and I didn't even know who he was and I was like, "This dude is [cf] tight . . ."
K: Yeah . . .
C: Cuz like Jay-Z don't [3a] even produce—I don't think he produces [3p] any of his songs, you know. But like I'm [cDC] just wondering like what makes [3p] a artist like Jay-Z thee man?

K: Well, for me it was like, let's say I'm [cDC] listening to his CD, when I first listened to it, you know, looking for that beat that, you know, get [3a] my head bouncing or whatever, but then...

C: So, what's [cDC] an example, like "Big Pimpin," or, what's [cDC] that Neptunes song—[singin] "Give it to me / Give me that funk ..." you know, that one...

K: Yeah...

C: ... that party song...

K: See, those, though...

C: What's [cDC] a hot Jay-Z song?

K: ... like those two songs you just said is [cDC] more like, those is [cf] more like the, you know, for the beats or whatever, but lately like his last CD has been more, you know, lyrical. The stuff he [ca] rappin about is [cDC] just way...

C: Oh, you mean, Blueprint?

K: Yeah...

C: You like that album?

K: Yeah...

C: That's [cDC] a tight album. I mean...

K: It's [cDC] like every song on there—that album I wasn't really—the beats is [cf] cool, but the way he flows [3p]...

C: It's [cDC] his lyrics...

K: ... the way he flow [3a] just bring [3a] it out even more, and I just think, like I like the combination of both. Like, you could like, if somebody ain't [cDC] rappin right on the beat then that kinda take [3a] away from the song, so it's [cDC] like a combination of both together that I like...

C: I feel you, I feel you. I mean, I always thought Jay-Z was cool. I always knew he could rap. People always try to put him down, like say he only rap [3a] about, you know, bling-bling...

K: Yeah...

C: ... or like, but he doesn't [3p]...

K: Yeah...

C: ... like if you listen to his albums, I do think he covers [3p] the full spectrum...

K: What you think about all this, you know, upcoming, since Cash Money, the bling-bling stuff how—what you think?

C: [suck-teeth] [sighing] Ahhh, maaan, I'll be honest, man, when I first heard Juvenile's [pp] album, when I heard, "Back that Azz Up," and when I heard, "HA"—member...

80 K: Yeah...
81 C: ...member that song, "HA"?
82 K: Yeah [laughter]...
83 C: I was like, "Dude, this dude is [cf] crazy!"

For simplicity's sake, let's just look at K's copula variability, particularly his use of the variant copula absence. In lines 1–83, there are three instances of copula absence (lines 4, 7 and 52) and nine cases where copula absence COULD have occurred. The other six cases are all examples of full copula (lines 3, 8, 22, 25, 50, and 60), meaning there are zero instances of the contracted variant. So, out of K's nine possible occurrences of the copula, three are absent, zero are contracted, and six are full.

In addition, there are also eleven "don't count" cases. Again, these are excluded from the analysis for various reasons. Wolfram (1969, 166) explains: "In the quantitative measurement of copula absence, it is essential to separate environments where there is no variability from those where there is legitimate variation between the presence and absence of the copula. Failure to distinguish these environments would skew the figures of systematic variation." For example, the BL copula is never absent in the first-person singular. So, in line 14 where K says, "I'm [cDC] like," it is a "don't count" case because K can never say **I like.* He can only produce *I'm like* and *I am like.* Since the third variant cannot be produced, first-person singular cases are thrown out. Further, in line 4 where K says, "That's [cDC] what get [3a] me," it is a "don't count" case because the BL copula is rarely, if ever, absent for *it's, that's,* and *what's* (see Rickford 1998 for the relevance of these cases to studies of copula absence). Another case of "don't count" is *ain't* (line 64), since the copula is never absent in this negative form. More complicated is the case of the copula following relative clauses—in my data, as with other studies, the copula is never absent when immediately following a relative clause (lines 50 and 53, for example).

Once these notations are made on the transcript, each instance is coded for the various linguistic and identity constraints that we are examining (see appendix C for coding scheme and chapter 5 for the constraints on the copula). Each instance of the copula is coded and then entered into a statistical software program that analyzes the variation—in this case GOLDVARB 2001 (Robinson, Lawrence, and Tagliomonte 2001), based on GOLDVARB 2.0 (Rand and Sankoff 1990). This variable rule program runs a binomial up and down (logistic regression) to produce factor weights (see Cedergren and Sankoff 1974; Sankoff and Labov 1979; and Guy 1988), or probability coefficients, rather than simply the observed frequencies of the variants. Logistic regression is used by researchers where the dependent variable is "limited" (discrete, not continuous) and they want to see if a given "event" occurred or not. In our case, we are concerned with the question: Was a given variant absent or present? The binomial up-and-down runs allow us to determine more than just the frequency of copula absence, for example; we can also determine the relative ordering of constraints on our variable (i.e., ranking the constraints that shape the behavior of the copula).

This is the type of analysis performed in chapters 5–7. In the next chapter, we discuss how variationist studies can benefit from ethnographic methods. In particular, I will reflect on my role as a researcher in an ethnographically informed study of style. As we will see, more and more researchers are beginning to see the value of ethnographic methods in variationist studies.

3. HOW THE OTHER HALF SPEAKS: ETHNOSENSITIVITY AND THE SHIFTING ROLES OF THE RESEARCHER

In the previous chapter, I discussed sociolinguistic variation and a research design for the sociolinguistic study of style. This chapter focuses on the ethnographic approach to the study of style and focuses largely on the researcher as instrument, with particular attention being paid to the concept of ETHNOSENSITIVITY. I will address questions such as: How did I gain access to the field? How did my own speech shift according to my shifting roles as a teacher and researcher? What is the value of developing a sustained, genuine relationship with the community of study? As we consider both the language of both the RESEARCHER and the RESEARCHED, these questions will hopefully help us rethink sociolinguistic methodology and theories of style.

ELEPHANTS IN THE ROOM: FROM NWAV TO AnWAV

The widely announced slogan of the 31st Conference on New Ways of Analyzing Variation (NWAV 31) in 2002, the largest annual gathering of sociolinguists, was "elephants in the room." Generally, the phrase "elephants in the room" is used to suggest that there are some quite glaring objects in our midst to which we have not paid enough attention. The Stanford University NWAV 31 Planning Committee decided that it was time for sociolinguists to begin questioning some of our fundamental assumptions, such as the notions of "vernacular" and "the authentic speaker" (Bucholtz 2003; Coupland 2003) and the "critical age hypothesis" in language acquisition (Sankoff 2002; Clark 2003), as well as revisiting some of our unresolved issues, such as the historical development of "African American English" (Wolfram 2002), the concept and definition of a "Black Standard English" (Rahman 2002), and the role that variationists can play in the language education of linguistically marginalized groups (Hakuta 2002; LeMoine 2002; Ramsey 2002; Rickford and Rickford 2002; Siegel 2002).

As we enter the new millennium, this moment in NWAV history, and the history of the study of language in context, can be described as one in which sociolinguists and linguistic anthropologists are looking for ways to bridge the decades-old disciplinary divide between them. There seems to be a swelling wave of scholars who believe that new insights into the study of language in social life can be gained by integrating the quantitative analysis of variationist sociolinguistics with the interpretive framework of linguistic anthropology. This integration, I believe, as Hymes (1977) did a quarter of a century ago, would lead to both theoretical and methodological advancements. The growing belief is that the predominantly quantitative work of variationist sociolinguistics needs the perspective of linguistic anthropology, which views language as cultural practice and as a tool to be utilized by speakers to construct identities (Duranti 1997). In turn, the primarily qualitative research of linguistic anthropology can benefit from the empirical methodology often used in variationist studies.

Eckert and Gaudio (2002), recognizing and riding the new wave, write:

> While many variationists are now using ethnographic methods, there remains a perception across disciplines that the quantitative analytic methods of variation are somehow incompatible with the qualitative approaches of linguistic and sociocultural anthropology. This workshop will delve into the integration of the two traditions, showing how each can enhance the other, as we shed light on the embedding of variation in communicative practice and social life.

While it is clear how ethnographic methods can benefit the study of variation (by increasing rapport between the researcher and the researched, developing greater insight into the social meaning of variants gained from prolonged exposure to the speech community, providing greater understanding of how speech acts are situated within the everyday practices of speakers, etc.), it is not so clear how variationist analysis can benefit linguistic anthropology. In light of the growing trend to consider anthropological ways of analyzing variation (AnWAV), this chapter seeks to demonstrate how the approaches of variation and linguistic anthropology can be MUTUALLY beneficial.

Importantly, this chapter considers "how the other half speaks." At first blush, given the sometimes hierarchical, elitist nature of sociolinguistic research (as noted by Bucholtz 2003), this title may be perceived as meaning, "how the poor, disadvantaged speak." This misperception results from the almost exclusive focus on the speech of the RESEARCHED, and the regular neglect of the speech of the RESEARCHER. In the examination of speech style, the realization that style and meaning are coconstructed is essential. Therefore, limiting our empirical analysis to one speaker in what is fundamentally a DIALOGIC activity (conversation) has made sociolinguists to overlook approximately 50% of the speech situation. If we are to say anything about the speech style of a given speaker in a given situation, we must consider, equally, the speech style of both (or all) interlocutors. Of course, this problem is magnified when the methodology of the study is the sociolinguistic interview, which sometimes reduces style to a monologically produced entity. In looking out of only one eye and listening with only one ear, we have indeed not noticed the elephant among us. How does the speech style of the sociolinguistic researcher impact the speech style of the researched and vice versa? What methodological approaches can help us gain greater insight into this developing conceptualization of style? How can we begin to theorize style as a dialogic project that is continuously being coconstructed by speakers working together, rather than a monologic entity representing only one half of the speech situation?

EXPLORING ETHNOSENSITIVITY IN ETHNOGRAPHIC RESEARCH ON STYLE

Writing in a chapter entitled "The Scholar and the Street: Collecting the Data," Baugh (1983, 36) notes the challenges of collecting speech data in Black and other marginalized communities: "It is one thing to recognize the need to gather data from representative consultants, but it is another matter altogether to get the job done." To that, I say, "Amen!" He begins by explaining that the challenge lies in what Labov (1972a) termed "the observer's paradox," which recognizes that the sociolinguist can never truly be the proverbial fly on the wall. In other words, as sociolinguists, the paradox is that we hope to observe the type of speech behavior that occurs when speakers ain't bein observed. In marginalized speech communities, Baugh notes that given the "negative reactions to their behavior when they venture into mainstream domains, it is quite understandable that their suspicions are aroused by outsiders who suddenly appear, not to mention outsiders who also desire to record their conversations."

Further, if that outsider happens to be a "researcher," the suspicion is heightened due to the community's view of "scholarly research" that claims to accurately depict certain aspects, values, and experiences of that community. Even when contemporary scholars attempt to go beyond the "deficit approach" and invoke a "difference approach," community members oftentimes view their research as still working well within the deficit model. For example, in a discussion about the ethics and responsibilities of researchers, one Stanford professor recounted a research project conducted in Sunnyside that evaluated a high school negatively. While attempting to engage in socially responsible research, the research team inadvertently disappointed and angered the community, who had willingly volunteered their time and effort for the study's success. They depicted the community as improperly managing their own high school, and thus contributing to its demise, while ignoring major social and economic factors which they had not researched fully. This case demonstrates how ignoring larger structural factors can be problematic.

Add to this already complicated relationship the fact that youth are often a marginalized group within a marginalized population, and the study of speech in schools seems to be an inordinately difficult task. As one of my students asked in the very first days of my research, "Do they think we're disadvantaged at Stanford?"

I hesitated, as I was not prepared for such a question, while she answered it herself: "They better not." Of course, I realized that this was as much a critique of the manner in which elite university-trained scholars often describe oppressed communities as it was an indirect signification on, and testing of, my role as a "researcher" in the initial stages of the project.

This anecdote provides an opportunity to discuss what Baugh (1979) termed ETHNOSENSITIVITY, which "requires the fieldworker to collect the data ... in such a manner that the values and cultural orientation of the native consultants are taken into account" (1983, 40). Beyond the collection of the data, I would add that ethnosensitivity requires scholars to analyze and interpret the data within research paradigms and frameworks that are both rigorous and respectful (Ray McDermott, pers. comm, 2003). Rigorous analysis is the first step toward respect. A rigorous analysis that considers the "values and cultural orientation" of the community cooperating in the study is the ultimate demonstration of respect, particularly when that community done been harmed and hardened by previous research endeavors.

Ethnosensitivity is not to be mistaken as a construct that merely invokes a respectful attitude. It is not spoken; it is SHOWN. In Baugh's case, his comments seem to have been largely driven by Dillard's (1972) observations that Black adults tended toward "standard English" and that they were not representative speakers of African American Language (BL), an observation that Baugh's work soundly refutes. Baugh recognized that his own sociolinguistic study was rare in the sense that he was not faced with rigid time constraints, nor was his study based on "personal experience" or "fleeting visits to the ghetto." Rather, his results were based on over 200 hours of speech data from Black adults with whom he had developed relationships via annual interviews. Citing the fieldwork of John Lewis (who collected much of Labov's data in Harlem) and Walt Wolfram (who, as a white researcher, played basketball with Black community members in Philadelphia to earn "authentic respect"), Baugh (1983, 41) notes that ethnosensitivity further requires "acute self-awareness and an in-depth knowledge of the community under investigation." Other ethnosensitive work in Black American speech communities includes Stack (1974), Smitherman (1977), Folb (1980), Goodwin (1990), Rickford and McNair-Knox (1994), and Lanehart (2002).

Ethnosensitive procedures, then, are best employed when one has knowledge of self AND community and is willing to face the tensions that may arise during the course of the research, as well as the underlying reasons that give rise to those tensions. In this sense, one can see how ethnosensitivity extends beyond the establishing of RAPPORT between the researcher and the researched (a necessary component), however that relationship may be constructed. Ethnosensitivity, in a sense, is a prerequisite to the establishment of a solid rapport. It would be difficult to imagine any genuine rapport being established and maintained without an ethnosensitive orientation. In my case, I established rapport during my role as a teacher-researcher at the high school, which I will discuss in detail later in this chapter. First, I consider my own ethnosensitivity in relation to the present study.

There are several factors that enabled fluid interaction between me and my students. First, I am a member of the broader Black American Speech Community (BASC), not simply by ethnic origin, but by my familiarity with the Language of mass-based Black culture. Language (with a capital "L") here refers to both structure AND use. This means that not only am I familiar with syntactic features, such as invariant *be* (*They be sellin CDs out the trunk*), copula variability (*They are lying* or *They're lying* or *They lying*), third-person singular *-s* variability (*She walk(s) to school everyday*), and possessive *-s* variability (*I'm braiding Telisha('s) hair*)—but I am also familiar with ritualized forms of Black Language (BL) use, such as SIGNIFYIN, RAPPIN, FREESTYLIN, and others, as well as the everyday interactional styles germane to the speech community. Knowledge of both structure and use enabled me as a field-worker to both observe AND engage in the speech activity that occurred across various situational contexts. And it is here that I stress that familiarity alone does not suffice; facility of use is also crucial. The collection of the data was greatly enhanced by my ability to recognize both WHEN BL WAS BEING EMPLOYED and WHEN TO EMPLOY IT.

Within the broader BASC, which consists of various localized and specialized speech communities, I am also a member of the Hip Hop Nation Speech Community (HHNSC). The HHN employs syntactic features and discursive practices that simultaneously build upon and expand the African American Oral Tradition (Smitherman 1994; Alim 2004d). Aspects of Hip Hop Nation Language (HHNL) are more than slang or unique lexical items, though they, too, are important. What I am referring to is a whole set of shared norms and discursive practices of a specialized speech community that has a healthy respect for BL and emphasizes its use whenever possible. In fact, within the HHNSC, BL is the PRESTIGE VARIETY.

My ability to navigate through the broader BASC and within the HHNSC provided me a particular advantage in this type of ethnographic research. I remember distinctly how the students at Haven High responded to me the first time I met them. The principal of the school had asked me to present my course to the entire high-school class to gauge whether or not there was sufficient student interest. I walked into the cafeteria, where they were all seated, FITTED in a fresh Busta Rhymes (an extremely popular Hip Hop artist) T-shirt and loose-fittin FUBU jeans (a Black jean company that markets to the HHN). I could already notice eyes glued to my T-shirt as I heard a young sista (whom I now know as Shahira) whisper to her friend in excitement, "That's Busta Rhymes!" Soon as I was introduced by the vice principal, I said, "Aight, we gon talk about Hip Hop! Who hot right now? Who y'all REALLY FEELIN right now?" Immediately the conversation ensued. "Fabolous!" one student shouted. "Awww, Fabolous?! I don't know, who else?" I asked. "Ludacris!" "Aight, that's my dogg, Luda!" Everybody started callin out names of they favorite Hip Hop artists and wasn't long before the whole room erupted in multiple, simultaneous, highly energized conversations. "Jay-Z!" shouted another. "Ohhh, Jiggaman, that's what I'M talkin about, FLOW OF THE CENTURY!"

Rereading my fieldnotes, I now see that in addition to the Language commonality, I had not previously noted that I shared a broad range of musical knowledge and cultural aesthetics with my students. I knew that "Ludacris" also referred to himself simply as "Luda." I also knew that one of "Jay-Z's" many monikers was "Jiggaman," and I even quoted one of his boasts, "flow of the century!" But, importantly, I didn't only QUOTE it, I MEANT it, forreal. Jay-Z DO got one of the SICKEST ('most excellent') flows in Hip Hop (*flow* describes the temporal relationship between the beats and the rhymes in Hip Hop lyrical production). The sharing of musical knowledge and cultural aesthetics is largely due to the generational overlap between me and my students. After all, I was only six years older than my oldest student, you know?! So, it wasn't unnatural for me to be wearin that Busta Rhymes shirt, nor was it unnatural for me to be quotin Jay-Z.

These observations reveal that there existed a broad cultural similarity between me and my students, at least on the SURFACE. I emphasize surface here for cultural and linguistic reasons. First, the generational overlap that helped to highlight the cultural similarities and aesthetic interests may have been a factor in enabling the fieldwork, but knowledge of Hip Hop Culture does not automatically grant one access to the speech community. I remember reading about the strange (to put it mildly) classroom practices of a fellow teacher when I was teaching in Philadelphia in the late 1990s. This teacher was well-versed in Hip Hop Culture, at least the commodified, commercialized media conceptualization, and decided to capitalize on this knowledge and use it to teach his students complex word problems in mathematics. Feeling comfortable with his knowledge and assuming that the students would, too, he proceeded to administer in-class quizzes with word problems that asked students to calculate how many BLUNTS ('marijuana') Snoop Dogg and his HOMEBOYS can smoke in a day if they each smoke at various rates of consumption. Titillated by the students' response, he continued administering these quizzes, asking the students to calculate everything from how many HOES ('prostitutes') a pimp owns to how many BRICKS and KIS (measurements of drug quantities) a dealer can move in an hour. Some of the students became upset, and it wasn't long before parents got hold of them quizzes. Needless to say, HOMEBOY had to pack his bags and look for another JOBBY JOB. Crazy? Yes. Well-intentioned? Perhaps. Any way you look at it, it was grossly insensitive. This example demonstrates that a surface-level knowledge of your students' contemporary culture is not sufficient. This teacher lacked deeper cultural awareness and familiarity, and as a result, his strategy backfired. That's what you call LACK OF ETHNOSENSITIVITY.

STYLESHIFTING AS CULTURAL PRACTICE

The second reason why I emphasized *surface* above is that when we examine the anatomy of styleshifting in the BASC, we recognize that it requires a sometimes subtle and oftentimes extremely sophisticated linguistic maneuverability. Styleshifting in the BASC, as we know from Baugh (1983) and Rickford and McNair-Knox (1994), is SITUATIONAL. Perhaps the most illuminating metacommunicative account of the situated nature of styleshifting is relayed to us by one of Baugh's (1983, 27–28) consultants. It is a lengthy passage, but as an excellent exemplification and interpretation of styleshifting as cultural practice, it is worth quoting in full:

> J: Have you come into contact with any other situations where you could see the difference [in dialect]?
>
> R: O.K. ... yesterday ... O.K. ... in my apartment building there are some New York poor white people ... O.K. ... Now, I know they don't live the best of their lives ... like most whites ... O.K. They can relate more than the California white person ... let's say like that ... O.K.?
>
> So, I'm sitting over there talking to them ... right? Two of my girlfriends come in, right? ... they come in, they come to their house [the whites' house] ... right? O.K. ... we introduce everybody ... I would sit there and see them trying to make the black girls comfortable when it wasn't really necessary. Y'know ... they want ... they try to make lots of conversation, lots of laughter ... and that's not necessary.
>
> J: So what did the sisters do? How did they handle it?
>
> R: The sisters ... they felt ... I could sit there, I saw them ... the way they felt, like, they was saying to theyself, like ... yeah, here some more white people trying to make us feel comfortable when it's not really necessary.
>
> J: No ... but what was their reaction?

R: O.K. ... their reaction was kinda like ... sit back ... and watch the show ... cause if you get up and try to dance with them [the whites], then they gonna step out and watch you act a fool ... and so, when you go around white people, you either gon be on stage, or you gon be in the audience ... y'know? ... 'n you got to sit back ... SAY LITTLE TO NOTHING, or you gotta be up there, which I call making a fool out of yourself; yackity yackity yack ... they already think they know too much about you anyway ... y'know ... and if they see you up there ... you just a mouthpiece ... most whites don't figure blacks think too well.

J: What kind of change did you go through?

R: Well ... for me ... it was even hard for me BECAUSE THE CONVERSATIONS WERE DIFFERENT.

J: What do you mean?

R: O.K. ... I have to sit ... right? I'm in the middle cause I know them both. They are both my friends ... like ... this. O.K., on this hand, I HAVE TO TALK TO THEM [the whites] ONE WAY AND THEN I HAVE TO TURN RIGHT BACK AROUND AND TALK TO THEM [the black girls] ANOTHER WAY ... AND TRY TO KEEP HIM [the white man] FROM FEELING LEFT OUT OF THIS CONVERSATION, AND THE GIRLS FROM FEELING LEFT OUT IN THE OTHER CONVERSATION ... SO ... it's kind of hard to sit in the middle of a situation like that.

In my experience, Blacks often note the differences in interactional style between Whites and Blacks, and as we shall see below, between some Blacks and other Blacks. The above account is important in that it clearly highlights the situated nature of styleshifting in the day-to-day experiences of Black Americans. In addition, it shows a sophisticated level of metacommunicative awareness, which clearly has developed from the unique social pressures born out of being Black in American society, or as Tupac Shakur (1996) once rapped, being "born Black in this white man's world."

My own experience in Sunnyside provides several examples of the cultural value placed on styleshifting in this speech community, particularly among Black Americans. Having lived in the community for the duration of my teaching experience, I established several close friendships with community members. One brotha, in particular, became my weightlifting partner, and we worked out several times a week at the local gym. Lonnie and I, both not being hardcore bodybuilders, often digressed into conversations that sometimes lasted up to several hours. We was doin what rapper E-40 call MARINATIN—a common Black linguistic practice that occurs mainly among intimates and close friends. MARINATIN involves interlocutors engaging in a free-flowing conversation with a relaxed interactional style, yet being fully and deeply involved in discussing a variety of philosophical issues. One night, after we done marinated for hours, we came across another brotha in the gym who had been listening to, but NOT PARTICIPATING IN, our conversation. So, Lonnie, thinking his silence to be a little strange (perhaps because he was shy or for some other reason), invited the brotha into the conversation with a "Ain't that right, brotha?" He didn't respond with words, rather, he just nodded and smiled, "Mm-hmm," all the while being very polite and seemingly interested in the conversation. He would add a "Yes" and an "I agree," every now and then, but his interactional style became increasingly distant. After several failed attempts to engage him as an interlocutor, the brotha left, with a smile. Soon as he rounded the corner, Lonnie was like, "See, he can't get INTO it like we can, Scream [one of my MANY nicknames]," and he just bust out laughin.

It wasn't long before I figured out that Lonnie's initial attempt to engage him ("Ain't that right, brotha?") was, in fact, initiating a linguistic assessment. Of course, in Black America, language is viewed by many as a direct indicator of one's personal background, social standing, level of educational attainment, and, importantly, cultural assimilation and political ideology (Morgan 1994). It is for these reasons that some Black Americans view the very act of speaking as a surefire way of "puttin yo business in the street." It was clear that Lonnie was privileging his own ability to "get into it" (or styleshift) and that he was evaluating the brotha based on his inability, or reluctance, to enter what he considered a familiar and familial linguistic space. "Oh, he probably a doctor or lawyer or something like that," he said, and we left the gym.

The next three personal instances demonstrating the cultural importance of styleshifting occurred on the Stanford University campus. During the course of this study, I developed a close friendship with a sista name Dee, who was one of the few sistas out of

Sunnyside to attend Stanford as a graduate student (in fact, she the only one I know). Largely because we had met in the Stanford graduate student context, and also due in part to our own comfort and facility with "mainstream English," it became the normative speaking style in most of our interactions. Several months into our friendship, as we were walkin on campus, I ran into a brotha I had known primarily from the Hip Hop cultural context—that is, we met on the basis that we were just REALLY big Hip Hop Headz. Our friendship was based around Hip Hop Culture, and he eventually enrolled in a class that I taught at Stanford, "The Language of Hip Hop Culture," a course where the knowledge and use of BL were highly valued. So, as me and Dee was walkin, we hear his voice from behind us, "Alim the dreeeaaaam!" Me and him get into it and do a lil reminiscin on the class, and he updates me on the new Hip Hop music he's been feelin lately (the new Styles and Clipse albums). We say, "Peace," and be on our way. Right after, Dee looks at me like, "Oooh, you sounded just like Carl there!" (Carl is a brotha who can styleshift from "mainstream English" to BL with ease.) I was surprised at HER surprise, because my styleshift, in this case, had occurred subconsciously. She proceeded to tell me all of the things that I did and said which she had never really witnessed me do or say before, offering commentary on my phonology, syntax, and interactional style.

This next instance is the mirror image of the previous one. It was this other sista name Jamila whom I had known for nearly three years. Over the years, we became real good friends and our preferred linguistic mode of being was "Black talk," as she put it one time. Well, one day I walk up to this professor door and knock on it, right. He come out and greets me, and I ask him if he busy so we can chop it up a bit about one of my papers. He told me to wait a coupla minutes and went back in the office. So, I wait a bit, and out comes Jamila with a funny look on her face. She sets up an appointment with the prof, smiles at me, and rolls out. Weeks later, after I done compLETELY forgot I even saw her, she came up to me like, "I got the funniest story to tell you. Remember when I was meetin with professor so-and-so a while ago, and I saw you comin in as I was goin out?" "Yeah, yeah," I said. "Well, when the prof came back in the office I asked him who was at the door. He told me it was you, but I swear I didn't believe him, Alim. It didn't make no sense. I just KNEW he was lyin to me! I coulda sworn it was a white man." I looked at her with a sideways glance, and she laughed, like, "I'm SERIOUS!" I was just laughin cuz I know I can flip it real White-like if I want to, you know what I'm saying? Curious, I asked her did she remember what I said to the prof. She started grinnin and MARKED (Mitchell-Kernan 1972) me in a real nasal-sounding voice, like, "Hi. Are you busy right now?" So, while my friend, Dee, was surprised to hear me shift into BL with my homeboy, Jamila was shocked to hear me shift into my "White voice."

This final instance is important because this experience occurred with someone whom I had not previously known. In response to the U.S. bombing of a wedding party that killed dozens of innocent Afghani civilians in 2002, the Black Student Union on campus was sponsoring a talk that critically examined the wide range of injustices caused by George W. Bush's "war on terrorism." After a fascinating dialogue, I exited with several of my friends and some others whom I did not know. After walking out to the parking lot, I spotted one of my homies, Muhammad, from Sunnyside. We greeted each other excitedly because we had been hoping to run into each other at the event. We do our linguistic thang (interact in a style valued in the BASC) and engage in a serious critique of the president's plans for war on what seemed to him to be the entire Muslim world. His ride pulled up and he said, "Peace," and was out. After he left, a sista whom I had not previously known (but who was standin outside wit us), turned to me and said, "I ain't know you could talk like THAT." "Like what?" I asked. She looked me up and down like only a sista could and said in a playful, yet sensual tone, "Like a BROTHA!" Turns out that sista had seen me on campus before where I was introducing myself to a group of students. She MARKED me with a nasally, formal voice, "My name is Alim, and I am a third-year doctoral student in educational linguistics." "You ain't right," I said, and we shared a hearty laugh. (These cases of MARKING, which I call performing "the Whitey voice," are identified as a Black American speech act of sociopolitical significance in Alim 2004e; MARKING is discussed at length in Mitchell-Kernan 1972).

These cases clearly show that Black American styleshifting can be viewed as cultural practice, as a linguistic tool employed to both CONSTRUCT and DECONSTRUCT identities. As a cultural practice, Black American styleshifting is embedded within a complex array of social, economic, and political factors, making it extremely difficult to study. Again the concept of reflexivity—speech as a reflex to past linguistic practices and ideologies and a means to construct future practices and ideologies—is important here, as evidenced by the several speakers' responses to my own speech above. It seems that the collection of speech data across the various situational and cultural contexts that occur in the everyday lived realities of representative speakers is a challenge for at least two reasons. One, it is extremely laborious and sometimes tedious from a purely methodological viewpoint, and two, Black American speech is not only the medium through which speakers' realities unfold, it also creates speakers' realities through identity construction across shifting contexts.

STYLESHIFTING AND THE SHIFTING ROLES OF THE RESEARCHER

Perhaps one reason that studies of Black American styleshifting are rare is that most linguists who study BL are not fully conversant in the variety or no longer have strong linguistic ties to the BASC. Labov clearly recognized this as a potential limitation of his study of BL in Harlem, and thus, he hired John Lewis as his field-worker. Rickford, conversant in other varieties of BL outside of the United States (Guyanese creole and other creoles, Rickford 1987), worked with the assistance of Faye McNair-Knox, a Black American member of the speech community that he was studying. Both Lewis and McNair-Knox demonstrated a type of facility with BL that was rare among researchers. Baugh, referring to Lewis's interactional style (1983, 41), was "struck by the fact that he [Lewis] was aware of the boundaries of acceptable verbal challenges, while taking care to minimize confrontations."

Baugh, who has conducted the only book-length study of Black American styleshifting, was aware that familiarity with and facility in BL were critical factors in determining the methodological approach to such a study. Rejecting a purely Chomskian, deductive approach to the study of Black street speech and preferring an inductive approach, Baugh chose to collect evidence from "Black street speakers themselves." As one of the few Black American linguists studying BL, he commented briefly on the utility of his own intuitions as a Black American scholar. He stated that the few Black Americans who do have access to academia, including himself, are fluent speakers of "standard English," and their intuitions about the dialectal boundaries of BL may be "clouded." While Baugh makes this point to underscore the need for inductive research on BL, I would like to consider it from another perspective.

It is rare in the sociolinguistic literature that we find a scholar analyzing his or her own styleshifting abilities. This would seem to be a crucial consideration in the study of BL and language in general. In other words, if we are studying the styleshifting abilities of speakers in a speech community, a major focus would have to be the styleshifting abilities of the researchers (or those collecting the data). A key point that cannot be overemphasized is that styleshifting occurs in interaction. Interaction, being a dialogic phenomenon—whether between researcher and speakers or speakers among themselves—requires the use of language by two or more interlocutors interlocking, as it were, in verbal and nonverbal discourse. This view of interaction assumes the necessity of collusion in conversation among participants (McDermott and Tylbor 1995). Thus, the language of the speaker collecting the data is as much a part of the study as the one providing the data.

While Baugh (1983) does not consider his own styleshifting abilities, one can discern a certain level of styleshifting based on the samples of his own speech provided in the text. In the long excerpt above, we don't see much of Baugh's speech, but from what we can tell, the style is formal. However, in recounting a confrontation with one of his speakers in the field, we can see that he has a strong command of BL and style as well (1983, 49–50). We join the conversation when JoJo offers Baugh a homemade alcoholic concoction:

J: Man, I don't want none of that shit.
JoJo: Oh ... you must be too good to drink my brew, huh?
J: I'm not sayin that ... I'm just sayin I don't want none. [smiling in an effort to diffuse the situation]
JoJo: [raising his voice] Well ... hold on then, motherfucker ... y'know ... cause some people just ain't born with no silver spoon in they mouth ... like you! [group begins to laugh]
J: Hey my man, I'm not nobody that knows nothing about no silver spoon ... but ... I ain't gon drink no jet fuel ... if you want to kill yourself ... tha's your business ... I got nothing to do with it.
JoJo: Shit ... you just gettin old ... can't take your drink no more.
J: Well ... I guess you're right, young blood ... the way you been drinking ... you must be right.

In this brief dialogue, we can see that Baugh uses not only double negation ("I don't want none"), but also multiple negation ("I'm not nobody that knows nothing about no silver spoon"). He also uses the future-tense form "gon," realization of final *-ng* as *-n* ("sayin"), and assimilation ("tha's" and "you been drinking"). Moreover, we notice that the entire interaction occurs in the uncensored mode (Spears 1998). The interaction itself is a verbal confrontation where one has to COME CORRECT with the language (to stand one's ground), while at the same time, diffusing any possible escalation in tensions. A defamation of character via the loss of a verbal challenge can have grave consequences for one's ability to collect further speech data. Notice that after JoJo raises his voice, Baugh responds firmly ("I'm not nobody that knows nothing about no silver spoon") and distances himself from the confrontation. JoJo then takes a direct shot at Baugh, commenting on his age ("you just gettin old"). In turn, Baugh sneaks a shot right back at JoJo, but again, only after feigning capitulation. The subtle signification on JoJo ("the way you been drinking ... you must be right.") gives Baugh a way out AND a way in. In other words, he manages to ameliorate a potentially inflammatory situation, while holding his ground. This type of verbal challenge is a means of testing someone's heart. When engaging in Black American discourse, you gotta have heart. Can't be no I'ma-lay-down-and-let-you-walk-all-over-me typa talker. Nah, GOTTA have heart. Brief dialogues such as these not only give us a window into the nature of Baugh's styleshifting abilities, but they also demonstrate the centrality of interactional style in maintaining and sustaining rapport with speakers.

More recently, Baugh (2001) has noted that he has begun to reanalyze the data collected for *Black Street Speech*, paying particular attention to his own speech and styleshifting abilities, which he strongly believes "played a major role in the nature and quality of the African American corpora" that he has gathered (2001, 116). This type of analysis is what is sorely needed in sociolinguistic research.

In Rickford and McNair-Knox (1994), the speaker, Foxy Boston, was interviewed by an "African American" researcher (Faye) and a "European American" researcher (Beth). In most studies, we are given an enormous wealth of quantitative evidence on the speaker PROVIDING the data, but very little evidence on the speakers COLLECTING the data. This, again, is problematic if one views interaction and interactional style as having central roles in the type of speech that is elicited from representative speakers. Rickford and McNair-Knox, however, do offer us some valuable information that serves our purposes for this discussion. They take up Bell's (1984, 167) theoretical question—"What is it in the addressee (or other audience members) that the speaker is responding to?" Bell posed three possibilities:

1. Speakers assess the personal characteristics of their addressees and design their style to suit.
2. Speakers assess the general level of their addressees' speech and shift relative to it.
3. Speakers assess their addressees' levels for specific linguistic variables and shift relative to those levels.

The summary statistics for Foxy's "vernacular usage," and that of her interviewers, are presented in table 3.1. Given that neither of the African American interviewers exhibits a high rate of absence—at least nowhere near Foxy's rates—it is more likely that speakers assess Bell's first two points, while the third possibility

TABLE 3.1
Vernacular Usage of Foxy and Her Interviewers

	Third-Person Singular -s	*Copula Absence*	*Invariant* be
Interview 3			
Foxy	73% (83/114)	70% (197/283)	385
Faye	30% (13/43)	22% (29/130)	5
Roberta	12% (2/17)	30% (14/46)	12
Interview 4			
Foxy	36% (45/124)	40% (70/176)	97
Beth	0% (0/17)	1% (1/81)	0

NOTE: Interview 3 was conducted by Faye and Roberta, both African American females; interview 4 was conducted by Beth, a white female.

is inconclusive. In other words, speakers may not necessarily be responding to SPECIFIC frequencies of absence in the speech of others; rather, they may be responding to general characteristics of the interviewer and his or her speech patterns.

In discussing the two interviews, we are given brief dialogic snippets from which we can conclude that Faye is a far more effective styleshifter than Beth. She is described as using a "bantering approach" in the interview (something which I see as a challenging stance in interactional style and term BATTLIN MODE later in this chapter), which excites the speaker.

> Faye: What kinds of plans you have for college? Where—where have you been thinking about going?
> Foxy: Prob— . . . I don't wanna go far away.
> Faye: Really? You wanna hang around with mom?
> Foxy: Mm-hmm ['yes'] [laughter]
> Faye: Are you scared to get out there on your own?
> Foxy: No! [laughter] I's [it's] just that . . . we just too close, I guess. [Rickford and McNair-Knox 1994, 120]

This bantering approach is contrasted with Beth's approach, which sometimes leads to awkward silences or misunderstandings:

Beth: I mean, do you think they maybe talk more to girls than they—
Foxy: Talk to girls?
Beth: Do you think they're like, yeah, like more open with other—with girls than they are with other guys? You see what I'm saying? Like do you think they, um—
Foxy: Do I think, um, guys are open with—girls than guys?
Beth: Yeah. [121]

INTERACTIONAL STYLE AND THE MEDIATION OF CONVERSATION

Recognizing that styleshifting occurs in and through interaction and that verbal interaction by definition requires the participation of two or more speakers, I seek to build upon such pioneering research and consider my own speech behavior as a participant in speech situations in the field. What becomes clear is that interactional style, as a possible variable both determining the speech style and serving the expressive purposes of a given speaker, plays an important role in mediating conversation.

It is clear from the excerpts above that Faye and Beth employ radically different interactional styles. What's also clear from the other brief speech samples in the text is that Faye has a much greater ability to styleshift using both structural features AND discursive strategies to accommodate to Foxy's speech. From the brief snippets of conversation available, we can see that Faye demonstrates copula variability and the use of several discursive strategies such as what I am calling the BLACK AMERICAN FALSETTO and the extended, affirming *mmm-hmmmm* found mainly in Black American female discourse. Faye's style appears to be much more familiar to the interactional styles that are germane to the speech community of which Foxy is a member. As a result, the two sistas can "get into it" in a much more familial way than, say, Beth and Foxy. As we can see in table 3.1, Foxy's speech exhibits higher rates of copula absence, third-person singular *-s* absence, and possessive *-s* absence when speaking with Faye.

I have already noted the value placed on styleshifting as a cultural practice in Black America and discussed the theoretical shift in viewing interactional style as a mediator in conversation. In this section, I examine my own speech as a field-worker who is both collecting and providing data. This sample of my speech occurred during what I have termed a STREET SESSION. Street sessions, as a methodological concept, were valuable to my fieldwork in that they allowed me to access the normative speech of this Sunnyside speech community. These sessions were devised with my dual role as a teacher-researcher in mind. Thus their purpose was twofold: (1) As a teacher, I was allowing students to participate in a hands-on "field research" experience so that they could gain the ability and confidence to conduct their own research in the field (the students were responsible for videotaping, audiotaping, and taking still photos). (2) As a researcher, I was gaining firsthand knowledge of the community and the various historical, cultural, social, political, and economic issues that concerned my students. The videotape, audiotape, and still photos were all used as data in this study. In addition, this discussion will focus on the ethnographic and sociolinguistic value of the street session, which allowed me to gain access to numerous issues of cultural importance while collecting a vast body of speech data.

It is important to note that student speech cannot be analyzed and appreciated for its vast stylistic range unless it is studied in both educational and community contexts. Street sessions, then, allowed me to access the type of peer, in-group speech data that occurs among Black American adolescents when they are LANGUAGING in their home-community context. In this particular street session, I walked with a group of five eleventh graders (all seventeen years old) from the school to a local plaza two or three blocks away. We had lunch at the plaza and walked back along the same streets. We were actively engaged in conversation about Sunnyside on the way to the plaza, during lunch, and on the way back to school. The entire session is 90 minutes long. The conversation addressed everything from the sociopolitical and sociohistorical (different sections of Sunnyside, race and ethnic relations/conflicts, the process of gentrification and the struggle for community survival, historical accounts of the city high school [the plaza now stands on the grounds of the old high school]) to the cultural (e.g., Hip Hop music and its relation to community concerns, Grammy awards and Black actors/actresses, recent movie releases).

Before analyzing my own speech, it is important to note that while few sociolinguists have analyzed their own linguistic accommodation, some have presented data that sheds insight on the role of the researcher in interviews (Jahr 1979; Trudgill 1981). Trudgill (1986), in particular, demonstrates—quite amazingly—the similarities between his speech and that of his Norwich speakers. Using the terminology of Labov (1972a), Trudgill notes that variable (t) is a MARKER that is higher in speakers' consciousness than variable (a:), an INDICATOR. Trudgill's remarkable shifts in variable (t) occur because of this higher level of consciousness associated with the (t) variable, he argues, while variable (a:), being lower on the level of consciousness of most speakers, does not play an important role in accommodation.

What is important for this discussion is that Trudgill is responding to Giles's (1973) concern that the process of accommodation may lead to "circularity" in the research of sociolinguists. Giles suggests that perhaps sociolinguists are prejudging the speech of

FIGURE 3.1
Variable (t): Selected Scores in Trudgill's (1981, 225) Norwich Study

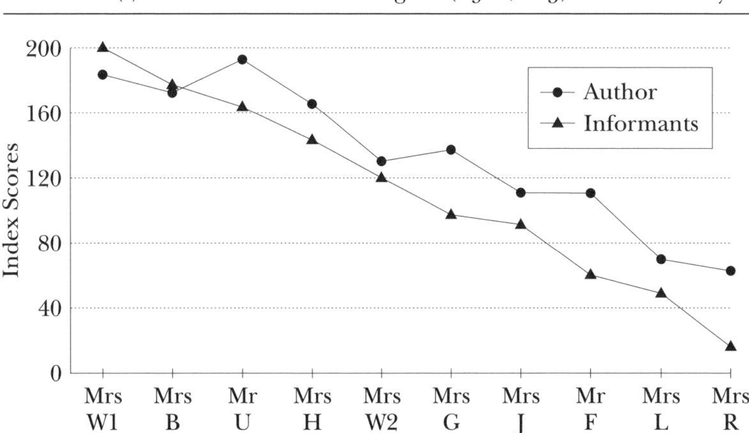

NOTE: Index scores range from 0, indicating use of the prestige pronunciation [t], to 200, indicating consistent use of the glottal stop.

FIGURE 3.2
Variable (a:): Selected Scores in Trudgill's (1981, 227) Norwich Study

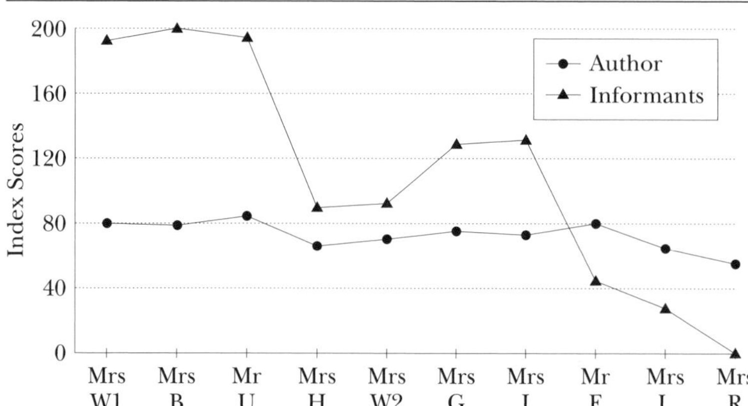

NOTE: High index scores indicate a low-prestige front vowel [a:]; low index scores indicate a high-prestige back vowel [ɑ:].

their informants based on prior knowledge of their social class status (and other factors) and are thus, in plain terms, getting back the speech that they put out there. By pointing out an interesting crossover pattern in his data (notice in figure 3.1 how the author uses the variable with lower frequency than his first two speakers and then higher with the remainder), Trudgill argues that, in fact, it was HE who was accommodating to his individual informants' speech, rather than they accommodating to his speech. Realistically, and critical to the theorizing of style in this paper, accommodation is a BIDIRECTIONAL phenomenon. This is especially true when speakers share the variable in question (if the variable is not shared, bidirectionality is less likely, but it may still occur). Unfortunately, there is no way to REALLY determine who is accommodating to whom by looking at aggregated speech data. What is needed to determine who is accommodating to whom, how, and when is an interactional analysis of discourse to determine the use of certain features over time by both speakers in question. We will return to this point later, as it reinforces the need to construct a more dialogic, interactional conceptualization of style.

Now, I will focus on my own speech in the street session, paying close attention to my styleshifts and to how my speech accommodates to that of the speech community. Before I begin, I must say that this analysis was not part of my original research design. One can see from the anecdotes above that I always knew that I had the ability to styleshift. However, after transcribing the first street session with my students, I was struck by the range of my shifting. In other words, it's one thing to know that you have the ability to styleshift, but it is quite another to see the empirical evidence supporting it. I also knew that I, like many speakers who belong to multiple speech communities, was sometimes conscious and sometimes unconscious of my shifts. In general, I was conscious of the fact that I would make various stylistic adjustments depending upon the situation, context, audience, and so on, yet through this analysis, I have come to learn that I never knew exactly which features I tweaked (and to what degree) and which features I left alone. In this respect, I am like most speakers of any language. In one important respect, however, I am not. Being a sociolinguist who studies the variable nature of speech, with a focus on BL, I am particularly attuned to the variation in that language variety. Beyond most speakers' intuitions, I can list the syntactic features that exhibit variation and the ones that don't. In other words, while I may share the consciousness of my stylistic adjustments with most speakers, I also have access to sociolinguistic language and theory to engage in a more precise metalinguistic analysis of my speech. In previous research (Alim 2002), I demonstrate that Hip Hop artists consciously control their copula variation to construct a street-conscious identity, but I make no claims about their metalinguistic abilities to discuss these adjustments. Further research is required in this area.

I have analyzed my speech with respect to both structural (syntactic) and functional (discursive) components. Syntactically, I chose to examine variation in (1) the copula, (2) third-person singular *-s*, and (3) possessive *-s*, as the literature on BL considers these features to be the variable, syntactic hallmarks of the language variety. Other features, discussed below, also became important in the analysis. Discursively, I discuss several discourse strategies that help characterize my interactional style, including the use of slang terms and idiomatic expressions, suck-teeth, Black American falsetto, and a particular mode of interaction (battlin mode).

Table 3.2 presents empirical data on my speech in three columns. Column one, RESEARCHER, refers to my speech when I am engaging in a conversational mode as a researcher, while column two, TEACHER, refers to my speech when I am engaging in an instructional mode as a teacher. Column three, TOTAL, refers to the total combined body of speech data. The data for the three main features are shown. The italicized percentages in table 3.2 are important for our discussion. The TOTAL column describes the variability in the total corpus of my speech, that is, my speech during the entire 90-minute street session. In this speech situation, I exhibited copula absence (e.g., "She mad at us") in 60.9% of all possible occurrences of the copula, and 66.7% in both third-person singular *-s* absence ("All of a sudden he win a Oscar") and in possessive *-s* absence ("It's Cash Money house"). The data is further broken down by my shifting roles as a teacher-researcher. As a researcher, I exhibited a higher rate of absence in both the copula and third-person singular *-s*, 67.6% and 70.0%, respectively. As a teacher, I had rates of absence that fell to 41.7% in copula (a decrease of 26.0%) and 55.6% in third-person singular *-s* (a decrease

TABLE 3.2
Alim's Variation across Shifting Roles as Teacher-Researcher and Total Body for This Session

Feature	*Researcher*	*Teacher*	*Total*
Copula			
Absent	46/68 (67.6%)	10/24 (41.7%)	56/92 (60.9%)
Contracted	12/68 (17.6%)	13/24 (54.2%)	25/92 (27.2%)
Full	10/68 (14.7%)	1/24 (4.2%)	11/92 (12.0%)
Third-person singular *-s*			
Absent	21/30 (70.0%)	5/9 (55.6%)	26/39 (66.7%)
Present	9/30 (30.0%)	4/9 (44.4%)	13/39 (33.3%)
Possessive *-s*			
Absent	4/6 (66.7%)	—	4/6 (66.7%)
Present	2/6 (33.3%)	—	2/6 (33.3%)

of 14.4%). While these figures may not be quantitatively significant, they are qualitatively significant. The limitations of this sample are (1) an unequal number of tokens as teacher and researcher (it's clear that I operated as a researcher much more than as a teacher), and (2) the number of tokens for possessive *-s* variability is admittedly low—the construction simply did not occur that frequently in the corpus.

Several additional BL features appeared in my speech. One extremely salient feature was the use of *y'all* to mark second-person plural ("I WOULD let y'all pick the topic") and second-person plural possessive ("What are y'all top picks for school?"). Of the 50 *y'all* occurrences, 48 mark second-person plural and 2 mark second-person plural possessive. Of the options available for marking second-person plural, *y'all* is used almost exclusively, with one occurrence each of *you, you all,* and *you guys.* Additional syntactic features include: negative inversion ("It ain't no McDonald's ... ain't really no McDonald's"); multiple negation ("I'm not tryina FIGHT with you or nu'in"); use of *ain't* as a general preverbal negator ("That ain't [isn't] really Sunnyside," "We ain't [don't] got nobody from where?" "Nah, I ain't [haven't] seen it"); invariant *be* ("You gotta watch out cuz sometimes that's where the loonies be at"); use of existential *it* ("It's AIDS here, too!"); formation of direct questions without inversion of the subject and auxiliary verb ("Why that's the only part they had to keep is the gym?"); *they* to mark third-person plural possessive ("How you know they got they doors locked?"); *yo* to mark second-person singular possessive ("Yo dad went?"); use of past-tense or preterite form as past participle ("Like the whole videotape ain't gon get ate up?!"); use of past-participle form as past-tense or preterite form ("I never seen a Tongan OR a Samoan before I came here"); generalization of *was* and *were* ("Hey, they was gon buy the whole apartment where they was from"); use of unstressed *been* for *has/have been* ("Maaan, I been under a CAVE"); *a* for *an* ("It's just a age range"); and use of *'nem* usually after a proper name to mark associative plurals ("Cash Money 'nem, too, though").

In addition to the syntactic features above, numerous phonological features common to BL appear in my speech, including the highly salient glottalized vowel. For example, in "I'm not tryina FIGHT with you or nu'in," the *th* in *nothing*, is realized as a glottalized vowel. There are numerous examples of other phonological features, including reduction of word-final consonant clusters (*last* to *lass*), realization of final [ŋ] as [n] in gerunds (*documenting* to *documentin*), realization of voiced *th* as *d* (*though* to *dough*), realization of *thr* sequence as *th* (*through* to *though*), deletion or vocalization of *l* after a vowel (*school* to *schoo*), absence of postvocalic *-r* (*holler* to *holla*), absence of *d* or *g* in certain tense-aspect auxiliaries ("I 'on [don't] know what y'all talkin about," "I'ma [gonna] let y'all know", "I'mon [gon] definitely be there"), realization of *z* as *d* ("It wadn't [wasn't] even about that"), monophthongal pronunciation of *ay* as *ah* (*I* to *Ah*), realization of *-ing* as *-ang* (*everything* to *everythang*), realization of *everybody* as *e'ybody* and *with you* as *witchu*, and varying intonation, pitch, and stress (discussed below).

SUNNYSIDE STREET SPEECH

I have so far shown my own speech data during the street session, but how does my data compare to the speech of the Black youth in the Sunnyside speech community? Below, we see that the aggregated data for all five speakers exhibits higher rates of absence in all

TABLE 3.3
Students' Variation in Copula, Third-Person Singular *-s*, and Possessive *-s*

Feature	*Variability*	
Copula		
Absent	173/212	(81.6%)
Contracted	11/212	(5.2%)
Full	28/212	(13.2%)
Third-person singular *-s*		
Absent	45/52	(86.5%)
Present	7/52	(13.5%)
Possessive *-s*		
Absent	6/6	(100.0%)
Present	0/6	(0.0%)

three variables: 81.6% for the copula (as compared to my 60.9%); 86.5% for third-person singular *-s* (as compared to my 66.7%), and 100.0% for possessive *-s* (as compared to my 66.7%). These higher rates of absence indicate that, while I certainly was accommodating to Sunnyside street speech, I exhibited a lower-than-average rate of absence. What is interesting, and least discussed in sociolinguistic studies (perhaps because it is less conducive to quantification within the variation paradigm), is my use of discursive strategies to complement my analysis of variable features.

DISCURSIVE STRATEGIES: INTRODUCING BLACK AMERICAN FALSETTO AND BATTLIN MODE AND REVISITING SUCK-TEETH

In addition to these syntactic and phonological features, I employed several DISCURSIVE STRATEGIES which are linked to Black American INTERACTIONAL STYLES. These discursive strategies will be discussed in relation to my interactional style in this speech situation. Such discursive strategies include the use of slang terms and idiomatic expressions, SUCK-TEETH, BLACK AMERICAN FALSETTO, and a particular mode of interaction (BATTLIN MODE).

I not only used slang terms and idiomatic expressions, but I reinforced them when I heard them. The reinforcement of terms is tied into the Black American practice of REPETITION in conversation, where a speaker repeats the words of another to show agreement and/or emphasis. For example, one of my students, Bilal, used the terms *dirty* and *grimy* to describe a particular section of Sunnyside. In the following dialogue, we can see both the knowledge of slang terms and their reinforcement through use:

> Bilal: That section is basically the middle of the whole city, basically.... It's the dirtiest, it's the dirtiest, you know, the GRIMIEST.
>
> Researcher: [laughter of recognition] What you mean, the dirtiest and the grimiest?
>
> B: It's the grimiest, basically [laughter] ... [describing other sections of city] ...
>
> R: Like you said that section was GRIMY, right...

B: GRIMY!
R: Does that—why is it different from other places?
B: I ain't gon get into all—can't touch on that on camera, cuz, you know what I mean [laughter]—nah, every SET grimy...

These two terms, *dirty* and *grimy*, are semantically related, *grimy* being an extension of *dirty*. In BL, the phrase *doin dirt* refers to committing what is considered to be an immoral and usually illegal act. So, *dirt* becomes a cover term for discussing immoral, illegal acts without actually getting into specifics. A section of town that is *dirty* is known for its illegal activity (the section is known as a *set*). *Grimy* takes it up a notch and intensifies the meaning of *dirty*. Both terms are widely used in Black American mass-based expressive culture. Members of the current generation of Black Americans in the South, particularly those heavily influenced by Hip Hop Culture, refer to their region of the Hip Hop Nation as the *Dirty Souf*, cementing their street credibility. More recently, they have used *dirty* as a noun and extended the term to mean something like *brotha* 'brother', *potna* 'partner', or *homie* 'homeboy'. So, you might can hear a young brotha say, "Wassup, dirty [pronounced 'dutty']?" meaning, "What's up, man?" The term *grimy* has been used by New York rapper Noreaga who, as Hip Hop Headz are known to do, FLIPT THE SCRIPT and inverted the meaning. He refers to those who are GRIMY as "God's favorite." His motivation for the semantic inversion came to him in a self-reflective moment. Lookin back on his life, he realized that he done led a DIRTY, GRIMY life, riddled with HELLA setbacks, a gang of shootouts, the death of family members and time spent BEHIND THE WALL (jail time). Young brotha was STEADY gettin into trouble. His reasoning—if a grimy brotha can survive ALL THAT and still be here to ROCK THE MIC today, he GOTTA be "God's favorite!"

Turning to SUCK-TEETH (Rickford and Rickford 1976), this discursive strategy is used by speakers of BL, Caribbean creoles, and other African-derived languages (Guyanese, Jamaican, and Barbadian creole, Krio, Cameroon pidgin, and others), as well as several African languages (Mende, Luo, Yoruba, and others). Suck-teeth is a loud sucking sound made with "the lower lip against the upper teeth, or with the tip or blade of the tongue just behind the upper teeth, on the alveolar ridge" (1976, 196). Rickford's Black informants described the use of suck-teeth in various ways—as showing disgust, defiance, disapproval, disappointment, frustration, or impatience. To my knowledge, no study has shown how suck-teeth operates in interaction across contexts and in conversation as a way to coconstruct meaning.

In the dialogue below, the use of suck-teeth by me and one of my students illustrates the way that suck-teeth is used in Black American discourse. This interaction occurs when my students are asking me to borrow my video camera for a trip they about to take, and I ain't tryina hear it. The following is their attempt to convince me to let them borrow the camera, beginning at the point where I'm tellin them how much the camera cost and how they tellin me how much deposit they would give me in order to hold it for a coupla days:

> Researcher: About, between three fifty and four hundred [dollars] . . .
> Bilal: So, tell them a hundred dollar, a hundred dollar deposit . . .
> Yesmina: Yeahhh . . .
> R: [suck-teeth] Maaan, that ain't nu'in! What am I gon get with a hundred dollars if y'all . . .
> Y: That's twenty dollars EACH . . .
> B: And then if they break it, you got yo hundred dollars in there, they owe you two fifty . . .
> R: What am I gon get with a hundred—yeahhh, I won't NEVER see that two fifty . . .
> B: Oh-hooo-hooooo!
> Aqiyla: Don't you TRUST us—yes, you will!
> Y: I WORK!
> A: You gotta write permission slips so the parents gotta sign it . . .
> R: I wish y'all could do a documentary over there . . .
> Y: [suck-teeth] C'mooon . . .

From the dialogue, we can see that the street sessions provided a linguistic space where BL was the language variety of choice. In that linguistic space, suck-teeth is used on numerous occasions. You can see that I am NOT about to give up my video camera to no group of teenagers, despite their extremely persuasive ways. Their attempt to convince me to let them put down a hundred dollar deposit is met with a loud suck-teeth, showing my complete and utter rejection of the idea ("[suck-teeth] Maaan, that ain't nu'in!"). A hundred dollar deposit don't mean I'm gon see all my money if they mess around and break it, you know what I'm sayin? ("yeahhh, I won't NEVER see that two fifty"). Aqiyla makes the matter one of trust, while Yesmina emphasizes that she got herself a job (meaning, she can pay for it if they bust it). At this point, they can see me startin to give a lil bit, and Aqiyla say, "You gotta write permission slips so the parents gotta sign it," using yet another approach to try and persuade me. At my weakest point, I admit that I really WOULD like to see them do a documentary while they on the trip, but I still don't give them the green light they lookin for. Frustrated with my hardheadedness, Yesmina delivers a suck-teeth and follows it with a "C'mooon," like she all whinin and whatnot. In the end, I hold my ground, and they decide to borrow a video camera from they school instead. This is but one interactional sequence in which suck-teeth was employed in this street session. The nature and communicative function of this discursive strategy need further examination.

Another discursive strategy that I employed in interacting with my students is the BLACK AMERICAN FALSETTO. It has been noted by researchers that BL has a more varied intonation and a "higher pitch-range and more rising and level final contours" than any form of American English (Wolfram 1993; cited in Rickford 1999). An example of the function of this strategy illustrates also a brief discussion of a particular mode of interaction that I employed in these street sessions (battlin mode) in order to create an interactional style germane to the speech community. The discourse begins just after the point when Amira expresses a great desire to go to Africa to "be with her peoples." Bilal trippin like that's the last place on God's green earth he would wanna go to. Aqiyla, tryin to convince him, proposes that he may be able to go for free. Let the games begin:

> Aqiyla: What about a basketball scholarship?
> Bilal: To Africa? FUCK that!
> A: YEAHHH . . .

Researcher and Kijana: [laughter]...
A: You get to play ball...
B: I don't give a damn! [Black American rhythm and intonation]...
A: ...and get paid for it, AND you go to Africa...
B: I don't give a damn!
R: Hey, that would be tight...
B: [suck-teeth] If you got a basketball scholarship to go to Africa—FUCK THAT!
R: [Black American falsetto] Why don't you wanna go?
B: [increased volume] A basketball scholarship to play in Africa?!!
A: [laughter] That's good!
B: [increased volume] Is you CRAZY?!!
A: What's wrong with that?
R: I bet if you spent, I bet if you spent like a WEEK, a WEEK there, you probably wouldn't even wanna come back...
B: SHIIIIITTT...
Amira: I KNOW he would!
B: Too many diseases and shit, FUCK THAT!
R: It ain't even like that, man!
Amira: It's NOT everywhere in Africa!
B: [laughter] We'll see...
Amira: If you go to have sex...
B: Y'all don't know what it's like...
A: ...if you don't have sex with people then you don't have to worry about diseases...
B: But, shit, I wanna have sex!
A and R: [laughter]...
B: What you MEAN? What the hell...
Amira: You go with somebody you wanna have sex with, so you can...
B: You can't have sex—maaaaaan...
R: Hey, hey, look, y'all—if you think everybody got diseases over there...
B: I didn't say everybody. I didn't say everybody got diseases...
R: ...it ain't more than here, it ain't more than right here...
B: WhatEVER it is...
Amira: No, they, they, they got AIDS, that's the real only disease you gotta worry about...
B: That's the disease I'm talkin bout, SHIIIIT!
R: [Black American falsetto] It's AIDS here, too!

Amira: Here, HERE, HERE, you got AIDS; you got syphilis [banging table], you got gonorrhea [banging table], you got [banging table]—what the fuck?—tuberculosis! [banging table] Shiiitt... [laughter]...

B: The fact of the matter is, the fact of the matter is...

R: WHAT is the fact of the matter?

B: ...I wouldn't go. Right now I [banging table] cannot [banging table] see [banging table] myself [banging table] going [banging table]...

R: Regardless? Hey, hey, hey, I bet you...

B: A-ha-haaaaaaaaaaaaa!

From a sociopolitical perspective, Black Americans have long been conflicted about their opinions regarding the "Motherland." Wherever you have an Amira, you also got a Bilal. Amira has been educated about Africa in a consistent manner from her childhood in the home, community summer programs she's participated in, and in her African dance classes. Bilal, on the other hand, has not had enough education about Africa to combat the Eurocentric miseducation, and the racist media portrayals, received by most American students. But Amira cannot convince Bilal of the value of visiting Africa. Much of this has to do with Bilal's communicative skills and his ability to cleverly manipulate the situation with words.

From a sociolinguistic perspective, I use the Black American falsetto for two different purposes in this stretch of speech. However, as we gon see later, both usages contribute to a specific BATTLIN mode of interaction. I enter the BATTLE in an attempt to understand why Bilal was not interested in a free ride to Africa. In the first instance of falsetto ("Why don't you wanna go?"), I am posing a challenge to Bilal. If he gon sit there and act all crazy talkin bout "Fuck THAT!" and "I don't give a damn!" then I'ma challenge his ass, you feel me? He gotta offer some sorta explanation. In other words, in this battle of the minds and war of words, he has to defend or substantiate his anti-Africa position. So, in this case, the falsetto functions as an INTERROGATIVE CHALLENGER.

Bilal answers my challenge not with facts, but with increased volume and a marked phrase in Black American discourse, "A basketball scholarship to play in Africa?!! Is you CRAZY?!!" Next, I try to convince him that, if he only spent some time there, he would enjoy it. His response, again, is another marked phrase in Black American discourse, "SHIIIIITTT," used here to show added emphasis and strong disagreement with the verbal opponent. Finally, Bilal offers up a reason why he don't wanna go: "Too many diseases and shit, FUCK THAT!" At this point, Amira enters the battle and takes a high moral ground with Bilal, "If you don't have sex with people then you don't have to worry about diseases." This don't even phase Bilal, as he turns to humor and turns the tables on Amira, "But, shit, I wanna have sex! What you MEAN? What the hell ... You can't have sex—maaaaaan." Bilal scores major points here as he gets the desired reaction from the audience, who are, themselves, important coconstructors of the dialogue. Amira, in an unsuccessful attempt to regain her footing, offers the idea that he can bring his own partner with him and not have to worry about catchin no sexually transmitted diseases. She then tries to tell him that he only has to worry about one disease in Africa—AIDS, whereas in America, we got HELLA diseases to deal wit. Bilal, again, is not to be outdone, "That's the disease I'm talkin bout, SHIIIIT!" Thinking I now had Bilal trapped, I attempted to show him that AIDS is also found in increasingly high rates in Black America. And seeing as though he had no trouble chillin in Black America, why should Africa be a problem? This is the line of thinking that produces my second instance of Black American falsetto ("It's AIDS here, too!"). Here, the falsetto is used as a DECLARATIVE EMPHASIZER, highlighting what one believes to be, or is attempting to get others to believe to be, a cogent argument.

The battle continues with Amira runnin down a list of diseases that he could very well catch right here in the good ole U. S. of A. She accents each disease by bangin on the table and delivers her own, "Shiiit," though not as loud or prolonged as Bilal's. I finally think that Bilal bout to give a real defense of his position when he begins with, "The fact of the matter is, the fact of the matter is..." Challengin him once again and attempting to capitalize on his hesitation, I'm like, "WHAT is the fact the matter?" He responds, "I wouldn't go. Right now I [banging table] cannot [banging table] see [banging table] myself [banging table] going [banging table]." Bangin on the table is Bilal's attempt to show that he is invested in his position, but importantly, we see that he still has not offered up any real justification or substantiation of his position. Despite this, he has won the battle—"A-ha-haaaaaaaaaaaaa!"

Why did he win the battle? Never did Bilal, anywhere in the dialogue, offer any real argument for his position. This is important. Being the one with the least knowledge of Africa, Bilal relied purely on his ability to verbally manipulate all parties. Here's the critical point: in Black American discourse in the battlin mode, it is of primary importance to know when your opponents are genuinely trying to present a cogent argument or when you simply bein played like a Sony PlayStation. In other words, for Bilal, this wasn't even ABOUT "to go or not to go to Africa?" It was about his skillful, verbal orchestration of his opponents. We see time after time how he uses verbal play to dismantle any attempt at cogent argumentation. Through his use of Black American rhythm and intonation ("I don't give a damn!"), marked Black American expressions ("Is you CRAZY?!!") and discursive strategies (suck-teeth, among them), and humor to engage the audience and to skillfully avoid being jammed up, we realize that all of the other participants (including myself) have been manipulated. From the GIT it was his game.

As a field-worker, I was participating fully in the battle, yet I was also conscious of the fact that this type of verbal battlin was a common practice in Black American discourse activities. Having seen it so much during my experience in the field, and from my life experiences, I took it to be a normative practice. From the dialogue, we see that the Black American falsetto is but one discourse strategy often used in the battlin mode. It is important to recognize the battlin mode as a major component of interactional style in the BASC, where it is learned along with other modes through everyday engagement in discursive activity. The battlin mode is both a norm and a means of interaction shared by the speech community and requires shared language attitudes and ideologies about language for full participation (Morgan 1994, 1999). One could easily see how, if viewed from a different cultural frame or if the words were just read off the page without the extended commentary, the verbal battle might actually be mistaken for a very serious confrontation. The fact that the whole speech event occurs in the UNCENSORED MODE (Spears 1998)—with expressions like *fuck that, I don't give a damn, shiiiiit,* and the rather open talk about sex—and that the voices are raised to a high pitch and volume, members of other speech communities may not know how to enter, engage, or interpret the speech activity. From THIS speech community's perspective, this speech activity is both COMPETITIVE and COMMUNAL. Speakers are simultaneously constructing community as they construct their arguments/linguistic maneuvers.

From the perspective of an ethnographic field-worker, it was important for me to be able to enter, engage, and interpret the normative speech behavior of this speech community. Participating in these speech events provides a clear advantage to the ethnographic field-worker in a community where so much value is placed on verbal interaction. Being able to enter and participate in a BLACK LINGUISTIC SPACE (Alim 2004d)—a competitive and communal language space where BL is the PRESTIGE VARIETY—enables and mediates the actual (TALK) and metaphorical (RAPPORT) conversation between the researcher and the researched. By this, I mean that one is able to gain respect as a speaker and is thus able to engage speakers in speech situations that might otherwise be inaccessible. As a researcher, I set out to engage fully in the normative speech behavior of the Sunnyside community. It was out of respect for the speakers AS BEINGS that I made a great effort to pay close attention to their speech. Towards the end of my fieldwork, I was told by more than one student that they noticed how I had accommodated to their speech patterns. I received the ultimate compliment—"You don't talk like the other teachers. You talk just like us." This may sound trivial to some, but I argue that language in the Black American community is SO CLOSELY TIED to identity that a deep, abiding respect and admiration for someone's language translates to a deep, abiding respect and admiration for that speaker, they mama, they grandmama, and even they great-GREAT-grandmama! On the serious tip, then, a statement such as "You talk just like us" is clearly more than a comment about my syntax; it is a reciprocal showing of respect and admiration.

SELF-CONSCIOUS LINGUISTIC ADJUSTMENTS

The previous point leads me to explore the conscious manipulation of language on my part. Earlier I stated that, in general, I was conscious of the fact that I regularly make various stylistic adjustments depending upon the situation, context, audience, and other factors. Yet, through this analysis, I have come to learn that I never knew exactly which features I tweaked (and to what degree) and which features I left alone. Baugh (1983, 27) writes that although his consultants "were not always able to pinpoint the exact nature of their linguistic adjustments, they were well aware of the process." I probably differ from most of Baugh's consultants in that, as someone who often writes IN and ABOUT BL (as you can see by the writing style of this chapter), I am keenly aware of the various linguistic features and often go to great lengths to represent them accurately on the printed page.

Whereas I came to this present study with the clear intention to accommodate to the language behavior of the Sunnyside speech community, I never intended to analyze my own speech. Analyzing my own speech behavior was incredibly revealing in that it allowed me a window into WHAT IT IS I ACTUALLY DO AS A FIELD-WORKER WHEN I ACCOMMODATE. Out of the entire 68 single-spaced pages in the transcript of the street session, one line jumps out at me above all others. In that line, I am engaging in what I call SELF-CONSCIOUS LINGUISTIC ADJUSTMENT, always a meaningful speech act. Most times, we hear about how speakers of varieties that are stigmatized by the dominating group engage in self-corrective behavior in an effort to modify their speech from their variety to what the dominating group considers the prestige variety. This sometimes leads to what has been termed HYPERCORRECTION (Labov 1966), where speakers are so concerned with getting the grammar "right" that they often get it "wrong." HYPOCORRECTION (Baugh 1992) is a similar process, yet "getting the grammar 'right,'" in this case, means modifying one's speech to a variety that the dominating group considers less prestigious. Hypocorrection clearly shows that, to some speakers, it is important for them to be able to connect with others who speak a different variety, even if that variety is not considered prestigious by the dominating group. The linguistic margin becomes the center. In other words, the speakers fly in the face of standard language ideology in an effort to bond with speakers whom the dominating group devalues.

In this dialogue, I am engaging in neither hypo- nor hypercorrection, yet my conscious linguistic manipulation is more in line with the ideological stance of hypocorrectors. In the following dialogue, we are fidgeting around with the video camera, and I ask Yesmina to help Bilal figure out how to work it.

> Researcher: Yesmina, can you teach him how to use it since you know how to use it all?
> Bilal: Hold it down longer? Okay, I got you...
> R: Zoom, and what else do you need to know?
> B: That's all I need to know...
> Yesmina: Um, you need to know how, do you know how to turn it on?
> R: Does it—do it say record on it?
> B: Yes, it say record...
> R: Okay, that's all you need...
> B: That's all I need...
> R: That's all you need.

This speech sample occurred a little over halfway through the street session. My second utterance is the ONLY line in the entire transcript where I self-correct on a syntactic feature, and thus the act is extremely salient. Given my exposure to and interaction in multiple speech communities, I have come to view myself as a speaker who can styleshift across dialectal boundaries with relative ease. This instance, though, is the one moment that reveals my conscious attempt to styleshift toward the speech of the Sunnyside speech community, as I understand it to be. In Sunnyside, as in the broader BASC, the third-person singular *-s* is variable, as we have seen. In the quantitative analysis of my speech above, I exhibited absence in this feature 66.67% of the time, and I showed a higher frequency of absence as a researcher than as a teacher. As informative as these figures are, they do not say anything about the cognitive processes involved in constructing my speech for this particular speech situation. This example is especially revealing because the shift from the presence to the absence of third-person singular *-s* also requires a vowel change (compare the shift from *runs* to *run*, for example). Again, further study is needed in the area of the conscious manipulation of language by styleshifters, codeswitchers, and diglossic switchers, as well as the relevance of these linguistic abilities to ethnographers, sociolinguists, anthropologists, and field-workers in other disciplines.

CONCLUSION: WHAT WE DONE DID

In this chapter, I have presented a case in which linguistic anthropology and variationist sociolinguistics can be mutually beneficial, particularly within the framework of an ethnographic study. I have also attempted to draw attention to an issue in sociolinguistics that can be referred to as an elephant in the room. Namely, I have urged sociolinguists to consider how the other half speaks, that is, their own styleshifting abilities when collecting data on stylistic variation. This issue is of concern to sociolinguistic theory and methodology. Methodologically, in addition to attention paid to speech, audience, race and familiarity of addressee, topic of conversation, setting, and other determinants of style, we need also consider and develop new ways to analyze INTERACTIONAL STYLE as a variable influencing styleshifting (see chapter 8). The language and interactional style of the researcher (or whoever is collecting the data), as well as the researcher's self-conscious linguistic adjustments, need to be analyzed empirically if we are to present a fuller picture of stylistic variation. Furthermore, the language and interactional style of the researcher need to be examined across the shifting roles of the researcher.

Future research on BL needs to consider ethnographic approaches to styleshifting in order to describe the linguistic abilities of its speakers, to determine WHEN and HOW styleshifting is made relevant in everyday verbal interaction, to reveal the level of metalinguistic abilities in speakers, and to investigate styleshifting in connection with underlying language ideologies within the speech community and among individuals. More specifically, future research on BL needs to consider the discursive functions of SUCK-TEETH, BLACK AMERICAN FALSETTO, and the various modes of interaction in the BASC (such as MARINATIN and BATTLIN MODE). There is a need for more research that records speakers across various naturalistic contexts and situations—and for that research to consider the language ideologies of the speech community and individual speakers as a starting point for interpretation or development of any framework. Ethnosensitivity here cannot be overemphasized. Whether researchers are engaged in survey research or developing sustained relationships in the field, consideration of one's ethnosensitivity has clear methodological implications, as we have seen.

By examining styleshifting as a means by which speakers construct and deconstruct identities, we are also recognizing the centrality of interaction. Thus far, linguistic accommodation has been studied largely by the quantitative analysis of variable features. However, if we are sincere in ascribing a central role to interaction, we must also begin analyzing accommodation on the level of discourse. Interactional styles are considered in this study to be represented by both sociolinguistic variables and discursive strategies. All of this, I believe, would add tremendously to developing a theory of stylistic variation, and a view of styleshifting in particular, as cultural practice.

Now that we have spent some time examining my speech as a researcher, the next chapter presents the living language of the students within an ethnographic narrative that details the community context.

4. "THIS IS CORPORATE AMERICA TAKIN OVER": SCHOOLING, SURVIVAL, AND THE SOCIOHISTORICAL CONTEXT OF LIFE IN THE OCCUPIED TERRITORIES

> Grabbin' up your hats, coats, boots and everything
> leave your worries on the doors step cuz we's goin bye and bye
> just direct your feet, you look neat, on the sunny side of the street
> Can't you hear the pitta and the patta
> of the rain drops tricklin down the fire 'scapin' ladda
> life could be so fine, fine as MMMMMMMMM... wine
> I used to walk, walk in the shade with my blues on parade,
> but I'm not afraid, It's ova cassanova
> If I neva had a cent-a I'd be rich as rockyfella,
> gold dust at my feet
> On the sunny... On the shady... On the sunny side of the street
>
> —Dizzy Gillespie, 1957

SUNNYSIDE IS SOMETIMES SUNNY, sometimes shady. Or like Dizzy Gillespie seem to be sayin, it bees sunny and shady AT THE SAME TIME, you know what I'm saying? As we will see in this chapter, the racial, economic, and political tensions that have shaped Sunnyside historically continue to shape the community today, but in new and unexpected ways. In this chapter, I provide the community, educational, and historical contexts in which Sunnyside street speech activity is embedded. Providing the community context is necessary in any ethnographic study, but in this case, it is also necessary to paint a fuller picture of the educational context. The educational context cannot be discussed in isolation from the community context. As a linguistic correlate, student speech cannot be analyzed and appreciated for its vast stylistic range unless it is studied in both educational and community contexts. The language used by my students throughout this chapter—in-group, peer Black street speech in a community setting—will be analyzed further in chapters 5–8 when we analyze styleshifting. Collecting student speech in school and the streets ain't easy, but it's like you gotta go outside AND inside the classroom in order to see what's really goin on wit this Sunnyside speech.

It is for these reasons that I begin this chapter with a discussion of the linguistic context of the Black American Speech Community (BASC) in "Black Street Speech, Straight Talkin, and Silence in the Occupied Territories." After placing my students' speech within the larger contexts of the Black American Sunnyside speech community, and the broader BASC, I then provide an account of my students' speech in a community context in "In Them Sunnyside Streets..." Both of these sections, while immersing the reader into the field both physically and linguistically, also serve to provide readers with a way to contextualize the varied and rich speech activity in my students' conversations in this chapter and throughout the text. The next section, "Back in the Day," provides both the ethnic and the educational history of Sunnyside. As we will see, the rapidly increasing ethnic diversity and economic development that has taken place in Sunnyside in recent times is linked to historical developments and broader demographic and educational trends.

Beginning with "'We Call It 'Over the Ramp': Sunnyside and Shadyside," my students enter the history and tell their own story, in their own voices and in their own language. In this section and the following sections, my students struggle to come to terms with ethnic diversity, economic development, and gentrification in the occupied territories—topics that are continually discussed and debated by community members in the "new" Sunnyside. Questions that drive the conversations include: What do Sunnyside youth know and think about the changes that are taking place in their community? How are they both experiencing and making sense of the rise in ethnic diversity and economic development? What do they see as the social position and status of Black Americans in this "new" Sunnyside? How do they explain the relative and perceived differences in the socioeconomic status of the various communities both IN and OUT of Sunnyside? What do they see as the role of race and class in the process of gentrification? Most importantly, how do they FEEL about these changes?

This chapter is written with the intent of integrating the educational, historical, and community contexts within which my students BE. The reader will get a view of the community as my students understand it. Their understanding is a sharp critique of a contemporary community in flux, but it is lacking in some historical detail, which will be provided by a factual, historical account in order to place their observations in perspective. My students attend Haven High, which as we will see, is the first high school that Sunnyside has seen in two decades. However, this ethnographic account takes us well beyond the confines of Haven High and into the dynamic social worlds of Sunnyside youth.

BLACK STREET SPEECH, STRAIGHT TALKIN, AND SILENCE IN THE OCCUPIED TERRITORIES

Before we provide a historical, ethnographic account of Sunnyside as understood by the students of Haven High, I'd like to provide a narrative of the Sunnyside community. As I stated in an earlier chapter, I lived in Sunnyside for the duration of my teacher-researcher experience. Beyond that, I visited the community barbershop weekly for a period of three years, and as a result became a regular in the community. I ain't gon sit here and lie—it wadn't all about research, you know what I'm saying? It just be hard to find a decent Black barbershop round herre (as in most predominantly White areas) where we can get our herre cut, you feel me? Nah, just playin. But seriously, though, the barbershop experience served multiple purposes for me. Not only was I gettin a tight fade every week (gotta stay sharp), but I was immersing myself in the community to which my students belonged, most of them born and raised in Sunnyside. As a participant in the rich speech activity of the community, particularly in this barbershop setting, I developed a keen sense for community ideologies of language and life, everyday linguistic practices and communicative norms, and the ways of speaking and modes of being central to membership in this community of speakers, who are living in what I have come to call the occupied territories of the East Bank. You gon see what I'm talkin bout in a minute.

Recent events in Black popular culture help to illustrate the role of the Black barbershop and its place in the Black community. In Ice Cube's *Barbershop,* a film that depicts the Black barbershop as a community-building institution, one of the main characters, Eddie (played by my mans, Cedric the Entertainer), is a 70-year-old brotha who just be tellin it like it is. Straight up and down. It's like he be droppin wisdom on the youngens at the same time he be splittin they sides, you know what I mean? The combination of humor and seriousness earns him respect among the community, but really, it's his straight-talkin that folks seem to hold in high regard. In the following dialogue, he takes on the know-it-all college boy, Jimmy, and the rest of the brothas in the shop, as he presents his take on Black political issues. The conversation occurs in BATTLIN MODE, a highly charged and highly animated mode of interaction within the Black American Speech Community.

> Eddie: What I'm saying is Black people need to stop LYYYING. There's three things that Black people need to tell the truth about. [Brotha: "Lyin bout what?!"] One, Rodney King shoulda got his ass beat for bein drunk and drivin a Hyundai... [Brothas: "Ooooh!!!"] Two, OJ did it! [Brotha: "OJ did it?! Awwww, maaan!"] And three, Rosa Parks ain't do nuthin but sit her Black ass down! ["Awww, maaan!"] That's right, I said it! I said it...
>
> Youngen: Hey, I'ma back you up on that, cuz see, look, he was on the bus back in the day AND he on the bus NOW!
>
> Jimmy: [in a condescending tone] Eddie, not only is what you're saying not true, it's wrong and disrespectful for you to discuss Rosa Parks in that way.
>
> Eddie: Wait, wait, wait, hold on here. [looking around the shop] Is this a barbershop? Is this a barbershop?! [Brothas: "Yeah, it is."] This is a barbershop. [Brothas: "Yeah!"] Wait, I mean, if we can't talk straight in a barbershop then where can we talk straight? We can't talk straight nowhere else and, you know, this ain't nuthin but HEALTHY CON-VER-SATION...

Brotha: Yeah, but not that Rosa Parks stuff!

Eddie: Maaan, ain't nobody exempt in the barbershop! You know that! Ain't NOBODY exempt. You can talk about WHOEVER and WHATEVER, WHENEVER you want to in the barbershop.

Importantly, Eddie touches on something that many Black people in the postintegration era can readily identify with—the sanctity of Black-owned public spaces. It is in these rare, Black-owned public spaces where Black folk can collectively, as Sunnyside Hip Hop artist Jubwa say, find "a place where you can be yoself." In the film, Eddie hits us with a moving metaphor of the Black barbershop as "the Black man's country club," a safe place to fraternize, build and maintain genuine relationships, and express yourself freely, without fear of being censored or censured by external forces. Eddie hittin on some major ishhh right here. The barbershop is a place where society is openly contested, critiqued, and criticized. In this sense, the barbershop is very much a postmodern space, where received notions are always under contestation.

The key phrase in Eddie's final words of wisdom is, "You know that!" Implicit in the defense of his straight-talkin is the notion that the communicative space created by the barbershop and its participants operates by a set of unwritten yet understood communicative norms. In other words, "You should know about straight-talkin, young Blood, cuz this how we do things around here. You ain't gon find too many places where you can express yo Black mind." Eddie is appealing to this shared set of speech norms as a means of emphasizing his previous point about straight-talkin. As Eddie engages in the rhythmic desyllabification of "CON-VER-SATION," he's also pointin out that the interactional mode is one that is germane to the BASC of southside Chicago. There are certain things one must come prepared to do with language. Wideman (1976, 36) put it so nice that it's worth quoting in full. Referring to "African American speech," he writes:

> And it's not words and intonations, it's a whole attitude about speech that has historical rooting. It's not a phenomenon that you can isolate and reduce to linguistic characteristics. It has to do with the way a culture conceives of the people inside of that culture. It has to do with a whole

complicated protocol of silences and speech, and how you use speech in ways other than directly to communicate information. And it has to do with, certainly, the experiences that the people in the speech situation bring into the encounter. What's fascinating to me about African American speech is its spontaneity, the requirement that you not only have a repertoire of vocabulary or syntactical devices/constructions, but you come prepared to do something in an attempt to meet the person on a level that both uses the language, mocks the language, and recreates the language.

Clearly, Eddie's recognition of shared communicative norms also recognizes historically rooted ways of speaking. So, not only, "This the way we do things round here," but also, "This the way we BEEN doin things around here." Loaded inside of this short dialogue are the experiences of a people. Clearly, the content of the conversation deals directly with well-known events in Black American history, but more importantly, the experience Black Americans have had in reshaping the English language to align more closely with their native languages and linguistic practices is packaged all up inside the syllables of every word. You can't just walk up in the shop without an understanding of these historically rooted practices. Like Wideman said, you gotta come WIDDIT! And he not only talkin about the structural dimension of what you say out yo mouth, but HOW you say what you say out yo mouth (i.e., discursive practices) and yo attitude toward it (i.e., linguistic ideologies). So, not only is "Ain't NOBODY exempt!" an example of negative inversion within a Black American system of negation, but Eddie uses stress, repetition, and rhyme ("You can talk about WHOEVER and WHATEVER, WHENEVER you want to in the barbershop") to drive his point home. Further, the brothas at the barbershop who are waitin to get their haircuts are participants in this competitive and communal BATTLE, serving as a contributing audience for the main speakers and emphasizing the importance of shared norms.

A final point on this dialogue involves Jimmy. Throughout the movie, he is portrayed as this know-it-all college-boy who done lost his soul, that is, lost touch with his community and makes every effort possible to distance hisself from Black ways of being, thinking, and speaking. Interestingly, Jimmy's speech ain't only hella condescending, but it's real "standard," too. "Standard" speech in and of itself ain't the thing that's outside of community norms and ways of speaking. Rather, it's the use of this "standard" form, in this particular setting and interaction, that breaks the rules. Thus, we see the connection between speaking in "standard" English and breaking the set of shared communicative norms—the brotha just ain't widdit. Having been raised up in the south side of Chicago, he quite possibly in fact had access to these norms and simply refused to styleshift. This refusal (if we assume it to be the case), as much so as Eddie's Black American speech, has to do with the indexical relationship between the use of language in Black America and the cultural conception of Black Americans within the broader society. Here, Eddie and Jimmy are clearly in opposition, representing vastly different language ideologies within the BASC.

In the barbershop in Sunnyside, The Right Price, the type of speech witnessed above is a daily occurrence. It ain't never a dull moment in that place, that's fa sho! In fact, after the release of Ice Cube's film, we couldn't STOP talkin about the many similarities between the shops. Each character in the movie had his correlate at The Right Price. Mr. Black, an older brotha who had a knack for BATTLIN, dubbed for Eddie. Mr. Rice, the owner and one of the barbers, referred to him in these terms: "Yeah, he just like Eddie cuz he always got something to say out his mouth!" The youngest barber, known as P, dubbed for Ice Cube's character, Calvin. Even the brotha in the movie who always looked for a way to get a free haircut was represented by the neighborhood clown character, Vin. This dude always be pissin the barbers off cuz he be STEADY tryina get a free haircut, you know what I'm saying? It's craaazy. But, anyway, even the Arab storeowner across from the barbershop in the film was represented by the Palestinian storeowner right next door to The Right Price. In an eerie similarity, both shops were once broken into using the same method of drilling a hole in the back wall to get in! And if that wadn't enough, both robbers ain't get a dime!

The Right Price is one of the few Black-owned businesses in Sunnyside, and serving a predominantly Black American clientele made it one of the few Black-owned public spaces in the city. It's a small shop, but it does the job, you know. All the barbers line they walls up with pictures of they wives, brothers, sisters, aunts, cousins, nephews, nieces, and friends. Historical newspaper clippings of all kinds can be found on the wall next to Mr. Rice chair, such as the Arabic-language article with a photograph of former South African President Nelson Mandela embracing Palestinian Chairman Yasser Arafat. The three old, brown leather barber chairs are lined up against the back wall, which is one long stretch of mirrors. A coffee table stacked with everything from the local newspaper to *Ebony* to *The Source* Hip Hop magazine is at the center, surrounded by about ten orange cloth waiting chairs. Up in the corner hangin off the wall is a old TV that stays runnin all day long—most of the time it be tuned in to the news. It's a nice, community-oriented place that has special meaning in this particular neighborhood, especially for the brothas. One sista relayed a sentimental story to me one day about how her lil brother, and all other young bucks on the block, viewed they first haircut at The Right Price as a rite of passage of sorts, the day they became men. For most folks, the shop is where you go to catch up on all the latest happenings within the neighborhood. "Did you hear about Ronnie?" "Ronnie who?" "You know, Ronnie stay up in the B [a section of the city]." "Oh, Ronnie Rollins?" "Nah, man, Ronnie Johnson, you know, BIG Ronnie, Talisha cousin." "OHHHH, oh, yeah, yeah, what about him?" "He done moved all the way out to the west side." "Oh, yeah, his wife go widdim?" "Nah, they not together no more.... You know how that go [laughter]." "Yeah, a good woman sho is hard to find." "I feel you, brotha, I feel you." The next stretch of dialogue may contain several minutes of folks BATTLIN about what makes a "good woman." Most of the time, brothas be laughin so much and havin such a good time, that the barbershop can serve as a therapeutic safe haven in a hostile world. Like one brotha said on his way out the shop one time, "THERAPY! Ahhh love this barbershop!"

Other moments in the barbershop can be real serious, you know, with critiques of U.S. foreign policy, international affairs, and their relation to Black Americans and their history. One day we was watchin the TV and the voice of a newscaster cut through—"We interrupt this program to bring you a special report"—and got everybody attention. "In the first sign of military action in response to the September 11th attacks on the Pentagon and the World Trade Center, the United States has initiated a bombing campaign in Afghanistan, where Osama bin Laden and his associates are believed to be seeking refuge." A brotha say, "Oh, shit, we at it again," in a matter-of-fact voice. "Long as no terrorists come down my street, my backyard, or whatever, I ain't fightin in no war." Another brotha questions his isolationism, "Man, what?" He responds, "Look, I got me a gun and I'm ready if they crazy-ass come knockin on my front doe, but other than that, I'ma stay my ass right here. Real Talk. I'ma stay my ass right here in Sunnyside." The phrase "Real Talk" is similar to what Eddie and others refer to as "straight talk." It's like the Hip Hop Nation Language version of this metalinguistic discourse. In the Sunnyside speech community, the phrase "Real Talk" be takin on multiple meanings. Not only is you expressin yoself freely (as in "straight talk"), but you allegedly speakin the truth as you see it, understand it, and know it to be. In addition, you stand ready to defend Real Talk. This is why the phrase is often used to punctuate statements. Notice its positioning: "I'ma stay my ass right here. Real Talk." He serious, like, he ain't playin. In other circumstances, the phrase "Real Talk" is used to question or verify the authenticity of someone's truth claims. For instance, if the brotha woulda made that statement, "I'ma stay my ass right here," and left off the "Real Talk," somebody mighta jumped in with a "Real Talk?" "Yeah, that shit is Real Talk." So, while the phrase is used by speakers to punctuate and emphasize truth claims, it's also used by listeners to engage and verify the truth claims being made.

The dialogue continues: "Maaan, look, if them terrorist think they can do all this crazy shit and get away with it, it's only gon get worse! I say we bomb the HELL outta Osama AND his mama!" The shop breaks into laughter, appreciating the rhyme. Another brotha joins in with a recognizable Black American falsetto, "And then it ain't gon BE NO MO DRAMA!" The shop breaks out into laughter one mo gin! The news "analyst" keeps rollin: "This bombing campaign should signify to the rest of the world that when President Bush says he will go after the terrorists AND THOSE WHO HARBOR THEM, he means it." Then I break into the discussion, "Nah, forreal, though, what if they turn around and say all the folks in Sunnyside is harboring criminals? The next thing they wanna do is drop a big-ass bomb right on top of us!" A brotha responds, "Maaan, they wouldn't do that!" "They did it in Philly not too long ago, AND they bombed out Black Wall Street in Oklahoma back in the day, you know what I'm saying? It's possible." "Nah, you crazy, man," he responds. Another brotha from the chair, who had been silent up until this time, jumps in with passion, "Anything is possible when you dealin with this typa enemy, you know. Them CRACKAS did some evil shit to us, you know what I mean, when they brung us over here in slavery. That's what I call TERRORISM, you know what I mean? Not THIS shit." At that moment, the shop got kinda quiet, you know, cuz here was this brotha who ain't said nann word about nuthin and he just bust in and drops the C-BOMB and levels a heavy critique linking slavery with Western Imperialism and the "War on Terror." Mr. Black, the elder barber, breaks the tension, "Yeah, he right about that now. Plus, like Ali said, ain't no Afghani ever called me no nigger!" Another round of laughs!

What this dialogue above shows is that Real Talk can sometimes be realer than real, capturing events that are SO REAL that they seem SURREAL. What I mean by that is that barbershop talk in Sunnyside IS Real Talk. It covers the gamut from mundane, daily conversation to profound analyses, producing a text of societal critique that be HELLA funny at the same time that it be DEADLY serious. In fact, one can say that both humor and gravity are necessary, coexisting components of Real Talk in this barbershop. The gravity of the brotha's statement about slavery left virtually no wiggle room for humor, which often provides a safety valve for unexpected tension. To return to the earlier part of the dialogue, Mr. Black was quick on his feet and smoothed it right on out. In this case, even though we was dealin wit real serious issues of war, international affairs, and their relationship to Black America history/reality, we still had TIME to appreciate the RHYME, you know what I'm saying? The Black American penchant for rhyming in everyday discourse is valued in the speech community (Lee 2002). A prime example of the everydayness of rhyming in the BASC occurred when a older brotha—say 60 years old—walked into the shop and took a number (to get in line). "Hey, hey, what's happenin?" "Alright, how you doin?" The brotha replied, "Hey, Jesus leadin, welfare feedin!" and everybody cracked up, appreciating the wit. He added, "If it wasn't for bad luck, I'd have none at all, and all that stuff, you know."

As another example, P, the youngest barber, was cuttin dude's hair one time, and they was talkin about this other cat who they could see out the window. Not really bein able to place him, dude made the assumption that he was probably a new dealer on the block. "Have rock will travel," he said, *rock* being the street name for 'crack cocaine'. P looked at him like he was crazy and started crackin up, "Nigga said, 'Have rock will travel!'" As folks started laughin, dude put on a pissed-off face and was like, "I know it's 'Have gravel will travel!'" This only made P and the others laugh harder cuz he was visibly upset. Laughter can be used as a means of testing someone's linguistic fortitude. Dude finally gave in, joined the shop, and laughed at himself. In another instance of rhyme, I came into the barbershop one day and hopped into P's chair. He like, "What you want? Same thing?" "Yeah, yeah, high bald fade, with a 1A on top." I'd been peepin how P been gettin a lil bit bigger over the last few weeks so I'm like, "Damn, P, you gettin swole." He pull up his sleeve and flex his bicep with these words, "That's the one-hitter quitter right there. Real Talk. One-hitter quitter," and we both started laughin. "That's dangerous, huh? You betta slow down before you hurt somebody." "Yeaahhh, that's Real Talk, homie," and we laughed again.

P, a street-affiliated brotha, worked out to keep himself in top condition. When asked about how he maintain so good while so many other brothas be fallin off, he say, in an example of Black American indirection, "Well, let's put it this way. When all of them was bein SERVED I was the one doin the SERVIN!" As he laughed, "Nah, I never touched that stuff." The barbershop for P was a way outta the trappings of street life that too many young brothas get caught up in (one is too many). P brought that streetified (Smitherman 1977) Black street speech up in the shop widdim. On several occasions, he would be chastised by Mr. Black for usin the word *nigga* in the barbershop. Mr. Black, from the older generation, used the word himself in his younger days but gave it up as he got older, or so he says (I heard him usin it a coupla times when talkin to some older buddies of his). He developed a language policy that outlawed the usage of the word in the shop—really, directed only at P—but P never did curb his usage. This went on for months until Mr. Black started collectin money from P each time he heard him say the word. Mr. Black challenged P, "I bet you can't go a day without usin that word, P." "Yeah, right, whatever." "Well, I'ma collect a dolla from you every time you say it then." "I'm cool, man, I ain't bettin." "See, told you you couldn't stop yoself from sayin it." "Man, whatever, Black, let's do it then." "Fine, I get a dollar every time you use it." "Cool, I ain't gon use it. What you think you gon get rich off me, huh?" "Everybody heard that?" (Brothas: "Yeah.") "Okay, I'ma hold you to it."

It wasn't no less than five minutes before P said the word! Mr. Black, "Hah! That's a dolla right there, P!" "Awww, MAN!" and we cracked up. A minute or two later, "That's another dollar—whooo-hoooo!—that's two dollas already," Mr. Black exclaimed as P reluctantly handed the dollar over. Mr. Black, triumphantly, "Hey, hey, you keep this up and I be done collected $600 by the end of the day!" (Rounds of laughter.) As time went by, the rules of the game begin to shift, or perhaps I began noticing what the rules of the game ACTUALLY were. I started noticing that P would "get way" with saying the word a dozen times while I was in there gettin my cut, but only be called out on it one or two times. At first, I figured that Mr. Black was just slackin on the rules or he wasn't really payin attention—but that didn't make no sense, cuz as unassuming as Mr. Black may appear, he don't miss a THANG. A pattern began emerging. P would only be called out for usin the word *nigga* when he was usin it in a disparaging way against another brotha. For instance, phrases like this one in reference to a local entrepreneur went by "unnoticed," "Oh, that's my nigga, I support that cat in whatever he do. He makin moves, you know what I'm saying?" Or, in reference to Barry Bonds's smashing the home run record, "Did you see that nigga mash that ball out the park? That ball was like, 'Don't hurt me, Barry, PLEASE don't hurt me!'" However, statements like the following often earned him severe rebuke from both Mr. Black and Mr. Rice, who was also in on this. One time P was talkin to the cat known as the neighborhood drunk, Vin. P and him been friends for a long time, you know, but sometime, Vin be gettin on P nerves. One day, while P was eatin ice cream, he noticed Vin starin at his food and damn near salivatin. He turned to Vin in a harsh voice, like, "What you lookin at, nigga?! Is this yos?! This ain't yos!" Mr. Rice responded with, "Hey, hey, hey, P, cut that out. Don't say that!" Vin like, "Damn, P, chill out, it just look good that's all." "Well, get your own then!" Recognizing his use of *nigga*, P ameliorated the situation with, "I didn't even say it. I said 'NINJA!'" "Oh, yeah, right," said Mr. Rice with a smile. P went on to explain that that's what one of his homies be doin to avoid sayin that word around his grandma.

What's important here is that in order to capture the talk in this speech community and the subtle yet integral rules and communicative norms of interaction, one has to LISTEN BETWEEN THE WORDS, so to speak. For an ethnographer, one of the most under-discussed aspects of methodology is LISTENING. A real close listen reveals not only the content of what is said, but the situational and contextualized nature of speech, along with patterned behavior of specific language usage. Listening between the words requires that one not only hear what's bein said out the speaker's mouth, but also "hear" what is intended by the speaker given a range of illocutionary and pragmatic possibilities and subtexts. It's the aural version of reading between the lines. In the above description, for example, we see the need for both humor and seriousness in Real Talk, the way the phrase "Real Talk" operates in Black American discourse, the penchant for and value placed on Black American rhyming practices, the subtle rules of interaction, the linguistic negotiation of controversial language, and, of course, the norm-driven use of BL in this localized community.

The following passage, in another case of listening between the words, demonstrates that silence can be as loud, if not louder, than words. It is not an unusual sight to see several young brothas hangin outside the shop and around the corner during regular business hours. These participants in the informal economy, street entrepreneurs if you will, have been effectively blocked out of the public education system, and subsequently, blocked out of the formal economy for various reasons. As one brotha once put it, "It's sad, but they makin it the only way they know how." It's a regular thing to see the po-po chasin brothas down the street, into backyards, over fences, and around the block. Chases have been normalized, right along with the activity that leads the officers to give chase.

One day, we was sittin in the barbershop on what was a pretty slow Thursday morning. I walked in the shop and wasn't no line, so I just hopped up in the chair. "Hey, hey, what's happenin?" P was ready and he started doin his thing. As more customers began rollin in, the shop was beginning to get a lil more lively. A group of young females in they twenties was standin cross the street actin like they wasn't up to nothing. Well, needless to say, they were the subject of conversation that morning. "Look at that one in the black—you know who that is?!" "Nah." "That's Lakisha's daughter." "That's Lakisha daughter?" "Yeah, member ha? She useta be YAY BIG walkin around with her thumb in her mouth, and now she look like THAT. Lord have mercy." (A round of laughter.) "C'mon, now, Mr. Black, get it together." "Oh, I'm workin on it—me and HER gettin it together," and he bust out laughin so hard I thought he was gon chop up dude's hair with his clippers!

Out of the blue, the one-time come rollin down the street and park they cars right outside the shop, but across the street. P, "Woah, where they come from? You see how they just rolled up like that?" Before P could finish, a gang of brothas rushed into the shop and acted like they was gettin they haircuts. Mr. Rice, peepin they game, shouts, "Oh, no, no, noooo, y'all not gettin yo hair cut today! I know what you doin." "Nah, Mr. Rice, I'm gettin a facial," one says. "Yeah, just a quick cut," says another. And about three or four more young Bloods take seats. Now, the shop FULL, right. Mr. Rice just shakin his head. The air gets a lil thick, but the conversations continue. Nobody seems to know that what's about to happen next is akin to a military incursion. The door to the shop creeps open and in walks this big, white, Irish-lookin police officer—ominous as all get-out! Immediately, a hush falls over the entire shop. I mean, you would literally hear a pin drop in that mug, you know what I'm saying? Quiet. The officer, thumbs in his belt loops like we sometimes catch George W. Bush doin on TV, walks around the shop in silence, his big, awkward body cuttin through the tension. Still silence. He moves from one end of the shop to the other, with everybody he passes avoiding eye contact. Makin his way from the door to the other side of the shop, he stop to look at the personal photographs on the wall next to Mr. Black's chair. "How you doin, officer?" says Mr. Black, breakin the silence at last with a phrase that oozed with unnatural niceness. "Fine, thanks," was the terse reply. Still silence. He walk over to Mr. Rice side and glances at his photos for a while, scrutinizing the young Bloods in the shop the way a cop might do in a police lineup. Then he turns to a small six-year-old, the young brotha in the chair gettin his hair cut. He bends down with his hands on both knees, "You're getting your hair cut today, huh?" he asks the young boy with a smile. The young brotha, in an amazing display of acquired norms, looks from side to side as if indifferent to the officer's question (and his overbearing presence)—and doesn't say a WORD! By now, the silence is deafening, and it seems to be ringin loud in the officer's ears. He turns around, defeated, and walks out the shop.

Soon as the doe slams behind him, the brothas that ran into the shop to escape the long arm of the law start cappin on him in a major way. All usin their version of a nasally white voice, they begin imitating and MARKIN him. One like, "You're getting your hair cut today, huh, little boy?" (round of laughter). Another, imitating what he heard the cop sayin outside, "You boys really need to stay off of the street. That's why you don't get anywhere in life" (nother round of laughter). Even Mr. Rice, who had initially resisted the use of his shop as an escape route, gets in on it and mocks his career choice of police officer in this community, "Yeah, right, look who talkin!" P was just about through with my haircut. As I left the shop, I noticed that the cop had now pulled into the parking lot and had two young Bloods up against his car. "You have a warrant, and you have a warrant." There was no resistance from the brothas. Just another day. I hear Mr. Rice shoutin in the background at one of the brothas, "But, see, that's why I don't want y'all runnin up in here like that—cuz I don't want THEM up in here!"

Both silence and humor play an important role in the speech situation above. Again, humor here serves as a means to release the tension. Only here, it is also used as a way to cope with what can oftentimes be a humiliating experience for those regular folks who just tryina live a decent life in this East Bank Sunnyside community. Homes, community businesses, and other institutions are subject to scrutiny whenever. Police incursions such as this one, including ones organized by the FBI, are not an uncommon occurrence. Rather, they are an unwelcome danger that most folks have to live with. When one considers the rate at which officers kill Black men in U.S. cities (since 1995 in Cincinnati alone, police have shot 15 Black men; and in a neighboring city near Sunnyside, a group of four officers were indicted for forming a police gang that shot Black men as they planted drugs and arms at the scene of the "crime"), that danger is real.

What we notice in this incredible power play is the role of silence as a form of articulation. As Wideman (1976) noted, Black American speech "has to do with a whole complicated protocol of silences and speech, and how you use speech in ways other than directly to communicate information." Well, when that six-year-old brotha gave the officer the "silent treatment," I think the message was loud and clear—"Get outta my face, cuz I ain't tellin you NU'IN!" Importantly, we see that even at six years old, the brotha had already picked up on the use of silence in situations where the community feels threatened by an oppressive police presence, particularly a white police presence. Silence, as a form of articulation in this manner, is a subtle communicative norm. In this case it's not what you SAY, but what you DON'T SAY. The fact that everybody in the shop participated in orchestrating this SILENCE EVENT all but turned the tables on the officer. It usurped his power and reversed the humiliation. Although the residents of this speech community remain effectively under occupation, speech AND silence function as face-saving devices. These moments reveal so much about the speech and communicative practices of a community that it's hard to imagine uncovering the subtleties and nuances of this speech activity without extended time in the field. It is through immersion that one can begin to place these speech events, and silence events, within the context of the overall communicative behavior of the speech community and, more broadly, within the context of the (sur)reality of this community's experiences. I mean, that's some surreal shit right there...

IN THEM SUNNYSIDE STREETS...

We walkin in them Sunnyside streets. We just left the school grounds and IT AIN'T NUTTIN NICE, as the locals like to say, a phrase that simultaneously represents some folks' reality in this small, suburban neighborhood and challenges outsiders or enemies who may consider approachin they block. But today IS a nice day. And as if to cosign my thoughts, an old '67 Chevy rolls by, baby blue with a white stripe on the sides. With the music playin loud out the window, we hear Jimmy Cliff sing to us: "It's gonna be a bright, bright, bright, sunshiny day." With the late March afternoon sun shinin long and hard against these hot streets, I silently hope for shade as we walk toward our destination.

Today is our first street session. My students (Amira, Aqiyla, Bilal, Kijana, and Yesmina) are embarking on what is about to be a hands-on field research experience. But before we even make it one hundred feet from the school grounds, I hear the VROOOOOM of a car that's soundin like it BEEN needed work, you know what I'm sayin? From behind me, Yesmina shouts, "Shit, get out the way ... Bucket!" We all scatter quickly to the side of the road. No sidewalks on this street. Dirt. Rocks. Gravel. Parked cars. A large muddy puddle fills the pothole big enough to take a bath in. "It ain't nuttin nice, we used to it," says Bilal. He pauses for a second, then he adds, reflectively, "But, damn, how come we the only ones wit no SIDEWALKS?" Before I respond, I turns around to see who drivin down this narrow street that fast, and Yesmina was right. That car sho nuff IS a bucket! Lil old red beat-up sports car with the muffler hangin so low made you wonder how on earth it even stayed on, you know what I mean? We had to laugh as them cats whipped by all fast...

"Hey, yo!" SCREEEEEEEEECH! To our surprise, the car suddenly screeches to a halt, peels out, and with a loud spin of the tires, the dude kicks it into reverse. Yesmina, as if speaking for me, hollas,

"Oh, Lord!" "Yeah, exactly," I think. "What we about to get into, you know?" The dude yells something out the car, and Yesmina like, "What did he say? What he say?" Bilal laughs, but it's a mixture of humor and nervousness. We hear the driving bass beatin out the car from the sounds of a local underground rap crew. Now the car has backed up all the way next to us and dude in the passenger seat motions over to Amira. He got on a black T-shirt, black stocking cap, and black sunglasses with a cheap-lookin thin, gold chain. You shoulda seen it, thing looked like dental floss! It quickly becomes apparent that dude tryina spit some game at Amira. I can see that my students ease up a little bit, cuz apparently, like India.Arie be singin, they done heard it all before. Of course, this form of Black American rappin, where a male attempts to win the heart of a female through a dazzling (or sometimes lackluster, if you don't got game) display of verbal skills is a common practice in the neighborhood. So, they ain't trippin, but me, as the one responsible, I got my antennas up for any signs of trouble, you know what I'm saying?

Amira responds, "Me? Why? Who are you?" I now see that there are three brothas in the car. Dude, "Hey, don't I know you?" "Huh, do you know me?" she asks. "Don't I know you?" he persists, failing to come up with another line. She blows him off with a low, "I don't know," and turns away. Now, Kijana walk up with the video camera, and Aqiyla snaps a photo of the three brothas in the car. The driver shouts, laughing, "Hey, why you gotta do all that? Hold on, hold on, hold on, hold on!" The passenger in the back seat chimes in, "She filmin and everything!" As we all begin to laugh, I recognize dude's shame in being caught on tape and say, "We got somebody in trouble over here. He said, 'Why you gotta do all that?'" Homeboy tries again, this time, actin all innocent, "What yo name is?" "Monique," Amira shoots back, playin him like a ukulele. Now the brotha, thinkin he got something, leans out the car with his arm hangin out the window, smilin, like, "Monique, where you stay at?" "In Parkside," another lie. "In Parkside, forreal?" "Forreal," says Monique, beginning to get visibly annoyed. Then dude say, "Can I call you?" And that's when I step in, cuz this has gone on for too long. Over all the voices, I intervene, "Hey, look, look,

look, look, look, hey, hey…" By this time, Amira ready to give him a phony cell number so he can drive off, and homie whips out his Palm Pilot like he ain't got a number in years. I steps in again like, "Hey, brah, this is a class project." Thankfully, another car rides by and they happen to know the three stooges, so they become distracted. We walk off and I turn to my students like, "Y'all gon get into some TROUBLE."

We keep walkin and, naturally, my students start cappin on dude and, indirectly, poking fun at Amira (cuz he's attracted mainly to her). Bilal starts it off, "You know he a dopefiend, Amira, you know that, right?" She ignorin him, crackin up replaying how she deceived him. Yeah, it's funny, but still I warn her and the others to cut off all communication with them, cuz these types of encounters don't always end up being funny, right? Despite my attempt to enforce a serious tone, the cappin continues. Bilal, again, "You know he a dopefiend." Yesmina joins in, testing Amira further, "He a dopefiend, Amira," and she cracks on the dude, "Look at that perm—that shit dry-y-y-yyy!" as we all break into laughter. We continue walkin down the street and finally, I think, we can really get into our street session.

It wasn't even fifty feet before we heard that local underground rap crew ONE MO GIN! I'm like, "Is this dude forreal?!" Amira cuts him off before he can even get started, "My boyfriend said I can't give you my number," pointing back at me. Not wanting the situation to get outta control, I walk up to the car and let it be known that I wasn't havin it. "Hey, we in school right now," I said firmly. "Oh, that's yo class?" he asks. "Uh-huh." "Oh, okay, I respect that." And the car rides off as fast as it came. I'm thinkin, wheeeewww, that coulda got ugly, you know what I mean? All this and we ain't even hardly left the school, really! Maaan… The students may have thought that the first time was "cute," but the second time, everybody agreed, was over the line. "Old-ass man, he the same age as my dad," says Yesmina. Bilal joins in, "He like 30-something." "YOU KNOW WHAT I'M SAYIN?!" I say to Bilal in agreement. "Rapists," he adds. "High school students?" I say in disgust at the thought of sorry older men drivin around a high school tryina score wit some teenagers. Aqiyla provides closure, "PLEEEAASE!" And we walk….

This type of interaction in the street is a ritualized form of talk in Sunnyside, where the street can be a place where the RAPPIN event witnessed above occurs, where friends and neighbors greet each other like they long-lost family members, where lil girls jump rope as they walk to school and teenagers roll dice, where older men conversate outside the barber shop, and where garage sales and the crowd from a family barbeque spills out from the front yard. The streets, however, can also be a place where drug deals are made in broad daylight as mothers push they babies by in carriages, where one may witness a young brotha runnin from the PO-lice hoppin fences in backyards ("Damn, he was on probation, too," a concerned onlooker might say), where the homeless sleep only to be awakened by the blast of a gunshot (fired by police or gang members, viewed as a thin line), and where the cracks in the pavement signify the crack-filled and fragmented nature of a community where far too many find themselves strung out on crack cocaine.

Sunnyside is a community where many of the Black residents are quickly becoming "strangers in their 'own' land" due to the silent, yet sweeping, process of gentrification. The educational history of Sunnyside cannot be told without considering the processes of segregation, desegregation, and gentrification. Desegregation and gentrification, in particular, have had and are continuing to have severe economic and social consequences for what was once a predominantly Black community, as my students recognize. As we tell the story of the occupied territories of the East Bank, of which the Sunnyside community is a part, the voices of my students will be supplemented by historical research. In fact, it was the collective memory of my students, the vividness of their stories, and the passion with which they told and retold them that led me deeper into the community to construct an oral history, to find out what REALLY went down, you know what I'm saying? While my students may only be teenagers, they have lived long enough to be able to describe life in the occupied territories. Life experience for this set of teenagers, as ahistorical and decontextualized as it is often depicted in the United States, is supplemented by the fact that countless tales told by the elders are etched in their minds. You ain't gon find these stories in no textbook. This the SHADY side of Sunnyside's history, and like rapper DMX be sayin, my students "got a story to tell." Their stories reveal the complex racial, political, and economic tensions between communities in Sunnyside, the students' ideologies of race, and a great sense that they are living in a community that, as alive as it once was, is now just tryina live. Clear in their accounts is both the struggle against, and the internalization and projection of, racism. In the latter cases, stories lead to what can be described as the occupation of the mind. These accounts, brief as they are, will hopefully provide some context for viewing the language data in chapters 5–8.

Of course, the Sunnyside story begins WAY before my students arrived on the scene. It would be damn near impossible for me to do justice to the Sunnyside story, but best believe I'm makin every effort to do RIGHT by the Sunnyside community (past, present and future generations). In the next section, I provide an outline of Sunnyside's complicated and contentious history.

BACK IN THE DAY: THE RISE AND FALL OF AFRICAN AMERICAN NATIONHOOD

(The historical sources in this chapter can be found at the small but very helpful Sunnyside archive. Readers interested in the history of Sunnyside should feel free to contact the author at writealim@yahoo.com.) Sunnyside's recent history, as we gon see in a minute, is the history of many Black communities throughout the United States—the occupied territories, as I call them. Don't matter if you in Chi-town, Oaktown, or the Boogie Down, this how it go down. At the same time, though, Sunnyside got its own story to tell, one that sees a community rise in status as the nation's Black-consciousness capital in the 1960s only to be abased as the nation's murder capital some three decades later. The story is a long and complicated one, and my brief account here clearly will not do any real justice to the complex history of this community. The idea is to give y'all a sense of the big picture, in particular, how this community, my students included, continues to survive, to resist occupation. It's an everyday thang. We call it MAINTAININ.

Black Americans came to Sunnyside in great numbers during the years of 1945 through 1960 in what's known as Sunnyside's "boom period." The Black American challenge to racial segregation resulted in their coming to Sunnyside in large numbers in search of housing. This is right around the time when White real estate agents began bustin up the block, BLOCKBUSTING they call it (and we ain't talkin bout movie rentals). Older Black American migrants to Sunnyside were eager and excited to begin livin the "American dream," or so they thought, and from 1945 to 1950 Sunnyside's Black American population had quadrupled. Blacks were told that they would be beginning a new life out of the major cities and into the suburbs, but when they tried to purchase homes outside of Sunnyside the real estate agents wasn't tryina hear it. Despite this, blockbusting, a racist strategy designed by real estate developers to rake in as much loot as they possibly could, changed the face of Sunnyside almost overnight. Dramatically, ten thousand Whites fled Sunnyside in the decade from 1950 to 1960—that's a thousand heads a year.

While the Black population was steady risin, several economic developments transpired. Immediately after World War II, a new freeway was built to accommodate the population boom in the area. The freeway, as in the case of several new freeways being built around the country, ran through the center of Sunnyside, effectively destroying the business district and predicting years of hard times ahead. Yo, it's serious—the freeway construction removed 53 businesses, only five of which were able to relocate within the city. While developers over here busy splittin up the area and destroyin its economic base, nearby White cities, witnessing the rise in the Black population and the increasing housing development, began annexing major sections of Sunnyside. This annexation of land by neighboring White cities, in conjunction with the devastation caused by the new freeway, resulted in major losses in property tax revenue for the area. So, as the Black population rose, they were also being set up for economic failure.

Blacks in Sunnyside was knowin what was goin down, too, cuz they done developed a "Black Action Council" in Sunnyside to try and counter the looming danger up ahead. In 1967, when groups like the Nation of Islam and the Black Panthers were developing strongholds in nearby cities and the Black Arts Movement poets and playwrights was spittin rhymes about "nation time," Sunnyside's Black Action Council wrote a "Black action paper" that emphasized seven aims: (1) to aid Black people in setting up businesses, (2) to encourage Black people to run for public office, (3) to involve the entire community in striving for the economic betterment of all Black people, (4) to focus on Black youth and unemployment, (5) to focus on getting industries with federal contracts to hire Blacks, (6) to facilitate the employment of Black people in the public schools on all levels, and (7) to focus on Black culture and communication. Interestingly enough, land ownership and control were not highlighted in the agenda, though the lack of land ownership appears to be a major factor in the continuing disenfranchisement of Black Americans in the area.

On the educational front, Black parents began developing programs and strategies in response to the failure of Sunnyside's White-owned and -operated schools to educate their children. The community organized independent Black schools and sought an educational ideology of self-determination.

In 1969, the same year that Blacks in Sunnyside established the first and only Black-controlled K–college educational institution and one year after the ousting of the White principal at Sunnyside's public Raven High, Sunnyside area schools were ordered to DESEGREGATE. While Black parents eventually complied with the legal mandate, many White parents refused. The combination of Black compliance and White refusal hindered the proposed bidirectionality of busing, and Raven High was forced to shut down due to low enrollment rates in 1975. Sunnyside residents were not to see a public high school in their area for the next two decades. Black students didn't fare too well in White schools, with dropout rates as high as 73%—White schools' dismal Black student graduation rate continues nearly three decades later, hovering at around 65%.

Against this backdrop of the community's struggle to MAINTAIN, an unexpected event knocked the wind out of Sunnyside. "Crack cocaine hit this community, I mean, like, like a tornado," one resident recalls. Increasing unemployment and poverty, the unavailability of jobs in the city, and 17 years of educational underdevelopment of Black students by White schools laid fertile ground for the rise of Sunnyside's informal economy. In 1992, Sunnyside was rocked by drug-related violence and won the infamous title of "murder capital of the United States." In that year, in that small two and a half square mile city, 42 bodies were buried out of a population of 23,939. In desperate need of some way to develop a solid tax base, many Sunnyside residents were elated to hear about the inking of a major deal between the city and developers. The developers, with their proposed 28-acre shopping mall, promised to raise one million dollars in sales tax revenue for the city. According to one inside informant on the community team of the development planning committee, Sunnyside residents never did agree on a comprehensive strategy for development, nor did they agree about the limits of commercial development by outside, White real estate companies. While some residents supported the development and viewed it as their only salvation for building a tax base, others protested the fact that the giant mall would bring increased traffic to the residential area, not be in the interest of the community, and cause the removal of community sites, businesses, and hundreds of families who lived on the proposed construction site. In addition, some residents feared that the lack of community control and involvement in the process would cause more harm than good in the long run. After years of protest and stalling, the developers moved ahead with their project in 1998.

The next section takes us "over the ramp" and right on up to the present day. The stories told by my students paint a picture of Sunnyside from the perspective of the NEXT generation of Blacks in the community, which although nobody wants to say it right now, could also be the LAST, as more and more Black families are being forced to move out due to the recent annulment of rent control laws. Figures 4.1 and 4.2 show how Sunnyside has changed ethnically in the decade of 1990–2000, and figure 4.3 shows the current ethnic demographic information.

The most important points to highlight in these figures are the dramatic shifts in the Black and Latino populations. From being an almost all-Black city decades ago, the Black population was

FIGURE 4.1
Population Change by Ethnic Group in Sunnyside, 1990–2000

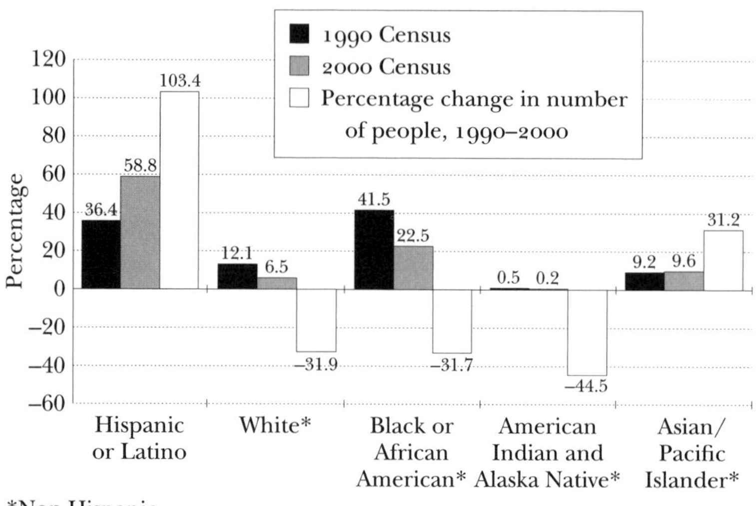

*Non-Hispanic

FIGURE 4.2
Population Change by Ethnic Group in Sunnyside, 1990–2000

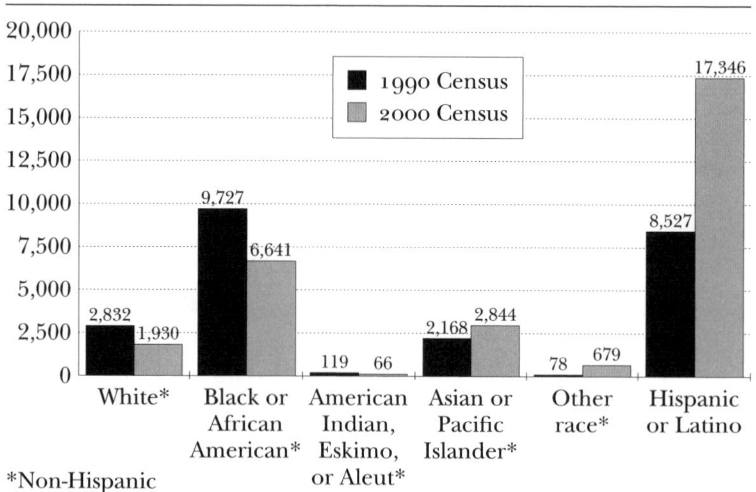

*Non-Hispanic

FIGURE 4.3
Ethnic Diversity in Sunnyside, 2000

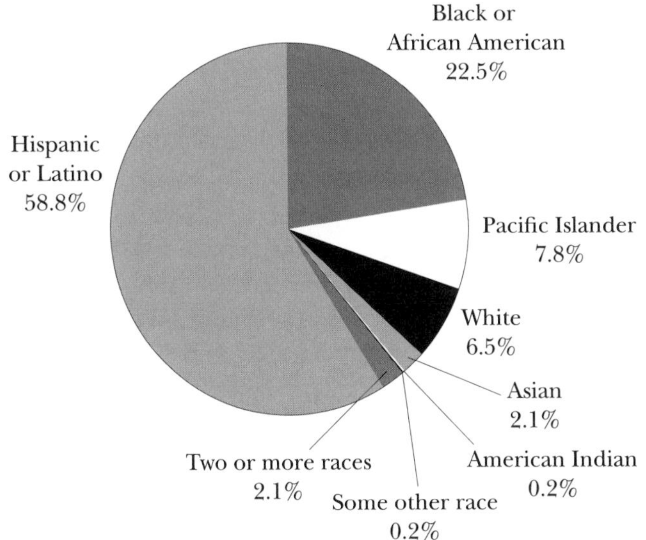

the predominating population in 1990 (making up 41.5% of the population) and decreased even further by 2000 (making up only 22.5% of the population). In the same decade, the Latino population continued its rapid rise in 1990 (making up 36.5% of the population) and rose even more dramatically by 2000 (making up 58.8% of the population). This rapidly increasing ethnic diversity, as we will see, can be interpreted as a signifier for increasing and increasingly diversified competition for limited resources in the occupied territories.

"WE CALL IT 'OVER THE RAMP'": SUNNYSIDE AND SHADYSIDE

People walkin by me. Black. Tongan. Samoan. Mexican. Palestinian. El Salvadorian. Indian. Chinese. Filipino. White. I see distinctive faces, worn by the work involved in maintaining. I hear the voice of the big homie Pac beatin out the mobb, "You just tryina maintain, and go head, cuz I ain't mad atcha." Survivin. Laughin. Smilin. Strugglin. Lots of work goin on in these streets. Bits of the world's tongues catch my ears. "YELLEHHH! WEIN RAYEHH?!" "Yeahhh, tha's what she be doin, rogue!" "Real Talk?" "Fa shiiiiiizzzzyyyy!" (laughter) "Que coche mas chingo!" Cars honkin they horns. Buckets, Beemers, and Benzos. Flipped out whips that be chromed OUT. The concrete that I stand on was once dirt, once clay, once mud, once plains. The names and faces may have changed, but the land remain the same. Like it say in the Bible, "Generations will come and go, but the earth abideth forever." I stand still, yet time rushes by me. I get this ill feelin like I'm standin at the crossroads of histories. It's all whippin by me like the wind. I see it all through the eye of the needle. I'm talkin hi-definition vision. Right here, right now, I'm in the middle of centuries of crossed paths, crossed bridges, crossed and double-crossed lives. Lost in the whirlwind. History continues to whip by me while the present, all around me, moves in slow-ow-ww-w mo-o-o-tion. I ask myself, "How did I get here?" Then I think, "No, how did WE get here?" DJ-J-J-J-J-JJJJJJJ!!! DJ-J-J-J-JJJJJ!!! It's at this moment that the machine-gun-like firing of a jack hammer suddenly brings me, as Soul II Soul sang, back to liiife, back to reality…

As we ride up to Sunnyside, we gon go the scenic route, you know, through the surrounding neighborhoods. This is so y'all can get a picture of what it be like "over the ramp," as the locals say, referring to the ramp entrance of the freeway that splits Sunnyside. The term is this community's, and this generation's, "other side of the tracks." The term itself reifies the dividing line along color, class, and educational opportunity. One afternoon while eatin lunch with some of my students, we got into a conversation about Shadyside, the city that exists in that other space "over the ramp," and the differences between it and Sunnyside. So, I'm like: "What y'all know about that?" and the following dialogue ensued:

Yesmina: The neighborhood just like…

Amira: White!

Y: Yeah, you know how like, like they be having like million dollar houses that be hella BIG and beautiful and shit. They don't be

like our houses, you know, or like—those new ones worth millions...
A: Once you cross that, over the ramp, after the bus stop...
Y: Yeah...
A: ...well, after the potholes, that's the White part...
Y: [shaking her head] It's like it ain't even worth it...
A: The streets is just smooth, all the houses look different...
Y: MM-HMM!
Researcher: As soon as you get over...?
Y: As SOOOOON. It says "Welcome to Shadyside."
A: Yep...
R: Does it say, does it really say, "Welcome to..."
A: They let you KNOW you leavin Sunnyside...

Here, the physical street sign welcoming you to Shadyside is both a sign and a symbol of very noticeable class and color lines. Ridin up through Shadyside is quite an experience. The neighborhood streets, extra wide and freshly paved, are lined with large, leafy oak trees and tall palm trees that seem to be reaching for the sky. The trees form a breathtaking natural canopy covering the width of the streets and providing for a pleasant drive. Rollin down these cool, shady streets, we see wealth all around us. Large Spanish- and Victorian-style homes line both sides of the street, one of which recently sold for $3.6 million. They "mansion-type cribs," as one of my students calls them. I mean, MTV Cribs ain't got NUTTIN on these Shadyside mansions, you know what I'm saying? Driveways lined with forest green BMW X5s, navy blue Jaguar XJ6s, new silver Audi TT Roadsters, Lincoln sports utility vehicles, and other high-status autos. I mean, that's just how Shadyside cats be ROLLIN.

As we head closer to Sunnyside, we can see the broad, congested eight-lane freeway through the trees. This is where we get to the ramp. Comin up over the ramp, we are immediately struck with a brand new development called College Circle, a complex of fancy hotels. Construction crews wrapping up they work. Maaan, this useta be the site of Sunnyside's business district—the only section of Sunnyside that was technically over the ramp. As a result of the construction of the new freeway, the business district ended up on the other side of the ramp. The district was TORE UP and demolished soon after developers inked the deal in 1998. One can't help but notice that the enormous hotels looks a lil bit outta place. As we make our way over the ramp, we can hear the freeway roaring beneath. Big cranes, lookin like the long arms of a robotic Godzilla, greet us with an almost ominous presence. Noises of loud hammering and drilling fill the air. Trucks, turnin fresh cement, rumble around the site. Dozens of men in bright orange construction gear move about the place, dwarfed by the magnificent structure looming over them. Sunnyside, despite a series of protests, had voted by a slim margin (1,562 to 1,419 votes, or 52.4% to 47.6%) in favor of the new furniture store. Ain't that some ishhh? Residential apartments that housed Black and Latino families once stood on that same land not too long ago. Like the business district over the ramp, they were demolished several years earlier in the name of development.

As we head down the other side of the ramp, we come to the first intersection in Sunnyside, which is lined with stores that serve the needs of the community. Two mom-and-pop neighborhood shops with Spanish names. "Beepers for 99 cents!" one sign reads. Then we get to one of the many meat-and-liquor stores found in damn near EVERY Black and Brown hood in the United States. And, if you hungry, you can always grab a fish taco at the local taqueria next door. On the other side of the street are a small animal hospital and the neighborhood mechanic. STEADY workin. Further down, you got one of the most lucrative Black businesses in the city—the funeral home. It's like every weekend you see them bright, lime-green Cadillacs and that old, black Hearse pulled up out front as brothas and sistas gather in they Sunday best to see their loved ones off (see Holloway 2002 for Black mourning and burial practices). The question is almost always asked: "Why we always gotta wait till somebody DIE to get together?" And life goes on.

Adjacent to the funeral home is the largest real estate development this city has seen in all of its history. Symbolically, the huge 28-acre shopping mall stands facing the freeway with its back turned away from the community. The mall so big that you can see it from Shadyside and peep it over the trees while you ridin down the freeway. The brand new establishment, made of pink and pastel stucco and freshly paved and painted, stands out like sore thumb. No joke. The back of the mall faces a residential area of Sunnyside that presents a stark contrast to the wealth suggested by the presence of this retail establishment. Given that the average income in Sunnyside is about one-third that of the neighboring cities, the number of high-end stores in the mall confirms some residents' fears that the mall would not be in the best interest of the community; the building of this 28-acre plaza is a hotly contested issue in the community, both celebrated and despised. Most of the people who shop AND work in the extraordinarily large plaza are not from Sunnyside. Ironically, the mall stands right on top of where the old Raven High useta be.

In addition to living in Sunnyside for the duration of my teaching experience in Haven High, I have been visiting the community for over three years. The community has changed drastically since my first visit in 1999. The two main topics of discussion in the community regarding the "new" Sunnyside are "ethnic diversity" and "economic development." Though usually discussed separately, the two are in fact inseparable. What do Sunnyside youth know and think about the changes that are taking place in their community? How are they both experiencing and making sense of the rise in ethnic diversity and economic development? What do they see as the social position and status of Blacks in this "new" Sunnyside? How do they explain the relative and perceived differences in the socioeconomic status of the various communities both IN and OUT of Sunnyside? What do they see as the role of race and class in the process of gentrification? Most importantly, how do they FEEL about these changes? We really got INTO it in one of our street sessions. As we will see, the raising of a seemingly simple question—"Have you noticed Sunnyside changing since y'all were little kids, like, little baby kids?"—opened up the floodgates of racial, ethnic, and class ideologies, all discussed on the grounds of what useta be the neighborhood's public high school. You ready to ride wit us?

ETHNIC DIVERSITY, ECONOMIC DEVELOPMENT, AND GENTRIFICATION IN THE OCCUPIED TERRITORIES

Male: C'mon, celeBRATE!
Female: Yeah, we gon celebrate this day!
Reporter: What are you celebrating?
F: We are celebrating the demolition of Raven High School.
M: We're celebrating hope for the city! That's right, a MAJOR milestone. It's the beginning of our economic independence, which we hope. That's what it seems like, a great opportunity for us.
F: Right! Right on!
[clapping and cheering]

—50-year-old Black couple in Sunnyside, 1996

Bilal: This is the, the, the white part of Sunnyside now...
Researcher: Yeah, so what IS all of this?
Yesmina: The WHITE part!
B: This BULLSHIT right here!
R: Is this Sunnyside?
B: Hell naw! This is, this is corporate America takin over...
Aqiyla: Yeah...
B: This is the sunny side of Sunnyside...
Amira: This whole area, right here, where ALL this new, all these new buildings are, this useta be Raven High School...

—17-year-old Black youths in Sunnyside, 2002

We walkin again in them Sunnyside streets. Conversatin. Choppin it up about Sunnyside. The streets is lined wit small, neat houses, each one havin a fence of some sort that clearly demarcates the property lines. We ain't talkin white picket fences here, you know what I mean? Sun still beatin down on us pretty heavy. Yesmina holdin the video camera right now, scannin the potholes she like, "Raggedy streets, raggedy STREETS!" We in the B right now, the section of Sunnyside where most of the remaining Black folks live at. See, Sunnyside divided into five different sections, or SETS. These divisions were created by White folks long time ago; however, the names of the sections have been adapted—sometimes I be thinkin about how no matter where you go or what city you be in, if it's Black people there, they done managed to rename the entire city, its various sections and even streets, and what's deep about it is that somehow these names actually signify a parallel existence for most Black people in the hoods of America. This nationwide network—a United Streets of America, as my lil man, Lil Wayne be sayin—sometimes signifies the "black market" within the Black community, you know what I'm saying?

So, as we roll through the B, everybody start throwin up signs and claimin they shit, like, "YEAHHH, I'm from the B!" you know, representin they different lil hoods like some straight-up GANGSTAS. Amira, noticin how we got all five sets covered within our group, exclaims in what can only be described as an AfroAmericanism: "We got REPRESENTITATION from everywhere!" I'm laughin like, "Representitation!" Interested in these terms and the meaning of REPRESENTIN these sets, I'm like, "Why do people feel like so strong that they gotta say where they from?" Aqiyla, as if recognizing the leading nature of the question, like, "I just be playin!" Bilal, "I don't—it's nothing that, it's NUTHIN that, how it USED to be, cuz people useta DIE over stupid stuff like that. But now, everybody see it as, you know, that's WHERE YOU FROM, basically, that's where you LIVE . . . not gangs and shit." Recalling the grim and grimy "murder capital" days of Sunnyside, he adds, "They useta battle over sets and shit like that, set-trippin and stuff. . . . When you go to other hoods and stuff, people be trippin. But here, we don't really trip off, 'Oh, he from this set or whatever, so I'ma do this. He from that set, I'ma do this.' It's nuttin like that." Amira, makin it plain, shows a more generalized, functional usage of set names. "That's just how you identify people. 'Oh, he from Da V. Oh, you from the B. Oh, you know, Marcus from the B?' Cuz it could be like hella Marcuses."

All of a sudden, we bend a conah, and the streets is hella smooth, paved with fresh tar and lined up with bright yellow paint. We at the edge of the B right now, and outta nowhere we see the back of this BIG pink and red stucco structure. I mean, this jawn HELLA big! The lil houses seem like they all pushed up against it, cuz the structure completely dominates the area. This the buildin that they was puttin up when I first came to Sunnyside. It wasn't nuttin but construction trucks and tractors rollin around a basic cement foundation. Now, it's THIS. Bilal, "This is the, the, the white part of Sunnyside now." I'm like, "Yeah, so what IS all of this?" Yesmina shouts, "The WHITE part!" We crossin the paved street and Bilal, obviously pissed off, emphasizes, "This BULLSHIT right here!" Noticin the stark difference from where we just was to where we at now, I'm like, "Is this Sunnyside?" Bilal, "Hell naw! This is, this is corporate America takin over... This is the sunny side of Sunnyside." Bilal tellin it like it is—I mean, clearly he know it's Sunnyside, but he's rejecting it being identified as such. Instead, he runs it down as a corporate America takeover, an occupation of Sunnyside territory by White real estate developers. I'm like, DAAAMMMMNNN, what was here, on this land, that he feel so STRONGLY about? I ask, "Now what is all this stuff? When I first came here, there was just buildings. When did this all get started?" "A couple years ago." Yesmina, "It's still fresh."

As we walk up through the back parking lot and around the side, Bilal explains, "They tore down the lil—I mean, they BEEN tore down the lil Raven High, but they started..." Yesmina interrupts him quick, like, "They coulda built that right back up!" "O-KAY!" exclaims Amira, in a signature affirmation used mainly by the sistas. "My mama useta go there. She MAD!" I'm all out the loop, not knowin WHAT's goin on. "What was here? What was here?" I ask. Bilal explains, "Originally, a long time ago, Raven High." In disbelief, I'm like, "THIS was Raven High?" Bilal, "This big-ass lot, ALL OF THAT!" I'm still like, "This whole place?!" I mean, y'all don't even underSTAND—you'd NEVER be able to tell it was a high school on this land back in the day. In a high-pitched Black American falsetto, I'm not believin it just yet, "Get the hell outta here?!" "ALL OF THAT..." Bilal's voice trails off. Amber picks it up, "My mom useta go to high school—this whole area, right here." Pointin all the way out across the 28-acre property, she adds, "Where ALL this new, all these new buildings are, this useta be Raven High." Yesmina, in a reflective, reminiscent tone, "Everybody useta come here."

Turns out that folks had just had a reunion for the last graduating class of Sunnyside. While everybody's talkin about it, I'm pissed like, "They said it was NUTTIN over here!" Yesmina turns around like, "SHIIIIIT, it was a high school." You gotta understand that most folks I talked to about this development—mostly outsiders or University folk, come to think about it—acted like it wasn't nuthin ever over here. And here I am findin out about all of this for the first time, connecting the fabled Raven High with an actual site, you know. Shit was mind-blowin! Meanwhile, they still reminiscin, "YEAH, aunties, uncles, they all went here!" says Bilal. Here go Amira again, "O-KAY!" Aqiyla adds, "My dad, my aunties, uncles, EVERYBODY... It was cool as hell—had a big-ass track and everything..." Hearin all this, I had to stop and ask, "Hold on, why'd they tear it down?!" Bilal repeats the oft-told reason with suspicion, "They said nobody was graduating and shit, SOME bullshit," and Amira follows up, "It was hecka Black people and minorities that went there, and they said that the graduation rate wasn't up to par, so they, so they shut it down. And then homeless people started living in there..." "Livin inside of that shit," Bilal adds. Amira, "So they just didn't attempt to rebuild it back."

Young Bloods in remiNISCIN mode now. "I useta go to camp there." "I useta play little league basketball there... They useta have summer school and, like, stuff, the YMCA and, maaan, they had tennis courts." Amira, a legend in her own mind, and destined to get her shine on, recalls, "I went to a summer performing arts program there. That's where I did my first acting debut... I helped portray some of the olden-day people who were tryin to do civil rights stuff, and we did a—[here, she launches into exaggerated, falsely modest speech, as if she were already a superstar—picture that animated sista, Cita, on BET]—WHOLE LIL SECTION ON MARCUS GARVEY AND EVERYTHANG, and we did like a song and it was a musical..." Wayblackmemories just flowin and flowin. Time continues to march on in this late March afternoon sun. We walkin now through the heart of the parkin lot and Bilal takes over. "If I remember, if I remember correctly, the gym and stuff was over there, tennis courts was like right over here, you know what I mean, if I remember correctly." Yesmina helps out, "The track was all around," and Amira adds, "And this part right here, right here in that middle part, that was the gym. That was the gym, and the swimming pool was right there [pointing to a HIGH-high end remodeling design store, Expo]. Where the Expo is, that's where the swimming pool was at."

I'm sittin here listenin to all of these memories flow, and I'm like, man, young bucks really FEEL the loss of this place—DEEP sense of loss. And the thing about it is, it wadn't even they school! Picture a Expo, where something as little as a bathtub sliding door can cost up to $25,000 (no JOKE!), sittin right up on top of the old school swimming pool. Now, understand that the per capita income for Sunnyside residents in 1999 (one year after this development went up) was $13,774, about one-third of the per capita income of the surrounding White cities, and about one-half of the price of that damn bathtub door. Why they gon put up a Expo HERE? With the development being so close to the "ramp," Shadyside folks slip in and out the store without having to interact with Sunnyside folk at all. Given the exorbitant prices, it's clear that the design center was not designed for Sunnyside. Amira and her homegirls tell an interesting story and exemplify the feeling of displacement in one's own community. She continues, "Me and Sharonda went in there and was like [in that exaggerated speech again], 'OOOH, I think this would go GOOD with my NEW BEEEEDDD. I think THIS would go GOOD with the refrigerator we just got,' you know," she laughs, knowing full-well the ridiculousness of her situation. She goes on to describe how they were followed around the store, out into the parking lot.

Pickin up on this feeling of displacement, I ask them, "Have you noticed Sunnyside changing since y'all were little kids, like, little baby kids?" Aqiyla like, "YEAHHH! A lot!," then she adds, "it got WORSE!" Now, this clearly is contrary to how most outsiders talk about Sunnyside. Like, most folks be like, "Yeah, isn't Sunnyside great now? It's cleaner, and I feel much safer there, especially with that new plaza and all of those new homes being built." "Hispanics!" shouts Amira. Then, agreeing with Aqiyla, she gets heated, like, (pointing to the new furniture store construction site described in the beginning of this section) "All this wa'n't even here! It was a bunch of houses, like..." Then she drops it, "... BLACK FACES." Bilal cosigns, "It was a lot more Black people!" Yesmina, "Yeppp." Amira repeats again, "Black faces." She continues, "It was like, it would be, like, like, kinda be more on the sides of yo stereotypical ghetto, BUT without the like..." Bilal jumps in, "It was more of a ghetto, basically. It wasn't as clean, you know what I mean?" Amira, again, pounds the point home, "And it wasn't all this—all these buildings, all this shit wa'n't here!" Trailing off, "It was a high school..."

By now it's becoming clear to me that the demolition of Raven High ain't just about the physical removal of a high school, you feel me? Wrapped all up inside of this symbolic structure is my students', and the Sunnyside community's, ideologies of race, class, and ethnicity, and their sociopolitical stance vis-à-vis the rapid ethnic diversity and encroaching economic development. Here they stand, amidst all of these alienating symbols of wealth and power, dealin wit the fact that they ain't got neither. To make matters worse, from their perspective, what was once a majority Black city has witnessed the economically coerced exodus of Black folk and the silent and sweeping forces of gentrification. In this case, the two phenomena—ethnic diversity and economic development—go hand in hand.

By now, we comin up on the brand new McDonald's, and the major construction sites over the ramp come into view. Sparkin another round of wayblackmemories, Bilal says, "Only shit we had over the ramp was the lil business district." "Yeppp, yep! I remember that!" Bilal continues passionately, engaging all others by rhetorically emphasizing his rhythmic *you know that I mean?* Everybody gets all into it, as they punctuate his statements in a conversational call and response sequence:

> Bilal: Hey, we used to—it was restaurants there, YOU KNOW WHAT I MEAN?
> Aqiyla: Yeah!
> B: The food mart was over there, YOU KNOW WHAT I MEAN?
> J: MM-HMM!
> Amira: It had hecka liquor stores...
> B: Number One Liquors, YOU KNOW WHAT I MEAN?
> J: UH-HUHHH!
> Aqiyla: I useta go over there and get my nails done and shit...
> B: It's called, they call it—we call it "over the ramp," basically...

J: Yeahhh, over the ramp...
B: Right where they buildin them hotels and stuff at...

I start flashin back to one of my earliest visits to the business district, and I'm rememberin how it useta be a Hip Hop record shop there, a community-based computer learning center, and all these other lil stores right in that one strip. All this reminiscin got me reminiscin, too, I guess, huh?

I'm brought back to the here and now when Amira responds WITH FORCE to Bilal's mention of the new hotels. "What the fuck we need a hotel for?! What the fuck?!" The passion in Amira voice is felt by everyone. She asks again, "Why we need a hotel?!" And the thing about it, she got a point—ain't no Sunnyside folk gon see the inside of no $150-a-night hotel, just like they probably ain't gon see the inside of no crazy HIGH-high-end Expo, you know what I'm saying? "What are people sayin about all this stuff that's comin up?" I ask. Bilal got the answer, "Because it's gonna bring in revenue—economics and shit—to bring the economics to Sunnyside." Yesmina, "Yeah, people say it's money." Amira, unwilling to accept any mercenary justification for gentrification, persists, "I mean, that's takin part of our heritage outta there, cuz I mean, we, we, that's where people was RAISED and stuff! Goin into donut shops, into the fish & chips spot over there, and the fried chicken spot." Yesmina shouts, "I know, I miss that!" Amira pauses for a brief second, glaring over the ramp, and adds, "and now the hotels." Bilal offers up an idea, "All they had to do is improve the buildings over there.... All they had to do was make the buildings more nicer." Amira, "O-KAY!" "That's all they had to do," repeats Bilal. "And just get them promotion, maybe they would sell stuff," Amira proposes.

It's at this point that we hit the Mickey D's and turn the recorders off. "We don't want anybody knowin what y'all eatin," I joke, and we step inside the joint. I think to myself, you know, these young brothas and sistas is not only familiar with what's goin on, but they got real strong feelins about it, too. Genuinely offered solutions like makin the buildings more nicer or givin the businesses more promotion are naïve, of course. And while they may not have ALL of the historical details accurate, they tryin hard as hell to make sense outta what's happenin in they hood. In the dialogue, the sense of community and belonging fostered by the old business district is contrasted with the sense of displacement and alienation given off by the new development. Within these pages, we have a clear sense of how gentrification is impacting today's Black youth in Sunnyside. This snapshot in time paints a picture of the way that they are experiencing these sweeping changes, and also, their powerlessness to affect it. I can't help but wonder what the 50-year-old Black couple quoted in the beginning of this section would think, say, or feel upon reading this account. Did they have any idea how the next generation of Black youth—who have grown up without a public high school in the city—would feel about them saying, "We are celebrating the demolition of Raven High School." For now, the gentrification and occupation of Sunnyside continue, as does the Black exodus.

Alright, let's get back into this thang. So, we roll up six deep into Mickey D's, and I'm thinkin the recorders were off. Well, turns out that, while I was busy orderin food, young Bloods was busy makin they own lil comedy video about the fast-food joint. Check it ... Aqiyla and Amira grab the video camera and start scannin the whole place, zoomin in on all the folks that's there, and providing narration. Scannin the back corner of the restaurant, a Mexican family comes into view and Aqiyla makes some comment like, "Dag, why they always be bringin they whole families in here like it's a real restaurant?" (laughter), as they continue scannin the restaurant. Next in view is a Asian man sittin alone talkin on his cell phone. He got on a black jacket, black slacks, and his hair parted to the side. They zoom all the way in on him. And after several seconds of silence, Amira bust out with, "Jackie Chan," and they all crack up. "Ohh, you crazy, Amira!" The camera keeps rollin. Next in the line of fire—a thin Black man, sittin by hisself, lookin straight up homeless. Clothes all raggedy-like, ill-fitting, and torn and whatnot. He lookin up at the ceiling with his head cocked to the side, concentratin real hard. Lord knows what he was lookin at, you know what I'm saying? Amira say to Aqiyla, mockin her star-struck love for rapper DMX, "That's how DMX gon look like when he get older." "Fuck that," Aqiyla fires back, "That's how yo boyfriend gon look like when HE get older" (laughter by all). They zoom in on the poor, homeless brotha even closer, noticin the bugged out, dreamy look on his face as he just STUCK on that ceiling. They all just bust out laughin when Amira start role playin like she gettin into his thoughts and shit. "Mmm, burgers," she says, in a longing voice, and it's almost too much for folks to handle!

I ain't just writin this to make y'all laugh or get upset at this lack of ethnosensitivity (dependin on how you take this lil comedy video). In our street session, this skit provides the perfect entree into a discussion of Sunnyside's increasing ethnic diversity. I mean, when I really think about it, Mickey D's, in a funny way, is almost the ONLY place in all of Sunnyside where you can see the full range of ethnic groups all in one small place. I guess the "D" stand for "Diversity," huh? Nah, just playin. But lookin around the restaurant, I realize that it's probably the one place in the whole plaza that Sunnysidaz shop at the most! That, and the other fast food joints, you know. So, we grab our food and head out back where they got this nice patio with all these shaded public tables. As we walk toward the tables, Bilal turns to me and says, "You see that car, Alim?" I nod with a, "Mm-hmm," as a White woman in a black Mercedes Benz rolls by, you know, one of them new jawns with the weird-lookin headlights. "Never was around a long time ago," he adds. "Never," agrees Yesmina, and Amira emphasizes it even further, "All these nice-ass cars, never."

Being that you can see the infamous "golden arches" from the freeway, and that White folk shoppin at the high-end stores in the same plaza, I'm like, "Daaammmn, this may be the only place in Sunnyside where I really see White people out in public like that, mixin with the locals, you know." So, I ask if anybody know people that live in Shadyside, where most of the White folk live at, and we launch into a discussion about ethnicity in both Shadyside and Sunnyside.

If we flash back to my students' discussion of houses in Shadyside (pp. 104–5), we already get a sense of the racializing of economic disparity. Let's check that dialogue again. "White" enters the dialogue pretty forcefully in the second line, and again when Amira describes Shadyside as "the White part." Both times, "White" is equated with wealth and a better quality of life. Yesmina's comments about the Shadyside houses "that be hella BIG and beautiful and shit," and Amira's humorous, "well, after the potholes," show that the students view Shadyside as not only a White town, but a WEALTHY White town where the people be "livin lavish," as Bilal like to say, that is, with HELLA economic resources.

In addition, Yesmina and Amira's comments about the "Welcome to Shadyside" sign not only demonstrate their knowledge regarding the color and class divide that exists between them and their neighbors; the students seem also to be ascribing some level of intentionality on the part of Whites in Shadyside in keeping the two cities separate. In their eyes, the signage is political—that sign doesn't just HAPPEN to be there, it was PUT there by Shadyside people as a deliberate divider, as a way of saying to visitors, "We ain't like them OTHER folk down the street." So, despite the fact that these signs are posted on the boundaries of nearly every city in the nation and the fact that Amira herself probably done seen dozens of them in other cities, she feels real strong about the undercover motive behind the signage. Whether she right or wrong ain't the issue, although (again) Shadyside and other neighboring White cities have undercut through construction of the freeway and annexation. In addition, residents of Shadyside actually voted to change the county line to exclude Sunnyside. It's not difficult to see how Black youth can read intentionality in the signage that lets people know where Sunnyside ends geographically and Shadyside begins.

Is the question on some of y'all minds whether Shadyside actually IS a all White town? I was curious, too. Check the dialogue:

> Researcher: So, basically now Shadyside is mostly White. Do other people live in Shadyside or is it just mostly White?
>
> Bilal: Asians...
>
> Yesmina: MM-HMM!
>
> B: ...the Uncle Toms...
>
> Y: [laughter] it be Black people—just like the RICH, like OLDER Black people...
>
> B: Yeah...
>
> Y: ...not no young...

R: Older, rich Black people?
Y: Yeah, they be cool, though…

So, I'm sittin here listenin to my students describe Shadyside in almost purely White terms, and I'm like, "I wonder how accurate their assessment is," you know? Turns out that Shadyside DO be mostly White. In fact, according to the 2000 Census, it's approximately 82% White, 10% Asian, 4% Hispanic, 3% Black, and less than 1% Native American out of 600,000. What's deep about Bilal's comments is how he describes the 18,000 Black folk that be livin in Shadyside—"the Uncle Toms"—in a way that distinguishes them. Their gaining of economic resources practically excludes them from in-group membership. Yesmina gotta step in and be like, "Yo, hold up, Bilal, they be cool, though," bringin them back into the group. Of course, such in-group tension along class lines occurs with Whites, too (and other groups), and as with Blacks, sometimes in the opposite direction, with lower-class Whites being referred to by wealthier Whites as "White trash." Both terms, *White trash* and *Uncle Toms*, can be used to OTHER in-group members that don't match the stereotype attached to the group's socioeconomic status.

Outside of they teachers, 90% of whom are White, my students ain't got no daily contact with White people, as this lengthy dialogue demonstrates. What begins as Bilal describin the kind of White folks in Shadyside ends up revealing some pretty HEAVY stereotypes about White people, and as we gon see, a near direct confrontation with White passerby:

R: So, Shadyside is like all White?
Bilal: Old-ass white people…
R: [laughter] They all old?
Y: MM-HMM!
B: HELL, YEAH! Retired, you know, just livin lavish [laughter]…
R: [laughter]…
Y: Yep…
A: That's why…
B: [?]…
A: …we go hit 'em up on Halloween…

Y: Halloween, we ALWAYS go there, don't we?
R: [laughter] Oh, yeah?
Y: "We goin TO SHADYSIDE..."
R: [laughter] Y'all raid, raid Shadyside...
Y: They got the good stuff, king-size stuff...
A: MM-HMM! They be givin MONEY if they run out of...
R: They be givin out money, huh?
Y: MM-HMM!
R: ...run out of candy, they give you money...
B: [suck-teeth] Dumb-asses be settin they whole basket of candy out like ain't nobody gon take that junk...
Y: MM-HMM!
R: [laughter]...
A: They set it on the porch cuz they don't wanna come to the door, [laughter]...
R: [African American falsetto] Why do they do that?!
A: They think we gon be honest...
B: They be like [mocking a "White voice"], "Just take one pleeease."
A: They think we gon be honest...
R: They probably put a sign in it, too, right?
Y: UH-HUHHH! "Take one."
A: Yep!
R: We useta do the SAME thing, maaan...
B: But see at the same time, they be puttin shit IN the candy, so...
Y: MM-HMM! Them White people...
A: Yep...
R: What do you mean puttin shit in the candy?
B: [laughter] They be puttin stuff in the candy...
A: That's why when you go over there you gotta check yo candy after, cuz they be putting razor blades and shit...
Y: Yep, they be doin that...
R: NAHHHH...
B: ForREAL!
Y: Mm-hmm...
A: One year, somebody put a razor blade in like this candy apple thing and a kid...
Y: MM-HMM!
A: ...bit into it and they tongue got cut off...
R: Over in Shadyside?
A: Yep!

Y: Yep...
R: You gotta watch out cuz sometimes that's where the loonies be at...
Y: MM-HMM!
B: Hell yeah, rapists and stuff...
A: O-KAY!
R: And so, basically, okay—hold on [laughter]... [as White couple walks by to get into their shiny, black Volvo]...
A: What?! Say it!
B: Go head!
A: Don't be—they in OUR TOWN...
R: I was just gonna ask you where do you think they from right there?
Y: Shadyside...
A: Ooh, her eye gone [woman was wearin a patch over her left eye] so maybe Sunnyside [laughter]...

There's so much we could say about this dialogic excerpt that it's hard to decide where to start. Forreal. After describin the White folks as "livin lavish," they break into a narrative about how they be gettin over on them by raidin they candy during Halloween. Not only do Shadyside folks display their wealth by givin out the "good stuff, the king-size" stuff, but they also "be givin money" out if they run outta the good candy. That very practice is an indicator of wealth, one that Sunnysidaz view as RIDICULOUS. Like Bilal say, after suckin his teeth in disapproval, "[suck-teeth] Dumb-asses be settin they whole basket of candy out like ain't nobody gon take that junk..." Further down, he further highlights the ridiculousness of this practice by markin Shadyside people in the common nasally voice used by Blacks to mock White people (as we saw in the barbershop scene earlier in this chapter): "Just take one pleeease."

The next two lines are critical in revealing the depths of White stereotypes held by Blacks in Sunnyside:

Bilal: But see at the same time, they be puttin shit IN the candy, so...
Yesmina: MM-HMM! [knowingly] Them White people...

These two lines introduce a shift in the stereotype. We move from Whites being viewed as naïve ("dumb-asses") and a fairly common marking of the "White voice" to Whites being viewed as sick, insane criminals, another fairly common stereotype held by some in the Black community (used to explain everything from centuries of enslavement, servitude, and free labor to the predominantly White makeup of serial killers in the United States). In this case, Bilal and Yesmina's comments were not rejected. Rather, Yesmina's emphatic, affirming, "MM-HMM!" and her knowing, "Them White people..." received a, "Yep," from Amira and a round of nods from the others. This, then, leads to talk of White people as the type to put "razor blades and shit" in Halloween candy and to be "rapists and stuff." Interestingly, my comment, "You gotta watch out cuz sometimes that's where the loonies be at," said to warn my students that danger could lie around ANY corner during Halloween (White, Black, whatever), was taken to confirm the view that White people are, in fact, "loonies" (and more than that, "rapists and stuff"). To cap it off, Amira drops one of her signature affirmations—one that many sistas use to show emphatic agreement—"O-KAY!"

So, we sittin outside Mickey D's havin this convo and a White couple come walkin by—and right when I was about to ask a follow-up question about White people in Shadyside, too. They bout to hop in their shiny, black Volvo, so I held up my question, like, "hold on," you know, not wantin to be rude, you know what I'm saying? My students automatically know what I'm doin, as it's common practice for Black Americans to lower they voices when talkin about White folk, specially if they right there, you know. My students ain't tryina hear it, though, as they get all loud and raise they voices. Clearly, the resistance to White presence in what useta be a predominantly Black city while these Bloods was growin up is only sometimes masked. Amira, in a verbal act of reclamation, gets mad at me ("Don't be—!"). Her claim, "they in OUR TOWN..." positions Whites in the status of outsider/occupier. Given the obvious wealth of the couple, I wait a sec (the White couple was well within earshot) and ask them where they think they from, a question that's taken as rhetorical. Amira, with characteristic humor, notices that the woman was wearin a eye patch, sometimes associated with knife wounds in the hood, and jokingly adds, "so maybe Sunnyside."

The convo continues: Bilal say they probably from Shadyside or some other town where rich White people live at. He like, "It might be Shadyside—there's no McDonald's in Shadyside..." Kijana, who hadn't contributed much to the convo, jumps in with, "They got the high stuff," and starts namin expensive Japanese and French restaurants in Shadyside. Everybody start laughin. Yesmina, shakin her head, like, "Nine dollar sandwiches..." Yo, forreal, a decent lunch cost you at LEAST ten bucks over there. If you ain't prepared to spend some doe, you ain't gon get no dough, basically. Amira, thinkin back to several years ago, "They useta have a Burger King but they shut that shit down." True enough. And, yo, that Burger King wasn't yo ordinary, run-of-the-mill Burger King neither. It was done up all nice with like stone walls and shit, lookin like a castle on the corner, but even THAT was shut down. Shadyside folks useta say it attracted "the wrong crowd," usually referring to those hue-mans of darker hue. I remember seein that Burger King during one of my first visits to Shadyside and bein like, "DAAAMMMN, even they Burger King is five star!" Yesmina affirms, "You know!" Amira one mo gin, "O-KAY!"

So, I'm like, wait a minute, y'all. I'm tryina figure out how they even see White people in Sunnyside, you know what I mean, cuz like I said before, I don't be seein them at all cept when they at Mickey D's or shoppin at them new, high-end stores. So, pointin to the nice cars in the parkin lot, I'm like, "So, like let's say, a couple of years ago or whatever, you might not have seen that..." and the following dialogue ensues.

> Bilal: HELLLL NAW!
> Researcher: ...the Volvo station wagon...
> Amira: Never!
> R: ...and the Mercedes and all that?
> B: Never...
> R: Never? Forreal?
> A: Mm-mm...
> B: EVER! Only time you...
> A: They scared or they buyin drugs...
> B: Only time you see them, only time you see them is when they crossin over the bridge, if they commute...

Yesmina: Oh, yeah, the commuting...
B: [suck-teeth] That's ALL they do...
A: And they got they doors on LOCK! [laughter]...
R: Oh, yeah? [laughter]
A: Yep...
R: How you know they got they doors locked? You can't see...
A: They don't look—they don't look at you. They be like this [making a scared face]...
Y: MM-HMM!
A: ... and start flyyyin!
R: Forreal? Where do they drive through? Where do they drive through?
Y: Through Da V...
A: They useta go through our streets and stuff...
B: Yeah, in Da V...
Y: They can go through C Street, too...
B: Oh, yeah, right...
Voice: [suck-teeth]
R: But now they have to...
A: No, they cain't go down that way...
Y: They cain't go like in Da V...
A: They gotta go—They can't go in the residential area in Da V...
Y: Yeah...
R: I know that they closed that road off right there, um...
B: Yep...
R: What is that?
A: Too much traffic...
Y: Yep, too much traffic...
R: Man, that's crazy, so people just basically be ridin through...
Y: Mm-hmm...
A: Usin our streets...
B: We should put a damn toll on THEM, SHIIITT!
Y: [laughter]...
R: [laughter] A toll every time you drive through...
B: YEAHHH, I'll toll they ass two dollars [laughter]...
Y: We'd make a lot of money...
R: [laughter] Hey, you know what I mean?
B: ... two dollars...

What's clear is that my students in Sunnyside have very little contact with Whites, outside of their teachers. This is exemplified by the fact that, as they teacher, I assigned them to go out and interview one of they White friends about Hip Hop Culture. Well, needless to say, I had to drop that assignment, cuz only ONE of my students actually had access to White youth (she had gone to a White school when she was younger and thought that she could look some of them up and interview them). From this dialogue, and other interviews, the only contact my students have with Whites in Sunnyside is either through commuter traffic or drug trafficking. Even within this limited context, Whites are portrayed as scared, distrusting, and disinterested in chillin wit the locals for any other reason than to buy drugs. One of my students reported that drug sales outside her mama house would nearly disappear if it "wasn't for all them White folks that be steady buyin coke and herron..." She paused and added, "and the niggas that be steady SELLIN it to 'em." Expressin some kinda empathy for the dealers, she adds with a shrug of the shoulders, "SHIIIT, if they buyin, why not?"

What's interesting, in economic terms, is that White folk are seen as being implicated in both the formal AND informal economy of Sunnyside. Not only is they buyin merchandise at them high-end stores, but they also buyin merchandise on them low-end streets, you feel? In the end, Bilal proposes to "put a damn toll on THEM, SHIIITT!" He like, if they gon drive through all day and night, for legal and illegal purposes, Sunnyside should flip the tolls and make 'em pay for their activity.

From here, we continue the discussion of ethnic diversity, but this time, with a focus on ethnic groups WITHIN Sunnyside. Throughout this dialogue, you gon see HELLA stereotypes bein thrown around about Whites, Blacks, Tongans, Samoans, Mexicans, Asians, and, maaan, I don't know WHO else. Again, even though we just choppin it up about "ethnic diversity," the wedge between the polarized and residentially segregated ethnic groups is driven in deep by perceived threat in a competition for economic resources. Yo, brace yoself. It's about to get real up in this jawn:

Researcher: And what about in Sunnyside, how many different kinds—it seem pretty diverse around...
Yesmina: It's VERY diverse...
R: Who are the different people that live here?
Bilal: Old-ass Black people...
Amira: Hispanics...
R: Old-ass Black people everywhere!
B: Hell, yeah!
Y: Blacks and Samoans, Tongans, Fijis...
R: Say it again, Samoans, Tongans...
Y: Tongans, like a lot of cities ain't got Samoans and Tongans, though...
B: Hindus...
Y: ...don't even know what it IS...
A: Punjabs...
Y: ...like in this other city, where my best friend from...
B: Talibans...
R: [laughter]...
Y: ...they don't know what Samoans and Tongans is...
A: A-rabs...
Y: They don't have that...
B: Al-Qaeda...
A: Afghanistanians—Oh, my gosh, you ain't NEVER seen as many cars that go through here with like ten or seven heads in they car...
[laughter]...
B: A-haaaa, pack it up!
[laughter]
A: ...it be a two-seater...
[laughter]...
R: Who is usually in the seven- to ten-person car?...
A: Uh, Mexicans [laughter], and you can't even say Hispanic cuz the Latinos don't even do that, cuz some Latinos be havin them whipped out cars...
B: THAT I will say—somehow, how the HELL they ballin more than us?...
A: O-KAY!
B: ...you know what I mean?
R: How the hell they WHAT?
B: ...they got more money than us?
A: O-KAY!

B: I mean, I understand they IS smart. They fix they own shit...

A: But it ain't that many, it ain't that many yards in the world that they can clean up...

Kijana: Who?

B: The Mexicans...

A: ... and that many houses they can redo to get that much money...

K: That's just cuz they WORK more...

B: They don't work more than us [fast rhythm]...

Aqiyla: BECAUSE what they do, if like twelve of them live in one house...

K: ... they take jobs that we don't take, rogue...

B: True, BUT...

K: They work in here [Mickey D's]...

Aq: ... that's like twelve incomes paying...

B: But listen, but listen...

Aq: ... one rent, then they save up they money...

B: Exactly, exactly...

A: Yep...

B: They got like twelve...

R: Wait, say that again, say that again...

Y: Twelve people in one house...

B: [clap] Cross the street [clap] from [clap] my [clap] house...

A: [laughter]...

Y: Next DOOR to my house...

B: Oh, my God! Oh, my God!

A: YESSS...

R: What? What?

B: It's like eight, it's like eight cars there, well, actually more than twenty people [laughter], more than twenty people gotta be livin there!

A: Yep...

B: ... but see they all come together with all they incomes and...

Y: Stay in the same house...

B: ... pay rent...

R: Like take over a house?

B: They buy another house...

Y: MM-HMM!

A: And they got theirself a GOOD line...

B: ... you know what I mean?

A: They all know the same line so they don't NEVER get caught up...

K: I knew somebody who...

Y: And they don't know no damn English!

B: They turn the garage into a little room, you know what I mean?

Y: Yep...

B: But that's normal, that, that's normal...

R: And they do that, they do ALL of that without knowing English, you said?

A: [referring to a Hispanic female nearby] She look hella hurt. She's like, [mimicking voice] "Ooooh, they're talking about me..."

Y: They CLAIM they don't...

B: Hell, yeah, but still, like if they know somebody in construction, they gon build they own shit...

Y: Yep...

B: They ain't gon pay for nobody to do it...

Y: Like Mexicans, a lot of Mexicans do construction, too, so...

B: That's why they shit always nice...

A: Yep, that's why they house be lookin nice and they cars be fuckin FLIPPED...

Y: ...they benefit from that...

B: If we get our house, if we get our house flipped or whatever, we ain't gon pay, cuz we know it's gon get messed up in coupla years...

Y: Yeah, that's true...

Aq: [laughter]...

B: We ain't gon pay to get it done again [laughter]...

Y: MM-HMM!

B: Basically, they fix they OWN shit! [clap]

A: Yeah, they, they do they own yard...

B: ...they own garden...

A: Yep!

R: They do their own yards, their own houses...

B: Hell, yeah...

R: That's deep...

Y: Like the Mexicans next door to my house, it's like, I say about three families in that house, and they expanded they house, EXPANDED, and they got like six rooms...

R: They expanded six rooms?

Y: Expanded, NOW they have like six rooms...

R: Where is that, right across...

Y: No, it's right next door...

R: Right next door?

B: To her house...

R: Do y'all like talk to your neighbors or it's just...

Y: Um, not really cuz they claim they don't speak English...

A: Ooh, these—okay, there's this, MY next door neighbors...

R: What do you mean they CLAIM?

Y: That's what they say...

A: But they never...

Y: But if you, like if you say something to them, like smart, they'll understand...

B: They know what the hell you talking about! [fast rhythm]...

Y: [mimicking] "Fuck you, man!"

R: [laughter] They know what THAT mean, huh?

Y: That's right...

A: But look, there's these Mexicans, they live next door to me. They do SOMETHING. They got some big-ass dogs and stuff, and they got hella cars. They doin SOMETHING over there, breeding them...

R: They live next to you?

A: MM-HMM!

B: Pitbulls and shit...

A: They be, they be gettin loose in my yard...

B: Drugs...

Y: They be doin something...

B: Importing, exporting everythang, they GOT it...

R: Do people say that—I mean, are they doin okay for themselves or are they...

B: HELLLL, YEAHHH!

A: Mm-hmm...

Y: MM-HMM, hell yeah...

B: Because they stick together; they ain't selfish...

A: O-KAY!

R: Are you sayin that in reference to Black people here, or are you just saying that...

Y: Shady, yeah, uh-huh...

B: Pretty much, but that's why we so different from everybody...

Y: We can't share money like...

R: What do you mean?

B: Because you ain't gon find too many houses where you see...

Y: Hella Black people...

B: ...forty damn Black people...

Y: ...sharing money and shit...

B: . . . in one house . . .
A: Because we don't get along . . .
B: And most of them ain't gon have a job!
Y: Yep!
B: All they need is for one person to pay the rent!
Y: Yep!
B: As long as [laughter], if one person payin the rent. . .
KandY: [laughter] . . .
B: . . . they gon freeload, sit there all day . . .
R: [laughter] Freeload . . .
B: . . . and feed off they grandma all day . . .
R: . . . in the front yard, huh?
B: . . . all the granddaughters just CHILLIN, doin nuthin, watchin TV . . .
Y: MM-HMM!
R: But why isn't that same mentality—I mean, why not takeover mentality . . .
B: Laziness . . .
R: . . . the take-over, forreal, it sound like they got a takeover mentality . . .
B: Yep . . .
A: Because Mexicans, throughout history, they done built up some kinda history with each other . . .
B: Yep . . .
A: . . . where they so close. Black people done did each other wrong for a long time . . .
B: Jealousy . . .
A: . . . and that's why it's like that. Like the Polynesians, they got MUCH love for every single person . . .
Y: MM-HMM!
A: . . . even if you ain't related to them . . .
Y: They hella cool. They deep in they religion, too, HELLA deep . . .
R: Who's all Polynesian?
A: Tongans, Samoans . . .
Y: They're like, yeah, islanders . . .
R: Is that just Tongan and Samoan . . .
A: Pacific Islander . . .
R: Yeah, what are they like in comparison . . .
Y: They hella cool . . .
A: Hecka cool to each other . . .

Y: They look BLACK but they just...
B: Stick together...
Y: ...I don't know, they got our nappy hair, they just...
B: Stick together...
R: So, you, do people make a difference between if you Black or if you Tongan or Samoan? People don't look at it as all the same?
Y: No, we just DIFFERENT from them, like...
A: They from the islands...
Y: ...totally different...
A: It's not that they Black, that's not the thing...
Y: They speak a whole different language. All of them hella deep into they religion...
R: What's they religion?
Y: I don't know, what is that, the M one?
A and Aq: Mormon...
Y: Mormon...
R: Mormon, forreal, they all Mormon?
A: But not, no...
B: Not ALL of them...
R: So...

Perhaps the best place to begin deconstructing this dialogue on ethnic diversity is this question by Bilal:

> Bilal: THAT I will say—somehow, how the HELL they ballin more than us?...

Much of this dialogue centers around perceptions of Mexicans, particularly their perceived ability to be BALLIN (succeeding economically, but with some degree of independence) more than Blacks. Before we begin focusing on stereotypes of Mexicans, it's important to note that the dialogue contains stereotypes of Arabs, Asians, Samoans, and Tongans, and even Blacks as well. While our central focus is on the link between ethnic diversity and the struggle for economic resources, we will also consider the reinscription of White American racist ideology as it operates in this group of Sunnyside youth. For example, in the beginning of the dialogue, we see a lot of terms used to describe people of Arab and South Asian heritage—Hindus, Punjabs, Talibans, A-rabs, Al-Qaeda, and

Afghanistanians. "Talibans" and "Al-Qaeda," used frequently in the U.S. government-media to describe the former "oppressive" government of Afghanistan and the international "terrorist" network of Osama bin Laden, respectively, are mixed in with legitimate ethnic/religious terms. This, of course, has the effect of equating certain groups of people with "oppressive governments" and "terrorism," as the U.S. government-media has often been criticized for blanketing Muslims and Arabs with similar labels.

Returning to Bilal's question, it's significant that it is elicited immediately by Amira's comments about how "some Latinos be havin them whipped out cars." Bilal tryina figure out, and apparently so is Amira ("O-KAY!"), how Mexicans be ballin more than Blacks. But, yo, stats from a recent Census say that Blacks is actually makin mo money than Mexicans. In 1999, Mexicans was makin a average of $38,118 a year, which was 34.4% less than Blacks, who were makin $51,220 a year. The issue here is not average income, but INDEPENDENT BALLIN—a level of self-reliance and economic independence. Some of the explanations that they offer are that Mexicans work more, conduct more independent and intragroup business, share economic responsibilities, and take lower status jobs. Sounds mild, right? But the stereotypes of White American racist ideology are all up inside of this. In fact, some of this ishhh sound like the straight up racist jokes I heard White boys tellin when I was in high school, except this ain't joke-tellin time, you know what I'm saying? Most obvious is they focus on how many Mexicans live in one house. It's like each one got a story about this, beginning with Aqiyla's explanation: "BECAUSE what they do, if like twelve of them live in one house, that's like twelve incomes paying one rent, then they save up they money..."

Bilal, Yesmina, and Amira all got they own stories about this, which often reveal more reinscribed White racism. We get a hint of what Amira referrin to when she say, "But it ain't that many, it ain't that many yards in the world that they can clean up, and that many houses they can redo to get that much money." She insinuates illegal activity again when she say, "But look, there's these Mexicans, they live next door to me. They do SOMETHING. They got some big-ass dogs and stuff, and they got hella cars. They doin SOMETHING over there, breeding them…" Bilal completes her thought, "Drugs… Importing, exporting everythang, they GOT it." Amira's conviction is seen in her belief that Mexicans always got a ready answer to cover up their illegal acitivity: "And they got theirself a GOOD line… They all know the same line so they don't NEVER get caught up." Yesmina story got a different twist to it, but it's still full of suspicion. Followin up, generally, she wonders how they can NEVER get caught up, in Amira's words, specially when "they don't know no damn English!" The suspicion is clearer when she describes her own neighbors as CLAIMING not to speak English. Highlighting the communication gap between the two largest ethnic groups in Sunnyside, Blacks and Mexicans, both Yesmina and Buck claim that they DO know English and that their claim is verified by cussin them out and drawin a response from them.

Perhaps the most insidious aspect of White American racist ideology is the OCCUPATION OF THE MIND that comes along with it. Not only does this group of Black youth hold White racist ideas about OTHER groups, but they also reinscribe White racist ideas held against their OWN group. Their explanations for why Mexicans be ballin more than Blacks rest upon several self-denigrating beliefs: (1) Whereas Mexicans "fix they OWN shit," Blacks not only don't know how to fix they shit, but if they do get it fixed, it's gon be messed up in a coupla years, and they "ain't gon pay to get it done again"; (2) Whereas Mexicans "stick together" and share economic responsibilities, Blacks are "shady," "don't get along," and "most of them ain't gon have a job"; (3) Whereas Mexicans got a hardworking, independent spirit ("takeover mentality"), Blacks just be "lazy"; and (4) Whereas Mexicans done built up tight historical relationships with each other, Blacks "done did each other wrong for a long time" and "jealousy" prevents them from developing friendly relations. Some of these reasons also make Blacks different from Tongans and Samoans, who are described as havin "much love for every single person" in their group, "even if you ain't related to them."

Within this dialogue, both Bilal and Yesmina state that Blacks are just SO DIFFERENT from everybody else. The differences they mention have to do with various abilities and characteristics, yet are clearly about other things, such as not having a heritage language that's still spoken and not having common spiritual beliefs. Their comments, in my view, are on point in one sense—Blacks are the ONLY group among all of those mentioned that have suffered from centuries of enslavement. Slavery, that peculiar institution, stripped Africans of they cultures, languages, religions, histories, customs, values, and mores. For centuries, livin and dyin as chattel slaves, Africans in America suffered from the most inhumane treatment, including the destruction of the family and the destruction of a sense of history and place in the world.

"THIS *OUR* HOOD!": RESISTANCE IS IN THE WAY WE WALK

Researcher: Y'all gon get run over...
Bilal: Look at them 20s! 15s, 14s—they cool, though. I'd push them...
Kijana: Ooooh, is that Maurice mama?
R: [starts running to cross the street]
Amira: Why are you runnin?
R: [to entire group] Let's cross...
A: WHY IS YOU RUNNIN?
R: I'm not tryina get hit...
A: This OUR hood. WE RUN THIS SHIT!
R: Oh, yeah?
B: You don't run, you just walk across. They gon move...
A: Yeah...

Despite the continuing gentrification and occupation of Sunnyside land and the occupation of Black minds by White American racist ideology, there are some signs of resistance. Belonging to a people without land, economic independence, and nationhood, Black youth in Sunnyside continue to resist occupation with what is perhaps one of the only weapons available to them—their culture and language. Black culture and language can be useful tools to resist occupation of land and mind precisely because they are the only entities that Blacks create and control. Black cultural acts (Blacks in their everydayness) and Black cultural artifacts (Black cultural production, such as music, poetry, writing, etc.) provide subtle and not so subtle examples of resistance and reclamation.

For Black youth in Sunnyside, the powerless within a powerless group, subtle acts of everydayness can be seen as resistance to the threat of occupying forces. Flash back to the barbershop scene in The Right Price where the brothas marked that police officer soon as he left the shop (pp. 91–92). As I said earlier, this use of the "white voice" created a humor that is often a face-saving mechanism in the face of occupation. Other Black cultural acts of everydayness are more subtle. Take, for example, the opening quotation of this section. It wasn't till after I watched the video of this street session several times that I realized what was goin on. So, we're on our way back to the school from being out all afternoon, and we gotta cross a street in the neighborhood. It just so happens that it's one of the streets that we was just talkin about, where White folk and others commute through the hood. So, I get to the street and, naturally, as the one in charge, I'm rushin across the street, like, "Y'all gon get run over." The cars was comin in a steady stream, so I'm thinkin that everybody gon start movin, right? Wrong. Instead, Bilal takin his time, pointin out the rims on people cars and mockin them, too. He see some small set of rims and he like, "Look at them 20s! 15s, 14s—they cool, though. I'd push them." Kijana takin her time, too, payin more attention to who around her from the hood than the cars in the street: "Ooooh, is that Maurice mama?" I mean, she and Amira was just walkin all SLOW across that street, you know. As for me, I start breakin into a run to cross the street, right, cuz like I said, I wasn't tryina get hit by a car. Amira like, "Why are you runnin?" I ignore her and keep rollin, urgin everybody, "Let's cross." She get loud, like, "WHY IS YOU RUNNIN?" After explainin to her that I wasn't tryina get hit, she come back with some serious words, "This OUR hood. WE RUN THIS SHIT!" Thrown off, I ask, "Oh, yeah?" And Bilal makes it plain, "You don't run, you just walk across. They gon move."

Now, I done seen this a thousand times before and never was able to make sense of it until now. Black youth in Sunnyside be takin they TIME when they be crossin the street, rogue, for REAL. Same kinda way. Indifferent. Almost oblivious to the cars comin by. Walkin slower than normal and not givin a blank about it, you know what I'm saying? Nonchalant. Not gettin moved by NUTTIN. And definitely not runnin. That's a no-no. "You don't run, you just walk across." Why? Cuz "This OUR hood. WE RUN THIS SHIT!" The full import of Amira and Bilal's statements is understood only when placed in the context of the entire street session. Possessive *our,* particularly in reference to the hood, came up several times in the conversation about Sunnyside. Both Amira and Bilal were pissed at White commuters who create traffic for Sunnyside by cuttin through the hood. "Usin our streets..." they said, and then proposed to charge them a toll. Member when we was sittin outside at the Mickey D's and they wanted me to go head and speak about the White couple as they walked by? "What?! Say it!" and "Go head!" "They in OUR TOWN," Amira said. These comments, including the "street-crossing incident" just described—Black cultural acts of everydayness—are subtle signs of resistance toward the occupiers. Powerless in their own land, these youth take up the battle the only way they know how, as subtle as it might seem, and seek to reverse this powerlessness, even if only momentarily. What seem like insignificant events, may in fact be instrumental to mounting a defense.

In the conclusion of this chapter, I wanna wrap this thang up with a couple more observations. On our way back to the school, you can't help but notice several BRAND-SPANKIN NEW residential developments. Funny, but they're stuck to the side of the retail development on the right side and the freeway on the other side—as if to separate them from the rest of the community. I mean, these cribs is NICE. You walk in there and you see them all lined up, kinda cookie cutterish, you know what I mean, but yo, they look so new and nice. All the same beige color. About a hundred or so brand new units. I'm like, "What are those apartments?" Amira correct me, like, "Not apartments, they're like townhouses." Yesmina, suckin her teeth all loud, "Yeah, like a little city!" They exchange looks at each other:

A: A little White suburbia...
Y: MM-HMM!

A: . . . in the middle of Sunnyside . . .
Y: That's what it look like . . .

They ain't lyin, y'all. Now INSIDE of Sunnyside you can see the wealth creepin in. College Square it's called, probably to make the new residents feel some sort of affiliation with the nearby elite, private university. The townhouses are designed in a square with a big green park in the middle, with park benches and a big jungle gym for they kids to play on, swing sets, monkey bars, a rec club, the whole nine. Sunnyside's parks was all shut down due to drug- and gang-related violence, but somehow, this one seems impenetrable. A over-sized maroon SUV come zoomin by—a White woman with blonde hair is behind the wheel. She don't look, just rides by with her black shades on. Amira, "If you knock on them doors, you'll find Hispanics, them Punjabian Talibans, and White people." But no Blacks.

We keep movin and, finally, we on the street that the school is on. Amira gets Yesmina attention, "Aight, get the tape, get the big houses . . ." Bilal, "This the houses we talkin about right here." I'm lookin at what looks like a little peninsula of beautiful new homes, all the same, stucco or stone. Again, it's funny to see this group of seven or eight new homes right in the middle of Sunnyside. It don't even look right. In what amounts to no more than a cul-de-sac, they got sidewalks, fresh-paved streets (no potholes), front lawns, street lamps—I mean, totally different than all that's around them. I'm like, "Okay, now what is this over here?" Amira, pointin to some folks in the yard, "You can see the Punjabs and stuff—see them?" Bilal explains, "They built these, you know, like different kinda ethnic groups live in there. Asian people, Latinos . . ." Amira, "Talibans . . ." Bilal trails off, ". . . but I don't think any Black people over there." I ask, "Now, do they say people CAN'T live there, or is it just . . . ?" Bilal pushes on, with a as-if-you-don't-know tone in his voice, "People with the money live there . . ."

Yesmina goes on to explain that the developers removed older, low-income housing to build many of the new homes in Sunnyside. In an agreement with the predominantly Black city council, the developers agreed to have what they call "set-asides" for low-income minorities, but the process ain't that easy. Yesmina, "They make you fill out a application!" Amira, "Yep, they put—saved us like twenty houses." Turns out that most Black people from Sunnyside can't afford the new homes that have been so-called "set-aside," as very few Black families can manage the $500,000–$600,000 prices.

Further down the street, on the other side, we get to what look like a open lot of land. Old-lookin greenhouses, small houses out front. Just like a big-ole lot. "Fleas and shit up in there," say Kijana. I ask, "Hey, now what's this all here?" Kijana yells, "This Haven High land!" Now, this land stretch clear across the block, so I'm like, "Haven High own all of this?" "Yeahhh," says Yesmina. Nobody seem to know what's goin on in this plot of land, though. "I don't know what this is right here, though, old-ass greenhouse and shit...." Bilal adds, "Farms, pesticides and shit up in there." "Mm-hmm, I don't know WHAT they doin... Sunnyside be havin a whole bunch of just, just land, just stupid stuff..." Kijana jumps in, "It's about to be dorms," she explains. I'm lookin at this whole block of land and wonderin why they gon build dorms on it when Sunnyside only 2.5 square miles big. Check it:

Researcher: Nahhh...
Amira: Yeahhh...
Bilal: HELL YEAH...
R: Forreal?!
Yesmina: Yep, that's gon be our dorm...
B: In like three or four years...
R: [Black American falsetto] Why y'all need dorms for?!
A: They gon make us live...
B: Because they want us to be connected to Haven High...
Y: They want people to live on the school...
B: All this shit over here gonna change...
A: College prep—you wanna be prepped for college, you gotta leave yo ass in the dorms...
R: All this gon change, too?
B: Yep, cuz they ain't gon have people comin by here and donatin money and the streets looking this. They gon do ALL this over... [pointing to the potholes in the streets; dirt covering the streets, no sidewalks]
A: Over, yep...

B: Basically, they gon own this whole damn block...
A: This gon be Haven High street school! [laughter] Haven High School Street...
Y: Yep, they probably gon block off this whole damn thing...
B: They paid my friend—I'll show you the house. My friend, they paid him like a million dollars, whatever, to leave and move out the house...

Interestingly, Haven High done got so much money from investors that it plans to use the same strategy as the developers. While there are no concrete plans to own the whole block, student fears are clearly justified. "They probably gon block off this whole damn thing." They done seen this all before, and they know friends families that's bein pushed out. The school, wittingly or unwittingly, is actually contributing to the gentrification of the city.

As we started wrappin up our street session, we got into a conversation about the various colleges students was thinkin about attending (they was feelin the stress of this big decision, and the discussion of dorms brought it up). Bilal, in the middle of describing how he wanted to go to any one of the historically Black colleges or universities, breaks the flow of the convo to point out a Mexican man pushin a red cart cross the street:

Bilal: Historically Black...—see, look at this right there, selling oranges—BAM! Right there!
Yesmina: Yep, I told y'all...
Researcher: Who that, who that, who that?
Amira: Stereotypical...
B: Mexican makin LOOT. You ain't gon find no Black person out here sellin oranges...
R: Hustlin, maaan!
Kijana: Hustlin, doin what you gotta do—doin what you can to get by...
R: Hey, that's forreal, though...
A: [mimicking a Latino accent] "Oranges, oranges, oranges!"

Just in this short five-minute stretch of our street session (contained within this section), we see again and again why Blacks in Sunnyside feel like strangers in their own land. What was once a predominantly Black city is witnessing the building of more and more new retail developments and residential settlements. As Whites and others continue to settle in Sunnyside, it's painfully clear that all of this new development is happenin to the exclusion of Blacks. So, few Blacks are able to participate in this new Sunnyside. Today, more Blacks have moved out of the city and more Black families are being scattered throughout the region. Time, like the construction trucks filled with fresh new cement, keeps rollin, and the physical and mental occupation of Sunnyside continues in 2004...

In this chapter, I have presented the language of my students—in-group, peer Black street speech in a community setting—without in-depth linguistic analysis. In chapters 5–8, we gon analyze the language used in these conversational street sessions (and other settings) as we discuss styleshifting based on race, gender, Hip Hop cultural knowledge, and interactional style. In this chapter, I have placed my students—all 17-year-old Black Sunnysidaz—in their community and historical contexts. Their stories, which describe the sociohistorical context of life in the occupied territories, are moving narratives in which a group of youth is trying to come to terms with their powerlessness. The discussions of economic development and ethnic diversity presented here reveal insidious forms of racism—the reinscription of White American racist ideology against other groups and the internalization of White American racist ideology against their own group. In this vein, I'm reminded of two comments relating to how we gon deal with this increasing ethnic diversity and the continuing gentrification and occupation of Black neighborhoods and minds:

> White folk spend all this money building... [pausing and using stress for rhetorical effect] ...BUILDINGS, and not enough money building BEINGS. You can put up the nicest buildings money can buy, but you know what, if we don't have the right kinda teachin, and start dealin with the problems that we face as human BEINGS, we gon tear ... them ... build ... ings ... DOWN! [said by an African American minister in relation to the gentrification of Black neighborhoods]

> What's happening here in Sunnyside, in some ways, politically and how we relate to each other and how we go through our growing pains as a com-

munity, the fact that we have diversity here, it's something that the whole state is going to go through very soon. The extent that which we can move ahead is a reflection of, you know, where our country's going. [said by a Hispanic resident of Sunnyside in relation to the community tensions over the rapidly increasing ethnic diversity]

As we move into chapters 5–8, this chapter should serve as a reference point, as a way of understanding what language and life is like for young Bloods in Sunnyside. As we analyze styleshifting, this chapter should provide the necessary contexts within which to interpret our findings and proposals. Yeah, we just gettin started...

5. WE SOME BAAADDDDD STYLESHIFTERS: THE COPULA IN STYLISTIC VARIATION

THIS CHAPTER, along with chapters 6–8, presents the major sociolinguistic findings in this study. In this chapter, we'll be focusing on the stylistic variation of the copula based on race, gender, and Hip Hop cultural knowledge (see full details of research design in chapter 2). In chapter 6, we focus on third-person singular *-s*, possessive *-s*, and plural *-s* absence, while invariant *be* and be_3 are the subject of chapter 7. In chapter 8, we synthesize the findings of previous chapters and present an interactional analysis of style.

THE CONTROVERSIAL COPULA

Copula absence refers to the absence of *is* and *are* in some present-tense forms. We are following previous studies by subsuming what is technically copula *be* (before a noun phrase, adjective, and locative) and auxiliary *be* (before Verb + *-ing* or *gon(na)*) under one term, *copula*. In nonlinguistic jargon, the copula is the linking verb that connects the subject of a sentence with its predicate. In Black Language (BL), a speaker can produce sentences like *He is the leader* (full form), *He's the leader* (contracted form), and *He Ø the leader* (absent form), all of which have the same semantic meaning (but differ in social meaning). The BL copula ain't ALWAYS absent, but only in SOME present-tense forms. This speech sample is illustrative: "The Black Man Ø on the rise, and the White man, he Ø runnin scared now, because we Ø wide awake today and he know we Ø not just gon lay down and accept things as they are." While the copula can be absent before prepositional phrases and locatives (*on the rise*), progressive verbs (*he runnin scared*), adjectives (*we wide awake*), negatives, and *gon* (*we not just gon lay down*), it cannot be absent when it is in sentence-final position (*as they are*). The copula also can't be absent in the first-person singular form. A sentence such as *I the boss* is ungrammatical in BL; the present-tense form must be *Uhm the boss, I'm the boss,* or *I am the boss.*

Rickford et al. (1991) refer to the BL copula as the language variety's "showcase variable." This pattern is one of the most extensively studied sociolinguistic variables (Labov et al. 1968; Labov 1969; Wolfram 1969; Fasold 1972; Rickford 1997, 1999; Walker 1999), so much so that a linguist once made this joke at a conference: "Let the copula *be*!" (Only funny to linguists, you know what I'm saying?). The BL copula has been a controversial variable for several reasons. First, it is one of the features that give BL its distinctiveness, setting it apart from other varieties of American English (with some exceptions in White Southern speech where it has been hypothesized that Whites have been influenced by Blacks; see Feagin 1979; Labov 1969; Wolfram 1974). Oddly, in today's conservative political environment, many Americans seem to find distinct Black linguistic features or practices "controversial." Perhaps recognition of a distinct language pattern for Black Americans reveals an American history where Whites made it illegal for Blacks to read and write and where Whites mandated racial segregation—both of which were parts of a racist system that developed numerous means of social control (as we've seen in chapter 4; see also Baugh 2000a). Second, the BL copula has been used to support the notion that BL is diverging (growing further away) from other varieties of American English (Bailey and Maynor 1989; Butters 1989; Fasold et al. 1987; Rickford 1992).

Thirdly, the BL copula plays a crucial role in heated debates about the historical reconstruction of BL, as it is perhaps the best indicator of BL's Creole-like origins. The feature has been analyzed extensively to draw support for the Creole origins of BL (Bailey 1965; Stewart 1968; Baugh 1979, 1980; Alleyne 1980; Holm 1984; Singler 1991; Winford 1992, 1998; Rickford 1998). Labov (1969 and since) has maintained that BL speakers exhibit copula absence only where White English speakers can contract the copula, thereby concluding phonological constraints as primary. Recent research (Poplack and Tagliamonte 1991; Walker 1999) also argues in favor of the copula's Anglican origin. While this debate is beyond the purview of this chapter, I will present an analysis of Black peer, in-group talk as a potential BL baseline from which copula patterns in different contexts derive.

The last two reasons why the copula is an important variable for the study of style in BL, and more generally, have direct bearing on this study. Fourthly, recent research on the BL copula in Hip Hop Nation Language (Alim 2002) suggests that speakers can, in fact, consciously vary their usage of copula absence based on issues of identity and ideology. Wolfram and Thomas (2002) have found that the younger Blacks in Hyde County, North Carolina, who identify strongly with Black culture seem to be aligning their copula pattern away from the localized regional norm and toward a national norm. This finding perhaps adds more evidence to Alim's (2002, 2003b) suggestion that the artists and participants in the Hip Hop Nation (HHN), in seeking to present a "street-conscious" identity, are the main preservers and maintainers of BL. Further support for the HHN's potential impact on BL is found in Rowe (2003), who suggests that Hip Hop artists employ a "performance register" and increase speakers' awareness of BL features.

Lastly, the findings on the stylistic behavior of the copula have been inconclusive to date. Some studies have shown that Black Americans vary their copula usage stylistically, although the data is not exactly comparable with the present analysis. Wolfram (1969), for example, found that Detroit Blacks exhibit copula absence much less when READING (7.9%) than when speaking in an interview (41.8%). This data is not comparable with the present study for two reasons: (1) there is no reading task in this study, and (2) reading constitutes a different modality than speaking. For example, in the case of the copula, a brotha is much more likely to pronounce the copula if it's lookin right back at him, as it would be on the printed page. The reader is interacting with the printed page, rather than an interlocutor. The other study that showed significant styleshifting in the copula was Alim (2002). While these data show that Black American Hip Hop artists increase their rates of copula absence in their lyrics versus their normal conversation, the lyrical data is only indirectly interactive and NOT equivalent to conversation, which requires the direct participation of an interlocutor.

Two other studies, with more comparable data sets, both suggest that the copula is not stylistically sensitive. Labov et al. (1968) presented data that showed that Black male adolescents do not vary their copula usage significantly in one-on-one versus group contexts. Baugh (1979, 1983) concluded that situational factors (familiarity and Black street culture membership) did not significantly affect the copula and found the internal linguistic constraints to be more significant.

The one study that did find the copula to be stylistically sensitive was Rickford and McNair-Knox (1994). Although this study had a limited sample, the findings were strongly in support of the hypothesis that the copula varied stylistically based, in part, on the identity characteristics of the interviewer. With the familiar, Black interviewer, Foxy Boston used copula absence 70% (197/283) of the time, but only 40% (70/176) of the time with the White, unfamiliar interviewer (significant at the $p < .001$ level). So, clearly, the studies on the stylistic behavior of the copula are inconclusive. This study builds upon previous studies and adds tremendous support to Rickford and McNair-Knox's findings. It is also the first study to isolate the effects of race, gender, and Hip Hop cultural knowledge on speech style.

In the next section, we gon break down the data for copula absence on multiple levels. First, we gon present a detailed linguistic and social anatomy of styleshifting in the entire corpus of 32 semistructured conversations (SSC). Second, we gon look at how the Sunnysidaz, as a group, styleshifted across the eight Stanfordian interlocutors. Third, we gon see how Sunnysidaz, as individuals—Amira, Bilal, Careem, and Kijana—shifted they styles up according to the eight Stanfordian interlocutors. Examining individual variability in style at this detailed level of analysis increases our understanding of how different speech styles emerge for any given speaker.

We will first look at an unresolved methodological issue that deals directly with the supposed need to separate *is* and *are* in our analyses of the BL copula.

COPULA ANALYSIS FOR 32 SEMISTRUCTURED CONVERSATIONS

Table 5.1 shows the output of the analysis of the speakers' copula absence data using the variable rule program, GOLDVARB 2001, which is described in chapter 2. I have separated the results for *is* and *are*, as well as presented a COMBINED run, to determine if *is* and *are* are similarly constrained. Rickford et al. (1991), citing previous work by Wolfram (1974), concluded that *is* and *are* are similarly constrained, with some minor differences. This study, in part, seeks to test their justification for the conflation of *is* and *are*. The runs show probability coefficients for internal linguistic constraints as well as external identity constraints.

Examining the internal linguistic constraints first, table 5.1 shows us that the copula forms of *is* and *are* are constrained by the same factor groups in exactly the same ordering. This data provides clear-cut evidence for the positing of a single copula absence rule. Practically, this means that we have the advantage of analyzing more tokens of the copula in each run, and that our data can be represented in a single copula absence run with probability coefficients presented for the person-number factor group.

Beginning with following grammatical category, we see that the ordering of the factors within the group follows the main pattern presented in the BL copula literature, in decreasing order: *gon* > Verb + *-ing* > locative > adjective > noun phrase. I also coded *gon* and *gonna* separately, as they showed extremely divergent probability coefficients for the rule. Research on the copula has traditionally combined *gon* and *gonna*, but it is clear from these results that *gon* strongly favors absence while *gonna* strongly disfavors it. The ordering of the factors in the subject type factor group was also similar to previous studies with personal pronouns favoring absence. Phonologically speaking, preceding vowels strongly favored absence, while preceding consonants strongly disfavored the rule. The following phonological environment, as in most studies, was not chosen as significant in the best run.

Turning to the external identity constraints, the table shows us that all three identity factor groups exhibit significant effects

TABLE 5.1
Probability Coefficients for Best Runs for Speakers' Copula Absence in 32 Semistructured Conversations

	is	*are*	*Combined*
Overall frequency	160/846 (18%)	233/692 (33%)	393/1,538 (26%)
Input probability	.190	.340	.254
Following grammatical environment			
gon	.935	.960	.944
Verb + *-ing*	.718	.598	.655
Locative	.542	.548	.564
Adjective	.424	.305	.389
Noun phrase	.403	.260	.354
gonna	—	.080	.107
Miscellaneous	.283	.672	.423
Subject type			
Personal pronoun	(.589)	(.568)	(.578)
Other pronoun	(.547)	—	(.460)
Noun phrase	(.355)	(.178)	(.315)
Person-number			
2nd-person plural			.637
3rd-person singular			.387
Preceding phonological environment			
Consonant	.213	.158	.213
Vowel	.644	.573	.606
Following phonological environment			
Consonant	(.480)	(.497)	(.486)
Vowel	(.589)	(.520)	(.578)
Interlocutor race			
Black	.633	.783	.716
White	.315	.183	.259
Interlocutor gender			
Male	.638	.647	.638
Female	.312	.329	.325
Interlocutor Hip Hop familiarity			
Hip Hop	.601	.637	.619
No Hip Hop	.371	.328	.350
Significance of best run	.000	.000	.000

NOTE: Parentheses indicated that factor group was not chosen as significant by best run.

on speech style. Black speakers tend to use more absence when speaking with Black versus White interlocutors; male versus female interlocutors; and interlocutors who are more familiar with Hip Hop Culture (HHC). See figure 5.1 for a graphical representation of the external identity constraints.

We are now in a position to determine the relative impact of linguistic and identity constraints on absence. By examining GOLDVARB's ranking of groups selected during the best run, we see that internal linguistic constraints interact with external identity constraints to produce the stylistic shifts. Three linguistic constraints and three identity constraints were selected in decreasing order: following grammatical category > race > preceding phonological environment > gender > HHC knowledge > person-number. These data show the value of including both linguistic and identity constraints in our analyses, as we see that, at least for this feature, the variation is affected by both types of constraints. Linguistically, while following grammatical category and preceding phonological environment interact, absence is affected most greatly by the following grammatical category. In terms of identity, while race, gender, and HHC knowledge were all selected as significant, race has the greatest impact on the rule.

FIGURE 5.1

Effects of Interlocutor Race, Gender, and Hip Hop Cultural Knowledge

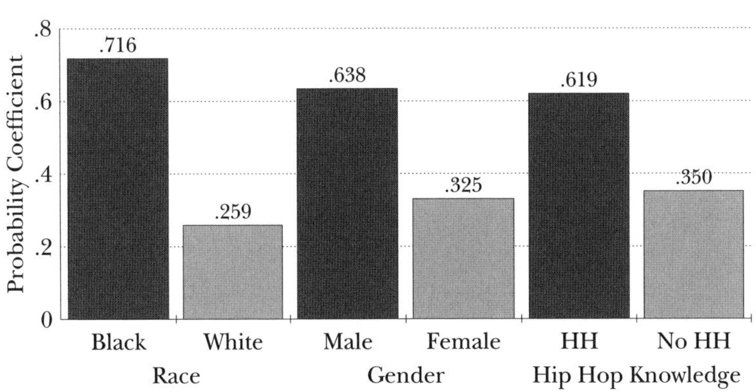

COPULA ANALYSIS FOR 32 SEMISTRUCTURED CONVERSATIONS ACROSS 8 INTERLOCUTORS

In this section, we present the data for copula absence as it varies by interlocutor. In other words, these data show how, as a group, the Sunnysidaz spoke to the eight Stanfordian interlocutors. Given the primary significance of race, the secondary significance of gender, and the tertiary significance of HHC knowledge, we can hypothesize that the ordering of the interlocutors would proceed in this manner, with decreasing rates of absence: (1) BMH, (2) BMN, (3) BFH, (4) BFN, (5) WMH, (6) WMN, (7) WFH, (8) WFN. In the run, the identity characteristics of the interlocutors are subsumed under the numbers 1–8. When we look more closely at the interlocutors as individuals, we can begin to see a finer level of analysis emerging. Table 5.2 displays the observed probability coefficients for the best run by interlocutor adjacent to the hypothesized ordering.

Remarkably, the observed ordering of interlocutors matches up almost precisely with our hypothesized ordering. Even more remarkably, the one interlocutor who veers from the hypothesized ranking is the White male Hip Hopper, who superseded his race category due to his familiarity with HHC. This finer level of analysis

TABLE 5.2
Observed Probability Coefficients for the Best Run by Interlocutor Adjacent to the Hypothesized Ordering of Interlocutors

	Hypothesized Ordering	*Observed Ordering*	*Probability Coefficient*
Increasing Absence ↑	BMH	BMH	.833
	BMN	BMN	.684
	BFH	BFH	.663
	BFN	WMH	.444
	WMH	BFN	.426
	WMN	WMN	.311
	WFH	WFH	.194
	WFN	WFN	.171

NOTE: Significance in best run .000.

allowed us to see what the previous level of analysis had obscured—the interaction of the three identity characteristics. That is, despite the ordered significance of race, gender, and HHC knowledge, the White male Hip Hopper was able to invite more copula absence from Blacks than the Black female Non-Hip Hopper.

COPULA ANALYSIS FOR 32 INDIVIDUAL SPEAKERS ACROSS 8 INTERLOCUTORS

Thus far, we have examined the internal linguistic constraints and external identity characteristics for all speakers in all 32 SSCs, and determined that both types of constraints were significant in styleshifting. Then we provided a more fine-grained analysis to see how the Black speakers, as a group, responded to each individual interlocutor. In this section, we look even more closely at each individual Black speaker to reveal his or her personal rankings of the interlocutors with regard to this feature. In other words, the overall pattern suggests that the WMH was ranked fourth, but we might ask: Did the WMH invite informality from each individual to the same degree? More broadly, is there any individual variation in the way that individual Sunnysidaz rank the interlocutors? Table 5.3 displays the observed ordering of the interlocutors for each individual Sunnysida—Amira, Bilal, Careem, and Kijana—and the probability coefficients. Based on the data presented in the previous section, the hypothesized ordering of interlocutors now becomes: (1) BMH, (2) BMN, (3) BFH, (4) WMH, (5) BFN, (6) WMN, (7) WFH, (8) WFN.

Table 5.3 reveals several pieces of information that may have been obscured had we not performed this even finer level of analysis. For one, we can see that the WMH does not, in fact, occupy the fourth position for any of the speakers and that, generally, there is a considerable amount of individual variation that can be obscured by looking at the larger, undifferentiated analysis. We also see that the WMN was able to supercede our racial expectations by ranking fourth among interlocutors in Careem's 8 SSCs.

This table leads to more questions: Is the ordering of race, gender, and HHC knowledge the same for the Black male and female Sunnysidaz? If we examine the copula absence data for each individual, we can begin to see what appears to be a once-obscured gendered pattern. Table 5.4 shows the probability coefficients for identity characteristics for the individual speakers.

Table 5.4 provides a much more nuanced picture that may help us further probe the reason why the identity characteristics of race, gender, and HHC knowledge ordered the way that they did. Further, by seeing what characteristics were significant to whom, we can begin to try to understand WHY this particular ordering for this particular individual. The first thing that immediately strikes us when the data is presented in this fashion is that race (Black) is the one identity characteristic selected by all speakers, and it is the primary indicator of styleshifting as it was selected FIRST in the GOLDVARB analysis. The second glaring item that strikes us is that gender was selected only by the males. Neither female selected gender in the best run. This indicates that gender of the interlocutor matters differently for Black males than it does for females. While both males exhibit a tremendous preference to use copula

TABLE 5.3
Observed Probability Coefficients for the Best Run for the Four Sunnysidaz by Interlocutor, Adjacent to the Hypothesized Ordering of Interlocutors

	Hypothesized Ordering	*Bilal*	*Kijana*	*Amira*	*Careem*
Increasing Absence ↑	BMH	BMH .861	BMH .823	BMN .821	BMH .963
	BMN	BMN .746	WMH .693	BFH .778	BFH .591
	BFH	WMH .612	BFH .690	BMH .760	WMH .272
	WMH	BFH .542	BMN .528	BFN .198	WMN .225
	BFN	BFN .317	BFN .424	WFN .113	BMN .214
	WMN	WMN .307	WFN .371	WMH .101	WFH .188
	WFH	WFH .131	WFH .233	WMN .000	BFN .187
	WFN	WFN .000	WMN .154	WFH .000	WFN .000
	Significance in best run	.000	.041	.000	.000

TABLE 5.4
Observed Probability Coefficients for Identity Characteristics That Were Selected in the Best Run for the Four Sunnysidaz

	Race	*Gender*	*HHC Familiarity*	*Order Selected*	*Significance of Best Run*
Amira	B = .863 W = .132	ns	ns	Race	.000
Kijana	B = .615 W = .368	ns	HH = .633 NHH = .381	Race HH	.012
Bilal	B = .688 W = .269	M = .691 F = .244	HH = .626 NHH = .378	Race Gender HH	.001
Careem	B = .814 W = .154	M = .723 F = .256	HH = .710 NHH = .174	Race Gender HH	.000

absence with male versus female interlocutors, females are not as selective. So, while all speakers tend to exhibit highly racialized styleshifts, it is only the males that produce significant gendered styleshifts. Thus, the performance of the males strongly influenced the overall pattern where gender was selected as a secondary identity characteristic.

HHC knowledge was selected by all Sunnysidaz except Amira. This leads us to search for an explanation as to why Amira did not produce Hip Hop Cultured styleshifts. Interestingly enough, while Amira is a big fan of Busta Rhymes, Lil Kim, and other Hip Hop artists, when she is questioned by one of the interlocutors about a Hip Hop detail, she claims: "Well, that's hard for me, cuz like I'm really a child of R&B, more than Hip Hop." A close reading of the transcripts reveals that Amira is not as well-versed in HHC as she seems to be, and relative to the other speakers, she is the least knowledgeable. While this is obviously not an airtight explanation, it provides an interesting qualitative detail that we would have to explore more fully.

Exploring Amira further, we see that she exhibits the greatest range of copula absence for race. It turns out that Amira is known for having the MOST OVERT race ideology out of any student at Haven High. She is known for trying to force other students to stop using the "n-word" around her, as she feels that White folks is steady laughin at Black folks callin themselves outta they name. I can recall one intense class discussion on the use of the words *nigga* and *nigger*, where Amira fervently argued that Blacks should not refer to themselves by that label. In extreme frustration at the end of the discussion, she let out an exasperated cry, "I hate White people!" Amira is, like many Blacks, frustrated with the everyday living conditions of the majority of her people (see chapter 4 for more details). An interesting moment occurred in one of the transcripts where the White female Hip Hopper used the word *nigga* with Amira—this dialogue on the subject may help to explain the development of her overt, race ideology:

A: ...I do not feel that you can just take the meaning off something just by saying that we've grown out of it, or...
C: Mm-hmm...
A: ...saying that the spelling has changed...
C: Mm-hmm...
A: ...or something like that ... so when someone says it it's like, you know that like your ancestors and that your people were hung being called that, and were lynched and just killed and beaten up and raped...
C: ...because they were that...
A: Yeah, and that, the whole white man who was oppressing us for so many years...
C: Mm-hmm...
A: ...was calling us that while he was killing us. Now you wanna call yo BROTHER that? You wanna call somebody who you supposedly LOVE that?
C: Uh-huh...
A: ...I mean, that's just stupid. Why would you...
C: ...you know...
A: I mean, and then, um, like I went to seminar, this is when I REALLY stopped using it. This man, Carl Ray or Carl Mack or something like that...
C: Uh-huh...
A: ...he was talking about it and how our whole history, how the whole history behind the word was and how like the whole Emmett Till story and how this woman was raped and they were calling her

a "bitch" and calling her "nigger" and then they killed her while she was pregnant and sliced her open as the baby—the baby was alive when it came out on the ground and they STOMPED on the baby and poured lighter fluid on her and, just, it was AWFUL...

C: I didn't know that story...

A: Tshhh, I didn't know it either. And then he was just like, "How are you gonna call somebody you love a nigga and just sit there, and then like the white man sitting up there laughing, saying that he can call you that 400 years and now you call, and now you use it against somebody. They're like, "Oh, we're getting the best of them, the whole African American race." So...

C: Woah...

A: ...just after that, the whole seminar thing, I just haven't used it and like...

C: Good...

A: ...and when people are around me using it, I'm like, "If you respect me and you are calling myself, I mean, calling yourself my friend, please don't use that around me, and like...

C: Good, good for you...

While Amira provides an interesting case study of how identity, ideology, and consciousness may impact speech style, more work is needed to pursue these complex issues.

DE-CONFLATING RACE AND FAMILIARITY

As I mentioned above, the copula plays a central role in the debate over the Creole ancestry of BL. While this is clearly not a historical study of the copula, I believe that the data for the present study can contribute to this discussion. In the interest of developing a BL baseline for the four speakers in the study, I set out to record their speech when they were among the primary in-group, peer network within the Black Sunnyside speech community. These data not only provide a BL baseline for these speakers; they are interesting for two additional reasons: (1) the data allow us to compare the speech of speakers when they are talking with unfamiliar interlocutors (in the 32 SSCs) to their speech when they're talking with familiar interlocutors, thus allowing us to test some of Baugh's findings based on his four speech event grids described above, and (2) the data allow us to compare the most significant linguistic constraint on the copula (the following grammatical category) in the differing situational contexts.

It should be pointed out that the data are not comparable in terms of number of copula tokens, with the number of tokens in the familiar, in-group, peer conversation being far less than the number of tokens in the 32 SSCs. Despite this, there are enough tokens in the group data to suggest some interesting preliminary findings. Table 5.5 shows the frequency of copula absence and the ordering of the most significant linguistic constraint on the copula (following grammatical category) in four contexts: (1) unfamiliar Blacks and Whites, (2) unfamiliar Blacks, (3) unfamiliar Whites, and (4) familiar Black peer group (BL baseline). The overall frequencies of copula absence in all four contexts are represented graphically in figure 5.2.

Given the significant impact that race has on speech style for Black speakers, as we've demonstrated above, it follows that Black speakers would exhibit higher rates of copula absence when talk-

TABLE 5.5
Frequencies and Probability Coefficients for Copula Absence across Four Speech Situations

	Unfamiliar Blacks & Whites	*Unfamiliar Blacks*	*Unfamiliar Whites*	*Familiar Black Peer Group*
Overall frequency	393/1,538 (26%)	310/819 (37%)	84/718 (11%)	190/235 (80%)
Input probability	.254	.375	.121	.762
Following grammatical environment				
gon	.944	.916	.957	[100%]
Verb + *-ing*	.655	.641	.590	.760
Locative	.564	.545	.451	.319
Adjective	.389	.399	.387	.463
Noun phrase	.354	.306	.467	.380
gonna	.107	.185	[0%]	[100%]
Miscellaneous	.423	.352	.417	.117
Significance of best run	.000	.043	.001	.010

FIGURE 5.2
Frequencies of Copula Absence across Four Speech Situations

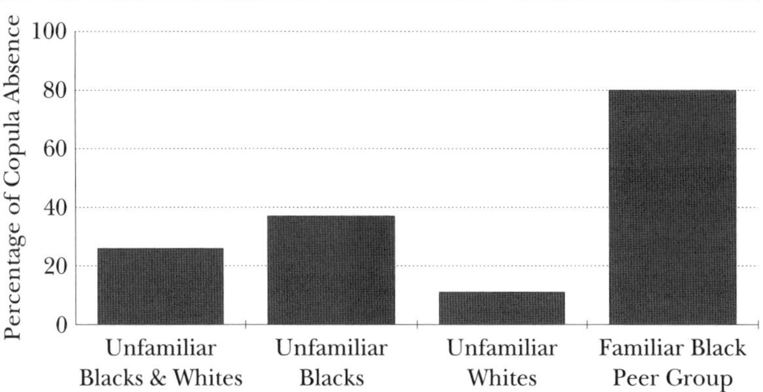

ing with unfamiliar Blacks versus unfamiliar Whites. We can also see that Black speakers exhibit greater rates of copula absence when talking with Black familiars (Black peer group) than Black unfamiliars. These results run counter to Baugh's (1979, 1983) data, where he found that level of familiarity and membership in the Black street culture did NOT have a significant impact on copula absence rates for Black speakers. Perhaps the difference lies in the fact that Baugh was studying the styleshifting of Black adults, whereas these data are for adolescents, but that's only speculation.

These results also remind us of the extreme importance of isolating race and familiarity in sociolinguistic studies of style. For example, in Rickford and McNair-Knox's (1994) study of Foxy Boston, as we pointed out previously, there is no telling how much Foxy was responding to the Black interviewers' race versus the level of familiarity, since she was both Black AND familiar. Although we recognize that the level of familiarity in a Black peer group is probably higher than that in the Black interviewers' relationship with Foxy Boston, it's the RELATIVE level of familiarity that's important. The point is they could have arrived at some less significant results had both the Black and White interviewers been unfamiliar to the speaker. Future research on sociolinguistic style might find it useful to develop tighter experimental controls.

COPULA IN THE CREOLE ORIGINS CONTROVERSY

As previously stated, the copula is perhaps one of the greatest indicators of a linguistic relationship between BL, African languages, and the Creole languages of the Caribbean, particularly when it is analyzed for the effects of following grammatical category. The following grammatical category is the most significant linguistic constraint on the distribution of copula absence. We've already seen that the FREQUENCY of copula absence in the BL baseline sample is much higher than in other contexts, but what about the DISTRIBUTION of the copula? Is it possible that the distribution of the copula in terms of following grammatical category could differ in varying contexts? If so, what does this mean?

Figure 5.3 shows the distribution of the copula based on following grammatical category when Black speakers are talking to familiar, peer group Blacks and compares this distribution with Jamaican Creole data (Rickford 1998). What we see is that the BL baseline distribution of the following grammatical category for copula absence is ordered in precisely the same way as for Jamaican Creole speakers. In fact, the distribution is so similar that most linguists would be willing to bet that the speakers represented by the two different lines are members of the same speech community. What does this mean? The data tells us that there is a strong relationship between the speech of this group of Black Americans and Jamaican Creole speakers. Unless one would be led to believe that this ordering is entirely random, one must see this data as further evidence that whatever process occurred in the restructuring of African languages (whether it be creolization, second-language learning, or a combination of the two) in the Caribbean also occurred in the United States, at least for this variable.

Figure 5.4 shows data for several sets of Black American speakers: New York City teenagers (Labov 1969), Los Angeles adults (Baugh 1979, 1980), youth in this study, and Jamaican Creole data (Rickford 1996, 1998). Interestingly, the data for the familiar Black peer group, which represents peers of the same speech community and friendship network, is the most closely aligned with the Jamaican Creole data.

FIGURE 5.3
Copula Absence in a Familiar Black Peer Group in the United States and in Jamaican Creole

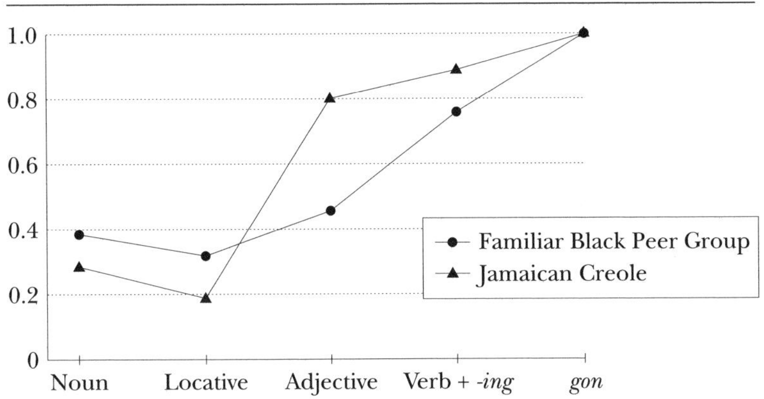

FIGURE 5.4
Copula Absence in a Familiar Black Peer Group in the United States, with Black Adults in LA, Black Teenagers in NYC, and Jamaican Creole

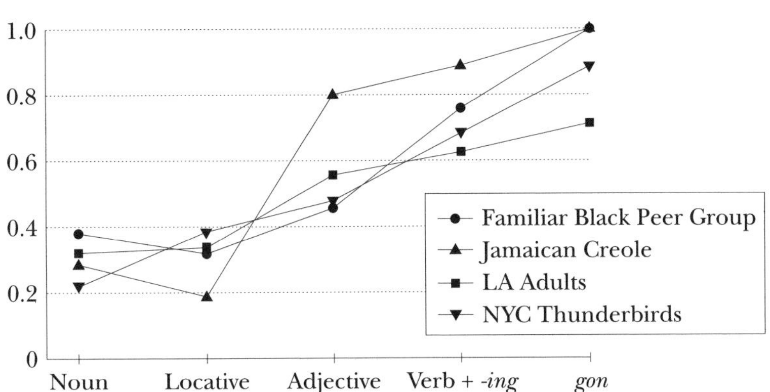

Earlier in this section, we asked if it was possible that the distribution of the copula in terms of following grammatical category could differ in varying contexts? This data appears to suggest that the answer to that question is yes. Table 5.6 re-presents the data from table 5.5. and shows the ordering of the following grammatical category when the Sunnysidaz talk with each other (the BL baseline group ordering), with unfamiliar Blacks, and with unfamiliar Whites.

It's important to remember that the following grammatical category is the most significant constraint on the behavior of the copula. We have seen in our data presented above that the Sunnyside interlocutors exhibited a much greater rate of absence in the BL baseline peer group session (similar to findings by Winford 1992). Some sociolinguists have claimed that FREQUENCY of copula absence is NOT a good indicator of the Creole origins of BL. Rather, they state that it's the DISTRIBUTION of the copula that really matters in the construction of the history of the language variety (Walker 1999; Poplack and Tagliamonte 2001). This argument is usually made when data collected by White researchers exhibits a LOW frequency of copula absence. These same data on Black speech collected by White researchers end up showing that the distribution of the copula is different in this group of speakers and, thus, that their language could not possibly have developed from an earlier Creole (or developed similarly to one).

To add some specific details to the statements above, this debate has played out with great fervor over the distribution of copula absence in following grammatical category for speakers of

TABLE 5.6

Ordering of the Final Grammatical Category for BL Baseline Peer Group, Unfamiliar Blacks, and Unfamiliar Whites

BL Baseline Peer Groups[a]		*Unfamiliar Blacks*[b]		*Unfamiliar Whites*[c]		
Locative	.319	Noun phrase	.306	Adjective	.387	↓ Increasing Order
Noun phrase	.463	Adjective	.399	Locative	.451	
Adjective	.463	Locative	.545	Noun phrase	.467	
Verb + *-ing*	.760	Verb + *-ing*	.641	Verb + *-ing*	.590	
gon	1.000	*gon*	.916	*gon*	.957	

a. Aligns with the ordering of Jamaican Creole speakers and closely approximates the ordering of the BL found in previous studies.
b. Aligns closely with the ordering of BL found in previous studies.
c. Does not align with the ordering of BL found in previous studies.

Samaná English, an African Diaspora community (see Rickford 1998 for an in-depth discussion of the issues). Two major studies have been cited in the literature, one where the data was collected by unfamiliar Whites (Poplack and Sankoff 1987) and the other where data was collected by an unfamiliar Black (Hannah 1996). Remarkably, as we see in tables 5.7 and 5.8, the ordering of the following grammatical category in Poplack and Sankoff (who were unfamiliar White researchers) aligns with the ordering found in my data for unfamiliar Whites. In addition, the ordering of following grammatical category for Hannah (who was an unfamiliar Black researcher) aligns with the ordering found in my data for unfamiliar Blacks. Further, neither data set matches the ordering of BL baseline peer group data in table 5.6.

While it would be premature to make TOO much out of these findings, the data seem to suggest that the distribution of copula absence according to following grammatical category in the speech patterns of African Diaspora speakers (including BL and Samaná English speakers) does in fact vary based on the situational context, with race of interviewer possibly being a major factor in that variation. Future research needs to be conducted to test these findings, as this could have serious implications for sociolinguistic

TABLE 5.7

Frequency of Copula Absence and Ordering of the Final Grammatical Category for Unfamiliar Whites and Poplack and Sankoff (1987)

	Unfamiliar Whites		*Poplack and Sankoff (1987)*		
	Adjective	.387	Adjective	.19	Increasing Order ↓
	Locative	.451	Locative	.23	
	Noun phrase	.467	Noun phrase	.41	
	Verb + *-ing*	.590	Verb + *-ing*	.46	
	gon	.957	*gon*	.59	
Overall frequency of absence	11%		20%		

NOTE: Neither ordering aligns with the ordering of BL or Creoles in previous studies. Both overall frequencies are lower than the unfamiliar blacks and the black peer group.

TABLE 5.8
Frequency of Copula Absence and Ordering of the Final Grammatical Category for Unfamiliar Blacks and Hannah (1996)

	Unfamiliar Blacks		*Hannah (1996)*		
	Noun phrase	.306	Noun phrase	.14	Increasing Order ↓
	Adjective	.399	Adjective	.43	
	Locative	.545	Locative	.47	
	Verb + *-ing*	.641	Verb + *-ing*	.88	
	gon	.916	*gon*	.97	
Overall frequency of absence	37%		48%		

NOTE: Both patterns align closely with the ordering of BL in previous studies. Both frequencies are intermediate between unfamiliar Whites and the Black peer group.

methodology. Those who argue that the race (or other identity characteristics) of the interviewer do NOT matter should produce data to substantiate that claim. What we have done throughout this chapter is produce data that strongly suggests that race (or other identity characteristics) DO matter, and significantly so. We've also shown that the frequency AND distribution of copula absence may vary from situation to situation, EVEN WHEN CONSIDERING THE MOST SIGNIFICANT LINGUISTIC CONSTRAINT ON COPULA ABSENCE.

6. OUR STEELO SWITCH UP: THIRD-PERSON SINGULAR -*S*, POSSESSIVE -*S*, AND PLURAL -*S* ABSENCE

THIS CHAPTER EXAMINES the linguistic and identity constraints on third-person singular -*s* in all 32 semistructured conversations (SSCs). Third-person singular -*s* variability has long been studied as a feature of Black Language (BL) (Labov et al. 1968; Wolfram 1969; Fasold 1972; Baugh 1979; Rickford and McNair-Knox 1994; Winford 1998). You might could hear a brotha or sista say something like *E-40 rapØ too fast*, and then turn around and say, *but Too Short raps too slow*. Some researchers (Labov et al. 1968; Fasold 1972) have posited that the earliest (and most "basilectal") forms of BL did not have subject-verb concord, while others insist that this feature may have its roots in Anglican sources (Poplack and Tagliamonte 1989). This may or may not be the case, but in some speakers (Rickford and Rickford 2000), third-person singular -*s* can be present ONLY 3–4% of the time!

In this study, we see that third-person singular -*s* variability appears to be fundamental in Black American styleshifting, confirming the results of Baugh (1979, 1983) and Rickford and McNair-Knox (1994) and arguing against the results of Labov et al. (1968) and Fasold (1978). Wolfram's (1969) study of BL in Detroit showed that this variable was a significant indicator of interview style versus reading style, but of course, those results are not relevant to this present study since, as we explained, reading constitutes a different modality than speaking. The choice of reading as a stylistic context can be contested on a number of levels, but suffice it to say that we should not be surprised if a letter on the printed page ("s") is pronounced more often than in spoken speech (the feature does not vary on the printed page, but it is variable by nature in speech). Put simply, while reading may approximate formal speech, there are serious doubts as to whether or not it is in fact speech at all.

Whereas we witnessed the interaction of linguistic and identity constraints in the variability of the copula, third-person singular *-s* seems to be constrained much more heavily by identity constraints. This finding confirms Baugh's (1979, 1983) findings that this particular variable was constrained more by his social categories (familiarity and Black street culture membership) than by internal linguistic factors. Rickford and McNair-Knox (1994) rightfully state that most studies of this variable do not include an analysis of internal linguistic constraints. However, this may be for a reason: the internal linguistic constraints for third-person singular *-s* are highly irregular (as Labov et al. 1968 found).

Baugh (1979) found that the linguistic constraints for this variable were less significant than the social constraints and that while familiarity AND Black street culture membership impacted its stylistic variability, the variable was most sensitive to familiarity. For the sake of comparison, table 6.1 shows Baugh's internal linguistic constraints for his adult Los Angeles speakers and the Sunnysidaz in this study.

TABLE 6.1
Internal Linguistic Constraints for Third-Person Singular *-s* in Los Angeles speakers (Baugh 1979) and Sunnysidaz

	LA Speakers (Baugh 1979)	*Sunnysidaz*
Overall frequency		296/934 (31%)
Preceding phonological environment		
Nasal	.490	.960
Voiced consonant	.567	.598
Voiceless consonant	.427	.548
ts-cluster	.430	.305
Vowel	.585	.260
Following phonological environment		
Consonant	.546	(.478)
Vowel	.454	(.555)
Pause	not reported	(.436)

NOTE: Parentheses indicate that factor group was not chosen as significant by best run.

It's clear from the data that the following phonological environment is not significant and that the preceding phonological environment, while selected in the best run for the Sunnysidaz, shows no resemblance to Baugh's data other than the possible favoring of absence by vowels.

Rickford and McNair-Knox's (1994) analysis of Foxy Boston's speech shows that verb type was the most primary internal constraint on third-person singular *-s* variability. While the verb types (regular verbs, *have, do, don't,* and *say*) turned out to be significant, there is no discussion of how these verb types were chosen. A run with different verb types could also turn out to be significant, as was the case in this study. In addition to verb type, I also examined subject type as a possible grammatical constraint and found it to be significant in the best run. Table 6.2 displays the probability coefficients of subject type and verb type from the best run of all 32 SSCs.

Both subject type and verb type were significant in the best run. Interestingly, the subject type pattern for third-person singular *-s* absence matches the subject type pattern for the copula in that personal pronouns favor absence more than noun phrases or other pronouns. Although these factor groups were chosen as significant in the best run, they need to be tested. While it does

TABLE 6.2
Probability Coefficients of Subject Type and Verb Type from the Best Run of All 32 Semistructured Conversations

	Sunnysidaz
Subject Type	
Personal pronoun	.630
Other pronoun	.347
Noun phrase	.555
Verb Type	
Regular verbs	.468
do/don't	.485
go	.658
want/wanna	.773
say	.532

not appear that internal linguistic constraints are very significant overall, future studies might find it useful to uncover more interesting details about the internal linguistic constraints that may govern third-person singular *-s* variability.

The remainder of the discussion on this variable will focus on the much more interesting and significant identity constraints. Table 6.3 shows us that all three identity factor groups exhibit significant effects on speech style for this variable, and were ranked in order of significance precisely as they were with the copula (race is primary; gender is secondary; Hip Hop Culture [HHC] familiarity is tertiary). Black speakers tend to use more absence when speaking with Black versus White interlocutors; with male versus female interlocutors; and with interlocutors who are more familiar with HHC. Figure 6.1 represents the identity effects graphically.

This shows the value of including identity constraints in our analyses, as we see that, at least for this feature, the variation is affected irregularly by linguistic constraints but significantly by identity constraints. Linguistically, subject and verb type need to be examined more carefully, but at this point, it is unclear how fruitful that would be. In terms of identity, while race, gender, and HHC knowledge were all selected as significant, race—again—has the greatest impact on the rule.

TABLE 6.3
Probability Coefficients for Identity Constraints on Third-Person Singular *-s* Absence

	Sunnysidaz
Interlocutor Race	
Black	.658
White	.289
Interlocutor Gender	
Male	.631
Female	.323
Interlocutor Familiarity with HHC	
Hip Hop	.615
No Hip Hop	.373
Significance of best run	.019

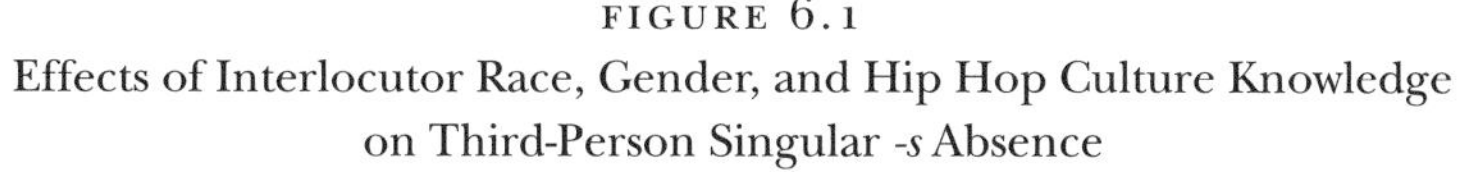

FIGURE 6.1
Effects of Interlocutor Race, Gender, and Hip Hop Culture Knowledge on Third-Person Singular *-s* Absence

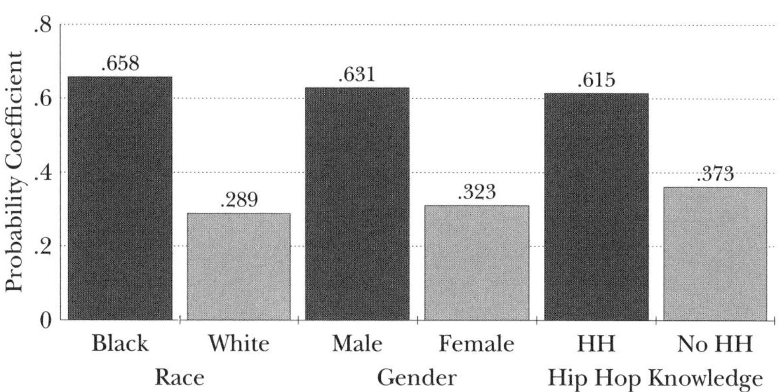

In the next section, we gon break down the data for third-person singular *-s* absence on the same levels as our analysis of the copula. We gon look at how the Sunnysidaz, as a group, styleshifted across the eight Stanfordian interlocutors. Second, we gon see how they, as individuals—Amira, Bilal, Careem, and Kijana—shifted they styles according to the Stanfordian interlocutors. Examining individual variability in style at this detailed level of analysis increases our understanding of how different speech styles emerge for any given speaker. Adding this second variable also increases our understanding of how different variables operate in the construction of styles.

THIRD-PERSON SINGULAR *-S* ANALYSIS FOR 32 SSCS ACROSS 8 INTERLOCUTORS

In this section, we present the data for third-person singular *-s* absence as it varies by interlocutor. In other words, this data shows how, as a group, the Sunnysidaz spoke to the eight different Stanfordians. Given the primary significance of race, the secondary significance of gender, and the tertiary significance of HHC knowledge, we can hypothesize that the ordering of the interlocutors would proceed in this manner, with decreasing rates of absence: (1) BMH, (2) BMN, (3) BFH, (4) BFN, (5) WMH, (6) WMN, (7) WFH, (8) WFN. As with the copula analysis, we find that when we look more closely at the interlocutors as individuals, we can begin to see a finer level of analysis emerging. Table 6.4 displays the observed probability coefficients for the best run by interlocutor adjacent to the hypothesized ordering.

Interestingly, the White male Hip Hopper Stanfordian was able to once again escape his racial cell and was the only interlocutor to veer from our hypothesis. This time, he escapes by a larger margin and is closer to the third position than to the fifth. In the next section, we gon look even more closely at each individual Sunnysida to reveal their personal rankings of the interlocutors with regard to third-person singular *-s* absence. In other words, the overall pattern suggests that the WMH was ranked fourth, but again we might ask: Is there any individual variation in the way that the individual Sunnysidaz rank the Stanfordian interlocutors? Table 6.5 displays the observed ordering of the Stanfordians for each individual Sunnysida—Amira, Bilal, Careem, and Kijana—and the probability coefficients. Based on the data presented in the previous section, the hypothesized ordering of interlocutors now becomes: (1) BMH,

TABLE 6.4
Observed Probability Coefficients for the Best Run by Interlocutor Adjacent to the Hypothesized Ordering of Interlocutors

	Hypothesized Ordering	*Observed Ordering*	*Probability Coefficient*
Increasing Absence ↑	BMH	BMH	.871
	BMN	BMN	.607
	BFH	BFH	.525
	BFN	WMH	.496
	WMH	BFN	.365
	WMN	WMN	.258
	WFH	WFH	.246
	WFN	WFN	.180

NOTE: Significance in best run .038.

TABLE 6.5
Observed Probability Coefficients for the Best Run for Amira, Bilal, Careem, and Kijana by Stanfordian Interlocutor, Adjacent to the Hypothesized Ordering of Interlocutors

	Hypothesized Ordering	*Bilal*	*Kijana*	*Amira*	*Careem*
Increasing Absence ↑	BMH	BMH .808	BMH .925	BMN .704	BMH .886
	BMN	WMH .581	BMN .701	BFH .561	BMN .637
	BFH	BMN .533	BFH .643	BMH .544	BFH .351
	WMH	WFH .519	WMH .511	WMH .430	WMH .273
	BFN	BFH .462	BFN .379	WFN .288	WFH .272
	WMN	BFN .456	WFN .212	BFN .159	BFN .246
	WFH	WMN .372	WMN .233	WMN .000	WFH .188
	WFN	WFN .222	WFN .141	WFH .000	WFN .000
	Significance in best run	.035	.016	(.012)	.049

NOTE: Parentheses indicate that factor group was not chosen as significant by best run.

(2) BMN, (3) BFH, (4) WMH, (5) BFN, (6) WMN, (7) WFH, (8) WFN.

Table 6.5 shows that the WMH actually occupied the fourth position in every run except Bilal's, where he came in second. Another interesting piece of information that was obscured by the previous run was the fact that the WFH also managed to escape her racial cell with Bilal. As in the copula, there is a considerable amount of individual variation that can be obscured by looking at the larger, undifferentiated analysis. Again, we ask: Is the ordering of race, gender, and HHC knowledge the same for the Black male and female speakers? If we examine the third-person singular *-s* absence data for each individual Sunnysida, we can begin to see what appears to be a once-obscured gendered pattern. Table 6.6 shows the probability coefficients for identity characteristics for the individual speakers.

Table 6.6 shows a remarkably consistent pattern for all the Sunnysidaz. The table shows racialized, gendered, and Hip Hop Cultured styleshifts for third-person singular *-s*. Bilal represents the only irregularity in what seems like a highly regular ordering of

TABLE 6.6
Observed Probability Coefficients for Identity Characteristics That Were Selected in the Best Run for Amira, Bilal, Careem, and Kijana

	Race	*Gender*	*HHC Familiarity*	*Order Selected*	*Significance of Best Run*
Amira	B = .635 W = .287	M = .613 F = .348	HH = .592 NHH = .335	Race Gender HH	.018
Kijana	B = .719 W = .237	M = .647 F = .307	HH = .661 NHH = .359	Race Gender HH	.009
Bilal	B = .579 W = .395	M = .571 F = .381	HH = .615 NHH = .429	Gender HH Race	.045
Careem	B = .739 W = .207	M = .693 F = .286	HH = .628 NHH = .307	Race Gender HH	.015

identity constraints. His case is explained by the fact that his identity shifts were nearly equal for each identity characteristic (race differential = .184; Hip Hop differential = .186; gender differential = .190). For all intents and purposes, Bilal's ranking of identity constraints maintains equality across all factors. This pattern contrasts with the others in that all of their identity differentials are far greater, all of them above .250 and as high as .532 (Careem's race differential). The primary reason for the difference in Bilal's ordering is his response to the WFH—he was the one Sunnysida to exhibit high absence with her. The fact that she's White AND female works against the hypothesis. Interestingly, the WFH ranks fifth on Careem's list, but LAST on Amira's and Kijana's.

Despite this, in the case of third-person singular *-s*, this level of analysis makes it plain to see the overall pattern of the primary effect of race, secondary effect of gender, and tertiary effect of HHC knowledge.

DE-CONFLATING RACE AND FAMILIARITY

As I mentioned above, third-person singular *-s* absence has been firmly established as a feature of BL. There have also been some limited studies that show the absence of third-person singular *-s* in some White dialects in the United States (Ash and Myhill 1986) and the United Kingdom (Trudgill 1998), with Poplack and Tagliamonte (1989), not surprisingly, claiming a British source as the origin of this feature in BL. The fact that many learners of English as a second language (including speakers of languages as diverse as Yoruba, Arabic, and Spanish) also exhibit third-person singular *-s* absence may lead us to consider the contribution of historically situated second-language learning.

Whatever the case may be, I set out, as with the copula, to record the Sunnysidaz speech when they were among their primary in-group, peer network within the broader Black Sunnyside speech community in the interest of developing a BL baseline for the Sunnysidaz. These data not only provide a BL baseline for these speakers, but the data also allow us to compare the speech of speakers when they are talking with unfamiliar interlocutors (in the 32 SSCs) to their speech when they're talking with familiar interlocutors. Again, we are in a position to test some of Baugh's findings based on his four speech event subdivisions described earlier.

It should be pointed out that the data are not comparable in terms of number of tokens, with the number of tokens in the familiar, in-group, peer conversation being far less than the number of tokens in the 32 SSCs. Despite this, there are enough tokens in the group data to allow us to make interesting comparisons. Table 6.7 shows the frequency of third-person singular *-s* absence and the input probabilities in four contexts: (1) unfamiliar Blacks and Whites, (2) unfamiliar Blacks, (3) unfamiliar Whites, and (4) familiar Black peer group (BL baseline). The overall frequencies of third-person singular *-s* absence in all four contexts are represented graphically in figure 6.2.

Given the significant impact that race has on speech style for Black speakers, as we've demonstrated above, we would expect that the Sunnysidaz would exhibit higher rates of absence when talking

TABLE 6.7
Frequencies and Input Probabilities for Third-Person Singular *-s* Absence across Four Speech Situations

	Unfamiliar Blacks & Whites	*Unfamiliar Blacks*	*Unfamiliar Whites*	*Familiar Black Peer Group*
Overall frequency	296/934 (31%)	221/540 (40%)	75/394 (19%)	52/61 (85%)
Input probability	.317	.409	.190	.852

FIGURE 6.2
Frequencies of Third-Person Singular *-s* Absence in All Four Contexts

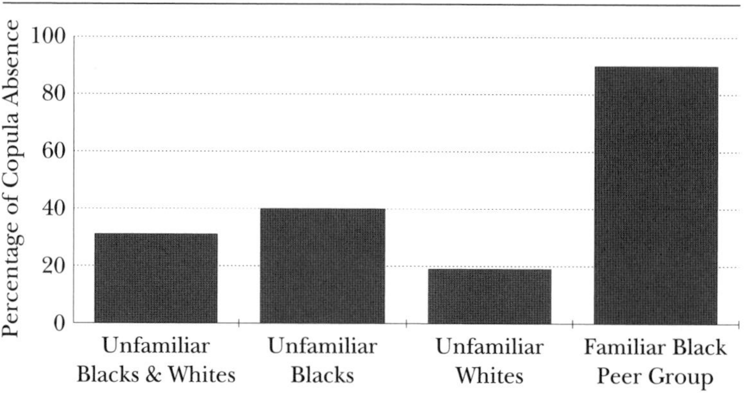

with unfamiliar Blacks versus unfamiliar Whites. Again, since both groups are unfamiliar, we have isolated race. The significance of race for these speakers differs from Baugh's earlier findings. We can also see that Black speakers exhibit greater rates of absence when talking with Black familiars (Black peer group) than with Black unfamiliars. These results confirm Baugh's (1979, 1983) finding that level of familiarity has a significant impact on third-person singular *-s* absence rates for Black speakers.

POSSESSIVE *-S* AND PLURAL *-S* ABSENCE

Although I began with the intention of analyzing the five features outlined earlier, the stylistic variation in possessive *-s* absence was insignificant, and there were NO tokens of plural -*s* absence in the entire data set. Any categorical feature is automatically excluded from a variation analysis, precisely because the feature does NOT exhibit any variation. In the case of possessive -*s* absence, there were too few tokens to take seriously in our consideration of style. For example, table 6.8 shows the rate of absence for this feature when the speakers are talking to Black versus White interlocutors. Importantly, there were only 41 tokens of the possessive for all 32 conversations, making it difficult to run a variation analysis.

Interestingly, none of the Stanfordian interlocutors, Black or White, exhibited absence in this feature. Contrast this with the 100% absence, albeit with only 7 tokens, with the familiar Black peer group, and perhaps we can consider the feature as an INDICATOR (Labov 1972b) of both race in American society and class in the Black speech community (since the feature is not found in any White speech communities). The feature is used only by Black speakers, and further, used predominantly by Black speakers who have spent the majority of their lives in Black working-class environments.

The only study to report Varbrul results for possessive -*s* variation was Baugh (1979, 1983). He showed that the feature varied primarily based on familiarity (frequency of contact) between the speakers, and secondarily on membership within the Black street culture. While we are presented with the factor weights for the variation of the feature, Baugh does not provide the total number of tokens for us to determine whether or not the variation is ACTUALLY significant. For example, Labov et al. (1968), who compared the speech of Black males in one-on-one and group contexts, reported 72% (23/32) possessive -*s* absence for one-on-one contexts

TABLE 6.8
Frequency of Possessive -*s* Absence with Black and White Interlocutors, and Peer Group

Unfamiliar Blacks & Whites	*Unfamiliar Blacks*	*Unfamiliar Whites*	*Familiar Black Peer Group*
12/41 (29%)	5/20 (25%)	7/21 (33%)	7/7 (100%)

and 57% (32/56) for group style. Rickford and McKnair-Knox (1994) point out that the apparent size of the percentage gap is misleading since the difference is statistically insignificant. In their study of Foxy Boston, they also found possessive *-s* absence to be a statistically insignificant indicator of styleshifting, showing 67% (6/9) absence with a Black, familiar interviewer and 50% (5/10) absence with a White, unfamiliar interviewer.

More studies are needed to investigate the stylistic significance of this feature and the possibility that it is an indicator of both race in the larger society and class in the Black speech community. As pointed out by Rickford (1992), researchers will have to find a way to overcome the relatively small number of tokens of nominal possessives that appear in speech.

In the next chapter, we will examine another hallmark feature of BL—invariant *be*—and describe a new form of invariant *be*—be_3, or the BL EQUATIVE COPULA.

7. WE BE WORD SORCERERS: INVARIANT *BE* AND THE EQUATIVE COPULA IN BL

VARIANT AND INVARIANT *BE*: BE_1, BE_2, AND BE_3

IN THIS CHAPTER, we take another hallmark feature of Black Language (BL)—invariant *be*—and analyze its stylistic sensitivity. We will begin first with a description of the feature and then follow with the stylistic analysis. In our analysis of the copula in chapter 5, we saw a different kind of *be* than what we see here. To give the reader a sense of how invariant *be* functions, there are nine examples of invariant *be* in the piece of dialogue below (lines 6, 7, 10, 18, 24, 28, 30, 31, and 42). Invariant *be* is used most often to convey an aspectual meaning of habituality. In other words, it's used to refer to something that happens over and over again. The two types of *be* discussed in most analyses of the BL copula are be_1 and be_2. In BL, as in English dialects in general, be_1 refers to the conjugated and variant form on the copula. For example, when Amira say, "They think we gon be honest," notice how the *are* ain't there. So, we would analyze that as copula absence (rather than a full copula or a contracted copula). So, be_1 is the form of the copula that varies (full = *we are gon be honest*; contracted = *we're gon be honest*; absent = *we Ø gon be honest*). Be_2, on the other hand, is called invariant *be* for a pretty straightforward reason—it don't vary. In other words, it always occurs as one form, just "be."

Let's take a look at this snippet of speech in a peer group conversation to get a sense of how invariant *be* works in BL. In this piece of talk, the Sunnysidaz is talkin about how they be raidin Shadyside during Halloween, cuz they got the best candy...

1 Yesmina: Halloween, we ALWAYS go there, don't we?
2 Researcher: [laughter] Oh, yeah?
3 Y: "We goin TO SHADYSIDE..."

R: [laughter] Y'all raid, raid Shadyside…
Y: They got the good stuff, king-size stuff…
Amira: MM-HMM! They BE givin MONEY if they run out of…
R: They BE givin out money, huh?
Y: MM-HMM!
R: …run out of candy, they give you money…
Bilal: [suck-teeth] Dumb-asses BE settin they whole basket of candy out like ain't nobody gon take that junk…
Y: MM-HMM!
R: [laughter]…
A: They set it on the porch cuz they don't wanna come to the door [laughter],…
R: [African American falsetto] Why do they do that?!
A: They think we gon be honest…
B: They BE like [mocking a "White voice"], "Just take one pleeease."
A: They think we gon be honest…
R: They probably put a sign in it, too, right?
Y: UH-HUHHH! "Take one."
A: Yep!
R: We useta do the SAME thing, maaan…
B: But see at the same time, they BE puttin shit IN the candy, so…
Y: MM-HMM! Them White people…
A: Yep…
R: What do you mean puttin shit in the candy?
B: [laughter] They BE puttin stuff in the candy…
A: That's why when you go over there you gotta check yo candy after, cuz they BE puttin razor blades and shit…
Y: Yep, they BE doin that…
R: NAHHHH…
B: ForREAL!
Y: Mm-hmm…
A: One year, somebody put a razor blade in like this candy apple thing and a kid…
Y: MM-HMM!
A: …bit into it and they tongue got cut off…
R: Over in Shadyside?
A: Yep!
Y: Yep…
R: You gotta watch out cuz sometimes that's where the loonies BE at…
Y: MM-HMM!

As we see in this case, the Sunnysidaz talkin about what generally happens every Halloween when they raid Shadyside. The use of invariant *be* lets us know that they not only talkin about a one-time thing, but rather, they talkin about what USUALLY be happenin every single year. So, when Bilal say, "Dumb-asses BE settin they whole basket of candy out like ain't nobody gon take that junk," he mean that that's what they REGULARLY or USUALLY do. And this is what they be sayin every year, too—"They BE like [mocking a "White voice"—again, see Alim (2004e) for a discussion of "the Whitey voice"], "Just take one pleeease"—never learnin they lesson.

Another snippet of talk between Careem and one of the Stanfordians reveals several different linguistic environments where be_2 can occur. Earlier studies (Labov et al. 1968; Bailey and Maynor 1987; Rickford and McNair-Knox 1994) have found that be_2 occurs most often with second-person and plural subjects (*you, we, they*, or *those girls*), then with first-person singular subjects (*I*), and least with third-person singular subjects (*he, she, it*, or *the girl*). In terms of following grammatical environment, these same studies have found that be_2 occurs more before Verb + *-ing* ("She be spittin lyrical flames") than noun phrases, adjectives, or locatives. As we saw in the dialogue above, be_2 can also be used as a quotative introducer. For example, when Bilal mocked the White folks in Shadyside, he began with "They be like," which means 'They usually say', and then he quotes them. Rickford and McNair-Knox (1994) also found other examples of these quotative introducers, such as, "They be going" and "They be saying." Let's join Careem (K) and the Stanfordian interlocutor (C) to see how Careem's be_2 usage displays many of these linguistic environments:

C: Do you think Jay-Z or—who else is kinda hot right now—Busta or Ludacris—do you think they would be as hot right now if Biggie and Tupac were still alive?

K: Um, I think they—it would be, you know, more even, but like right now, those people you said is like at the top or whatever like, to me, like I don't really like Busta Rhymes. I like—cuz like his CDs really don't BE that good [negative form, followed by adverb/adjective]. Like, he BE havin [Verb + *-ing*] like . . .

C: [laughter] . . .

K: ...his hit song that BE on the radio [locative (or prepositional phrase)]...
C: [laughter]...
K: ...and that BE, that BE the jam [noun phrase]...
C: That would be his best song?
K: ...But when you get the CD, it BE all to the bad [adverb/adjective], but...
C: [laughter]...
K: ...I think if Biggie and Pac was out, you know, I would—I would have to go with Pac or whatever...

The early research on invariant *be* also mentions durative and distributive functions of the feature. Baugh (1983, 72) gives examples of the durative function, which describes an action that endures "over a period of time but need not be of a habitual nature." For example, "...and we BE tired from the heat, but he just made everybody keep on working." Fasold (1972, 151) describes what he calls the distributive function of invariant *be*, which he explains as a rare occurrence. His one example is from a speaker describing some bikes: "Some of them BE big and some of them BE small." These cases are what Green (2000) would later refer to as "bicycle sentences." Green (2002, 49) writes that these invariant *be* examples "precede adjectives and prepositions that indicate permanent properties of a subject." Citing Fasold's (1972) description of this example, she explains that in these rare cases, "it is the subject of the sentence, not the event in the predicate" that is "distributed in time." So Fasold explains that "although any given bicycle is always the same size, one encounters different bicycles at different points in time and these will be of varying sizes."

In the last section of our discussion of invariant *be*, we gon talk about *be*$_3$—what I'm callin the EQUATIVE COPULA in BL. This form of invariant *be* differs from the descriptions of *be*$_2$ that we find in the literature in that there is no presupposition of habituality or distribution in time for the subject or the predicate. More details later, but for now, let's move on to our analysis of invariant *be* in the 32 semistructured conversations (SSCs) and peer-group data.

INVARIANT *BE* ANALYSIS FOR 32 SSCS AND PEER GROUP

There have been several studies (Fasold 1972; Baugh 1983; Rickford and McNair-Knox 1994) that suggest that speakers of BL exhibit stylistic sensitivity in their usage of invariant *be*. Fasold used both Black and White interviewers to collect data on BL and found that speakers averaged 4.7 tokens of invariant *be* with Black interviewers compared to 3.4 tokens with White interviewers. Not dramatic, but a shift in the generally hypothesized direction nonetheless. Baugh (1983) reports no statistics but comments that invariant *be* tends to be used in more informal contexts where all speakers are familiar with the form (i.e., all speakers are BL speakers). In the only study to show overwhelming evidence of invariant *be* in styleshifting, Rickford and McNair-Knox (1994) report that Foxy Boston used 385 tokens of the feature with a Black, familiar interviewer compared to only 97 tokens with a White, unfamiliar interviewer. Now, it's important to note that this study is the first in the literature to report such a high number of tokens for this feature by any one speaker. As the authors note, Foxy's 385 tokens is more than the number of tokens Labov et al. (1968, 236) reported for 18 speakers, AND the number of tokens reported by Wolfram's (1969) 48 speakers, AND the number of tokens reported by Bailey and Maynor (1987) for 20 speakers—COMBINED! Such a high number of tokens is extremely unusual and was not replicated in this study, although some researchers (Butters 1989; Bailey and Maynor 1987) argue that invariant *be* has increased in frequency and salience over the last three decades. This seems to be the general trend, but more studies with an authentic time-depth dimension are needed (that is, studies that compare Sunnyside youth's usage of *be* today with that of Sunnyside youth two or three generations ago, for example).

In this study, we are able to test how identity characteristics—race, gender, and Hip Hop cultural knowledge—impact the stylistic use of this feature. Given our tight experimental controls, we are in a position to determine the impact of these identity constraints on the use of invariant *be* in a way that no previous study has shown.

This analysis is much simpler than the one we performed on the copula (*be*$_1$) since, as we stated, this feature does NOT vary. It was, is, and always will be, *be*. As noted by Wolfram (1969), we cannot analyze *be* within the variation framework because we cannot quantify its usage in relative terms. Or as Baugh (1983, 73) notes: "For style shifting it is extremely difficult to identify contrastive elements in standard English that represent suitable options to distributive *be* in the vernacular." Invariant *be* just don't have a counterpart in "standard White speech," thus pointing to one of the limitations of the variationist framework in the study of style (see Winford 2003). This analysis follows Rickford and McKnair-Knox (1994) in reporting the occurrence of invariant *be* in absolute terms until the relationship of this feature to its full set of possible variants is better understood.

Figure 7.1 shows the distribution of the 72 total tokens of invariant *be* in the 32 SSCs. In the figure, we see that all three identity constraints seem to impact the stylistic use of invariant *be*. The Sunnysidaz had 56 tokens with Black Stanfordians and only 16 with Whites; 43 with males and 29 with females; 52 with Hip Hoppers and 20 with non–Hip Hoppers. Immediately, one would hypothesize that a BMH would invite the highest invariant *be* usage, and this is in fact the case. Due to the small number of tokens,

FIGURE 7.1
Effects of Interlocutor Race, Gender, and Hip Hop Culture Knowledge on Invariant *be*

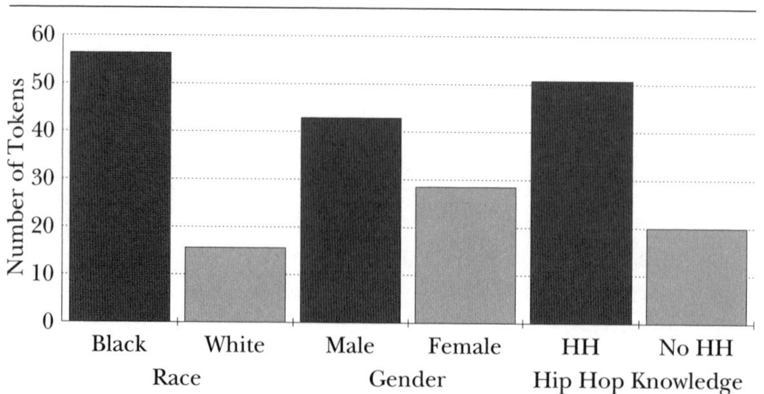

there is not much more we can say about this overall trend, except that this pattern is largely determined by the uneven impact of the BMH. Table 7.1 shows the number of tokens invited by each Stanfordian interlocutor. We can compare the use of invariant *be* in the 32 SSCs with its use in Black peer, in-group talk. In approximately 1.5 hours of speech, the Sunnysidaz used 30 tokens of invariant *be*. If we convert these figures into an hourly rate, we arrive at 3.43 tokens/hour for ALL 32 SSCs and 20 tokens/hour for the Black peer, in-group talk. At this rate, if the peer group were to talk for 21 hours, they would amass 420 tokens, which is far greater than the 72 total tokens found in the 21 hours of 32 SSCs. Figure 7.2 shows the hourly rates for the four situational contexts: unfamiliar Blacks and Whites, unfamiliar Blacks, unfamiliar Whites, and Black peer, in-group (BL baseline).

Figure 7.2 closely resembles figures 5.2 and 6.2 for the frequency of copula absence across these same four situational con-

TABLE 7.1
Number of *be* Tokens Invited by Stanfordian Interlocutors

BMH	32	(44.4%)	WMH	5	(6.9%)
BMN	4	(5.6%)	WMN	2	(2.8%)
BFH	11	(15.3%)	WFH	4	(5.6%)
BFN	9	(12.5%)	WFN	5	(6.9%)

FIGURE 7.2
Hourly Rates of Invariant *be* Use in the Four Situational Contexts

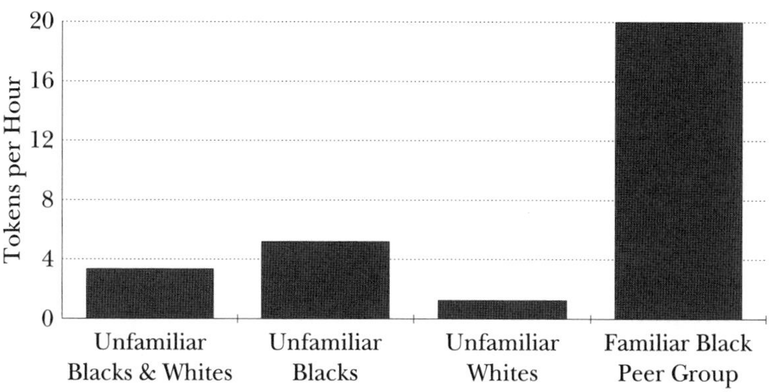

texts. The Sunnysidaz use all of these hallmark BL features—copula absence, third-person singular *-s* absence, and invariant *be*—at a higher rate with unfamiliar Blacks than with unfamiliar Whites, yet neither group is a match for the type of talk exhibited in the Black peer, in-group, where the Sunnysidaz is choppin it up with each other.

BE_3—THE EQUATIVE COPULA IN BL

As mentioned above, the sociolinguistic literature on invariant *be* in BL is well known to scholars of BL and language variation and change. Early studies of BL (Stewart 1965; Labov et al. 1968; Wolfram 1969; Dillard 1972; Fasold 1972) noted the occurrence of this feature and discussed its grammatical status. Fasold and Wolfram provide perhaps the greatest detailed account of this feature. Fasold (1972, 151) explains that this form, which he calls distributive *be* ("Distributive [or tenseless] *be* is only used in iterative contexts to refer to states or events which are periodically discontinued and resumed again"), occurs in five contexts: (1) as the auxiliary in the progressive construction *be* + Verb + *-ing* ("Cause sometime I be sleeping and I don't feel like doing the work"); (2) before adjectives ("Christmas? Everybody be happy"); (3) predicate nominals ("When you first come there, there be a lot of teachers"); (4) locatives and some nonlocative prepositional phrases ("Sometimes I be with Rudy") and (5) past participles ("Well, they be mixed up all kinds of way").

Fasold also states that *be* does not have a durative function like the conjugated forms *is*, *am*, and *are* (so *He is working right now* is grammatical, but **He be working right now* is not). He also states that it cannot be used with a purely past time meaning and warns us to be careful about counting contractions of *will* or *would*. Wolfram (1969, 183) also cautions us about this case of mistaken identity ("He be in in a few minutes" is interpreted as "He'll be in in a few minutes"). (Rickford 1974 and Bailey and Bassett 1986, 166, do offer past time examples, and Rickford explains them as a relic of a creolized form of BL when *be* signaled incompleted actions, whether nonpast of past.) In Fasold's description, **He be my brother* is rejected as ungrammatical because it refers to a "permanent state of affairs." Fasold, however, has a difficult time rejecting the three occurrences of *She be a rich lady* found in Henrie's (1969) data and attempts to make an argument for will deletion, which he admits is a "bit labored."

Making a similar point, Wolfram (1969, 187) states:

> Another reason for maintaining that the use of *be* in NNE [Nonstandard Negro English] is not a simple correspondence of present tense in the SE [Standard English] copula is that *be* cannot refer to a permanent continuous relationship. Reference to a continuing permanent relationship in a sentence such as **He be my father* is ungrammatical.... One can only conclude that this NNE category has no isomorphic correspondence in SE.

Wolfram (1991, 84) offers **She be my mother* as an ungrammatical form of "invariant *be*." The major difference between Fasold and Wolfram's analysis is that Wolfram does not see "distributive *be*" as "tense-less," where the choice of tense is optional.

As stated earlier, the literature on invariant *be* (Labov et al. 1968; Wolfram 1969; Fasold 1972) has deemed sentences like **He be my father* and **I be the head nurse* to be ungrammatical. Labov et al. (1968) and other studies (Dunlap 1977; Bailey and Bassett 1986, 173) have shown that *be* can specify instantaneous or definite time ("Oh, it be about four inches, three to four inches wide" [Bailey and Bassett 1986, 173]; see Green 2000 "bicycle sentences" above; "He be about six feet tall," Spears, pers. comm., 2001). While Green (2000) assumes that there must be an underlying presupposition of habituality, examples from my data reveal otherwise. We join a conversation that I had with two Sunnysidaz about the demographic nature of Shadyside (the extremely wealthy residential area next to Sunnyside, see chapter 4):

> Researcher: So, basically now Shadyside is mostly white. Do other people live in Shadyside or is it just mostly white?
> Bilal: Asians...
> Yesmina: MM-HMM!
> B: ...the Uncle Toms...

Y: [laughter] It BE Black people, just like the RICH, like OLDER Black people...
B: Yeah...
Y: ...not no young...
R: Older, rich Black people?
Y: Yeah, they BE cool, though...

In this dialogue, we see that Yesmina uses invariant *be* to refer to instantaneous or definite time ("it BE Black people, just like the RICH, like OLDER Black people") and to refer to a permanent property of the Black people in Sunnyside ("They BE cool, though").

No study, to my knowledge, has dealt with *be* as an equative copula. Throughout my fieldwork and experience in the Sunnyside and other Black American speech communities, I have documented several examples of this construction, which I am calling be_3. To review the different forms of the copula in BL:

be_1 = corresponds to the "standard English" finite forms of *be* (*am, is, are*)
be_2 = the form of invariant *be* often described as habitual
be_3 = the "new" equative copula (Noun phrase → *be* → Noun phrase)

In the remainder of this section on be_3, we will show examples of this equative copula construction from multiple data sources: (1) actual conversation, (2) Hip Hop Nation Language (HHNL) in the recorded lyrics of Hip Hop artists, (3) the poetry of the Black Arts Movement (BAM) and other literature, and (4) slave documents and slave narratives from the Federal Writer's Project (1936–38).

I have observed be_3 in the field on several occasions. The following examples all occurred in the years 2000–2002:

1. In a conversation between a Black journalist and a Black Hip Hop artist, who was approximately 30 years old, the journalist was commenting with amazement about how the Bay Area has managed to produce so many successful independent artists. The journalist asks: "How y'all do that shit, man?" And the artist answers, with obvious hometown pride, reppin for his hood: "We BE them Bay boys" (Bay Area's Mac Mall in conversation with a Black journalist, 2000).

2. In a similar example, the same journalist is talking to a Black Hip Hop artist in his 20s and asking him about his group's role in the development of Hip Hop in Nashville, Tennessee. The artist answers: "We BE the ones that first set it off down here" (Nashville, Tennessee's Young Buck in conversation with a Black journalist, 2001).
3. A Philly brotha-scholar in his 30s was talkin to me about his accomplishments and those of other Black scholars. In straight up boasting mode, he goes, "You know we BE some baaad brothas" (2001).
4. A young brotha, teenager, calls in to a Bay Area radio station, laughin and gigglin like he high. The DJ recognized this and asked him about his broccoli ('marijuana'). "What it BE like?" he asked with a laugh. The youngsta like, "Awww, it BE that good stuff!" (2001).
5. A Sista in her early 20s and three other friends was all ridin in the car one night back from hearing a speech in San Francisco. Somebody mentioned how a particular group of people at the venue were actually opposed to the speaker's strong, political message. She, obviously a lil pissed off, says, "They BE some WEAK-minded muthafuckas!" (2002).
6. A 17-year-old sista in Sunnyside was dribbling a basketball in front of me, playing wit me like she was about to school me. I'm like, "Whatever, you ain't got nuttin." She like, ""I BE the baddest baller on the court, Liiiim" (2002).

These examples of invariant *be* are clear cases of *be*$_3$. Let's take just the first two examples and show why they are NOT examples of *be*$_2$. In the first example, Mac Mall is representin for independent Bay Area Hip Hop artists with pride, "We BE them Bay boys." In the second example, Young Buck claimin his group's pioneering role in developing Hip Hop outta the Dirty Souf, "We BE the ones that first set it off down here." In both cases, there is no time dimension, or rather, *be*$_3$ occurs in instantaneous or definite time. Clearly, Mac Mall is not saying anything like "We are usually them Bay boys," or "Sometimes we are them Bay boys," or "We are them Bay boys at regular intervals in time." And Young Buck ain't sayin something like "We usually are the ones that first set it off," or "Sometimes we are the ones..." or "We are always the ones..." etc.

As with all of the other examples, THERE IS NO UNDERLYING PRESUPPOSITION OF HABITUALITY. A discussion of one example that I first mistakenly analyzed as a case of *be*$_3$ would be helpful here as a comparison. We was in class one day, and Amira and Kijana were talkin about this other girl, one of their classmates. Amira started raggin on Kijana for makin fun of the girl. Kijana got a little upset like she couldn't believe what Amira was sayin. Amira, pushin her even further, starts talkin about how she feel bad for the girl and how she sympathizes with her situation. Kijana busts out with, "You BE the main one that BE cappin on her!" At first blush, the first *be* occurs as NP → *be* → NP. However, this is NOT a case of *be*$_3$, because there is a clear underlying presupposition of habituality here. The presence of the second *be*, a classic case of invariant habitual *be*, impacts the interpretation of the first *be*, which might then be interpreted as, "You are usually the one . . ." The exchange presupposes some sort of recurring action, that is, the way students be steady cappin on this one girl.

Syntactically, examples (1)–(6) of *be*$_3$ could be replaced with the variants of *be*$_1$ ("We are them Bay boys"; "We're them Bay boys"; "We them Bay boys"). However, the semantic meaning of *be*$_3$ differs from *be*$_1$. We will discuss this semantic difference further once we have exhausted the current available data for this construction.

It turns out that among the earlier works on BL, Baugh (1979, 1983) was the only researcher to report what I have reanalyzed as *be*$_3$. Grouping *be*$_3$ with other *be*$_2$ examples, Baugh (1983, 74) provides two clear examples of this equative construction from his adult street speech speakers:

> They BE the real troublemakers
> The clovers BE the baddest ones around here

These two cases appear to be used in the same manner as the six cases above. A different example in Baugh's data—"Leo BE the one to tell it like is"—is more ambiguous, since there is an additional clause "to tell it like it is." The sentence can potentially have an underlying presupposition of habituality and can thus be interpreted as "Leo is usually the one to tell it like it is."

The second type of data we would like to turn our attention to is in Black lyrical production, particularly Hip Hop Culture and Black Arts Movement poetry. These two sets of data—Hip Hop in the 1990s–present and BAM poetry in the 1960s and 1970s—are important in that Black writers have, throughout history (and to differing degrees), consciously attempted to represent BL in their works. Do these poets provide us with any examples of be_3?

Beginning with the HHNL data, we can see that the feature is used widely by a variety of artists within the last decade or so who represent cities as diverse as New York, Los Angeles, St. Louis, and Philadelphia, to name a few. Some examples are provided below:

1. This beat BE the beat for the street. [Kelis, 2001]
2. I BE the truth. [Beanie Sigel, 2000]
3. We BE the ultimate lick. [Ice Cube, 1999]
4. Dr. Dre BE the name / Ain't a damn thing changed. [Dr. Dre, 2000]
5. I BE that insane nigga from the psychoward. [Method Man, 1995]
6. Yo, I BE the number one icon / Word to the holy Qu'ran. [Busta Rhymes]
7. Who BE the father of this? [Busta Rhymes, 2001]
8. With rhymes galore Busta Rhymes BE the ambassador / Explore my metaphor you beg for more. [Busta]
9. Yeah nigga this shit here BE the boss of me. [Busta]
10. This BE that put-you-out-of-your-misery song. [Busta]
11. We BE them new millennium prime time niggas. [Busta]
12. And I BE that nigga, that live nigga, Spliff, comin through right at you wherever the fuck you at. [Spliff Star]
13. My squad BE the official clique in this rap shit. [Spliff]
14. Too late, you BE the type of nigga that I love to hate. [Rampage]
15. The 9-8 people get this right / I BE a diamond in the rough like the Arabian Night. [Rah Digga]
16. I BE the mob fiance, about to marry it. [BIG]
17. Daddy Dearest, my vision BE the clearest. [BIG]
18. Everything you can imagine is real man / and revenge BE the dish I serve to cats cold. [Mark Curry]
19. We BE the outcasts, down for the subtle. [Black Sheep, 1993]
20. Now my dividends BE the new Benjamins (uh-huh). [Puffy]

21. I BE the B-R-A-T, her BE Missy / and we some bad bitches who be fuckin it up. [Da Brat]
22. I BE the G-I-F-T. [Gift of Gab]
23. It (music) BE the light, so open up. [Erick Sermon]
24. My gramma BEES Ebonics. [Nelly]
25. We BEES the baddest click up on this scene. [Queen Pen]

The examples found in Hip Hop lyrical production are too numerous to list. These examples are all clear cases of *be*$_3$. We see that this construction can also be used to form questions (7) and can also occur as *bees* (24, 25), as in some cases of *be*$_2$.

Given the overwhelming evidence of *be*$_3$ in HHNL, I wondered if there was any representation of *be*$_3$ in the Black Arts Movement poetry (one form of mass-based lyrical production in the previous generation). Baugh's adult street speakers would have been nearly the same age as many of the Black Arts Movement poets. As we see below with BAM poet Sista Sonia Sanchez, this form was also used in the 1960s and 1970s. Sista Sonia edited a book that used *be*$_3$ in the title: *We Be Word Sorcerers,* and could often be heard describing the poet's role in this way: "We bees the culture bearers." Sista Sonia, writing in a poem entitled "It Will Be Ours," provides us with two clear examples of *be*$_3$.

We ARE a new people
look at us walk. We walken
a New Walk. Its beat is the sound of Elijah
hurryen us to new frontiers
we BE a new people in a new land...
our talk IS new. It BE
original talk always prefaced by
As-Salaam Alaikum (a greeting of peace)...
[emphasis mine]

This poem is particularly interesting in that Sista Sonia not only provides clear examples of *be*$_3$, but she also uses *be*$_3$ near examples of *be*$_1$ in the same poem. I emphasized *are* in line 1 and *is* in line 6 because they serve as interesting cases of comparison. Why does Sista Sonia say first, "We are a new people," followed by "we BE a new people"? Why, "our talk is new," followed by, "It BE original talk"? As we shall see below, the answer lies in the semantic constraints of *be*$_3$.

Importantly, Sista Sonia was not the only BAM poet to use this construction. Don L. Lee, in "Mwilu / or Poem for the Living," gives us the line that beams with Afrocentric pride, "Musemi BE yr name," and Etheridge Knight writes, "We free singers BE voyagers and sing of cities with straight streets," in "We Free Singers Be." So, Baugh's few examples are given confirmation here by the use of *be*$_3$ by Black poets who, again, were probably around the same age as his adult Black street speech speakers. It is also important to note that, given these examples of *be*$_3$ in BAM and that both Hip Hop and BAM poets actively attempted to represent the "language of the people" (Alim 2000), *be*$_3$ seems to occur with MUCH greater frequency in Hip Hop lyrics than in the BAM poetry. This may have something to do with the fact that the majority of Hip Hop artists do not attain the same level of education as the BAM poets. Whereas BAM was consciously creating a form to reach out to the streets, Hip Hop artists were the recipients of that form—and are now producing verse in the language of the streets, almost by default.

DEEPER HISTORICAL ATTESTATIONS OF *BE*$_3$

Thus far, we have provided ample evidence to show that *be*$_3$ is used widely today (particularly in Hip Hop lyrics) and perhaps less widely in the 1960s and 1970s. But how far can we trace the history of this equative copula construction? What other sources are available to us? In this section, we present the few tokens of *be*$_3$ that we have found in other forms of Black literature and in slave documents and slave narratives from the Federal Writer's Project (1936–38).

Troutman (2002) recently published a paper entitled "We Be Strong Women," which, naturally, caught my eye immediately. The title comes from Lucille Clifton's short story "Lucy," in which the narrator was quoting a character using the equative copula construction in what would have been the 1930s or 1940s:

They tell me she was mean. Lucy was mean always, I heard Aunt Margaret Brown say to Mammy Ca'line one time. And Mammy just said no she wasn't mean, she was strong. "Strong women..." is what she said, "sister, we BE strong women...." [*Good Women: Poems and a Memoir, 1969–1980* (New York: BOA Editions, 1987), 4]

The slave narratives from the Federal Writer's Project (1936–38) offer some support to the idea that this construction was used during the same time period. Two examples follow from a formerly enslaved Black woman in Tampa, Florida, by the name of Josephine Anderson:

[describing a criminal man] Dis man BE a bad desper—you know, one o' them outlaws what kills folks. He some kinda foreigner, an jes tryin make blieve he a niggah, so they don't find him. ["Haunts," Oct. 20, 1937, 5]

[describing a "hant"] I looked back he was gone, like dat, without makin a sound. Den I knowed he BE a hant, an de next day when I tell somebody bout it dey say he BE de gommon what got killed at de crossin a spell back, an other folks has seen him jus like I did. [7]

Dillard (1972), in providing a historical sketch of "Black English," examines documents from the slavery period in an attempt to characterize the speech of Blacks "on the plantation." Dillard quotes from Hugh Henry Brackenridge. In his passage, Cuff, a "Guinea Negro," delivers a speech before the Philosophical Society:

Massa shentiman; I BE cash crab in de Wye rive; found ting in de mud; tone, big a man's foot: hole like to he; fetch Massa: Mass say, it BE de Indian Mocasson.—Oh! Fat de call it all tone. He say, you BE a filasafa, Cuff! I say, O no, Massa, you BE de filasafa. Well; two tree monts afta, Massa call me, and say, You BE a filasafa, Cuff, fo' sartan: Getta ready, and go dis city, and make grate speech for shentima filasafa. [*Modern Chivalry: Containing the Adventures of Captain John Farrago, and Teague O'Regan, His Servant* (Philadelphia: M'Culloch, 1792), 92]

Dillard describes these examples as "permanent (or at least long-term) attributes expressed with durative *be*; the zero copula of short-term attribution occurs elsewhere in the speech." Later in the text, Dillard cites Mrs. A. C. Carmichael's (a woman who claimed that "she worked until she perfectly understood the Negro dialect") recorded forms in *Domestic Manners and Social Conditions of the White, Coloured, and Negro Populations of the West Indies* (London: Whittaker, 1834).

> England BE very fine country
> She BE my sissy

In these examples, *be* represents long duration or "inherent" character. Dillard (1972) states that this construction was also heard in St. Vincent and Jamaica at the time of publication. This construction has also been noted in other African-European language contact situations. In Nigerian Pidgin English, one might hear, "I BE just a common shareholder," where *be* links two noun phrases in the same way. According to Sebba (1997, 132), this represents a more Anglicized variety of the language, because a less Anglicized variety would have *na* as the copula instead of *be*. The natural historical question would be: Could this relexification process have occurred in the African-European language contact situations in the Western Hemisphere?

The scant historical evidence that we have thus far does not paint a clear picture of the history of be_3 in BL. While the form is clearly used in the 1960s and 1970s and in the present day, the evidence is too sketchy to trace any kind of linguistic transmission of this form. What little evidence we do have suggests that there may have been an increase in the usage of the form since the 1960s (either that or an increase in the available evidence). We also might have what appears to be a semantic shift. Whereas the examples of be_3 in Dillard's description and in the slave narratives may have been examples of relexification, the present usage is clearly something different. In other words, there seems to be no semantic difference between the early forms of the NP → *be* → NP and be_1, while later forms appear to present new semantic information.

From the examples in conversation and lyrical production, we can posit situational and semantic constraints on be_3:

> SITUATIONAL: Appears predominantly in situations where all interlocutors are members of the Black street culture, or exhibit enough

communicative familiarity with the culture to be able to participate in many of its interactive speech events and activities; used widely by Black Hip Hop artists and poets whose works are directed at and derive from primarily Black audiences.

SEMANTIC: Usually used when a speaker attempts to speak an ultimate truth (and often emphatically in relation to one's identity), even if that "truth" is completely false; used to describe a permanent state or inherent characteristic of the subject in question. Ultimately, be_3 equates the subject and the predicate nominal in such a way as to reveal what the speaker believes to be a "realer than real" state of affairs. Not equivalent to be_1.

Certainly, more research is needed to determine both the historical development of be_3 as well as the current situational and semantic constraints on its usage. As it stands, there appears to be some semantic overlap between be_2 and be_3, and this needs to be explored further in future studies.

8. IT TAKE TWO TO MAKE A THING GO RIIIIIGHT: EXAMINING INTERACTION IN THE COCONSTRUCTION OF STYLE

THIS CHAPTER IS ULTIMATELY concerned with these two questions: What is causing the Sunnysidaz to styleshift, and how do interlocutors invite the use of Black Language (BL)? In pursuing these questions, the chapter attempts to accomplish two major goals, the first of which is to synthesize the main findings of this study thus far. Second, I will locate style within interaction by presenting speech data from the semistructured conversations (SSCs) in an effort to advance both our methodological approach to the study of style and our conceptualization of style as a coconstructed project. As I stated in chapter 3, sociolinguists have tended to view style as a monologic entity and have thus focused heavily on the speech of the RESEARCHED while neglecting the speech of the RESEARCHER. More recently (Rickford and McNair-Knox 1994; Bell 2001), studies have begun analyzing the speech of both the interviewers and the interviewees. This study does not use the traditional sociolinguistic interview technique and relies on what we have termed SSCs, meaning that our data set represents the efforts of interlocutors engaged in conversation (see chapter 2 for more on SSCs). Thus far, we have focused solely on the analysis of the SOCIOLINGUISTIC styles of our Sunnyside interlocutors. In this chapter, we will be analyzing the sociolinguistic styles of the Stanfordians, as well as beginning an examination of what we have termed INTERACTIONAL STYLES.

The demarcation of two broad categories of style derives from a conception of language that considers two broad categories of STRUCTURE and USE. For the analysis of linguistic structure, a sociolinguistic study of style would focus on the varying frequencies of particular sociolinguistic variables and how they correlate with social categories, identity characteristics, or some other sociological grouping. In this study, for instance, we analyzed the sociolinguistic styles of speakers in relation to the identity characteristics of race, gender, and Hip Hop cultural knowledge. An approach that integrates structure and use allows us to broaden our focus beyond the sociolinguistic variable and considers language use by analyzing the structure of talk in interaction. This chapter presents the beginning of an interactional analysis of the discourse particle *O-kay!*

Importantly, the introduction of INTERACTIONAL STYLES is an attempt to push our efforts at theorizing style forward. Recent work on style (Bell 2001; Coupland 2001) has attempted to develop research designs suited for the study of style and to theorize style outside of the variationist box. What seems to be missing from these approaches is an analytical perspective that locates style as a continually developing project, one that is built by and through the engagement of interlocutors in conversation. For instance, Bell (2001, 139), while developing a research design similar to the one in this study, states what he takes to be the sociolinguist's core question about style: "WHY did THIS SPEAKER say it in THIS WAY on THIS OCCASION?" While this question will surely get us part of the way to understanding style, we will see that asking another question may get us even closer:

> HOW and WHEN did THESE INTERLOCUTORS, INTERACTING in THESE WAYS, CO-CONSTRUCT speech styles on THESE OCCASIONS?

Asking this question leads us down a more interesting and complex theoretical road. Instead of WHY, we are asking HOW and WHEN. The WHY question, whether intentionally or not, locates style within the individual and presupposes that the analysis will most likely end with an attempt to understand a speaker's communicative purposes and motivations (e.g., solidarity, exclusion, etc.). Our question focuses not on THIS SPEAKER but on THESE INTERLOCUTORS, which sets up our view of style as COCONSTRUCTED on THESE OCCASIONS. We are focused on interlocutors INTERACTING in THESE WAYS so that we may locate style theoretically within the context of interaction. Interaction ITSELF becomes the context. Interaction, rather than situation, becomes the focus, or rather, an additional focus, which will take us one step closer to revealing style in process.

The focus on interaction is important because some researchers who have attempted to advance style theory (Coupland 2001; Rickford 2001; Alim 2002) have utilized data that is not exactly the best fit for the theoretical conception of style advanced in this study. Coupland (2001) and Rickford (2001) have provided supporting data from radio DJs in Cardiff and Guyana, respectively, while Alim (2002) provides data from Black American Hip Hop artists. As with Bell (1984), these studies have attempted to contribute to a theory of style as it is found in human speech behavior but have used data sources that are simply not comparable to the dialogic, face-to-face nature of conversation. By extrapolating from the stylizing of radio DJs and music artists, these studies are contributing more to a theory of style as PERFORMANCE, rather than style as INTERACTION, and future development in both theoretical directions (if, in fact, we can separate them) should prove fruitful.

We will return to these points later in the chapter, but before we begin we will find it useful to synthesize the current sociolinguistic findings in order to move beyond them. The presentation of the data in this chapter represents the evolution of my thinking on this issue, beginning with the analysis of the speech of one side of the conversation, then the speech accommodation of both participants, then finally, the interactional styles of interlocutors.

SYNTHESIS OF THE SOCIOLINGUISTIC STYLE ANALYSIS

Synthesizing the major sociolinguistic findings of chapters 5(copula absence) and 6 (third-person singular *-s*) serves as a starting point for our discussion. In short, we found that the identity characteristics of race, gender, and Hip Hop cultural knowledge were all significant indicators of sociolinguistic style. Figure 8.1 displays the graphical representation of the effects of these identity char-

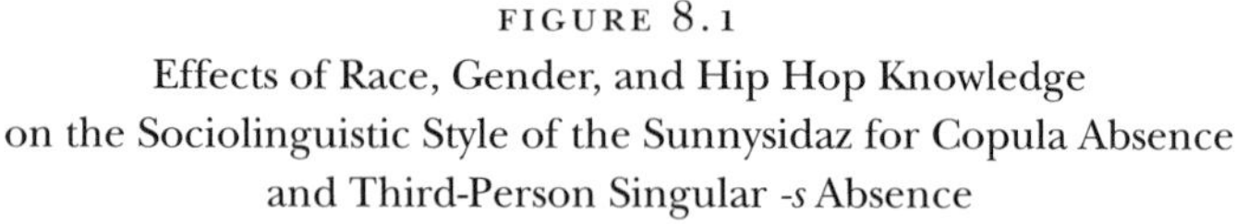

FIGURE 8.1
Effects of Race, Gender, and Hip Hop Knowledge on the Sociolinguistic Style of the Sunnysidaz for Copula Absence and Third-Person Singular *-s* Absence

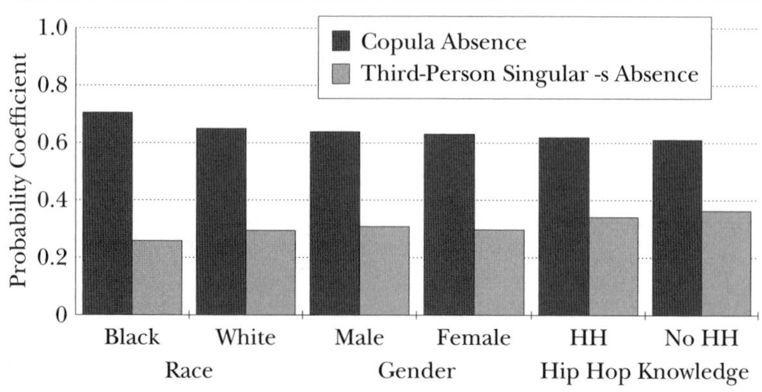

acteristics on the sociolinguistic style of the Sunnysidaz for the two variables. The first two bars within each identity characteristic indicate the rates of copula absence, and the second two bars indicate the rates of third-person singular *-s* absence. Figure 8.1 combines figures 5.6 and 6.1 presented in earlier chapters. The superimposition of these figures is done to show the remarkable, near-perfect match between the effects of the identity characteristics on the two variables.

We then analyzed the ordering of the probability coefficients to show how absence in the two variables was impacted by the eight Stanfordian interlocutors. We showed how the observed ordering of the probability coefficients for absence in each variable differed from the hypothesized ordering. As we see in table 8.1, the Sunnysidaz responded to the Stanfordians in precisely the same way for the two variables, with the notable crossover pattern of the White male Hip Hopper and the Black female non–Hip Hopper.

Figure 8.2 shows us that the BL baseline for the Sunnysidaz, which is found in the Black peer group situation, demonstrates considerably higher rates of absence than any of the SSCs with the unfamiliar Blacks and unfamiliar Whites. This suggests that there is a possibility that the Sunnysidaz would be accommodating

TABLE 8.1
Observed Probability Coefficients for the Best Run by Interlocutor Adjacent to the Hypothesized Ordering of Interlocutors

	Hypothesized Ordering	*Observed Ordering*	*Probability Coefficients Copula Absence Absence*	*Third-Person Sing. Absence*
Increasing Absence ↑	BMH	BMH	.833	.871
	BMN	BMN	.684	.607
	BFH	BFH	.663	.525
	BFN	WMH	.444	.496
	WMH	BFN	.426	.365
	WMN	WMN	.311	.258
	WFH	WFH	.194	.246
	WFN	WFN	.171	.180

NOTE: Significance in best run .000.

FIGURE 8.2
Frequencies of Copula Absence and Third-Person Singular *-s* Absence across Four Situations

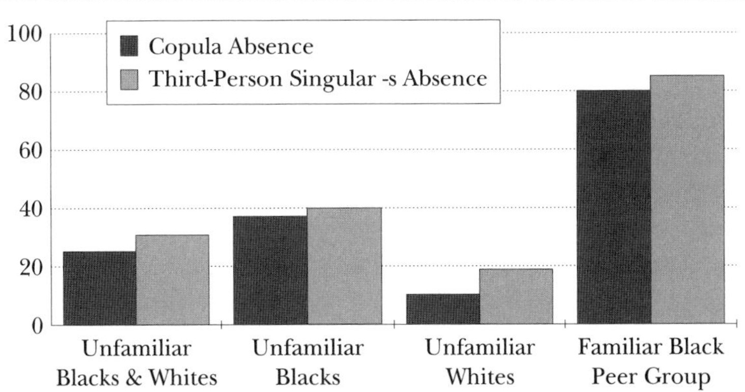

to the speech of the Stanfordians to a great degree, but this must be tested. The following section presents accommodation data for copula absence.

STANFORDIAN STYLESHIFTS

Thus far we have presented a detailed sociolinguistic analysis of the Sunnysidaz, but what of the Stanfordians? The section presents our first level of analysis, which asks the question: What is it about the Stanfordians that the Sunnysidaz are responding to? As I said in chapter 3, Bell asked a similar question in his initial formulation of "audience design" (1984, 167)—"What is it in the addressee (or other audience members) that the speaker is responding to?" He posed three possibilities:

1. Speakers assess the personal characteristics of their addressees and design their style to suit.
2. Speakers assess the general level of their addressees' speech and shift relative to it.
3. Speakers assess their addressees' levels for specific linguistic variables and shift relative to those levels.

We have, throughout this study, presented convincing evidence that supports (1), that is, the idea that the Sunnysidaz are responding to the personal characteristics (identity characteristics of race, gender, and Hip Hop cultural knowledge) of their interlocutors. We have not yet presented data that bears on (2) and (3). While it is unclear what differentiates (2) from (3), we will explore this possibility by seeing if the Stanfordians made any effort to style-shift in the direction of the Sunnysidaz. Since the process of accommodation is bidirectional, the graphs below show the copula absence rates for each Stanfordian as they interacted with each of the Sunnysidaz. Several things are immediately apparent when examining figures 8.3 through 8.10. First, while interlocutors are not accommodating to the rates of copula absence on a SPECIFIC level, there is some GENERAL accommodation being shown, particularly, though, on the part of the Sunnysidaz. Figure 8.11 represents a hypothetical display of specific, feature level accommodation, which we don't see in these data. In the figure, the hypothetical Stanfordian would be accommodating to the specific levels of absence in the speech of the Sunnysidaz. Again, this type of pattern is NOT seen in these data. Perhaps if we had examined a feature that

FIGURE 8.3
Frequencies of Copula Absence for BMH Stanfordian across Four Sunnysidaz

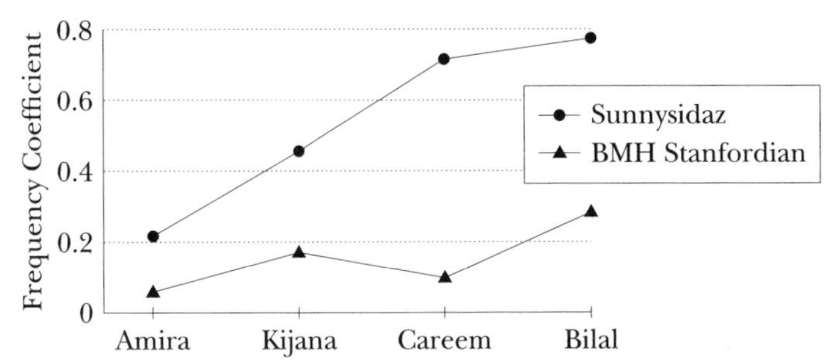

FIGURE 8.4
Frequencies of Copula Absence for BMN Stanfordian across Four Sunnysidaz

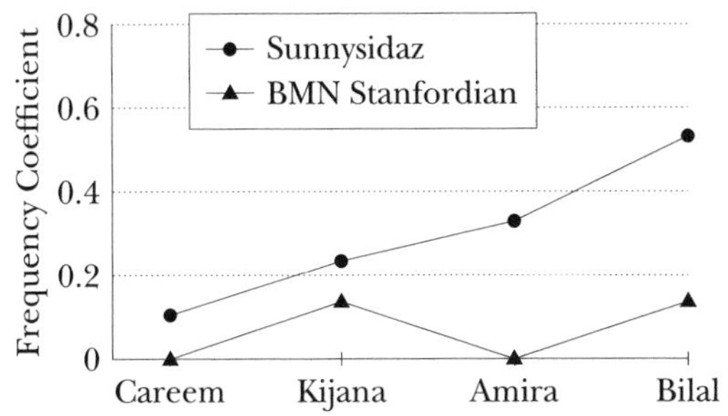

FIGURE 8.5
Frequencies of Copula Absence for BFH Stanfordian across Four Sunnysidaz

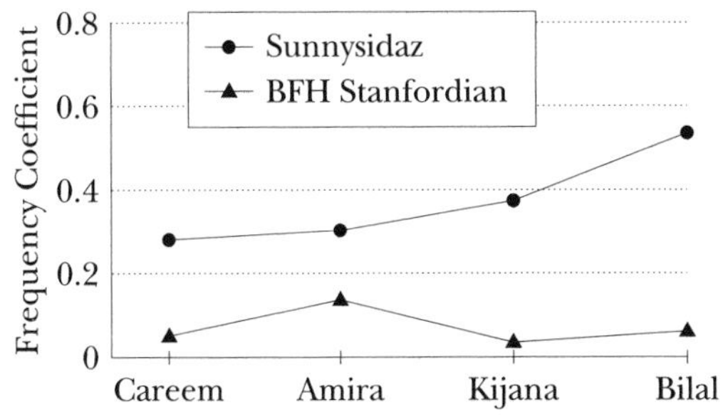

FIGURE 8.6
Frequencies of Copula Absence for BFN Stanfordian across Four Sunnysidaz

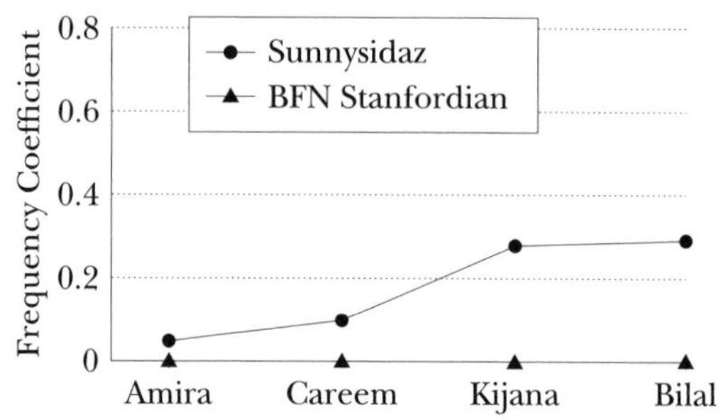

FIGURE 8.7
Frequencies of Copula Absence for WMH Stanfordian across Four Sunnysidaz

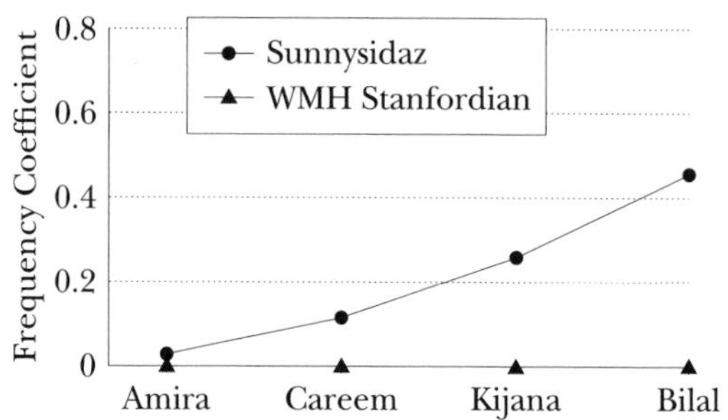

FIGURE 8.8
Frequencies of Copula Absence for WMN Stanfordian across Four Sunnysidaz

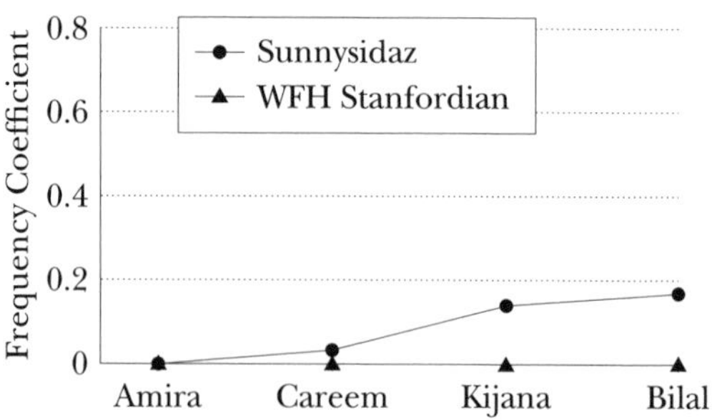

FIGURE 8.9
Frequencies of Copula Absence for WFH Stanfordian across Four Sunnysidaz

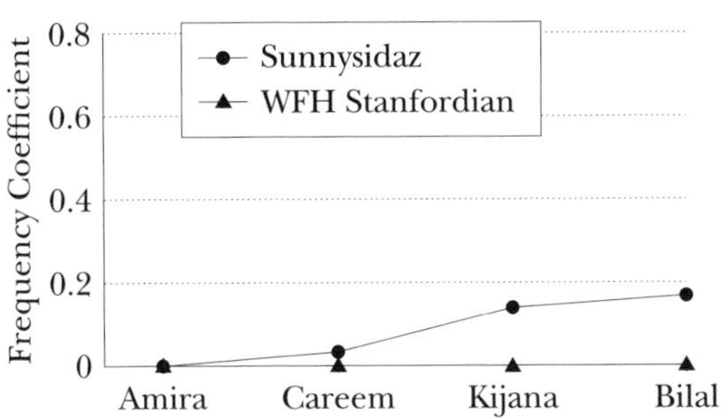

FIGURE 8.10
Frequencies of Copula Absence for WFN Stanfordian across Four Sunnysidaz

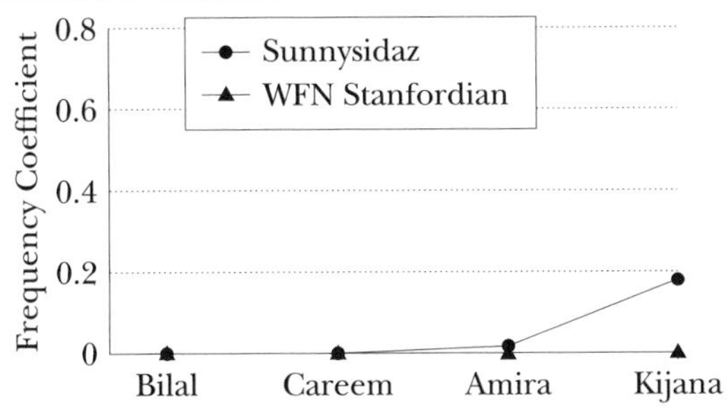

FIGURE 8.11
Frequencies of Copula Absence for Hypothetical Stanfordian across Four Sunnysidaz

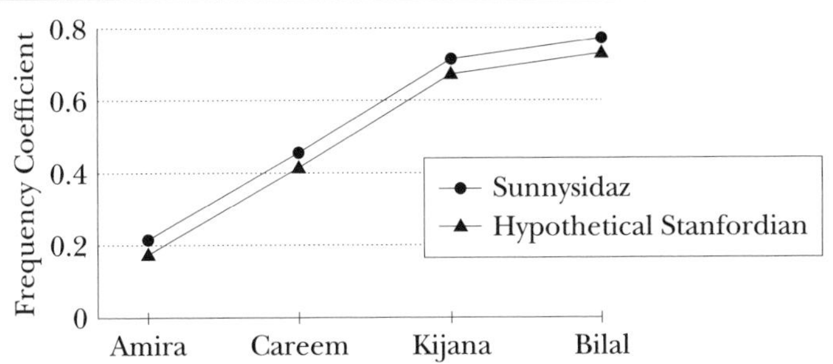

was a part of the speech pattern of all interlocutors we would have witnessed a pattern similar to this hypothetical one. None of the White Stanfordians (and the BFN Stanfordian) possessed copula absence. Only the BMH, BMN, and BFH Stanfordians exhibited copula variability.

THE SUNNYSIDAZ AND STYLISTIC FLEXIBILITY

In relation to this, the second thing we notice is that most of the accommodation is being done by the Sunnysidaz, who have a much wider range of stylistic flexibility with this variable. Take Bilal's rates of copula absence, for example. Figure 8.12 shows Bilal's varying rates of copula absence across each Stanfordian interlocutor and for his peer group.

In this remarkable case of styleshifting, Bilal displays an EXTREMELY broad stylistic range of copula absence. He goes from exhibiting 88.37% absence in his peer group to 0% absence when talking with the WFN Stanfordian (a difference of 88.37%)! If we examine his stylistic range among just the Stanfordians, we see that he goes from 77.42% absence when talking with the BMH Stanfordian to 0% again with the WFN Stanfordian (a difference of 77.42%)—a remarkable display of STYLISTIC FLEXIBILITY.

FIGURE 8.12
Frequencies of Copula Absence for Bilal across Eight Stanfordian Interlocutors and His Peer Group

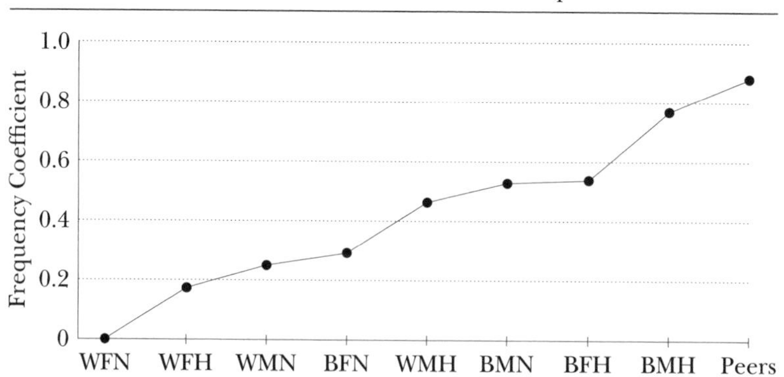

When we compare Bilal to the most stylistically flexible Stanfordian (BMH), we can see that the Stanfordians, by virtue of their lack of flexibility, are generally unaccommodating. The BMH Stanfordian's stylistic range pales in comparison to Bilal's. His highest rate of absence is 27.87% with Bilal, and his lowest rate of absence is 6.52% with Amira (a difference of 21.35%). The average stylistic range for the Sunnysidaz is 54.53%, while the average stylistic range for the Stanfordians is 5.64%. To be fair, let us remove those Stanfordians who do not exhibit copula variability. Then, the average stylistic range for the Stanfordians becomes 15.03%, still remarkably lower than the average range for the Sunnysidaz. Tables 8.2 and 8.3 display the stylistic range in copula absence for those Sunnysidaz and Stanfordians who exhibit copula variability.

Thus far, we have performed the first two levels of analysis. We have shown convincingly that the identity characteristics of the Stanfordians impact the style of the Sunnysidaz. We have also shown that the Sunnysidaz possess a vastly greater stylistic range than the Stanfordians. Given that speech accommodation is theo-

TABLE 8.2
Stylistic Range in Copula Absence for Sunnysidaz

Sunnysidaz	*Stylistic Range Calculation*
Bilal	77.42% (w/BMH) – 0.00% (w/WFN) = 77.42%
Careem	72.29% (w/BMH) – 0.00% (w/WFN) = 71.29%
Kijana	42.86% (w/BMH) – 7.14% (w/WMN) = 35.72%
Amira	32.96% (w/BMH) – 0.00 (w/WFH & WMN) = 32.69%
AVERAGE RANGE	54.53%

TABLE 8.3
Stylistic Range in Copula Absence for Stanfordians Who Exhibit Copula Variability

Stanfordians	*Stylistic Range Calculation*
BMH	27.87% (w/Bilal) – 6.52% (w/Amira) = 21.35%
BMN	13.79% (w/Bilal) – 0.00 (w/Amira & Careem) = 13.79%
BFH	14.29% (w/Amira) – 4.35% (w/Kijana) = 9.94%
AVERAGE RANGE	15.03%

retically bidirectional, we can say that it is the Sunnysidaz, possessing greater stylistic flexibility (particularly when we include the BL baseline), who are going out of their way to accommodate to the Stanfordians.

Once we recognize the bidirectionality of speech accommodation, things become infinitely more complex. Speech accommodation essentially locates the explanation of the convergence or divergence of speech styles within the individual, as psychological research tends to do. Along these lines, explanations of why speaker A is accommodating to speaker B, or each to the other, are often stated in terms of those speakers seeking some type of social approval. In this next section where we consider interaction, we can begin to move beyond cognitive explanation and towards a cultural analysis. We can also begin to move beyond variationist correlations. For example, did Bilal use his highest rate of absence with the BMH Stanfordian, and vice versa, simply because they were both Black, both male, and both Hip Hoppers? Did Amira use a high rate of absence with the BFH Stanfordian, and vice versa, simply because they were both Black, both female, and both Hip Hoppers? In general, can we REALLY explain style based on the identity characteristics of individuals? The next section will delve deeper into the conversational data to try to answer our initial question: How and WHEN did THESE INTERLOCUTORS, INTERACTING in THESE WAYS, COCONSTRUCT speech styles on THESE OCCASIONS?

LOCATING STYLE IN AND THROUGH INTERACTION: *O-KAY!*

In chapter 3, we emphasized that styleshifting occurs in and through interaction and that verbal interaction by definition requires the participation of two or more interlocutors interacting in a vast speech world (consisting of various speech communities). What became clear to me, after an analysis of my own speech behavior in the field, is that interactional style, as a possible factor in both determining the speech style and serving the expressive purposes of a given speaker, plays an important role in mediating conversation. In this section, we present an interactional analysis of the discourse particle *O-kay!* in an effort to demonstrate the need to look beyond cognitive explanation and variationist correlational explanations of style. Only then can we view style as a coconstructed, continually developing project.

In the previous section, we saw that the Sunnysidaz seemed to be doing the lion's share of the accommodating. But what about the few cases where it is undeniable that both interlocutors are accommodating to each other? We know that accommodation is theoretically bidirectional, but in some cases, we have both speakers using a high rate of absence in one, particular conversation relative to all others. For instance, we asked above: Did Amira use a relatively high rate of copula absence with the BFH Stanfordian, and vice versa, simply because they were both Black, both female, and both Hip Hoppers? The rest of the analysis will focus on this specific question.

In this interactional analysis, we will begin with a description of *O-kay!* as located within the SSC between Amira and the BFH Stanfordian. While this is not conversation analysis, our initial conception of "context" is the talk itself, as in traditional conversation analysis studies. While it is difficult to ascertain the relevance of the various kinds of "contexts," traditional conversation analysts have been criticized for not looking beyond talk to other possibly relevant contexts (such as historical context or community context). Since we have the advantage of possessing ethnographic speech data within the Sunnyside speech community, we can expand our context to include a description of HOW and WHEN *O-kay!* is used in in-group, peer interaction. (See Duranti 1997, 264–77, for a detailed account of the "context issue" from the perspective of conversation analysis and ethnography.)

First, we will present an analysis of *O-kay!* as it is used by Amira and the BFH Stanfordian in their SSC. Then, our analysis will move to the use of *O-kay!* by one speaker in the speech community context.

O-KAY! IN THE CONTEXT OF ONE SSC

We will be working with the following transcript throughout the remainder of this section. The transcript is a stretch of talk where the interlocutors, Amira (A) and the BFH Stanfordian (S), are discussing female rappers:

S: Yeah, yeah. Um, what do you think about—on the same token—like women rappers?
A: I, I, I listen to a lot of women rappers. I listen to Da Brat, Foxy...
S: Uh-huh, Da Brat...
A: ...and Lil Kim...
S: Mm-hmm...
A: ...and Rah Digga's like my favorite female...
S: Mmmmm, Rah Digga...
A: Yep...
S: ...everybody's sleeping on Rah Digga...
A: Yeah [laughter], cuz, and she writes everything that she, she, she raps...
S: Uh-huh...
A: ...and like not a lot of people do that. Foxy does that, but then a lot of, some of her stuff it IS written by males...
S: Right...
A: ...but for Rah Digga to be a MOTHER AND write her own rhymes AND be the only woman in Flipmode Squad AND be making movies now...
S: Uh-huh, and holding it down...
A: ...AND have a deep voice!
S: Right...
A: When, you, when, girls with deep voices are like, "Oh, that's manly. You a man!"
S: Mmmm-hmmm...
A: She, she comes out in one of her songs she's like, um, "They say, they say, my, they say I sound like a dude, but I'm still making more money than they are."
S: Mmmm-hmmm...
A: ...and stuff like that...
S: Mmmm-hmmm...
A: I'm like, "Just say it, just SAY it!"
S: "Speak the truth, speak the TRUTH!"

A: O-KAY!
S: [laughter] Mm-hmm...
A: And like, Foxy and Lil Kim, I like Lil Kim cuz she, she's not afraid to talk about stuff [laughter]...
S: Right...
A: ...and...
S: ...and put it out there...
A: Yeah...
S: Do you think that the women are—we were talking about, like I said that I like Hip Hop artists that are true to themselves...
A: Mm-hmm...
S: ...and you know, really speak from the heart. Do you feel like any of those, any of the women artists do that? Do you think that they are allowed to do that?
A: To be true to theirself?
S: Yeah...
A: Foxy, I think she does it the most. She, like her new album, she talks about how she's doing her own thing, how she came back from rehab cuz she tried to...
S: Right, right...
A: ...commit suicide and all that, and um, she just being true to herself now. She's not worried about all the people that done turned they back on her. She just doing this to make herself happy...
S: Mmmm-hmmm...
A: ...and she's not even, she's not even worried about the records in the past that have flopped...
S: Mmmm-hmmm...
A: ...and how bad this one's doing. She's just worried how she's gon get over...
S: Mmmm-hmmm...
A: ...different obstacles and how she's gon make herself better...
S: Mmmm-hmmm...
A: ...and I think that shows a lot about her character...
S: Right...
A: ...and how she, how strong she is...
S: Right...
A: ...and um, some people just like, a lot of male artists just think about how, how they gon sell records and how they just gon look in the eyes of the people who are buying their CD, but they, that

takes away from the impact of they music and what they're trying to say...
S: Mm-hmm...
A: ...cuz it's not reaching anybody if you just out to get money...
S: Right...
A: [laughter] and not trying to make yo public happy...
S: Right, right. Um, do you think for the most part—how do you think like—your friends and you, how much validity and respect are given to women rappers in the game?
A: Little to none [laughter]...
S: Yeah...
A: ...because there's a LOT of female rappers out there who have talent, but aren't just, just aren't exposed to people. They don't show enough skin or...
S: Right...
A: ...they aren't in with like some of the big names like Jay-Z or anybody like that, like Charli Baltimore, she, she's REALLY good and she, she useta have a lot of good stuff back in the day but then she, something happened...
S: I was like, "What happened?" [laughter]...
A: ...but now she came back, but now she wit Ja Rule...
S: Mmmm-hmmm...
A: ...and so now people are looking at her again, but she was still the same person in between them two periods...
S: Right, right...
A: ...and like Angie Martinez...
S: Mmmm-hmmm...
A: ...she's good, too, but you don't really hear anything about HER until she's with the Terror Squad or...
S: Uh-huhhh...
A: ...or with...
S: ...exactly...
A: ...somebody else...
S: ...exactly...
A: So...
S: Why do you think that is?
A: Because [laughter], it's been like that from history. Women don't get credit for [laughter], like males do, cuz they think women are inferior to men...

S: Do you, what, do you feel like—so you feel like they should have an equal place in Hip Hop, they just don't…

A: Yes, they should, cuz some women will blow some of these men out the water!

S: O-KAY!

A: Just, oh, my God!

S: O-KAY!

A: [laughter]…

S: [laughter]…

A: And, I mean, Eve, she has a lot of good things to say…

S: Mm-hmm…

A: …if you put her against like [suck-teeth] Fabolous…

S: Fabolous, right…

S and A: [laughter]…

A: Oh, no!

S: Right…

A: No…

S: Um, do you, do you see that changing or do you see what, like, what would have to—or maybe what would have to happen in order for those women to be getting credit?

A: I don't know, it is too much [laughter]…

S: Like, do you think just like more exposure so that women might, might do it, you know, because they don't get a lot of play, you know, except maybe Lil Kim, you know, like the WORST song that she might ever say would be the one to get play and then they sorta let that song speak for the rest of women rappers. Um, but I wonder, you know, is it just—is it cuz people don't have exposure to the women or is it that they just don't take what the women say?

A: I think it's both. There's not enough exposure and that people just feel, "Oh, that's a woman. She ain't talking about nuttin [glottal]. She just, just bringin more drama…"

S: Mm-hmm, so they have to listen a lot harder, huh?

A: Yeahhh…

S: …in order to get the message.

A: When the MEN are the ones bringing more drama then—cuz Nas and Jay-Z got a WHOLE BIG OLE BATTLE! Fightin [glottal] amongst each other…

S: BIG OLE BATTLE…

A: …and then everybody eatin it up, lovin it!

S: UH-HUHHH...
A: What's the difference between that and what Foxy Brown and Lil Kim is goin through?
S: Right...
A: You never heard about that...
S: Right, right...
A: You NEVER hear about that...
S: VERY true, huh? Very, VERY true...
A: And you wouldn't even know that Queen Pen didn't get along with Foxy Brown...
S: Right...
A: ...'nem...
S: [laughter] VERY true...
A: Everybody interested in like what Beanie Sigel and what everybody else is beefin over...
S: Uh-huhhh...
A: ...but when women got BIGGER beefs and they for BIGGER reasons than just...
S: Right, some radio talk-show incident [laughter]...
A: O-KAY!
S: ...or, you know, some shit like that. Um, yeah, do you have any younger brothers or sisters?
A: I have two younger sisters and two older sisters...
S: Okay, um, how, how old are your sisters, your younger sisters?
A: My younger sisters, one is thirteen, and one is nine, nine...
S: They listen to Hip Hop?
A: Yeah. My, the thirteen year old does. I don't know about the little one...
S: Uh-huh...
A: ... [laughter] she's weird...
A and S: [laughter]...
A: She's strange, but...

Before we begin analyzing *O-kay!*, an initial look at the transcript reveals that the BFH Stanfordian (S) is in control of the direction of the conversation. She introduces all of the topics, and with very direct questions (lines 1–2, 42–43, 79–81, 108, 129–31, and 172–73), while Amira responds to each question with a stream of talk. Amira's talk is punctuated repeatedly by S's moves of agreement—the extended "Mmmm-hmmm," "Right," "Uh-huhhh," and variations of these. Lines 50–77 are perfect examples of S's constant reinforcement of Amira's ideas. In these lines, Amira and S exchange an equal number of turns, yet Amira's the one expressing the ideas, while S's role seems to be strictly to show agreement. In fact, this pattern is largely the reason why Amira and S share a nearly equal number of turns (Amira 65, and S 64), despite S's command of the topic. This high level of agreement, as we shall see, appears to be a prerequisite for *O-kay!* usage.

The first instance of *O-kay!* is provided by Amira upon S's invitation (line 34). Before line 1, Amira and S are talking about the images of women in Hip Hop videos. In general, they are on the same page: Amira dislikes the images, and S supports her dislike. After hearing her out, she introduces the question of "women rappers" (lines 1–2). Amira mentions several women rappers and S repeats the ones that she likes as well (lines 4 and 8). In line 7, Amira mentions Rah Digga as her favorite female rapper, and S answers in agreement, "Mmmmm, Rah Digga" in line 8. Further, she expresses agreement with Amira by saying that "everybody's sleepin on Rah Digga," which can be translated to mean, 'everybody doesn't give Rah Digga the credit that she deserves'. Amira, in lines 11–21, then provides a litany of reasons why Rah Digga should be gettin that credit: "she writes everything that she raps, and like not a lot of people do that," Rah Digga's also a "mother," the "only woman in Flipmode Squad (a rap crew)," and she makes movies, "AND have a deep voice!" When Amira provides these reasons, S shows full agreement with "Uh-huh" (line 13), "Right" (line 16), "Uh-huh, and holding it down" (line 20, meaning, 'Uh-huh, and really good at it').

In lines 23–30, Amira delights in how Rah Digga flips the script on male hegemony in the rap game. Despite the prevailing ideology that women who have deep voices are ridiculed for sounding like men, Rah Digga confronts that ideology and mocks the men with a rap line that Amira paraphrases: "They say, they say, my, they say I sound like a dude, but I'm still making more money than they are." S again shows consistent agreement with a couple of "Mmmmhmmms." In line 32, Amira shows her total approval of Rah Digga's counterhegemonic lyrics with the repeated phrase, "Just say it, just

SAY it." S follows immediately after Amira with her own repeated phrase, and places stress on the repetition as Amira did: "Speak the truth, speak the TRUTH!" Now that the interlocutors have achieved full agreement and appear to be on the exact same wavelength, Amira follows with an "O-KAY!" in line 34, and then continues to give examples of women rappers.

The second instance of *O-kay!* is provided by the BFH Stanfordian. In lines 88–105, Amira is making a point about how female rappers don't get enough credit in the rap game unless they are associated with already successful males. She provides several examples of such female rappers and their male benefactors, if you will. The BFH Stanfordian is with Amira all the way on this one, providing multiple moves of agreement—extended "Mmmm-hmmm" (lines 94 and 99) and "Right" (line 97) and jumping in Amira's point midstream with "exactly" (line 104). They seem to be in full agreement when the BFH Stanfordian asks what can be considered a direct (even jarring) question: "Why do you think that is?" (line 108). This question throws Amira a bit, but she offers up an answer that sounds more like a "school" answer than natural response. The question—"Why do you think that is?"—could easily have been interpreted as a "school" question, where students are often asked this type of "Why" question. We can see that Amira offers two nervous laughters in her initial response (lines 109–10). The four starts to the BFH Stanfordian's next question reveal some sort of recognition of the awkwardness of her question in the context of this conversation. We can see that she shifts the verb in her first and second question from "Why do you THINK" to "do you FEEL like," in a further attempt to open up a space for Amira to express her emotions. The BFH Stanfordian's question never actually gets asked again. Rather it is rephrased in terms of the BFH Stanfordian's own beliefs: "So you feel like they should have an equal place in Hip Hop..." We can say that this rephrasing acts as a releasing of the pressure valve of direct questioning. Now we have Amira's genuine feelings (not intellectual musings) on the issue: "Yes, they should, cuz some women will blow some of these men out the water!"

It is Amira's emphatic opinion about the superiority of some women rappers that invites the BFH Stanfordian's "O-KAY!" (line

116). To this, Amira emphasizes her point with enthusiasm, "Just, oh, my God!" (which can almost be read as gratitude for the release of the pressure valve of direct questioning). The BFH Stanfordian fully approves and agrees with Amira's sentiment. In fact, it was so nice she hadda say it twice—"O-KAY!" (line 118). Amira continues her point and provides an example of a female rapper (Eve) who would out-rap a popular male rapper (Fabolous) and suggests that it would be no contest for Eve. In fact, she closes the door on the possibility, "Oh, no!" and repeats, "No."

The last instance of *O-kay!* is provided by Amira (as if exchanging *O-kay!*s with the BFH Stanfordian). Amira is responding (lines 141–69) to the BFH Stanfordian's question (lines 133–40) about whether it is lack of exposure or lack of serious attention to women that places them in an inferior position in the industry. Amira feels it's "both," and then launches into a tirade about how people pay WAY more attention to men's rap beefs than women's rap beefs. Even though some people say that females are "just bringin more drama" (meaning that they arguin over a nonsense issue that ain't worth arguin over), Amira believes that it's the MEN who have BIG OLE BATTLES over nothing. The BFH Stanfordian is showing agreement throughout Amira's talk by repeating phrases like, "BIG OLE BATTLE" (line 150), offering an extended, stressed "UH-HUHHH" (line 152), multiple uses of "Right" (lines 155, 157, 162, and 170), and even going so far as saying, "VERY true, huh? Very, VERY true" (line 159) and "[laughter] VERY true" (line 164) to show ultimate agreement. In lines 168–69, Amira is trying to express a thought about how women got "BIGGER beefs" for "BIGGER reasons than just . . ." The split-second pause allows the BFH Stanfordian to jump in with one of the stated reasons for male beefs: "Right, some radio talk-show incident [laughter]" (line 170). This example is particularly interesting in that there is perhaps no better display of agreement than completing one's statement exactly as the other person would have completed it by offering an idea that is directly in line with the other interlocutor's thinking. The only way the BFH Stanfordian knows that she "hit the nail on the head," so to speak, is by Amira's resounding, "O-KAY!" In this example, Amira's *O-kay!* acts as a crescendo to a steady stream of agreements.

Upon viewing these examples, we can lay out a possible structure for the invitation of *O-kay!* Importantly, there is an essential prerequisite of strong agreement. This agreement represents the interlocutor's recognition of "same-pagedness," that is, the fact that both interlocutors are working the same line of reasoning. *O-kay!* seems to occur in highly overlapping, rapid speech exchanges and is either immediately preceded or followed by laughter. *O-kay!*'s co-occurrence with laughter underscores the general agreeable/comfortable nature of the discourse.

Structurally, we can say that *O-kay!* occurs when an interlocutor is providing a stream of talk about a subject matter that the interlocutor feels strongly about. This strong opinion is shared in discourse that is interspersed with multiple moves of agreement (in this case, "Mmmm-hmmm," "Uh-huhhh," "Right," "True," etc.). *O-kay!* is deployed when one interlocutor recognizes and attempts to show ultimate or full agreement between the two interlocutors. *O-kay!* operates as an enabler of conversation, and thus, the talk almost always flows following its use. The following is a generic structure for the invitation of *O-kay!*

> Interlocutor A: Stream of talk about a subject matter that the interlocutor feels strongly about...
>
> Interlocutor B: Agreement move (a variable number of agreement moves can be provided by B—this "A-talk" and "B-agreement" pattern can be repeated)...
>
> Interlocutor A and/or B: Full agreement is realized by one or both interlocutors (either by an emphatic agreement move such as repetition, a series of ordinary agreement moves, or the completion of one interlocutor's thoughts by another) and possible laughter...
>
> Interlocutor A or B: O-KAY!
>
> Interlocutor A: Continuing related stream of talk (with possible laughter), and further conversation is enabled...

The breadth of our research design, and the incorporation of ethnographic techniques, has allowed us to gather speech in the community context. In the next section, this hypothesized generic structure, a conversational edifice, if you will, will be tested for consistency by examining the invitation of *O-kay!* in the speech community.

O-KAY! IN THE CONTEXT OF THE SPEECH COMMUNITY

In this section, we will present numerous examples of *O-kay!* as it is used by one speaker in the speech community context in an effort to determine both its discursive function (its semantic meaning through discourse) and the conversational structure that invites its use. In one 1.5-hour recording session, consisting of speakers A, B, C, D, E, and F, speaker A uses *O-kay!* on nine different occasions. From these nine instances, we can determine the discursive function/semantic meaning of *O-kay!* fairly certainly. We should point out that a complicating factor in the speech community context is that our examples move from a two-party conversation to a multiparty conversation. This, as we will see, contributes to the difference in the conversational criteria required for *O-kay!*'s invitation.

Let's take example (1). Speakers B and A have just explained to speaker F that people in the speech community have various names for different sections of town. Speaker B explains that these names used to represent "sets" (usually associated with some kind of criminal or gang activity on the streets), but nowadays, people just be usin them to identify folks. When speaker B describes one set as GRIMY, F asks about the difference between that section and the others:

EXAMPLE 1

1 F: Like you said that section was GRIMY, right...
2 B: GRIMY!
3 F: Does that—why is it different from other places?...
4 B: I ain't gon get into all—can't touch on that on camera, cuz...
5 A: O-KAY!
6 B: ...you know what I mean? [laughter]...
7 F: [laughter] FORREAL, is it like...
8 B: Nah, every set grimy, but it's just...

Speaker B avoids explaining why "the M" is considered GRIMY (associated with lots of criminal-gang street activity) with the line: "I ain't gon get into all—can't touch on that on camera, cuz..." As he pauses, speaker A reinforces his wish not to touch on that on camera with an, "O-KAY!" Speaker A is not only reinforcing speaker B, but A is also showing full agreement, as if to say, "we on the same page." Speaker B continues with a "you know what I mean?" and laughs.

Already, in this first instance of *O-kay!* in the community context, we are led to modify our hypothesized structure. This peer, in-group conversation differs from the SSC in two important ways. First, there are more than two interlocutors, so that the possibility of a third interlocutor acting as commentator on the discourse between two other interlocutors is present. Second, by definition, interlocutors who are members of a peer in-group share a higher level of common understanding than would be held between two strangers. These two main differences call for a change in our structural hypothesis. First, we see that no agreement moves are necessary in (1). The new subject is introduced by F (F is referring to a previous conversation), and F asks a question about this subject (line 3). B answers with a statement that trails off with "cuz...," allowing A to *O-kay!* B then continues the talk. Here the structure can simply be:

> Speaker F: Question about a particular subject...
> Speaker B: Answer to the question...
> Speaker A: O-KAY!
> Speaker B: Continues discourse...

Here, no prior agreement moves are necessary. However, agreement is still a prerequisite. *O-kay!* here expresses a shared, common understanding, rather than a final stage of building agreement. One can say that the building of agreement has already taken place in prior life experiences where both parties share a common understanding that "the M" ain't a nice place to be. One can also say that *O-kay!* is acting primarily as a cosigner.

In example (2), all of the speakers walk up to the current site of what used to be an old high school in the neighborhood. The participants are describing the now gentrified area ("the sunny side of Sunnyside") as a place where their parents attended high school. Speaker F, who is relatively new to the community, opens this snippet of dialogue by asking about what structure was previously located on the site of what is now a great, big shopping mall:

EXAMPLE 2

B: This is the sunny side of Sunnyside...

F: Now what is all this stuff? When I first came here, there was just buildings. When did this all get started?

D: Like, couple years ago...

B: Probably a couple years ago...

F: Couple years ago...

D: It's still fresh...

B: They tore down the little—I mean, they BEEN tore down the little Raven High School, but they started...

D: They coulda built that right back up!

A: O-KAY! My mama useta go there. She MAD!

F: What was here? What was here?

C: Wooooh, it feels good right here... [in the shade]

B: Originally, a long time ago...

A: It was a college and Raven High School...

B: Raven High School, everybody went to college...

F: THIS was Raven High School?

D: Yep...

A: Yeah, this whole area...

B: This big-ass lot, ALL OF THAT!

F: This whole place?!

B: ALL OF THAT...

A: This WHOLE area...

D: Ghetto high school...

F: [falsetto] Get the hell outta here?!

In the conversation, speaker B is describing how they (the city) tore down Raven High and built a monster shopping mall in its place. But before he can finish his statement, D jumps in with an emphatic: "They coulda built that right back up!" Speaker A hears D loud and clear and supports, affirms, and emphatically agrees with the anger she sensed in D's comment: "O-KAY!" Speaker A then continues to respond to D's anger by providing an example of community anger over the demolition of Raven High: "My mama useta go there. She MAD!" In this example, F is asking a straightforward question, and B and D are providing a straightforward answer. It is only when D expresses a strong opinion that A comments on the discussion with an *O-kay!*, cosigning D's opinion about what the city coulda done.

Example (3) occurs shortly after example (2) and begins with speaker A discussing how her mom attended Raven High:

EXAMPLE 3
A: My mom useta go to high school—this whole area, right here...
D: Everybody useta come here. It's like Sunnyside right here...
A: ...where ALL this new, all these new buildings are, this useta be Raven High School...
F: [falsetto] REALLY?
B: They just had a reunion a couple weeks ago...
D: Yep!
B: ...a couple months ago...
D: Yep!
F: They said it was NUTTIN over here!
C: I KNOW you ain't [?]...
D: SHIIIIIT, it was high school...
B: SHIIIIIT, it was Raven...
F: This was the REAL high school for everybody around...
B: Everybody...
A: Everybody useta go here. It was KNOWN...
B: [?]
A: It was no Sunnyside high school except...
F: Did any of y'all parents go to Raven?...
B: YEAHHH!
D: Yep, my mama did...
F: Forreal?!
B: YEAH, aunties, uncles, they all went here!
A: O-KAY!
C: My dad, my aunties, uncles, EVERYBODY...
B: This was the high school...
F: You mean the high school was THAT big that it filled up the whole place?

D: It was cool as hell—had a big-ass track and everything...
B: It filled up ALL OF THAT...
A: Yep!
F: Oh, yeah?!
A: It useta be—hell, I'll bring you a yearbook!

Speaker A is the one who opens up the subject of parents and Raven High by telling everyone that her mom attended Raven High. She further claims that EVERYBODY useta go to that high school and that it was KNOWN. Speaker B supports A's statement by saying "aunties, uncles, they all went there!" and gets an emphatic "O-KAY!" of agreement from speaker A, who later offers to bring in a yearbook to prove it. In this example, A, B, and D are all stating straightforward facts about who used to attend Raven High. It is when B takes it to the next level by providing a string of folks that he knows went there (and thereby supporting A's claim that EVERYBODY went there) that we get the *O-kay!*

Example (4) is nearly identical to example (2). The dialogue resembles (2) in that the speakers are all upset about the gentrification of their community. Again, we see speaker A expressing strong dislike with the current situation of the community. The others are also in agreement, and B offers up a solution other than removing the older community businesses: "All they had to do was make the buildings more nicer..." To this, A emphatically agrees: "O-KAY!" We enter the discussion where the speakers are describing the part of town known as "over the ramp":

EXAMPLE 4
F: When you say over the ramp, y'all mean right over there?
D: Yep...
B: Right where they buildin them hotels and stuff at...
F: What are people saying?...
A: What the fuck we need a hotel for?! What the fuck?!
F: Yeah, what are people saying about all this?
A: Why we need a hotel?!
F: What are people saying about all this stuff that's coming up?
B: Because it's gonna bring in revenue...
D: Yeah, people say it's money...
B: Economics and shit...

D: Yeah...
B: ...bring the economics to Sunnyside...
A: I mean, that's takin part of our heritage outta there...
B: ...revenue, basically...
A: ...cuz I mean, we, we, that's where people was *raised* and stuff!
B: All they had to do...
A: ...going into donut shops, into the fish spot over there, and the fried chicken spot...
B: ...is improve the buildings over there...
A: ...and now the hotels...
C: Ooooh, the fried chicken spot!
B: I forgot about the fish place...
C: I wish we had a chicken spot...
D: I know, I miss that!
B: All they had to do was make the buildings more nicer...
A: O-KAY!
B: That's all they had to do, all [?]...
A: And just get them promotion, maybe they would sell stuff...

Speaker A's use of *O-kay!* here follows B's suggestion that something else could have been done to rescue the older community businesses in much the same way that her *O-kay!* followed D's suggestion that the city could have just rebuilt the high school instead of tearing it down. In both cases, A is upset at the destruction of community institutions and welcomes, supports, and emphatically agrees with other solutions offered by the group. Again, agreement moves are not necessary due to a common understanding and life experiences (memories) of the community's recent history.

In example (5), the group is talking about how they useta go to Shadyside, the wealthy, neighboring town, for Halloween because they usually gave out better candy than Sunnyside folks (sometimes they even gave out money). But, as speaker B warns, "But see at the same time, they be puttin shit IN the candy."

EXAMPLE 5
B: But see at the same time, they be puttin shit IN the candy, so...
D: MM-HMM! Them White people...
A: Yep...
F: What do you mean puttin shit in the candy?

B: [laughter] They be puttin stuff in the candy...
A: That's why when you go over there you gotta check yo candy after, cuz they be putting razor blades and shit...
D: Yep, they be doin that...
F: NAHHHH...
B: ForREAL!
D: Mm-hmm...
A: One year, somebody put a razor blade in like this candy apple thing and a kid...
D: MM-HMM!
A: ...bit into it and they tongue got cut off...
F: Over in Shadyside?
A: Yep!
D: Yep...
F: You gotta watch out cuz sometimes that's where the loonies be at...
D: MM-HMM!
B: Hell yeah, rapists and stuff...
A: O-kay!
F: And so, basically, okay, hold on [laughter]... [as white couple walks by to get into their shiny Black Volvo]
A: What?! Say it!
B: Go head!
A: Don't be—they in OUR TOWN...

We can see that the conversation takes a turn when speaker B warns about the dangers of Shadyside during Halloween. After speaker A provides a real example of what can happen to you if you trick-or-treat there, speaker F warns, "You gotta watch out cuz sometimes that's where the loonies be at..." This example gives us a real sense of what *O-kay!* means to this community of speakers. In response to F's warning, D emphatically agrees, "MM-HMM!" and B emphatically agrees and offers a specific example of the types of "loonies" that may be out there: "Hell yeah, rapists and stuff." So, both D and B have shown emphatic agreement with "MM-HMM!" and "Hell yeah." It is then that speaker A responds directly with a resounding "O-KAY!" showing that she truly shares the sentiment. Again, although there are agreement moves prior to the *O-kay!*, the *O-kay!* serves primarily to co-sign the good example offered by speaker B.

At this point, it may seem redundant to offer more examples of the use of *O-kay!*, but this next example follows directly from the conversation in example (5) and provides us further, more concrete clues to *O-kay!*'s meaning. The group continues where they left off, as the white couple comes walkin by:

EXAMPLE 6

F: And so, basically, okay, hold on [laughter] ... [as White couple walks by to get into their shiny Black Volvo]

A: What?! Say it!

B: Go head!

A: Don't be—they in OUR TOWN...

F: I was just gonna ask you where do you think they from right there?

D: Shadyside...

A: Ooh, her eye gone [woman is wearing a patch] so maybe Sunnyside [laughter]...

B: Some rich town, Shadyside...

D: Shadyside...

B: It might be Shadyside—there's no McDonald's in Shadyside...

F: Oh, yeah, it ain't no—ain't really no McDonald's...

E: They got the high stuff that's like that expensive Japanese restaurant and...

B: That El-Camino...

D: I know!

F: Like the sushi spot [laughter]...

A: [laughter] Plutos...

B: Chilis and Taxis and shit, that's what they got...

D: Nine dollar sandwiches...

A: Taxis is they closest thing...

F: ...to McDonald's, right...

A: They useta have a Burger King, but they shut that shit down...

B: Subway and Pizza A-Go-Go [laughter]...

D: You know!

A: O-kay!

D: Yep...

F: So, like let's say...

A: Plutos...

F: ...a couple of years ago or whatever, you might not have seen that...
B: HELLLL NAW!
F: ...the Volvo station wagon...
A: Never!

All of the speakers are of one mind as they run down the list of restaurants that exist in Shadyside, noting how that town does not have cheap fast-food-type restaurants like McDonald's or Burger King. It's when speaker B offers some other names of restaurants like "Subway and Pizza A-Go-Go," and laughs, that speakers D and A respond simultaneously with different utterances. Since all speakers are in agreement, both of these utterances, "You know!" and "O-KAY!" are used to show emphatic agreement and to announce "same-pagedness." In fact, this example is especially useful in that D's "You know!" can be substituted for any one of A's *O-kay*'s. This is not a questioning "You know?" or a "You know what I'm saying?" It functions as if that person has said, "I know, you know, we all know!"

These next two instances of *O-kay!* provide even further evidence of the semantic meaning. The group is discussing, really mocking, Latinos/Mexicans by painting stereotypical depictions of them. After they have enough of that, speaker B asks an interesting question, and apparently it's a question that A has thought about before as well. We enter where speaker A is mocking Mexicans:

EXAMPLES 7 AND 8
A: Oh, my gosh, you ain't NEVER seen as many cars that go through here with like ten or seven heads in they car...
All: [laughter]...
B: A-haaaa, pack it up!
All: [laughter]
A: ...it be a two-seater...
All: [laughter]...
F: Who is usually in the seven- to ten-person car?...
A: Uh, Mexicans [laughter], and you can't even say Hispanic cuz the Latinos don't even do that, cuz some Latinos be havin them whipped out cars...

B: THAT I will say—somehow, how they HELL they ballin more than us? . . .
A: O-KAY!
B: . . . you know what I mean?
F: How the hell they WHAT?
B: . . . they got more money than us?
A: O-KAY!
B: I mean, I understand they IS smart. They fix they own shit . . .
A: But it ain't that many, it ain't that many yards in the world that they can clean up . . .
C: Who?
B: The Mexicans . . .
A: . . . and that many houses they can redo to get that much money . . .

A offers emphatic support and agreement for B's question—TWICE. This example further shows the use of *O-kay!* when a speaker feels that they are on the same page with another. A's use of *O-kay!* allows B to keep on goin. B offers an explanation, suggesting legitimate means as to how Mexicans can be better off than the speakers' group. Speaker A, still in line with a need to offer some sort of explanation for the Mexicans' perceived wealth, suggests that they must be doing something else (perhaps illegal) to make that money. Clearly, both speakers share a frustration at their group's poorer economic standing. Further, both speakers have a shared common understanding of the relations between ethnic groups in the community.

The final example only offers further support to what we have argued above. Again, the group is trying to come up with reasons for why Mexicans are in a better position than their group. Speaker F asks:

EXAMPLE 9
F: Do people say that—I mean, are they doin okay for themselves or are they . . .
B: HELLLL, YEAHHH!
A: Mm-hmm . . .
D: MM-HMM, hell yeah . . .
B: Because they stick together; they ain't selfish . . .
A: O-KAY!

Speaker A again here is showing emphatic support and agreement to B's reasoning.

Now that we have delineated the semantic meaning of *O-kay!* in the speech community context, we can begin to lay out a more detailed conversational structure for its invitation. By looking at the structure of the conversations where *O-kay!* occurs, we can begin to ask questions like: When is it okay for *O-kay!* to be used in conversation? When is it not okay? What has to be present in the conversation for *O-kay!* to occur? What conversational work are interlocutors doing to allow for O-*kay*? Or broadly, how and when does *O-kay!* occur?

O-KAY! AS A POTENTIAL SYMBOLIC MARKER OF BLACK FEMALE IDENTITY

Up until this point, we have not mentioned that fact that *O-kay!* is said only by Black females, at least in the data collected for the present study. Actually, in all 32 SSCs, *O-kay!* is used only by Amira and the BFH Stanfordian, and ONLY in that one conversation. Also, in the community context data, the only person to use *O-kay!* is Amira, although there are three other females present. One can hypothesize that *O-kay!* indexes Black female identity, but if so, how? In other words, how does the analyst know that Amira and the BFH Stanfordian are announcing their Black femaleness by using *O-kay!*? Is it enough to say that *O-kay!* is not said by any White speakers in the study or by any Black males in the study? Further, is it enough to say that this researcher has never heard *O-kay!* used by Black males in all of his three years in the Sunnyside speech community? One can assume that Amira and the BFH Stanfordian are doing their best conversational work to show that they are both Black females, SISTAS, and that they are using *O-kay!* as a strategic display of solidarity. But, how does the analyst know that this is the case, particularly when speakers are often not reliable interpreters of their own subconscious speech behavior (and many interactional norms are subconsciously learned)?

Schegloff (1991, 50–51) puts the analyst's dilemma in these terms, and is worth quoting at length:

> The alternative type of solution insists on something else, and that is that professional characterizations of the participants be grounded in aspects of what is going on that are demonstrably relevant to the participants, and at that moment—at the moment that whatever we are trying to provide an account of occurs [e.g., an instance of *O-kay!*]. Not, then, just that we see them to be characterizeable as "president/assistant," as "chicano/black," as "professor/student," etc. But that for them, at that moment, those are terms relevant for producing and interpreting conduct in the interaction.... Now let us be clear about what is and is not being said here. The point is not that persons are somehow not male or female, upper or lower class, with or without power, professors and/or students. They may be, on some occasion, demonstrably members of one or another of those categories. Nor is the issue that those aspects of society do not matter, or did not matter on that occasion. We may share a lively sense that indeed they do matter, and that they mattered on that occasion, and mattered for just that aspect of some interaction on which we were focusing. There is still the problem of SHOWING FROM THE DETAILS OF THE TALK OR OTHER CONDUCT IN THE MATERIALS that we are analyzing that those aspects of the scene are what the parties are oriented to. For THAT IS TO SHOW HOW THE PARTIES ARE EMBODYING FOR ONE ANOTHER THE RELEVANCIES OF THE INTERACTION AND ARE THEREBY PRODUCING THE SOCIAL STRUCTURE. [emphasis mine]

According to Schegloff and other formal conversation analysts, the talk ITSELF is the relevant context, and any other way of explaining what is relevant to speakers is "positivistic." However, as Duranti (1997, 266) points out, researchers such as Hymes (1974, 81) and Goffman (1976, 32) disagreed with this definition of context—with Goffman actually referring to such an approach as the "sins of noncontextuality." Whereas Hymes and Goffman, and linguistic anthropologists in general, would argue that ethnographic data (such as the knowledge of both speakers being Black female Hip Hoppers) enlarges the context and is relevant to that particular interaction, Schegloff and other conversation analysts would argue that such terms can hinder our analysis of social structure if they are not warranted by their application to that particular moment on talk.

Given that our data on *O-kay!* suggest that it is used only—or at least used primarily—by Black females, we can begin to ask an interesting set of questions. Since *O-kay!* is not used by ALL Black females, which Black females use it? Is there any other community that uses *O-kay!*, such as gay males, for instance? If so, is the structure of its invitation similar or different to what we have found? Are there ever any instances of *O-kay!* that are not responded to? More generally, what happens when *O-kay!* is used incorrectly, that is, when a speaker does not follow the appropriate rules of interaction?

In this data, it is difficult to determine what would happen if a speaker did NOT follow the appropriate rules of interaction for the use of *O-kay!* This is because all users of *O-kay!* are members of the broader Black speech community. As linguistic anthropologists have shown, for any given speech community, there are rules of interaction without which rules of syntax are useless (Hymes 1974). These rules of interaction, or communicative norms, are learned in and through language socialization within a community of speakers. They are unwritten and largely subconscious ways of speaking that authenticate one's membership within a given speech community. Amira and the BFH Stanfordian do not ever respond inappropriately to *O-kay!* because both females have been raised up in Black speech communities and participate actively in Hip Hop Culture, a cultural world that privileges distinctly Black modes of discourse and interaction. So, in a very real sense, I need to expand my database to obtain more *O-kay!* examples, beginning first with instances of *O-kay!* in two-party, peer-group conversations in the community context. This would be the ideal data set needed in order to compare the structure of *O-kay!* invitations in the SSCs and the speech community. One could also imagine a data set that had one of my Sunnysidaz in a multiparty, non-peer-group conversation, which could be compared to the multiparty, peer-group conversation presented above. More data across a wider variety of speakers is needed.

What I can do is offer cases in the present data where I think *O-kay!* could have been used, but wasn't. This may be one way to strengthen the current analysis of *O-kay!* usage. Let's take this example:

C: So, like, I only like Christian acts that have original music...
B: Yeah...
C: ...and I think that's what you can't do...
B: I don't like when they...
C: ...you can't sacrifice the music...
B: Maaan...
C: ...for saying, "Oh, Jesus, Jesus, Jesus!" Like, at least—don't like...
B: I hate, I hate...
C: [shuddering] Uuuughhhh!
B: I hate groups that copy the same beat off a rapper...
C: And just...
B: ...switch the words around...
C: YESSSS!
B: And God...
C: Dude!
B: Maaan, I hate that!
C: Dude!
B: I hate that!
C: Dude!
B: So much!
C: I hate that so much! Like there's this one rapper...
B: [shuddering] Uuuuuughhhh!
C: ...and he took the beat for, "Every other city we gooo..." and I'm like, "How you gon make a Christian song outta that?!"
B: [laughter]

In this conversation, we see that the conditions exist for *O-kay!* usage. We have speaker C, who is making a strong point about his dislike of unoriginal Gospel musicians. Throughout his point, B is making several agreement moves ("Yeah," "I don't like when they...," "Maaan," "I hate, I hate..."). Then we have an interesting sequence where both speakers are so in line with each other that they finish each other's thoughts (which we described above as an ultimate sign of agreement):

B: I hate groups that copy the same beat off a rapper...
C: And just...

B: . . . switch the words around . . .

This could very well have been one speaker saying: "I hate groups that copy the same beat off a rapper and just switch the words around." So, while C is making his point, B agrees by providing an example of unoriginality that he really hates. This supporting case is read by C as full agreement, which is shown by his use of "YESSSS!" This "YESSSS!" could very well have been replaced by "O-KAY!" Without telling the reader anything about the speakers, all of the necessary preconditions are there. Well, if it was made known that these speakers are Black males, would that make a difference in our interpretation? Could we say that *O-kay!* didn't occur because it was two Black MALES talking, rather than FEMALES? Well, since we do not have any instances of Black males using *O-kay!* within the everyday interaction of the speech community, we can argue (albeit cautiously) that the communicative norms of the Black speech community forbid this use by Black males.

But, does this argument hold any water if we have a similar case of possible *O-kay!* use by Black females? Can we conclude that *O-kay!* is part and parcel of the speech community's gendered communicative practices? Let's look at the next example:

S: How do you feel about—now that I said women—um, women in videos? . . .

A: Mmm-hmmmm, hmm, hmm [laughter], wow, um, I like the girls who dance in videos like Aaliyah's video, like "Rock the Boat" . . .

S: That DANCE . . .

A: DANCE! Not just . . .

S: Right . . .

A: . . . do all of this . . .

S: Right, right [laughter] . . .

A: "Oochiwallie, wallie . . ."

S: Mmmm-hmmm, mmmm-hmmm . . .

A: . . . [laughter] and all that stuff, no. That's not something—and like the "Big Pimpin" video . . .

S: Right . . .

A: . . . Don't you have respect for yourself? Because do you hear the words to the song? I mean . . .

S: And you're right up there like . . .

A: Yeahhh...
S: ... "Heyyyyy!"
A: ...and he's pointing to you and then like when you off camera, "Oh, oh, this song's not about me, I'm just dancing." ACTUALLY, you're the face of the girl...
S: Actually, right...
A: ...who's in the video...
S: Right...
A: ...being talked about...
S: Uh-huhhh...
A: ...and when somebody sees on the street, they gon...
S: Associate you with that...
A: ...identify you...
S: Right, right...
A: ...and that's not worth it. You can have respect for yoself and keep yo clothes on...
S: Mmmm-hmmm...
A: Why don't you be the girl in the video with Common or like Mos Def, being the girl who is just the center of they life?...
S: Right...
A: ...just they girlfriend. You can get just as much attention...
S: Right...
A: ...and not have to take yo clothes off...
S: Right...
A: ...and [suck-teeth], I mean, dancing is a art form, and I think that it takes some of the credit off dancing by just girls just doing...
S: Shakin...
A: ...yeah, just shakin...
S and A: [laughter]...
A: ...just to do it...

For the conversation analyst, "Right" here is used in a space where we would accept *O-kay!* The pattern of a speaker expressing a strong opinion in a stream of talk that is interspersed with agreement moves and recognizing clear agreement based on the completion of one another's thoughts is present. But why "Right" and not *O-kay!*? Importantly, these structural preconditions do NOT necessitate the use of *O-kay!*, they simply are mandatory if we are to hear *O-kay!* emerge. There are a number of alternatives for the same set of preconditions that speakers within the speech community may choose among, so the nonexistence of *O-kay!* in an *O-kay!*-relevant moment in the speech of Black females does NOT negate the argument that *O-kay!* is a symbolic marker of Black female identity. The case for *O-kay!* as a symbolic marker of Black female identity is strengthened by the fact that there are NO *O-kay!*-relevant moments in Black male discourse where *O-kay!* actually occurs. Instead, we see suitable substitutes such as "YESSSS!" "You know!" and "True dat!" ('that's true').

While *O-kay!* does not seem to occur in heterosexual Black male discourse, there is anecdotal evidence that suggests that it may be used by gay male speakers. A Black female in her 30s recently reported the use of *O-kay!* by a gay Black male in his 50s. They were discussing the educational struggles of non-English-speaking students when, according to her, "he busted out with it." I have also heard *O-kay!* being used by gay males of other ethnic communities, but I have not yet come across any recorded examples. Clearly, this needs to be followed up with further research in gay speech communities. Are gay males appropriating features of Black female discourse, such as *O-kay!*? Is the use of *O-kay!* invited in much the same way that it is invited in Black female discourse, or are there differing circumstances that lead to its use? What does the use of this discourse particle mean in relation to the performance of sexuality, gender, and race?

AN INTEGRATED APPROACH TO THE STUDY OF SPEECH STYLE

While we still need to investigate the use of *O-kay!* more thoroughly (using more sources of data), our point for this study is to demonstrate how an examination of interactional style can elucidate the ways in which style is coconstructed. By being familiar with the rules of interaction for the use of *O-kay!*, and communicative norms in general, the BFH Stanfordian was able to invite informality from Amira in ways that other Stanfordians could not. This takes us beyond examining sociolinguistic accommodation based on specific sociolinguistic variables and starts us on an increasingly complex mode of analysis that explores the work that speakers do in order to coconstruct style and meaning. While varying levels of copula absence may correlate with the identity characteristics of interlocutors (as we have shown), we have no way of telling HOW that is accomplished unless we examine deeply and thoroughly the structure of the talk that is produced. It is my belief that an approach to style that integrates sociolinguistic variation, interactional analysis, and ethnographic fieldwork will get us much farther down the road to understanding how and when speakers shift their styles. The central question for analysts still remains: How and WHEN did THESE INTERLOCUTORS, INTERACTING in THESE WAYS, CO-CONSTRUCT speech styles on THESE OCCASIONS?

9. THE GENTRIFICATION OF SPEECH AND SPEAKERS: BLACK LANGUAGE IN WHITE PUBLIC SPACE

> I mean, I think the thing that teachers work with, or COMBAT the most at Haven High, is definitely like issues with standard English versus vernacular English.
>
> —Teacher at Haven High in Sunnyside, 2003

> The crisis is not about education at all. It is about power. Power is threatened whenever the victim—the hypothetical victim, the victim being in this case, someone defined by others—decides to describe himself. It is not that he is speechless, it is that the world wishes that he were.
>
> —James Baldwin, National Symposium on the 1979 "Black English Case," 1981

Any study of Black Language (BL) must take into account the persistent racial tensions that exist between Black and White communities in the United States. Wolfram's (1974) paper on the controversial nature of Black-White speech relations begins with a comment that observed Black-White speech differences are "still interpreted by some" through the White ideological lens of Black inferiority. This is a point that has been understated in the literature and is now beginning to be newly interrogated by studies of "Whiteness" (see below). Further, to my knowledge, no study of BL directly examines the multiple reasons—historic and contemporary—for interracial tensions between the two groups in a given community. The next section provides the community context as a necessary precondition for examining Black Language in White public space. It is within this context that the following sections are to be interpreted.

THE GENTRIFICATION OF SPEECH AND SPEAKERS

As we discussed in chapter 4, Sunnyside was once a thriving Black community that led the nation in Black consciousness and nationalism, establishing the nation's only independent Black preschool-through-college educational system in the 1960s and 1970s. Since the government's forced closure of the city's only high school in the 1970s, the Black community has experienced an increasing sense of displacement in what was once known as "a Black city," as the Latino population rises and Whites begin to move in slowly. For two decades, the community did not have a high school and Black students experienced a 65% dropout rate in the schools of the neighboring suburbs, all of which were predominantly White and upper middle class. The gentrification of the community by White real estate developers is directly linked to educational concerns, since the city's new 28-acre, high-end shopping plaza (and several expensive hotels) stands on the grounds of the former high school (similar situations are occurring nationwide from Oakland to Atlanta to New York).

As we saw in chapter 4, the previous generation celebrated the demolition of the old, dilapidated structure of the city's only high school, while the current generation laments the displacement of Black people from a city that no longer HAS a public high school. As the city continues to raise revenue through continued development, rent control legislation is being overturned and more and more Blacks are being forced out of the area (the community is now about 20% Black in 2004, and needless to say, the economic independence of Black people in Sunnyside has not been attained). Tensions between Blacks and Whites, and other ethnic groups, continue to rise in this small city, as well as distrust for Whites. Whites are seen as outsiders who are "scared" of Blacks and who are only in Sunnyside to either commute to work or if "they buyin drugs."

In this context, Black youth in Haven High will often comment on how they see their teachers (mostly White) only when they are exiting or entering the community on the nearby freeway ramp. The fact that White teachers don't spend time in the community only reifies feelings of social distance and distrust between students and teachers, which can be a major source of tension in the schooling experiences of Black youth. As one student put it, "Man, they don't know what it's like here—they act like they know, but they don't know... they CAN'T know."

Just as economic institutions are gentrifying and removing Black communities around the nation and offering unfulfilled promises of economic independence, one can also say that educational institutions have been attempting (since integration) to gentrify and remove Black Language from its speakers with similarly unfulfilled promises of economic mobility. In both cases, the message is: "Economic opportunities will be opened up to you if you just let us clean up your neighborhoods and your language." Most Blacks in the United States since integration can testify that they have experienced teachers' attempts to eradicate their language and linguistic practices (see Morgan 2002 on "outing schools" and Smitherman 2000b) in favor of the adoption of White cultural and linguistic norms. I'll return to this point at the end of the chapter.

BLACK LANGUAGE STRUCTURE AND USE

We now turn our focus to language within this context, BL as a complex system of structure and use that is distinct from White Mainstream English (WME) in the United States. While it is true that BL shares much of its structure with WME, there are many aspects of the BL syntactic (grammar) and phonological (pronunciation) systems that mark it as distinct from that variety. If we examine syntax alone, sociolinguists have described numerous distinctive features of BL, such as those analyzed in this volume. Additional features include *steady* as an intensified continuative ("She STEADY prayin her son come home," meaning 'She is intensely, consistently and continuously hoping her some comes home'; Baugh 1983), stressed *BIN* to mark remote past ("I BIN told you not to trust that woman," meaning 'I told you a long time ago not to trust that woman'), *be done* to mark future/conditional perfect ("By the end of the day, I BE DONE collected $600!" meaning 'By the end of the day, I will have collected $600!'; Baugh 1983), aspectual *stay* ("She STAY up in my business," meaning 'She is always getting into my business'; Spears 2000), third-person singular present-tense *-s* absence ("I know who run THIS household!"; Fasold 1972), possessive *-s* absence ("I'm braidin Talesha hair"), multiple negation ("I ain't never heard about no riot big as the one we had in LA"; Labov 1972a), negative inversion ("Can't nobody touch E-40!"; Sells, Rickford, and Wasow 1996), and several other features (see Rickford 1999). It is important to note that many of these distinct BL features are used in variation with WME features as most speakers possess an ability to shift their speech styles, to varying degrees (not all BL speakers have the same stylistic range). I am conceptualizing BL to include the full range of styles, including WME, as speakers deem appropriate.

While much of the sociolinguistics literature has focused on distinctive phonological and syntactic features of BL, most researchers are aware that BL cannot simply be defined as a checklist of features that are distinct from WME (Morgan 1994). Aside from having an ever-evolving LEXICON (Turner 1949; Major 1970; Dillard 1977; Folb 1980; Anderson 1994; Smitherman 1994, 2000a; Stavsky, Mozeson, and Mozeson 1995; Holloway and Vass 1997), speakers of BL may participate in numerous linguistic practices and cultural modes of discourse such as SIGNIFYIN (and BUSTIN, CRACKIN, CAPPIN, and DISSIN) (Abrahams 1964; Kochman 1969; Mitchell-Kernan 1971, 1972; Labov 1972a; Smitherman 1973, 1977; Morgan 1996), PLAYIN THE DOZENS (Abrahams 1970; Brown 1972), CALL AND RESPONSE (Daniel and Smitherman 1976; Smitherman 1977; Alim 2004b), TONAL SEMANTICS (Smitherman 1977; Keyes 1984; Alim 2004c), BATTLIN and ENTERING THE CIPHER (Norfleet 1997; Newman 2001; Alim 2004c), and the use of direct and indirect speech (Spears 1998; Morgan 1998), among others.

BL, then, refers to both linguistic features and rules of language use that are germane to Black speech communities in the United States. In the following sections, we see how the richness of BL goes completely unnoticed and is regularly censored in White public space. We also see how speakers manipulate BL and how use of BL can often lead to misinterpretation and conflict for Blacks languaging in White public space, particularly educational institutions. While differing rules of language use are certainly part of what sometimes creates misunderstandings in intercultural communication, miscommunication often occurs in sociopolitical and sociohistorical contexts where communities (and their languages) are in conflict for economic, political, and social reasons as we touched on above (see Lippi-Green 1997).

BLACK LANGUAGE IN WHITE PUBLIC SPACE

The racial segregation present in American society has led some scholars to use the term "American apartheid" to describe the deliberate isolation and exclusion of Blacks from educational, occupational, and social institutions in the United States (Massey and Denton 1993). Perhaps it is centuries of persistent segregation between Blacks and Whites that accounts for the dearth of significant studies of Black-White intercultural communication, with the notable exception of Kochman's (1981) *Black and White Styles in Conflict*. Additionally, when Blacks and Whites do interact, as Kochman (1981, 7) points out, "Black and white cultural differences are generally ignored when attempts are made to understand how and why black and white communication fails." One could argue that most Black-White intercultural communication occurs either in schools or on the job, where Blacks and Whites are "forced" into contact and Whites tend to be in the position of power. In this sense, I will draw on "White public space" as used by Page and Thomas (1994; cited in Hill 1998, 683): "a morally significant set of contexts that are the most important sites of the practices of racializing hegemony, in which Whites are invisibly normal, and in which racialized populations are visibly marginal and the objects of monitoring ranging from individual judgment to Official English legislation." Whites in educational and occupational settings may exercise their power in obvious ways (such as giving an order or firing an employee) and less obvious ways. As research on "Whiteness" argues (Frankenberg 1993; Yancy 2000), Whites exercise power through overt and covert racist practices, which often reveal racist ideologies that even the "racist" may be unaware of (Hill 1998). In our case, WME and White ways of speaking become the invisible and unmarked norms of what becomes glossed as "communicating in academic settings." Further, White public space refers not only to physical space, but also to most interactional spaces in which Blacks encounter Whites, particularly White strangers or Whites in positions of power over them. In both cases, Blacks work to maintain a social face (Goffman 1967)—or the "mask," as poet Paul Laurence Dunbar described in his 1895 poem and rappers The Fugees rhymed 101 years later—"the image and impression that a person conveys during encounters, along with others' evaluation of that image" (Morgan 2002, 23).

The fact that it is the language and communicative norms of those in power, in any society, that tend to be labeled as "standard," "official," "normal," "appropriate," "respectful," and so on, often goes unrecognized, particularly by the members of the dominating group. This dialogue with a teacher from Haven High serves as the entry point to our discussion of how BL (and its speakers) are viewed in American educational institutions. We enter the dialogue as the teacher describes the "communication" goals of the school and the language and communication behavior of her Black students. We return to some of the key words and phrases emphasized in this passage:

> Teacher: They [Haven High] have a lot of presentation standards, so like this list of, you know, what you SHOULD be doing when you're having like an oral presentation—like you should speak slowly, speak loudly, speak clearly, make eye contact, use body language, those kinds of things, and it's all written out into a rubric, so when the kids have a presentation, you grade on each element. And so, I mean, in that sense, they've worked with developing communication. I mean, I think the thing that teachers work with, or COMBAT the most at Haven High, is definitely like issues with STANDARD English versus VERNACULAR English. Um, like, if there was like one of the FEW goals I had this year was to get kids to stop sayin, um, "he was, she was..."
>
> Alim: They was?

T: "They was. We be." Like, those kinds of things and so we spent a lot of time working with that and like recognizing, "Okay, when you're with your friends you can say WHATEVER YOU WANT but... THIS IS THE WAY IT IS. I'M SORRY, BUT THAT'S JUST THE WAY." And they're like, "Well, you know, it doesn't make sense to me. This sounds right." "She was." Like, and that's just what they've been used to and it's just...

A: Well, "she was" is right, right? You mean, like, "They was"?

T: "They was."

A: And "we was" and that kinda thing...

T: Yeah, "we was." EVERYTHING IS JUST "WAS."

A: [laughter]...

T: And like, just trying to help them to be able to differentiate between what's ACCEPTABLE... There's a lot of "ain't," "they was," "we ain't not..."

A: [laughter]...

T: And THEY CAN'T CODESWITCH that well...

A: Uh-huh...

T: Um, and I have to say it's kind of DISHEARTENING because like despite ALL THAT TIME THAT'S BEEN SPENT FOCUSING ON GRAMMAR, like, I don't really see it having helped enormously. Like, if I stop them in class and they're like, you know, "The Europeans, they was really blah-de-blah..." and I'd be like, "OH, THEY WAS?" And they'd be like, "they were," like they'll correct themselves, but it's not to the point where it's NATURAL... They're like, "Why does it matter?"

A: "You knew what I said, right?"

T: Yeah ... I'm not sure they understand WHY it's necessary...

A: Do you have any other ideas about language at the school, like maybe the way the kids speak to themselves versus the way they speak in class, or do you notice...

T: Well, I mean, of course, they're not gonna be as FREE as when they're speaking to each other when they're speaking to me. I mean, I guess the only thing is not so much spoken language as it's like unspoken language, like tone, like a lot of attention is paid to like tone and body language, in terms of RESPECTFUL ATTITUDES.... For a lot of kids, they don't see the difference. They're like [loud voice and direct speech] "Yeah, I just asked you to give me my grade. Like, what's the big deal?" And I'm like, "You just ordered me. I mean, you talked to me like that." Like, it's like, [loud again] "You didn't give me a grade!" like that, it's very ABRASIVE, but they don't realize that it's abrasive. And so, I mean, it's just like, I guess, teaching them like the nuances of like when you're talking with people, what's APPROPRIATE? Should you be sitting up, or should you be kinda be leaning over [and she leans in her chair]...

A: [laughter]...

T: Like that your body language and your facial features like speak just as loudly if not MORE loudly than what you ACTUALLY say... I mean, just even bringing awareness to that, like, it's upsetting to them and it's like shocking to them that we'll comment on that, like, MAYBE THEIR PARENTS LET THEM GET AWAY WITH THAT AND SPEAK TO THEM THAT WAY and having to be like, "Hey, you know what, like, maybe your parents let you, but here that's never acceptable." Like, there's just so many—I mean, thinking about it, it's just, it's asking a lot of them to do, not only to speak standard English but to know all these other like smaller nuances that they've never experienced before and never had to think about. Like, it's probably on some level pretty overwhelming to them to have to deal with all of these things at once. Because, I mean, their parents say "they was"...

A: Yeah, is there any talk about what they're being expected to do, and what they do ordinarily, in the community, in the home, or anything?

T: Um, I mean, not officially or regularly, but I'll always be like, "I know you might speak this way at home, but in an academic setting, or if you're interviewing for a job, or if you're applying to college, and you talk to someone like that, they will like not even give you the time of day"...

A: Do they ever ask why?

T: Yeah, they're just like, you know, "Why?" and I'm like, "I DON'T KNOW!" [laughter!] "YOU KNOW, THAT'S JUST THE WAY THAT IT IS! YOU HAVE TO LEARN HOW TO PLAY THE GAME GUYS! I'M SORRY."

A: Right, and I can see that being such an inadequate answer for a student who doesn't care about "they was" or "they were," being like, "What's the difference? What's the big deal? Like what's the overall picture?"

T: Right, and I DON'T KNOW HOW TO PROVIDE THAT...

A: Yeah...

After several years as a teacher-researcher at Haven High and in Philadelphia schools, I marvel at how remarkably consistent teachers' ideologies of language are, particularly in response to the language of their Black students. The language of the Black child is consistently viewed as something to eradicate, even by the most well-meaning teachers. In fact, this particular teacher is genuine about her commitment in seeing as many of her students attend four-year colleges as possible. And when she states, "I have to say it's kind of disheartening because like despite ALL that time that's been spent focusing on grammar, like, I don't really see it having helped enormously," one gets the sense that she is actually disheartened and saddened by her lack of results.

What teachers like this one are probably not aware of is how they are enacting Whiteness and subscribing to an ideology of linguistic supremacy within a system of daily cultural combat. It is revealing that the teacher describes the language of her Black students as the thing that teachers at Haven High "COMBAT the most." In fact, her attempt to eradicate the language pattern of her Black students has been "one of the FEW goals" she has had throughout that academic year. The teacher not only works to eradicate the language pattern of her Black students, but responds negatively to what she calls "unspoken language," or the students' "tone." Black students and their ways of speaking are described with adjectives like "abrasive" and not "respectful." This attribution of negative characteristics due to cultural differences has been noted frequently in studies of intercultural communication (Gumperz 1982a, 1982b).

Interestingly, the teacher notes her students' failure to speak "standard English"—particularly in the case of what's known as the generalization of *was* to use with plural and second-person subjects (Wolfram 1993)—while she fails to make several linguistic distinctions herself (her own language being only marginally "standard"). Not only does the teacher erroneously point out "he was" and "she was" as cases of BL (this is actually WME) and imply that BL has a random system of negation ("we ain't not" is actually not found in BL or any other language variety in the United States), but she is clearly not aware of the stylistic sensitivity in the use of *was* and *were.* When the teacher says, rather exasperatedly, "Everything is just 'was,'" she is not recognizing the subtle stylistic alternation of *was* and *were* that is employed by BL speakers, where speakers alternate their use of *was* and *were* based upon various contextual and situational factors, including the race of the person with whom they are speaking. In fact, the teacher goes as far as to say that her Black students do not have the ability to "codeswitch." Somehow, despite the vitality of BL, teachers continue hearing what's not said and missing what is (see Piestrup 1973; Smitherman 1981).

The teacher's claim that her Black students do not possess stylistic sensitivity in speech (what she calls "codeswitching" and I call "styleshifting") is erroneous, given the remarkable stylistic flexibility we witnessed in chapters 5–8. The following section reports on misunderstood Black linguistic practices and the resulting conflicts with Whites.

BLACK LINGUISTIC PRACTICES

Not only do Black youth possess and deploy a variety of sociolinguistic styles, but there are numerous Black linguistic practices that are misunderstood and misinterpreted in White public space. As part of my experience as a teacher-researcher in Sunnyside, I trained students to become "hiphopographers"—that is, ethnographers of Hip Hop Culture and communication. As such, they were responsible for documenting and describing the linguistic practices of the most recent instantiation of Black American expressive culture: Hip Hop Culture. Several examples of linguistic practices that they described follow. Terms in small capitals indicate other practices and lexical items also described by the class. The first practice is BATTLIN, a form of Black verbal dueling associated with Hip Hop Culture and the verbal art of rhyming (Spady, Lee, and Alim 1999). The second is HUSH MODE and SCRATCH THAT GREEN OFF YO NECK, two phrases associated mostly closely with Black female interaction, argumentation, and play. Both of these entries highlight the value placed on verbal creativity and competition in the Black speech community. The third is ROGUE, a localized example of semantic inversion (where the negative meaning proscribed by the dominating group is flipped on its head) used ONLY within the 2.5 square miles of Sunnyside. All of these examples below are taken from student writing that is part of a larger project where students describe and document their own linguistic practices.

BATTLIN (noun) (verb) and FLOW (noun) (verb). Battlin involves more than one person. A FREESTYLE rapping contest when a group of people take turns rapping lyrics. They don't write the lyrics; they say them as they think of them off the top of their heads. As they take turns rapping back and forth, they're actually competing. In the end, the judges or the people watching the competition vote who won the competition and who had the better lyrics. Sometimes it is just obvious to the contenders who won by who DISSED/ CLOWNED the other better. Also judged by who had the better meaning behind his/her words.

> JT and T-Reezy were battlin in the grass last week; they got on each other. JT got on T-Reezy's braids and face and T-Reezy got on JT about his height and women/girls.

The term comes from the idea of fighting with words. A battle is set up like a fight. One contender takes one side and the other takes the other. They rap at each other (in turn, though) until one gives up or a specific winner is announced. Usually done by males—those who tend to be street affiliated. Males talk about guns, women, SETS (areas of affiliation), and other topics. Done at clubs, social events, on street corners, etc. Takes the place of actual fights at parties where people FLOW—to have a smooth current of rap lyrics. If a person messes up their rap lyrics while saying them, then they ain't flowin. Flowin does not necessarily have to rhyme, as long as your words go good together.

HUSH MODE and SCRATCH THAT GREEN OFF YO NECK (phrase). Hush mode is when you get CLOWNED (get talked about rudely) and don't have a remark or comeback for that person. To be dumbfounded. Usually used when instigating or talking about a fight or argument.

Aisha: Shut up, Tee!
Tee: [doesn't say anything]
Tereese: She got you on hush mode!

When somebody get CAPPED ON, and that person don't have anything to come back with, then the person who capped on them would say, "I got you on hush mode."

> For example, say Shahira and Bibi are capping on each other and Shahira says to Bibi, "Yo mamma so old she used to gang bang with the Hebrews." If Bibi can't come back with something, then Shahira would say to her, "I got you on hush mode."

While we were defining the word, Jamal got on Tereese nerves and she said she was gon hit him…

Tereese: I'mma bust you in yo mouth.
Jamal: [silent]
Aisha: Oooh, Jamal, she got you on hush mode.
Jamal: She ain't got me on hush mode.
Tereese: I'mma hit you in yo mouth.
Jamal: I WISH YOU WOULD.

Females use this phrase a lot because they tend to instigate more than males. Males sometimes use it when they want to start something. Someone might tell you to "scratch that green off yo neck" after you been hush moded. Not sure of the origin of this phrase, but it's used after someone has been proven wrong.

> For example, say two people are arguing and one of them got proven wrong, then someone would say to them, "Oooh, scratch that green off yo neck."

ROGUE (noun). A word that people use as a substitute for another person's name. Originated in Sunnyside, California, and mainly used in Sunnyside. JT uses it a lot to say hi to people. "What's up rogue?"

Waz up rogue?
Dang, rogue, what you doing?!

See DOGG, HOMIE, PATNA.
Males use it more, but females do often use it. Used by all races in Sunnyside. Used mainly with the younger generation.

> Aisha was CONVERSATIN with Shahira on the phone and at the end she said, "alright, rogue." Then her mom asked her why they call each other rogue.

All of these linguistic practices can be misunderstood by Whites not familiar with Black culture and language. For example, while Black youth place extreme value on the verbal inventiveness and competition involved in battlin, teachers broke up the biggest rhyme battle in the school because, as one student relayed, "Whenever they see a group of Black folks they automatically think it's a fight!" One teacher described the event in these words, "Whatever they were doing, it wasn't appropriate on school grounds." If Whites were more aware of the verbal creativity of Black youth and their penchant for verbal games, perhaps their linguistic practices would not be so misunderstood. Rather, they would be utilized for pedagogical purposes. As Labov (1972a, 212–13) wrote plainly decades ago:

> The view of the black speech community which we obtain from our work in the ghetto areas is precisely the opposite from that reported by Deutsch or by Bereiter and Englemann [verbal deprivation]. We see a child bathed in verbal stimulation from morning to night. We see many speech events that depend on the competitive exhibition of verbal skills—sounding, singing, toasts, rifting, louding [and battlin]—a whole range of activities in which the individual gains status through his use of language. We see the younger child trying to acquire these skills from older children, hanging around on the outskirts of older peer groups, and imitating this behavior to the best of his ability. We see no connection between verbal skill in the speech events characteristic of the street culture and success in the schoolroom.

The incident above is not merely a matter of communicative misunderstanding. An issue that is often not taken up by studies of intercultural communication, but is certainly central to them, is the fact that Black verbal competition was interpreted as VIOLENCE. This interpretation must be understood in relation to the White racist view of Blacks as violent, despite the fact that it is Whites who commit most of the violent crimes in American society. This misunderstanding is particularly poignant when the students' definition of *battlin* includes the notion that it often "takes the place of actual fights at parties."

Several questions for studies of Black-White intercultural communication remain: Why is it, despite ample evidence from sociolinguistic studies and theory that different speech communities possess different, yet theoretically equivalent, linguistic rules and rules of language use, that BL and linguistic practices continue to be denigrated and underappreciated by Whites, particularly in educational institutions? What is at the ROOT of this denigration and misinterpretation? How is it that the ideology and practice of LINGUISTIC SUPREMACY—the unsubstantiated notion that White linguistic norms are inherently superior to the linguistic norms of other communities, and the practice of mapping White norms onto "the language of school," "the language of economic mobility," and "the language of success"—persists, even WITHIN the subjugated group? What is the role of communicative misunderstanding in maintaining and perpetuating tensions between communities? How do we understand communicative differences not as the source of tensions but as a means of perpetuating and reinforcing those tensions? How do we move beyond searching for communicative mismatches to explain intercultural tensions and conflicts that already exist due to the larger and systematic social, political, and economic subjugation of a group? Or worse yet, as we see in Eades (2004), will greater knowledge of communicative differences be used FOR or AGAINST justice? As overt forms of racism begin to be publicly sanctioned in most areas of the United States, linguistic differences are currently being used to exclude Blacks from full participation in society in a number of ways (see Baugh 2003 on LINGUISTIC PROFILING in housing discrimination based on "Black-sounding" voices and Bertrand and Mullainathan 2003 on differential access to employment based on "Black-sounding" names). Studies of language need to address these questions if sociolinguistics is to remain relevant to dominated populations. Such studies are essential since the problem with BL has more to do with Black PEOPLE than Black LANGUAGE. Given the emerging studies addressing the role of BL in various forms of discrimination, more scholars are beginning to see the BL "problem" as one that is part and parcel of a sociostructural system of White racism in the United States.

For this generation of Black youth, how do we avoid explanations of Black academic failure as the result of Black "opposition" to formal schooling and begin interrogating the daily cultural combat (conscious or unconscious) against Black language and culture in White public space? How do we go beyond the oft-heard and inadequate teacher's response to Black resistance to White cultural and linguistic norming: "I don't know!" [laughter!] "You know, that's just the way that it is! You have to learn how to play the game guys! I'm sorry"? Responses of this type are enactments of Whiteness that put the onus on the oppressed group at the same time as they alleviate the dominating group of any responsibility. In this case, when pushed, the teacher is willing to admit that she is not equipped to provide an answer for the underlying reasons of what I have called the gentrification of BL—this is a start. The continued gentrification of BL is the cultural analogy to the physical removal of Black communities by White developers. As one of my students so passionately expressed her resistance to the gentrification of the community in which she was born and raised, "I mean, that's takin part of our heritage outta there, cuz I mean, we, we, that's where people was RAISED and stuff! [she pauses for a brief second, glaring over the freeway ramp, and adds] ... and now the hotels."

While Blacks around the nation continue to be removed from their communities, BL persists despite every attempt by Whites to eradicate it. The community continues to resist these efforts to "renew" its language for reasons so clearly articulated by Black writers and artists.

> The language, only the language.... It is the thing that black people love so much—the saying of words, holding them on the tongue, experimenting with them, playing with them. It's a love, a passion. Its function is like a preacher's: to make you stand up out of your seat, make you lose yourself and hear yourself. The worst of all possible things that could happen would be to lose that language.... It's terrible to think that a child with five

different present tenses comes to school to be faced with books that are less than his own language. And then to be told things about his language, which is him, that are sometimes permanently damaging.... This is a really cruel fallout of racism. [Morrison 1981]

A Black teacher in Philadelphia provides a different perspective: "The reason why Black students continue to speak their language is because, really, if you think about it, it's the ONE THING that they own in this world. It's the one thing that NOOOOBODY can take away from them. NO-body."

CONCLUSION: FACING AND FIGHTING THE CHALLENGE

By this point, if the responses to my teacher workshops are any indication, there are probably many of you who are asking a "philosophical" question: "What are you saying, Alim—are you proposing that teachers should NOT teach 'standard English'"? Here's what I'm proposing. First and foremost, we must begin with an understanding that there is nothing STANDARD about "standard English." Standard simply means that this is the language variety that those in authority have constructed as the variety needed to gain access to resources. What we have, then, for a "standard" in the United States is nothing short of the imposition of White linguistic norms and ways of speaking in the service of granting access to resources to Whites and denying those same resources to as many others as possible, including poor Whites (LINGUISTIC SUPREMACY goes for VARIETIES of a language as well as languages other than the dominating language, whatever it may be).

Secondly, I take the statement that I've heard from so many teachers, linguists, and scholars—"Well, fair or unfair, that's just the way the world works"—as a STARTING point for the discussion that we need to be having, not as an END point. This is truly where philosophical interrogation begins. Rather than agreeing, for one reason or another, that we HAVE to provide "these students" with "standard English," I ask: By what processes are we all involved in the construction and maintenance of the notion of a "standard" language, and further, that the "standard" is somehow better, more intelligent, more appropriate, more important, etc., than other varieties? In other words, how, when, and why are we all implicated in LINGUISTIC SUPREMACY?

Thirdly, many well-meaning teachers and scholars who insist on the teaching of "standard English" to Black youth are under the assumption that BL is a monostyle, that is, that BL can be described as one style of speaking that is identifiably Black. As these data have shown, Black youth possess a broad range of speech styles (review Bilal's stylistic flexibility when talking with a White female non-Hip Hopper and in his peer group, for example). It makes more sense, that is, it is more in line with the data on Black stylistic variation, to consider BL as the whole range of styles within speakers' linguistic repertoires. Part of speaking BL is possessing the ability to styleshift in and out of in-group ways of speaking. This is not astonishing. But somehow, when it comes to Black youth, some are under the impression that they are mired in this monostylistic linguistic ghetto (this is certainly a contemporary strain of linguistic deprivation thinking). But the ghetto can be a beautiful thang—that is, speakers such as Bilal, who have had a full range of experiences as Black youth, naturally (and quite obviously) vary their speech styles in different situations and contexts. Any time spent in Black communities would reveal that Bilal speaks to his minister and the Nation of Islam mosque in one way, to his White teachers in another, to his grandmother in another, to his girlfriend, father, brothas on the block in yet another. And certainly, since he's forced to look for employment outside of his community, as a sporting goods store employee he will speak to White customers and non-English-speaking customers in yet another style. And why should we expect him not to? The question is: If the Black speech community possesses a range of styles that are suitable for all of its communicative needs, then why the coercion and imposition of White styles?

Lastly, while it may be true that many Blacks would resist a pedagogical approach that did NOT focus on "standard English," it is ALSO true that there are many Blacks who view access to White ways of speaking as part of "playing the game" (Urrieta forthcoming).

That is, as one of my informants put it, "If you livin in the White man's world, you gotta play by the White man's rules. At least as long as THEY runnin shit." As is often the case, subjugated populations develop survival strategies that seem antithetical to linguistic emancipation. This does not mean that it is futile to attempt to develop ways to eradicate LINGUISTIC SUPREMACY. This means that scholars dedicated to LINGUISTIC EQUANIMITY—the structural and social equality of languages—have to work equally as hard among both the oppressors and the oppressed. This is the challenge—and it is one worth fighting for.

APPENDIX A: TRANSCRIPT OF ONE SEMISTRUCTURED CONVERSATION

C AND BILAL, MAY 4, 2002
(approx. 40 min.)

ABBREVIATIONS

ca = copula absence
cc = copula contraction
cf = copula full
m = singular-plural mismatch
3a = third-person singular *-s* absence
3p = third-person singular *-s* presence
pa = possessive *-s* absence
pp = possessive *-s* presence
AAf = African American falsetto

C: Hot topics.
B: Hot topics... Uhhh, Suge Knight.
C: WOAH! Suge KNIGHT!
B: [laughter]
C: I didn't go there, but uhh, word, aight, Suge...
B: Yep...
C: Kid's scary, maaan...
B: Yeah, I was just—I look at this little Web site every day hiphopdx.com...
C: hiphopdx?
B: Yeah...
C: Aight...
B: It's a little thing that gives news and stuff, and it was asking Suge Knight how he feel [3a] about Eminem, Snoop, Dr. Dre, and Puffy or whatever...
C: Aight...
B: ...and Jennifer Lopez...
C: [laughter]
B: So, for Eminem, he was like [laughter], "He a little funny little kid," or whatever...
C: Serious?

B: He said he had NEVER signed Eminem or whatever, because…

C: [AAf] Forrreeeaaaalll?!

B: That's what he said. He was like, "He [ca] more of like a funny comedian," whatever. He was like, uhh, he wanna give a opportunity to the people out the hood, out the hood, give them the opportunity or whatever to…

C: Like he's saying Eminem ain't out the hood?

B: …blow up. That's what he was saying.

C: Aight [laughter].

B: He wanted to give ghetto people a opportunity…

C: That's true, he always been like that…

B: Yep, and then Dr. Dre, he was like he respect [3a] him, you know, he ain't got nuttin against him; he just, you know, he haven't [3a] talked to him, yet, but he said he ain't got nuttin against him, he ain't got nuttin to say; he said he's [cc] a good person and stuff like that…

C: [AAf] He did?!

B: Yep, he said he didn't have nuttin to say about him.

C: What about Snoop Dog?

B: Snoop!

C: Daaaaag! My boy!

B: He said the main reason why he [ca] mad at Snoop, really, because, you know, when Snoop had that little murder trial or whatever…

C: Yeah…

B: …he said he put up like $4.5 million to get him out, you know, get him out of what he did.

C: Forreal?

B: He didn't say he really did it, but he was like, "I put the money up for you and this is how you treat me?"

C: Daaaag!

B: And stuff like that. Then he was like…

C: Shhhhhhhh…

B: …he was like, "Snoop [ca] scared to come out with stuff. I ain't seen Snoop since I been out!"

C: [laughter!]

B: "I go to clubs and stuff and he [ca] scared to be out, you know, I ain't gon do nuttin to him…"

C: [laughter!]

B: …you know what I mean? So…

C: I don't know, maaan, I mean, cuz I'm from LA, duuude…

B: Yeah…

C: ...and like, Suge is [cf] scary, dogg.
B: He is, really?
C: Straight up...
B: He really is, huh?
C: I mean, [AAf] that fool will shoot...
B: [hand clapping and laughter]
C: I'm even scared to put something on tape cuz I don't know where this might end up!
B: [hand clapping and laughter]
C: I'ma use a fake name...
B: [laughter]
C: I'm SERIOUS!
B: I'm serious [laughter]
C: [AAf] Suge got connections! I ain't messin with Suuuuge!
B: He do, he do got connections...
C: [to tape recorder] I ain't got nuttin bad to say about Suge.
B: [to tape recorder] Me either.
C: [to tape recorder] I'm scared of you. I mean...
B: I'm just quoting...
C: [laughter] I mean, but the way I think is like, sometimes, I mean, Suge is [cf] pretty smart...
B: Yeah...
C: ...as far as a business man, so, he knows [3p] he won't—he can't say anything bad about Snoop...
B: Yeah...
C: Dre, Eminem, or anybody...
B: Yeah...
C: ...Nas, because they're [cc] the tops.
B: Yeah...
C: ...you know what I'm saying?
B: The tops.
C: So people got they back right now...
B: Yep...
C: ...like the public got their back. So if he disses somebody—that's why...
B: ...then it's gon make him look bad...
C: ...that's like, "Death Row's [cc] against," you know, "who the top people are..."
B: Yep...
C: ...you know, that's gon make people pick sides...

B: Yep...
C: ... and that's dumb to like divide up...
B: Yeah, that's true...
C: ... yo customer base like that...
B: [laughter]
C: He's not gon do nuttin like that...
B: Yeah...
C: So, but every now and again he'll say som'in, and he'll just have like a little twinge of like animosity in his voice...
B: Did you—were you at—did you hear about the West Coast Summit thing?
C: Yeah, didn't he like, he, didn't he call Dre [AAf] gay or something like that?
B: Yeah, it was like, I mean, he [ca] poseta be one of the pioneers of Hip Hop, where he [ca] at? Where Snoop and Dre at? Why they ain't here? Why Master P 'nem ain't here?
C: That's what he saiiiid?
B: Yep.
C: Damn, I didn't know he like went off like that...
B: But then everybody forgot about what he was saying about how we should invest money into more independent labels and stuff like that, and have the money for—something like that...
C: Yeahhh, yeahhh...
B: Something positive he was saying. Russell Simmons was like, "Everybody don't forget that, what he said..."
C: That's true...
B: It's the NEGATIVE stuff people always remember...
C: Always wanna hype up...
B and C: So...
C: So, do you think, umm, do you think he had anything to do with like Biggie's [pp] death at all?
B: [laughter] Honestly, I feel that, he had—not, I really can't say, it's hard, cuz I don't wanna say like he did...
C: [hand clapping and laughter]
B: ... but I kinda get the feeling that he did have something to do with it.
C: ForREAL?
B: I don't... [laughter]
C: ... or at least like allowed it to happen or something like that...
B: Allowed it to happen. I think he coulda...
C: [laughter]

B: I don't know, man… I mean…
C: [He knew about it (?)]
B: That's all…
C: [That's a lot of coincidence (?)]
B: He knew about what was gon happen…
C: Daaaag…
B: I think at least…
C: [Do you think he knows who did it? (?)]
B: Yep, I think he know [3a]…
C: Wow, that's powerful…
B: Yep…
C: …man…
B: He had—man, cuz my cousin—not my cousin, but my friend, Brian—he goes [3p] to Longbeach State…
C: Oh, forreal?
B: Yeah, he said Suge Knight, like you was [m] saying, he got a lot of connections out there…
C: [AAf] I mean…
B: …so, like with police officers and stuff like that, so I was like, "Maaan, like THAT?" I didn't know it was LIKE THAT! So…
C: He has peoples, man, I mean, that's how it—I mean, basically, if you look at anybody that like runs the city…
B: Uh-huh…
C: They got people EVERYWHERE. They'll have some kinda like affiliate or connection in any…
B: [laughter]
C: …influential area, whether it's courts…
B: Yeah…
C: …or whether it's the police…
B: Yeah…
C: …politicians or like businesses. And I mean, there's a reason why he has such a reputation, like and you know, he might use that reputation for good…
B: Mmm…
C: …or for bad, whatever, but he uses it to benefit himself…
B: Yeah…
C: …but to me, man, like, it's smart like—I'm all for supporting people that come out the hood…
B: Yeah, me, too…
C: …because it's, you know, [AAf] that's what we should do…

B: Yeah, that's what we should do...

C: ...each one, teach one... BUT, what I'm NOT for is when people like get a better life and they still act ignorant...

B: Yeah, exactly...

C: Like, and I'm not gon diss you—I'm not dissin Suge, but I'm saying like, you own Death Row, you got multimillion dollar artists...

B: Mm-hmm...

C: ...on you, and you [ca] goin around beatin up people in casinos...

B: For what?

C: I don't know. Like, I don't know...

B: [laughter]

C: ...and, I mean, I don't know, like, I'm tryina figure out, you know, a hood mentality, but I can't...

B: Yeah...

C: ...cuz that's just—like I don't know, maaan!

B: Sometimes, to me, it's always like when they get this money or when they get all this national fame, they want people to still remember, "I'm from the hood." They wanna prove a point—and to me, it ain't even like that...

C: [laughter]

B: ...to me, when you get all this money and stuff, it should show that you [ca] getting wiser and stuff, and you [ca] smart...

C: Riiight...

B: ...like Master P, for example...

C: Yeaaah...

B: He's [cc] very smart, on how he handle [3a] things and stuff...

C: That's true, that's true, that's true...

B: So, that's how I see it.

C: So, when people—O.K., so you think, you know, artists from the hood... And I'm just gonna assume, they have pressure to keep it real...

B: Yeah...

C: ...They have pressure...

B: Yep, yep, that's true...

C: ...to stay connected to the hood, BUT, does being from the hood mean acting ignorant? And that's, that's, like I guess my big question would be like, do you think people sell out when they move away from the hood, and then not only when they move away, but like, how can a artist move away from the hood and still keep it real?

B: Ooooh!

C: Like do you think there's like a—cuz like, I'll speak on it—I'll speak on it first...
B: Go head...
C: Like, I love Ice Cube...
B: Yeah...
C: ...you know, that's my boy. And to me, like people can criticize him all they want, like he don't rock the same, or he don't live in the hood—[AAf] WHO...?
B: [laughter]
C: I don't—see, I mean, you know, my family lives in the hood, you know, it's cool...
B: Yeaaahh...
C: ...but I know if they could move out...
B: They would.
C: ...they WOULD.
B: [laughter]
C: Like why would you encourage somebody to stay in the hood? So, for ME, keeping it real was more like, "I'mo move out, I wanna show 'em!"
B: "I wanna..." Yeah, exactly.
C: "And I can help YOU move out!"
B: That's keeping it real!
C: "Let's ALL move out!"
B: That's keeping it real!
C: [laughter]
B: Who want to keep living like this? Or, even if it's not bad, people want, you know...
C: A better life.
B: A better life.
C: I mean, yeah, I don't know, thought like, but [AAf] it's pressure...
B: Yep, it IS pressure...
C: It's a lotta pressure for people to like, you know, like I was talking to Cyrus, he was like—I was just asking him like, you know, when people first come out on they first album, they're real HUNGRY...
B: Yep, yep...
C: ...like the way they rap is like PASSIONATE...
B: ...like they get ready...
C: Like they [ca] HUNGRY, like, "I'm literally, I don't have nuttin to eat...
B: [laughter]

C: . . . I'm rappin for my meal." And then, you know, when they blow up, on they second album . . .

B: Lacking, lacking . . .

C: They're just like chilliiin . . .

B: They got the money . . .

C: I mean, they're just more like lax with theirs, you know what I'm saying? And I'm like, I was like, that upsets me . . .

B: Yeah . . .

C . . . because I want like, I want that s— well, not skinny, but like the THINNER Biggie, you know what I'm saying?

B: Yeaaah . . .

C: Or like that real broke Nas . . .

B: That DMX . . .

C: Oh, yeah . . .

B: That DMX, that's the—oh, my goodness . . .

C: [laughter] Speak on DMX!

B: When I first heard his first album, oh my goodness!

C: What was that, *Hot*? . . . What's it called? *Hell Is Hot*? . . .

B: Yeah, *Dark* and sumthin, sumthin . . .

C: [laughter]

B: THAT, maaan, I was like, [AAf] "Who is THIS?! Why he . . . Why is he talking like this?! Why he so angry?!"

C: [laughter]

B: He was HONGRY!

C: [laughter]

B: Like you was sayin, he was READY.

C: [laughter]

B: Then the next album, you know, he [ca] a little hungry. And then, just from then on, it just—he's been in a comfort zone and like he ain't really ain't got nuttin to worry about . . .

C: Yeeaahh . . .

B: . . . and to me, that really, that really show [ʒa] me how people [ca] out just for money sometimes, and like they [ca] not really passionate about rap or whatever. But somebody like Nas or somebody, I think he [ca] really passionate—he just wanna get his word across . . .

C: Yeah . . .

B: . . . and I like that about him . . .

C: You like Nas?

B: Yeah, I like Nas.

C: So do you think when people aren't hungry no more it kinda like dilutes the ARTform of Hip Hop?
B: Yeah, I think, yeah...
C: But like, [AAf] Cyrus was like, "Well, how can he rap about being hungry if he's not hungry no more?"
B: That's true.
C: Because he was saying like, cuz he respects any artist that really raps about like what they, how they live...
B: Yeah...
C: ...so he was like, you know, "On somebody's first album, if they [ca] broke, you know, I expect them to rap about being broke, but then if they [ca] not broke no more, they [ca] gonna rap about not being broke no more."
B: That's true...
C: But then I look at like artists like Outkast, like that's my...
B: Yeah...
C: ...favorite group, right. When they first started, they was [m] broke, they hustled, you know, they slang, they did all that...
B: Yeah...
C: ...and to me, they're still inspired...
B: Mm-hmm...
C: ...to make good music, you know what I'm saying? So I think the difference between like somebody like Outkast...
B: Mm-hmm...
C: ...and somebody like DMX is like—I consider Outkast to be like true musicians...
B: Yeah...
C: ...and artists. [AAf] DMX...?
B: [laughter]
C: ...is like, I'm not gon take—cuz I think he has a connection to people...
B: Yeah...
C: ...like, he has a real strong personality, and I think he has a way of like—he has kind of a passion that like draws attention to him...
B: Yeah...
C: ...but he's not in it for the MUSIC, I don't think...
B: Yeah...
C: ...like, he don't sit down in front of like a board and say, "What we gon create?"
B: Yeah, I feel you...

C: ...or he doesn't like break out the guitar [laughter]...

B: Yep...

C: ...or like, or try to create music...

B: Yeah, that's what Outkast—that's what separates Outkast from ALL of them, cuz...

C: Mm-hmm...

B: ...they music is just—every time they come out with something, it's different!

C: Yeah, every single time!

B: It's different!

C: Yeaah, dogg...

B: Maaan, I don't...

C: You like them?

B: [nodding]

C: You think they're tight?

B and C: [laughter]

B: Yeah, I like that song with Slick Rick they have...

C: OOOhhh, "The Art of Storytelling"?

B: Yep, that was the song!

C: "It's like that now..."

B: Yep [laughter]

C: That one? I mean, [AAf] that's my group, dude!

B: "Old school playas to new school fools..."

C: Yeaaah!

B: [laughter]

C: Oh, yeahhhh, yeahhh!

B: [laughter]

C: Like for me, man, like, they're like, I think they're like a year older than me...

B: Yeah...

C: ...so when they came out, I was in high school and they were my age...

B: Yeah...

C: ...and they were rapping about like the SATs and graduating...

B: They was?!

C: Yeah, dude!

B: I haven't heard their first album...

C: Oh, my GOD! Duuude...

B: [laughter]

C: I gotta educate these… I mean, but like, they were rappin about, "I only got 300 on my SATs, I'm not gon be able to graduate…"
B: Yeah…
C: Like stuff like that or like—Andre wrote this rhyme where he was like, "Never smelt the aroma of a diploma, but I write the deep ass… rhymes…
B: [laughter]
C: …so let me tell you…" Like…
B: Yeahhh…
C: They was like, "I ain't graduate, but I can write." Like all this stuff I could relate to, like…
B: It's cool, yep…
C: …the pressures of what you [ca] gon do, like, growing up as a man and stuff…
B: Yeah…
C: …so for me, like, anybody I could really relate to…
B: Mm-hmm…
C: That's who I got they back…
B: Yeah…
C: Or anybody like I LEARN from, like Ice Cube…
B: Mm-hmm…
C: …when I was like y'all's age, Ice Cube was like the tops…
B: Yeah…
C: …like in the early 90s. And he would just drop knowledge, dogg, like being from LA…
B: Uh-huh…
C: …and South Central, and he rapped about the HOOD, like, what was going ON…
B: Yeah…
C: …giving it to you raw…
B: [laughter]
C: …like in yo face, like, and he was hard and he could flow…
B: Yeah…
C: …so for me like, I relate to somebody that either is going through something I'm going through…
B: Mm-hmm…
C: …or that is teaching me something…
B: Yeah…
C: … you know, like, who do you relate to? Like, do you relate to like…
B: Ummm…

C: Who you really feelin?

B: E-40, that's...

C: WORD?!

B: ...the biggest rapper...

C: 40-Water, really?!

B: [laughter]

C: Why?

B: Because, I don't know, it's just that, you know, he live [3a] in Vallejo or whatever...

C: Right, right...

B: ...and, I don't know, it's just, our—the Bay Area Hip Hop and LA, this whole West Coast Hip Hop—as far... is a lot different from East Coast...

C: Yeahhh...

B: ...like as far as beats and stuff...

C: Yeahhh...

B: So, like that's our, I don't know. It's just how he talk [3a] about he [ca] growing up and, you know, how he used to have, he used to look out the window and [snotty livin (?)] you know with a Navigator, I'm just sittin here with a Pinto and stuff like that...

C: [laughter]

B: I don't know, it's cuz of how he go [3a] about things, how he be talkin about cars and stuff like that. And he just—he has never let this music industry get to him and stuff like that...

C: You think so?

B: Yeah, so, I don't know...

C: Like he's always stayed the same...

B: Yep.

C: You think he's been consistent...

B: Yep.

C: Like Too Short... Like Too Short, literally...

B: I don't...

C: ... that fool has been rappin the same way...

B: The same exact way...

C: ...the same way for a good twenty years now, and granted like...

B: [laughter]

C: ...he raps about the SAME stuff...

B: The same stuff...

C: ...boning girls...

B: The SAME stuff...

C: ...like getting head, whatever, he raps about all that stuff...

B: I'm thinking when is you [m] ever gon get—when you ever gon run outta something to say?!

C: [laughter] How many times... [laughter] How many different ways can you rap about boning a girl? I don't know, I don't KNOW...

B: Twenty years of it!

C: ...but he keeps doing it. BUT, granted that's my criticism...

B: [laughter]

C: ...but then my, my, you know, I commend him...

B: Uh-huh...

C: ...just for like, he's been consistent...

B: That's what I like, too...

C: ...like the whole time, and I've never seen—there's few people I've seen that's rocked the same way for twenty years...

B: Yeah...

C: ...and still putting out albums, like, you just don't see that, you know what I'm saying?

B: You don't, you do NOT...

C: Like, I saw Ice-T give a interview one time, and he was like, "I'm not a rapper," he was like, "I'm a pimp."

B: [laughter]

C: Whatever, I'm not supporting pimps, but he was like, "I have game!"

B: Yeaahhh...

C: He was like, "People think this rap stuff is like, you know, fun and games, fairy tales," but he was like, "The way I rap, what I talk about, that's how I live..."

B: Hmmm...

C: He was like, [AAf] "I get by on game!"

B: Yeahhh...

C: He was like, "So, what I'm giving you on tape, I'm giving you GAME." And he was like, "You can call it whatever you want; you can critique it, but I got this phat house; my kids gon go to college; and my wife is...

B: Yep...

C: ...you know, comfortable; I live a good life, all off of game. So, whut?" You know, and I was just like...

B: Shhhhh...

C: ...damn, like, that puts it in a whole nother perspective...

B: Yep...

C: ...of like, you know, why so many different people are involved in Hip Hop. Like you got people trying to feed they families...

B: Yep...
C: You got people trying to like...
B: It's crazy...
C: ...you know, like...
B: ...yeah, it's a lot of different types...
C: ...do you think there's like a right motive or motivation to be in Hip Hop?
B: Ummm, for me, the song, "One Mic," by Nas...
C: Mmmmmm...
B: ... how he just summed it up when he was like, "All I need is one mic. I don't need no cars; I don't need no jewelry; I just wanna get my MESSAGE across."
C: Wowww...
B: "I want people to LISTEN." And that son really—I kinda really changed how I, you know, put things in perspective about Hip Hop, in general, because most nowadays you got a lot of Fabolouses and Nelly's and stuff...
C: [laughter]
B: ...that's more mainstream artists, but they [ca] trying to get paid and they wanna be famous and stuff like that. And then somebody like Ja Rule, where his first album, he was more of a street person...
C: Mmm...
B: ... and a thug and a murderer—Murder Inc or whatever, and then...
C: Yeah, what you think about Ja Rule, man, like, I say...
B: I don't know, maaann...
C: ...he's probably the most popular rapper out right now...
B: Yep, probably...
C: What do you think about his formula that he's milking...
B: [laughter]
C: ... all the WAY to the bank? I mean, he's getting paid off that formula like... I mean, how do you feel? Do you think like—you got any opinions on Ja Rule? I do, but I wanna hear yours...
B: Only criticism I have on Ja Rule is I don't think he [ca] being real with himself...
C: Ooooooh!
B: I feel that, I think, yeah, his albums, his first album, it did good. I think it went platinum, or whatever it went, but as for these last five six songs, it's been about love...
C: [laughter]

B: ...and he [ca] poseta be a murderer or stuff like that, but I don't know, cuz at the same time I respect him, because he IS A GREAT ARTIST! He produce—not produce, but he [ca] a great songwriter and stuff like that, so I respect him for that. But I just think he [ca] not keeping it real with himself...

C: So you think that's, ummm—like at least as far as like artists that you, you know, are drawn to...

B: Yeah...

C: ...you like the ones that keep it real...

B: Yeah, yeah...

C: So you like the ones who don't front...

B: I mean, but I respect the fact that, if this is how he choose [3a] to make his money, and how he go [3a] about writing his songs, then I respect that. I mean, I like his songs, but at the same time, you know, switch it up sometimes...

C: [laughter]

B: ...Don't, you know, put out one street album and then go head and just go turn mainstream on me...

C: [laughter]

B: ...and, you know, it's GOOD, cuz I think music should be universal...

C: Right...

B: ...for EVERYBODY...

C: Right, right, right, right, right, right...

B: ...So, I mean, it's cool, like, but I don't know...

C: So do you think, you know, people that—cuz I was askin Cyrus, I was like, "You like Jay-Z." Then I was like, "Do you think..." I was like, you know, "You from out here, and Jay-Z'z from Brooklyn, like, how—can you really relate to somebody that's not where you from?" He was like, "Yeah, cuz he keeps it real," and all this and that... And I was like, "Well, aight, my question would be like—Hip Hop is BIG –

B: [laughter]

C: You know what I'm saying? Like Hip Hop is in Germany...

B: Yep...

C: in, like, Asia...

B: Heck, yeah [laughter]...

C: Africa...

B: [laughter] Japan...

C: Do you think—would you honestly say—O.K. cuz when I, when I look at like Nas...

B: Uh-huh...

C: . . . I see East Coast . . .

B: Yeah [laughter] . . .

C: Cuz I ain't, I ain't really been to like, to New York . . .

B: I've been to New York, but I haven't been TO New York. I went sightseeing . . .

C: And I ain't spent no time, I never spent no time . . .

B: Yeah . . .

C: So, I can't lie, like, when I think of New York, I think of rappers . . .

B: I do, too!

C: I don't think of like . . .

B: I think of boots . . .

C: . . . the Yankees . . . What?

B: I think of boots.

C: [laughter]

B: Timberland boots.

C: [hand clapping and laughter]

B: I just do. I don't think of skyscrapers . . .

C: Right, right, right. I don't know New—I probably don't really know New York . . .

B: Yeah . . .

C: . . . but my IMPRESSION is like RAPPERS . . .

B: Yep . . .

C: . . . like, no lie, it's crazy . . .

B: DJ'ing, like a lot of DJs . . .

C: Yeaahh, like I just think of like, like, Wu-Tang!

B: [laughter]

C: I think of like fatigues and like . . .

B: [laughter and hand clapping]

C: . . . nappy hair, and like . . .

B: That's exactly what I think about!

C: . . . like aggressive men . . .

B and C: [laughter]

B: Maaan, that's exactly—looook . . .

C: So I'm wondering like . . .

B: I be thinking the same thing. I was about to say Wu-Tang, too. That's exactly what I think about . . .

C: [laughter] So, when I like, when I—when you just think about Hip Hop and it being so global, like, do you think it really paints a good picture of us, as like Black men, cuz if I go—

B: Mm-hmm . . .

C: I'ma be—I went to Costa Rica, like, I go somewhere every year...
B: Yeah...
C: Like, I go to like Latin American countries...
B: Uh-huh...
C: ...and like Mexico and stuff. Everywhere I go, somebody either compares me to a basketball player or a rapper. Like, cuz like, last year I had big hair...
B: Yeah...
C: ...and then I had corn rows...
B: Uh-huh...
C: ...and when I had my corn rows, people called me Allen Iverson.
B: [laughter]
C: ...or, like, Latrell Spreewell, I was like, "I don't look nuttin like..."
B: Ahhaaahaaaaah!
C: And then somebody called me Kobe when I had my hair out, and I was just like—or people would call me like, whatever like, Usher, WHATEVER, MAN!...
B: Yeahhh, yeah...
C: ...and I'm like, "Daaamn!" Like, that's all they know about us...
B: Yeah...
C: ...you know what I'm saying? And like, I wonder like, am I okay with that?
B: Yeah...
C: Like, cuz I'm not Usher; I'm not Kobe...
B: Not, yeah, Kobe...
C: I'm NEVER gon do that kinda stuff! And I just wonder like if it's good or bad? Like, how do you feel about that? Is it positive or negative?
B: To me, umm, it has positive and negative, but I think the negatives—cuz that's only one side they see of you. They see you as this person—like just by you saying, "We [ca] going to Coast Rica," and somebody saying, "Look, it's Kobe Bryant," or something like that...
C: Mm-hmm...
B: And you, "I'm not Kobe Bryant!" and stuff like that. The only negative about that is, you know, I would hate for somebody to see me as that person, cuz if I don't like that person, personally, then I wouldn't like somebody to call me that, but...
C: Right...
B: But the POSITIVE is that, I mean, just for us being Black or whatever...
C: Right...

B: ...that's a good impression that other people respect us and stuff like that, so...

C: Yeah, yeah, I mean, I think like, it's a double-sided coin...

B: Yeah, a stereotype, too...

C: ...like, if they [ca] like associating me somebody positive—like I have nothing against, I like Kobe Bryant...

B: Yeah...

C: ...I like Usher...

B: [laughter]

C: I think they're like upstanding men, you know, so like, it's cool if that's your impression...

B: Yeah...

C: ...or even Will Smith—like, people like clown him, but Will Smith is like...

B: I have...

C: ...one of my biggest...

B: He's [cc] a GREAT actor!

C: ...role models.

B: Yeah...

C: Yeah, because like you said, man, like, as much as he's done...

B: Uh-huh...

C: this soon...

B: [laughter]

C: ...like the acting and like the rapping and just like his wife...

B and C: [laughter]

C: ...and like his life...

B: Yeah...

C: ...like, [AAf] I want his life!

B: Yeah...

C: Man, I would LOVE—not saying I wanna be Will Smith, but like, just the level of success he has...

B: Yeah, yeah...

C: So, I don't have a problem when that's—if they associate me with somebody that's successful...

B: Yeah...

C: ...but I just don't want them to think...

B: All we do...

C: ...that like, we're one-dimensional...

B: Exactly! That's what I was gonna say. Everybody's [cc] a singer.

C: ...you know, like, the only thing I can do is entertainment.

B: Or only thing I can do—if you [ca] tall, they all maybe assume you play basketball...
C: Yeaah, yeaahh...
B: ...or if you [ca] swole, all maybe, "Oh, you play football?"
C: Yeah, yeah, yeah...
B: Nah, I hate it—you can't categorize me as one thing.
C: But do we do that—do you think we do that to other people, though? Like do we do it to Asians?...
B: [laughter]
C: ...you know what I'm saying?
B: That's true...
C: ...or do I do it to like Africans?
B: Yeah...
C: ...or like, you know, Mexicans or something like that?...
B: Yeah...
C: Do I think every dude that's Spanish is a bullfighter?
B: Yep [laughter], that's true...
C: You know what I'm saying? Like...
B: That IS true...
C: So like, whenever I go overseas, man, like, it really like helps me get like a...
B: Uh-huh...
C: ...a step back, and be like, "Damn, what's—how do I look at this world and society, like, how do people see me?..."
B: Yeah...
C: ...and how do I look at other people?" you know what I'm saying? Like, I think, I don't know, it just trips me out like how globalized Hip Hop has been, cause it's the most popular music right now...
B: Yeah...
C: Do you think—do you agree?
B: Yeah, I agree with THAT, but I mean, I haven't heard any rappers from Germany. I HEARD it—it spread, though, I know that for sure—it spread.
C: [laughter] So, do you think Hip Hop would be as big as it is if White people didn't like it? [pause] Like if White kids weren't buying albums, would Hip Hop be as big as it is?
B: It would be big, but not AS big, I think [laughter], because, I don't know. It's like, Eminem, for example, if he only had White supporters, he [ca] gon get that six or seven million REGARDLESS, then add on the Black people...

C: [laughter]

B: I mean, to me, I feel like, a album like, okay, Jay-Z [pa] album—no, let's say Notorious B.I.G.'s [pp] album...

C: Alright...

B: ...if he only, if only Black people support him, they [ca] gon be—they [ca] gon support him, but not support him as much as a White rapper or whatever. They [ca] gon—he [ca] gon sell two million or whatever...

C: [laughter]

B: [laughter] Eminem, he'll have seven million sold!

C: [laughter]

B: I mean, like, people [ca] gonna download and buy—

C: [laughter]

B: you know, Black folks ain't gonna pay no fifteen dollas! [AA rhythm]

C: [laughter and hand clap]

B: They [ca] shady! Not shady, but...

C: [laughter] That's just us!

B: That's just US! That's how we live!

C: [laughter]

B: We'll be like, "We support you, but, fifteen dollas for yo CD?!" [AA rhythm]

C: [laughter]

B: "I don't think so."

C: [loud laughter]

B: [laughter] We'll take the easy way out...

C: Oooh, boy!

B: I'm burning a CD or...

C: Boy, boy, boy, boy, boy...

B: ...you know, that's how I see things sometimes...

C: So, do you think that—I mean, cuz people wanna like compare—okay, basically, like I hear a lot of people talk about like, people don't wanna see Hip Hop be like jazz...

B: Yeah...

C: ...as far as like, jazz, back in the day, if it weren't for White people, musicians woulda starved. Like, jazz musicians woulda starved...

B: Yeah...

C: ...cuz Black people just wouldn't—either cuz of segregation...

B: Yeah...

C: ...or just transportation or location—they couldn't go see these people perform...

B: Yeah...

C: ...so they were totally dependant on WHITES, and like a lot of people wanna like say that, "Well, jazz artists sold out because they started like catering to the White audience..."

B: Uh-huh...

C: ...and like, for ME, I don't know if I think, you know, rap artists cater to the White audiences...

B: Mm-hmm...

C: ...but I do think a lot of them cater to like just the public, in general...

B: I think so, too...

C: ...or like what sells...

B: Yep...

C: ...you know, like a lot of people like, EVERYBODY got a Neptunes beat on...

B: EVERYBODY, EVERYBODY, just to sell a record...

C: ...just to sell—I MEAN...

B: [laughter]

C: How you feel about that, though? Like, I was in—I was taking a shower yesterday...

B: Maaan...

C: ...and like, there was a mix, right, there was a mix going on. They played Busta Rhymes song, Neptunes...

B: Every song...

C: They played Nelly's song, Neptunes. That... "It's getting hot in here, so take off..." And I was just like, "O.K., that's Neptunes, cool..."

B: [laughter] Yeah...

C: ...and then they played like N'Sync...

B: Neptunes...

C: Neptunes song. Then they played like, gosh, what else...

B: Probably played Jay-Z...

C: Yeah, I mean, I was just like, "Is that what it is?!" you know what I'm saying?

B: To me, it's crazy, it's [suck-teeth]...

C: I mean, does that make you upset? Like, do you even listen to the radio?

B: To me, yeah, I listen to the radio, yeah. To me, I just—sometime I get mad, like [suck-teeth], some people be pickin the rapper that's out right now and then put him on they album—they don't really like him...

C: [laughter]

B: ... they just—cuz he [ca] hot right now, they [ca] gonna put him on his album!

C: Yeah...

B: Like, for instance, when Master P, when they blew up, everybody wanted Master P on they record; everybody wanted Silkk on they album or whatever...

C: That's true...

B: ...and to me, that's just [suck-teeth]—it's crazy! Now everybody want [ʒa] Nas back on they album...

C: [laughter]

B: Now... That's just dumb, maaan!

C: Or like when everybody had like Jadakiss...

B: Yeah...

C: That fool was doing guest appearances on...

B: Fabolous [ca] on EVERY remix!

C: That's a good point.

B: On EVERY remix...

C: Fabolous is everywhere...

B: Maaan...

C: I mean, so does that upset you, as just a lover of Hip Hop—but also, you know what they [ca] doing, cuz it's a business, too...

B: Exactly, it IS a business...

C: ...you know what I'm saying?

B: It is a business.

C: So, like, how do you—it's weird how we like juggle all that...

B: Yeah, it's partly a business AND how we feel and stuff...

C: Yeah, yeah, yeah, and as a consumer, we KNOW what they [ca] doing!

B: You know! [laughter]

C: We KNOW what they [ca] doing! And like, it'll be a beat, and I might love the beat, but I'm like, "I don't wanna love the beat."

B: Cuz you know... Exactly!

C: I know why y'all did it...

B: [laughter]

C: ...or just like—it's so formulated, like, on the real, man, I hate Ja Rule!

B: [laughter]

C: [AAf] I just hate Ja-Rule.

B: Tell the truth...

C: But like...

B: I don't...

C: Every now and again, when I just hear like...

B: Some of his songs is [m] cool...

C: [laughter]

B: [laughter] and you didn't wanna watch it!

C: But I'm mad at myself, then I'm like...

B: [laughter]

C: ...I'm human. I'm human! [laughter] So, I'm just like, "Well, you got me."

B: You got—[laughter]... Ooooh, maaan...

C: You know, like, I don't know, man, like what do you do in that situation?

B: I don't know...

C: Like, do you really support Nas? Like, O.K., so what do you think about positive rappers, like Nas?...

B: Mos Def...

C: ...Mos Def, Talib Kweli, umm, Common, even like Outkast...

B: Yeah, Outkast...

C: ...and Goodie Mobb, like they're positive. Like, do you think that'll ever be as popular as the other stuff?

B: I think it NEEDS to be, because every [laughter]—it's like, anything that happen [ʒa] with violence, it always associates it with rap or whatever, or Hip Hop, in general. And I think they need to, you know, give more respect, give more respect, more publicity like, to people like Common and Mos Def and stuff like that, because they [ca] setting it positive or whatever. I mean, all rappers—I mean, most of the rappers, they ARE positive, but, Mos Def 'nem, they come from a different perspective. And all they music is positive, MOST of their stuff is...

C: Yeah, yeah...

B: ...So, I just—I want people to understand—like other people that don't, that think Hip Hop is nuttin—I want them to understand that there is rappers out there that is positive and stuff...

C: Yeah...

B: ...and have, you know, good music like Outkast and stuff.

C: Mm-hmm...

B: So, I don't know, I think they just, they haven't got the respect that they deserve...

C: Yeah...

B: ...like Mos Def 'nem...

C: Yeah...

B: ...the poetry and stuff like that...

C: Yeah, like I think like...

B: And we NEED that...

C: Outkast... [AAf] Heck, yeah, man! Like, people, I think people forget like how much we just need to be encouraged...

B: Yep...

C: ...and built up...

B: [laughter] Yep, that's what they do...

C: I think the good thing about Outkast is like, they know what it takes to grab your attention...

B: Yeah...

C: ...and then they hit you with a message. So, they're like, we're gonna have a tight beat...

B: A tight beat...

C: We're gon have a real cool video...

B: Like, [AAf] "What is that?"

C: Yeah, yeah...

B: And THEN whip the message out...

C: And then like, so I'ma draw you in with the video...

B: With the clothes...

C: With the clothes...

B: [laughter]

C: Or just a tight show...

B: ALL of it go [3a] together...

C: Yeah!

B: All the four elements.

C: Yeah, like they're really, really smart...

B: [laughter]

C: ...and I think that's why they're successful, and you know...

B: Maaan...

C: ... [AAf] and they're getting paid!

B: Yeah, they're [cc] getting paid...

C: And I love it, but like, I think the key thing—like when you were saying that, you were like, it needs to be more popular. And I think, you know, you gotta understand what people want...

B: Yeah...

C: ...but you still gotta give them what you think they need...

B: Yeah, that's true...

C: ...and I think that's what not enough artists do...

B: Yeah...

C: ...like, people don't wanna get stuff shoved down their throat...
B: Yeah...
C: You know, you gotta come and like welcome them, or make them more buy into a positive message. Like sometimes people ask me about like Gospel music like...
B: Yeah...
C: ...like, you know, "Don't you listen to Gospel?" And I'm like, "Weeell, kinda, sorta, but..." Like, I always say like, "It's the music."
B: Yeah...
C: You know, I love God and I'm a Christian...
B: Huh...
C: ...so like, I love hearing, you know, positive messages, but like, if the music's wack, it's just hard...
B: Yeah, it's hard...
C: ...it's just really hard for me to get into it...
B: [laughter]
C: So, like, I only like Christian acts that have original music...
B: Yeah...
C: ...and I think that's what you can't do...
B: I don't like when they...
C: ...you can't sacrifice the music...
B: Maaan...
C: ...for saying, "Oh, Jesus, Jesus, Jesus!" Like, at least—don't like...
B: I hate, I hate...
C: [shuddering] Uuuughhhh!
B: I hate groups that copy the same beat off a rapper...
C: And just...
B: ...switch the words around...
C: YESSSS!
B: And God...
C: Dude!
B: Maaan, I hate that!
C: Dude!
B: I hate that!
C: Dude!
B: So much!
C: I hate that so much! Like there's this one rapper...
B: [shuddering] Uuuuughhhh!
C: ...and he took the beat for, "Every other city we gooo..." and I'm like, "How you gon make a Christian song outta that?!"

B: [laughter]

C: [laughter] How are you gonna like take a song about hoes, and just, [AAf] I mean, and put in Jesus?!

B: That's what really upsets me...

C: But like, I'm like, one, that's not creative. You [ca] lazy!

B: [laughter]

C: And two, [AAf] don't talk—that's what you [ca] listening to?!

B: [laughter] You [ca] try to talk about this, and make people think that you [ca] it...

C: [laughter]

B: I mean, be true to yo—maaan...

C: I mean, right, right, just like, be true to—I don't know...

B: Maaan, that's crazy, man...

C: ...take a chance to like be original and creative and don't copy...

B: Yeah, what do you feel about sampling then?

C: Oooooh, oh boy, boy, oh, oh boy, oh boy, oh boy... I like, okay, I really like Puffy...

B: Yeah...

C: ...because he's a self-made man...

B: Yeah...

C: ...and I can't, I can't front on that. I can't front on like a young, Black man being a millionaire by the time, before he was thirty...

B: Mm-hmm...

C: ...and NOT coming from like money. Like he wasn't rich; he's from Harlem...

B: Yeah...

C: He went to college, you know. He was a real ambitious, young man, so I really support him because people don't give him credit...

B: Yeah...

C: ...for like, what he's done...

B: Like, that's smart...

C: ...but sampling had its moment...

B: [laughter]

C: ...and you can't do that anymore...

B: No [laughter]...

C: Like, and I think HE killed it...

B: Yep... [laughter]

C: [laughter] Like he could've stretched it out maybe a little bit longer, but he just got really greedy...

B: Yeah...

C: ...you know, and was like, "I'ma..."—you know, I just think that's the problem with...
B: He overdid it...
C: ...music, is people get greedy...
B: Yep...
C: ...and they overdo certain formulas...
B: Master P...
C: Yeah, yeah, you overdo certain formulas, man. Now, they [ca] gon overdue little kids.
B: Overdo it...
C: They [ca] gon like have a gazillion little kid rappers, because it sells...
B: Lil Romeo, Lil Bow Wow, Lil Sammy, Lil...
C: Yeahhhh, Lil J...
B: Yeah [laughter]...
C: Everybody, and it's like...
B: Even the little boy groups, too...
C: Yeaaahhh! And it's kinda like...
B: B2K and Lil, I don't know...
C: I mean, sometimes, I'm just wondering, or sometimes, do you ever think like they think we're stupid as consumers, or like—cause people still buy it. They wouldn't do it unless people buy it, you know what I'm saying?
B: That's true...
C: Like do you ever get upset?
B: I get upset ALL the time. It's like, it's crazy, how they, I don't know—it almost make [3a] me feel like we [ca] stupid. They think we're [cc] stupid; we don't know what they [ca] doing!
C: [laughter]
B: In reality, we [ca] two steps ahead of you! We KNOW what you [ca] bout to plan!
C: [laughter] Yeahhh!
B: And when Lil Bow Wow come [3a] out, OF COURSE, somebody else's [cc] gonna come out with a Lil Romeo. Who WOULDN'T?!
C: [laughter]
B: If they see Lil Bow Wow doing it, and somebody [ca] making his lyrics, who wouldn't?
C: Yeaahhh, so would you say this is...

[side 2]

C: Is this like uhhh... Like when Jay-Z and Nas [unclear] album came out?...
B: Yeah...
C: I was like, "This is a good time!"
B: Yep, this is a great time...
C: [laughter] "This is a great time to be a fan."
B: I would say one of the best times in a while...
C: And no it's kinda stopped, so let's kinda assess who's out there right now...
B: Yeah...
C: Ja Rule...
B: Ja Rule...
C: Who else?
B: Nas is [cf] out there, Jay is [cf] out there, Beanie is [cf] out there...
C: Mm-hmm, Nelly...
B: Umm, not Jermaine Dupri, a little...
C: Fabolous...
B: Fabolous [ca] out there...
C: Jadakiss, Ludacris...
B: Ludacris, yeah...
C: Big Tymers are out now...
B: [laughter]
C: Not a lot of West Coast right now...
B: Nope...
C: They kinda took a break...
B: Yeah...
C: Would you say it was a good time? Or, you know, would you look at all your options now when you listen to the radio—Busta—would you be like, "Yeah, I'm really pleased," or do you think there's been better times in Hip Hop?
B: There's been better times. I really, REALLY liked the Jay-Z and Nas...
C: Forreal?!
B: That was just, me, I was glued in—I was really—I have a CD, a *Street Warz* CD I got from New York...
C: Really?
B: I mean, from Washington, and it have [3a] all these different mixes on there where people [ca] talking about each other...
C: Serious?!
B: That's something you gotta—I'll let you use it if you want it...
C: I wanna hear that!

B: [laughter]
C: Just a bunch of people dissin each other? [laughter]
B: [laughter] They got this dude name Ali [Bargus] dissin Fabolous from DJ Clue...
C: Cluuuuee...
B: Jadakiss and Beanie Sigel going at it...
C: Daaaamnnn!
B: It's crazy, though, you can listen to it or whatever, but...
C: So, who did you like, Jay-Z or Nas?
B: I likedid Jay-Z.
C: REALLY?!
B: I likedid Jay-Z.
C: So you think Jay-Z won?!
B: I don't think he—
C: So...
B: Only reason why I say he won is because I support him—it only took him one line to have Nas write a whole song on him...
C: Mmm...
B: It only took him one, one, ONE verse to have Nas write a whole thing, and to me, I'm saying, the truth really hurt him...
C: Nas?
B: That's what I think...
C: About his mom, baby moms?...
B: About that AND about how he said, you know, "Four albums in ten years; albums went down," and stuff like that...
C: Yeah...
B: ...I think the truth hurt! For somebody to write a WHOLE song on you, and you only put out one verse about him? C'mon, now! That's telling me something right there!
C: [laughter]
B: And then he took the approach as somebody growing up looking up to Nas...
C: Yeah, that's true...
B: That's his approach, and to me, I just thought that was creative, because I feel like the fact that Nas took a whole five minutes and clowned Jay...
C: [laughter]
B: ...that's another story. It was good...
C: Did he do it well?
B: He did it well.

B and C: [laughter]

B: He did it well.

C: See, I'm a big Nas fan. And I told somebody, I was like, "I NEED Nas."

B: [laughter]

C: I don't need Jay-Z. I really enjoy Jay-Z, and I have every Jay-Z album...

B: Mm-hmm...

C: Like, I support him; like he's great, but I NEED Nas. I need Nas to succeed more than I need Jay-Z to succeed...

B: Ah-hhaaaa-ha-haaaaaaa! [hand clap]

C: Just because...

B: Do you have the *Illmatic*?

C: [AAf] Of course, dogg, I got it all!

B: Oh, I haven't heard that. I haven't hear it yet...

C: The first one?

B: [laughter]

C: [AAf] The first one?!

B: Alim keep [3a] telling me about it. I haven't heard it yet...

C: Okay... Let me back up...

B: Ah-hhaaaa-ha-haaaaaaa! [hand clap]

C: Let me—you haven't heard the first Outkast album; you haven't heard the first Nas... When did you start?—I keep forgetting how young y'all are...

B: Seventeen...

C: When did you really start listening to Hip Hop?

B: Maaan, I started listening to like local stuff, man. Like, my whole life I been...

C: See, I don't know anything about that...

B: Yeah...

C: So like who...

B: So, I been listening to local... Like Killa Tay...

C: [laughter]

B: Steve-O, e-40...

C: I know Steve-O. I know Brotha Lynch...

B: The Lunies, Too Short...

C: Forreal?

B: I listened to all of them, and then like, probably in '95/'96, I started listening to—I mean, I listened to Tupac, of course...

C: Right, right, right...

B: ...but '96 and '95 is when I started branching out...

C: Really?!

B: ...so I listened to Notorious B.I.G. and stuff like that...
C: So what was it about like local rappers that like—like why do you think you guys...
B: I don't...
C: ...cuz that's something I never understood, like, Bay Area really supports underground...
B: Yeah...
C: ...like HEAVY...
B: Yep...
C: ...and like, almost to the point where they don't even listen to mainstream; they only listen to underground...
B: But like...
C: WHY?
B: Like, if I'm riding in my car, I'm listening to, I'm gon listen to Keak Da Sneak or something, or Three X Krazy...
C: What's that?
B: That's the name of a local group...
C: Keak Da WHO?...
B: Keak Da Sneak! [laughter]
C: See, I don't even know who that is...
B: I'll, [suck-teeth] I don't know, I get the impression—I can't even put a Jay-Z disc in...
C: WHY?
B: I can't put in—I don't have Ja Rule...
C: [laughter]
B: ...but I'm just saying, for instance... I don't know, it's just different music...
C: You mean when you're rollin around the HOOD...
B: Yep, yep, anything...
C: ...you can't...
B: Like if I'm listening to Three X Krazy, I can't listen to Jay-Z for the rest of the day...
C: WHY?
B: I don't know, it's just, I don't know. It's like, the whole mentality, or the feeling, of the song...
C: Really?
B: ...it's just different. I don't know why I get that every time...
C: That's weird, man...
B: Right...

C: Is it because, I mean, is it, can you relate to them more than you can relate to Jay-Z?

B: Yeah...

C: Cuz they [ca] from up here?

B: Because they [ca] from here and I understand what they've been through...

C: Forreal...

B: ...and stuff like that, so...

C: Forreal, forreal...

B: Yeah...

C: ...that's a strong phenomenon, dude, just like, I guess that's why I love Ice Cube...

B: Yeah...

C: ...cuz I'm from LA, and I can just relate to bean pies being sold on the street corner, like, just EVERYTHING about South Central. But like, to me, he was like mainstream...

B: Yeah...

C: ...you know, like he wasn't underground. Everybody knew about Ice Cube, so to me, I guess like, I was listening to mainstream rap, you know. But like, when I came up here to visit my boy, he told me C-Bo, I was like [AAf] WHOOOO?

B: [laughter] Yeeahhh...

C: ...or like Celly Cell...

B: Celly Cell, all of them, yep...

C: I was like, or Brotha Lynch, I was like...

B: Brotha Lynch Hung, yeah...

C: ...this dude is crazy, you know what I'm saying? Like, I've never really understood like why they get so much support...

B: Yeah...

C: ...you know, as compared to like, I guess, LA is more commercialized. So, I mean, do you think the Bay Area has its own, unique...

B: Yep...

C: ...Hip Hop Culture?

B: Yeah, I think they do...

C: Do you think it's better?

B: Ahhhh, I mean, LYRICALLY, it's gon be people out there that's lyrically—Nas is [cf] a GREAT lyricist, Jay-Z is; Tupac is; Notorious B.I.G. is. I mean, I like Notorious B.I.G., but people put too much on him...

C: Think so?

B: I think so.

C: [AAf] Really?!
B: People put WAY too much on him!
C: You think?
B: I think so.
C: Why?
B: I don't know. I mean, I listen to *Life after Death*; I listen to *Ready to Die*; it was cool, to me, it was cool, but I would pick Nas and Jay-Z over Biggie...
C: Over Biggie?!
B: Yeah...
C: Worrrrd?
B: Yeah, in a quick, fast moment, I would pick Nas and Jay-Z over Biggie...
C: So who do you think is the tightest Bay Area lyricist?
B: E-40, no doubt!
C: Bottom line?
B: Bottom line. [laughter]
C: Can you understand half the stuff he says?!
B: [laughter] I gotta listen...
Alim interrupts: Who, e-40?
C: Yeah!
B: Sometimes...
A: I knew it!
B and C: [loud laughter!]
C: Wassup? Are we done?
A: You got a coupla minutes to wrap it up.
C: Aight.
A: Hey, you know what I'm feelin, though?
C: What?
A: How does it go?
B: He say [ʒa], "I'm not rappin too fast; y'all just listening too slow!"
C: That's what he says?
B: Yep...
A: Yeah, yeah, and then, "I'ma hafta slow down my game..." What he say? "So y'all squares can understand it..."
B: Oh, yeah, "Y'all squares..." [laughter]
C: I can't, maaan...
B: Why can't you squares understand, man? You can't understand him?
C: I can't...
B: [laughter]

C: . . . like, even when, he was like, "I be hippitahippitapotumus . . ."
B: [laughter]
B and C: ". . . like a neurologist." [laughter]
C: I'm like . . .
B: It's funny when he be saying it . . .
C: . . . but then, once I heard it, I was like—cuz I always feel like, "Oh, he's rappin so fast, he ain't sayin nuttin."
B: Yeah . . .
C: But then, he's really . . .
B: He really IS . . .
C: He puts time into like [AAf] writing his lyrics! I'm like, "He's really saying something!"
B: It's great, I think—like, have you heard the Fabolous song that he got?
C: Oh, that . . .
B and C: "Automatic, systematic . . ."
C: Yeah . . .
B: It's weird when he [ca] rappin slow . . .
C: [laughter] That's slow, huh?
B: It's different, yeah, he [ca] rappin slow. He kinda . . .
C: But to me, [AAf] that's fast!
B: Really?
C: Like, I might do—it's fast, but I can understand it . . .
B: Yeah, yeah . . .
C: . . . so that's probably, for him, slow, but for me I'm just like . . .
B: Maaan . . .
C: . . . cuz I'm used to like [runnin his lips] . . .
B: [laughter]
C: I have to TRY to like . . . Like, I'm like . . .
[laughter]
C: I got me ear like . . .
B: That's like Rashid Wallace's [pp] conversation . . .
C: Ooooh! I remember that one, I remember that one . . .
B: [laughter]
C: He was like, like AZ . . .
B: You know, [speakin really fast] "I was selling tickets on the show with AZ and Timbaland and . . ."
C: [laughter]
B: At first, when I first heard him, I was like, "Who is this? Where he [ca] from?!"
C: When you first heard E-40?

B: Yeah, cuz people don't talk like that...
C: [laughter]
B: Like the words he be comin up with, "woeples," like, we don't really talk like that...
C: Y'all don't say "woeples" and stuff?
B: Nawww, nawww...
C: Y'all don't say "Yay Area"...
B: Yeah, yeah, people from Vallejo probably speak like that...
C: [laughter]
B: But East Palo Alto, we will not...
C: Nobody says "smell me"?
B: Yeah, sometimes, but it's not common like the way he put [ʒa] it or whatever, but, I don't know...
C: How do you feel about people "pop they collar"? Okay...
B: Oh, my goodness! I'm in the engineering program, the National, the NSBE program...
C: Yeah, cool...
B: I was in that, yeah, and I went to the junior chapter a year ago in Indiana. Sooo, we [ca] having a little party or whatever, people [ca] poppin they collas, so it was like, "Okay whatever," and we did it, too. So, they were like, "Y'all can't be doin that. We invented that!"
C: INDIANA folks said that?
B: No, they was [m] from Florida...
C: Oh, REALLY?
B: So, I'm like, y'all just don't know where everybody get [ʒa] this from, huh?!
C: Daaaaaag!
B: And then, we didn't say nuttin about it, because, I wasn't really trippin. If that's how they feel, that's how they feel. But I know where it came from...
C: Yeah, man!
B: And e-40 had a little article about that, how people [ca] biting him or whatever, and don't give him credit...
C: They really, a LOT, from people saying, "Oh, boy!" to "Pop yo collar," to, you know, "smell..." all the...
B: Yeah...
C: ...That fool, I respect him for that, and it just goes to show like how people BITE so hard...
B: Yeah...
C: ...you know, they just start...

B: Master P...

C: Is he the king?

B: He's [cc] probably the king of biting.

C: Yeah, yeah...

B: He say somebody [pa] line in every one of his raps...

C: [laughter] He's a businessman...

B: And I used to like him, too...

C: Did you really?

B: Yeah...

C: Oh, he was big out here, wasn't he, back in the day?

B: Yeah, yep, yep...

C: He lived in like Richmond or something like that...

B: Yep, in Richmond...

C: Didn't he start out here, or something like that?

B: Yep, *West Coast Bad Boys*, I still got that CD...

C: The first one he put out?

B: Yeah, the compilation, yep...

C: Was he tight back then?

B: He was cool. I liked him a lot...

C: Forreal...

B: But now it's like, I mean, I respect him and I like him on a business standpoint as far as, I know he [ca] not a rapper...

C: Yeah, you KNOW that!

B: ...but just get—I'm sick and tired of it, that's all—when he tries [3p] to come out, try to save his company and, to me, he don't [3a] NEED to. He [ca] living off Lil Romeo. Lil Romeo gon...

C: God, darn... doing that to his son...

B: Man, he GOT money, maaan...

C: Do you think that's right or wrong? Do you think he should have his son in there?

B: Nah...

C: You think he's too young?

B: It's not right, man. I mean, the type of music that his son's [cc] making is good, for the younger crowd...

C: Right, right...

B: That's just him being another smart...

B and C: ...businessman...

B: Yeah, yeah... I mean, it's good in some ways and bad in some. Like, the chains and stuff, WHAT ten-year-old should be having a chain like that?

C: I don't know...
B: He got his own house. You seen "Cribs"?
C: YES...
B: See the Lexus he has?
C: And like, that's his house. I was like, "I'm twenty-five. I don't own a house!"
B: ...apartment...
C: [laughter]
B: And people may think we [ca] jealous—it's not about jealousy, it's about...
C: Being rational...
B: Exactly!
C: Like does your little kid, is that gonna destroy his idea of reality?...
B: Yeah, exactly...
C: ...you know what I'm saying? Like, is that healthy for a oyoung kid?
B: Having two BIG ole platinum chains on, Bugs Bunny—I mean, it's crazy, man.
C: Yeah, that IS crazy. That's crazy, man. Don't do that to yo kids...
B: Nah, shoot...
C: Don't do that to Buck, Jr...
B: [laughter]
C: Forreal, maaan...
B: Keep it real...
C: Aight, let's be done, man...
B: Yeah...
C: Aight, dude...
B: Nice talkin with you...
C: Nice...

APPENDIX B: SSC QUESTIONS: HIPHOPOGRAPHY CONVERSATIONS

1. What kinds of music do you listen to, and how often do you listen to them?
2. Do you remember your very FIRST Hip Hop experience (when you first heard or saw it, and what it was like)? What did you think when you heard it?
3. How often do you listen to Hip Hop music now?
4. Are people into Hip Hop music WHERE YOU ARE FROM? Where do you hear or see Hip Hop in your local area?
5. Do you know anyone that does Hip Hop or anyone that raps or makes music (just for fun or professionally)? Do you know any rappers in your area/school? Are they any good?
6. Do you watch any HIP HOP VIDEOS? Which ones are your favorites right now? Do you agree with people who say that Hip Hop videos are too violent? What about Hip Hop movies? Do you know of any?
7. Do you listen to any radio stations that play Hip Hop music? What stations do you listen to? If you could create your own Hip Hop radio station, what would it be like? Describe it.
8. Who is your FAVORITE HIP HOP ARTIST, and why? Who is your favorite artist out of any type of music? What makes them your favorite?
9. What makes a really good artist, to you? What three or four qualities do they have to have?
10. AS A MAN/WOMAN, do you think you view Hip Hop differently than the opposite sex? How are men and women rappers different? How do they get treated differently?
11. Who are the tightest female rappers? Pick one as your favorite, and why?
12. What do you think about girl R&B groups like DESTINY'S CHILD? Are they still together? What about AALIYAH, TLC, ALICIA KEYS, MARY J BLIGE and them? Are they Hip Hop, too? Who's the tightest? Do you relate to any of these artists?

13. Did you hear the news about Aaliyah and Left Eye (from TLC)? What do you make of that?
14. What are some of the biggest issues going on in Hip Hop right now?
15. What do you know about FREESTYLE BATTLING? What does freestyle mean? Have you ever seen a battle? What are some of the most famous rhyme battles (or beefs) that you have heard of? Describe them.
16. Do you think there needs to be new songs that are not just about the "BLING-BLING"?
17. Do you think what rappers talk about has an IMPACT ON KIDS? Does it have an impact on you personally? Why or why not?
18. What about when rappers talk about "ice" and "ridin on dubs" and all that stuff—how does that affect people?
19. What do you remember about the EAST COAST/ WEST COAST BEEF? Is it over, or do people still feel like there's beef?
20. How do you think the deaths of TUPAC AND BIGGIE affected the Hip Hop community? What do you know about these artists? How did they affect you personally? Who do you think will ultimately go down in history as the better rapper? Why? What do people like about these artists?
21. What do people like about NAS, JAY-Z, FABOLOUS, OR E-40? Do you know any of these artists? How are they the same or different?
22. Does a rapper's PHYSICAL APPEARANCE (weight, looks) matter? How much of a rapper's success depends on their looks, or their weight, or their image? Is image important in Hip Hop? Give examples.
23. What do you think about the content of lyrics and the videos for young rappers like LIL BOW WOW AND LIL ROMEO? Do you have a problem with anything they do? If not, what do you say to people who do have a problem with them talkin about sex, guns, drugs, etc.?
24. Is Hip Hop being messed up by lyrics about sex, guns, drugs, etc.? Why or why not? Does Hip Hop really reflect what's going on in THE STREETS?
25. Do you know anything about how Hip Hop got started? What do you know about OLD SCHOOL HIP HOP?
26. Should HOMOSEXUALITY have a place in Hip Hop? Do you think the rap community will ever accept a "gay rapper"? Why or why not?
27. What do you think about controversial artists like Eminem and his lyrics? Is EMINEM different from groups like N.W.A.? How? Who are some other controversial artists, and why are they controversial?
28. Do you think different regions—East Coast/West Coast/Dirty South—have different styles and slangs?

29. How important is SLANG to Hip Hop?
30. What is unique about the way Hip Hop artists use LANGUAGE? Do you think Hip Hop is POETRY, or like poetry?
31. Are there any RELATIONSHIPS (affairs) between music artists that you know about? What's the latest word on that? (gossip time)
32. Is Hip Hop a CULTURE, or is it just MUSIC? Why? Explain yourself and give examples.
33. What do you think about groups who come out like ONE-HIT WONDERS? Why do some groups just fade away after one hit, while others last longer?
34. What about WHITE ARTISTS in Hip Hop? Or OTHER RACES in Hip Hop? Is Hip Hop Black music? What does it mean to say that something is "BLACK MUSIC"?
35. Have you heard anything about the controversy over the word *nigger/nigga* in Hip Hop? What do people at your school think about it?
36. What do you think OLD FOLKS thinks about Hip Hop? How do their opinions differ from the youth's?
37. What role does Hip Hop play IN YOUR LIFE? WHAT DOES IT REALLY MEAN TO YOU?
38. Have you ever been to a HIP HOP CONCERT? What was it like? What was your favorite one? Who would you really LOVE to see in concert that you haven't seen already? Why?
39. Do you think that POSITIVE MESSAGES IN HIP HOP music can actually change things in the community? Do you know of any good examples? How? Why or why not?

APPENDIX C: CODING KEYS

COPULA CODING KEY

1. VARIANTS: (a) Ø; (c) contracted; (f) full
2. IS/ARE: (I) *is*; (A) *are*
3. MISMATCH: (y) yes; (n) no
4. SUBJECT TYPE: (P) personal pronoun, *I, you, he, she, we, you, y'all, they*; (N) noun phrase; (D) other pronoun, *these, those, one, whoever, who, whatever, everybody*
5. FOLLOWING GRAMMATICAL: (g) *gon*; (x) *gonna*; (z) *finna, bout to,* etc.; (v) V+*-ing*; (l) locative; (a) adjective; (n) noun phrase; (m) misc.
6. PRECEDING PHONOLOGICAL: (C) consonant; (V) vowel
7. FOLLOWING PHONOLOGICAL: (c) consonant; (v) vowel
8. CONVERSATION CODE: E113 = experiment 1 (E1), table 1 (1), conversation 3 (3); E241 = experiment 2 (E2), table 4 (4), conversation 1 (1)
9. SPEAKER ID: (A) Amira; (B) Bilal; (C) Careem; (K) Kijana
10. INTERLOCUTOR RACE: (b) Black; (w) White
11. INTERLOCUTOR GENDER: (M) male; (F) female
12. INTERLOCUTOR CULTURAL KNOWLEDGE: (h) Hip Hop; (n) no Hip Hop ("Cultural knowledge" is a social constraint/construct that attempts to describe the interlocutor's familiarity with the dominant cultural force in the lives of Sunnyside's Black youth, i.e., Hip Hop Culture.)

DON'T COUNTS: (1) *it's, that's, what's*; (2) *am, 'm*; (3) *there is/there's*; (4) *here is/here's*; (5) clause final (including relative clauses); (6) questions; (7) *be*$_2$ and *be*$_3$; (8) unclear/mergers (e.g., *he sittin* or *they runnin*).

EXAMPLE:

He's trying to be like Tupac.

CODING STRING: cInPvVcE111KbFh

THIRD-PERSON SINGULAR *-S* CODING KEY

1. VARIANTS: (a) Ø; (p) present
2. SUBJECT TYPE: (P) personal pronoun, *I, you, he, she, we, you, y'all, they*; (N) noun phrase; (D) other pronoun, *these, those, one, whoever, who, whatever, everybody*
3. VERB TYPE: (r) regular; (d) *don't*; (s) *say*; (g) *go*; (w) *want*
4. PRECEDING PHONOLOGICAL: (C) consonant; (V) vowel
5. FOLLOWING PHONOLOGICAL: (c) consonant; (v) vowel; (p) pause
6. SPEAKER ID: (A) Amira; (B) Bilal; (C) Careem; (K) Kijana
7. INTERLOCUTOR RACE: (b) Black; (w) White
8. INTERLOCUTOR GENDER: (M) male; (F) female
9. INTERLOCUTOR CULTURAL KNOWLEDGE: (h) Hip Hop; (n) no Hip Hop ("Cultural knowledge" is a social constraint/construct that attempts to describe the interlocutor's familiarity with the dominant cultural force in the lives of Sunnyside's Black youth, i.e., Hip Hop Culture.)

DON'T COUNTS: Unclear/mergers, such as *speaks softly, walks slow*

EXAMPLE:

Nas rap about what's real.
CODING STRING: aNrCvKbFh

POSSESSIVE *-S* CODING KEY

1. VARIANTS: (a) Ø; (p) present
2. PRECEDING PHONOLOGICAL: (C) consonant; (V) vowel
3. FOLLOWING PHONOLOGICAL: (c) consonant; (v) vowel; (p) pause
4. SPEAKER ID: (A) Amira; (B) Bilal; (C) Careem; (K) Kijana
5. INTERLOCUTOR RACE: (b) Black; (w) White
6. INTERLOCUTOR GENDER: (M) male; (F) female

7. INTERLOCUTOR CULTURAL KNOWLEDGE: (h) Hip Hop; (n) no Hip Hop ("Cultural knowledge" is a social constraint/construct that attempts to describe the interlocutor's familiarity with the dominant cultural force in the lives of Sunnyside's Black youth, i.e., Hip Hop Culture.)

DON'T COUNTS: Unclear/mergers, such as *Tupac's style*

EXAMPLE:

They go back to the projects and pay people bills.
CODING STRING: aCcKbFh

REFERENCES

Abrahams, Roger D. 1964. *Deep Down in the Jungle . . . : Negro Narrative Folklore from the Streets of Philadelphia.* Hatboro, Pa.: Folklore Assoc.

———. 1970. "Rapping and Capping: Black Talk as Art." In *Black America*, ed. John F. Szwed, 132–42. New York: Basic Books.

Ah Nee Benham, Maenette Kape'ahiokalani Padeken, and Ronald H. Heck. 1998. *Culture and Educational Policy in Hawai'i: The Silencing of Native Voices.* Mahwah, N.J.: Erlbaum.

Alexander, Neville. 2004. "Mother-Tongue Education (MTE) and the African Renaissance, with Special Reference to South Africa." Unpublished MS.

Alim, H. Samy. 2000. "360 Degreez of Black Art Comin at You: Sista Sonia Sanchez and the Dimensions of a Black Arts Continuum." *BMa: The Sonia Sanchez Literary Review* 6.1: 15–33.

———. 2001. "Diversifying Our Approaches to Language and Literacy Development." *Language Magazine*, Dec., 29–31.

———. 2002. "Street-Conscious Copula Variation in the Hip Hop Nation." *American Speech* 77: 288–304.

———. 2003a. "On Some Serious Next Millennium Rap Ishhh: Pharoahe Monch, Hip Hop Poetics, and the Internal Rhymes of *Internal Affairs.*" *Journal of English Linguistics* 31: 60–84.

———. 2003b. "'We Are the Streets': African American Language and the Strategic Construction of a Street-Conscious Identity." In Makoni et al. 2003, 40–59.

———. 2004a. "Combat, Consciousness, and the Cultural Politics of Communication: Reversing the *Dominating* Discourses to Empower Linguistically Profiled and Marginalized Students." Paper presented at the annual meeting of the American Dialect Society, Boston, Jan. 8–10.

———. 2004b. "Hip Hop Nation Language." In *Language in the USA: Themes for the Twenty-First Century*, ed. Edward Finegan and John R. Rickford, 387–409. Cambridge: Cambridge Univ. Press.

———. 2004c. "Hearing What's Not Said and Missing What Is: Black Language in White Public Space." In *Intercultural Discourse and Communication: The Essential Readings*, ed. Scott F. Kiesling and Christina Bratt Paulston, 180–97. Malden, Mass.: Blackwell.

———. 2004d. "Nation Language in the African Diaspora: Language Use in Contemporary African American Expressive Culture." Unpublished MS.

———. 2004e. "The Whitey Voice: Linguistic Agency, (Anti)Racism, and the Discursive Construction of Whiteness in a Black American Barbershop." Paper presented at the annual meeting of the American Anthropological Association, San Francisco, Nov. 17–21.

Alleyne, Mervyn C. 1980. *Comparative Afro-American: An Historical-Comparative Study of English-based Afro-American Dialects of the New World.* Ann Arbor, Mich.: Karoma.

Anderson, Monica Frazier. 1994. *Black English Vernacular: From "Ain't" to "Yo Mama," the Words Politically Correct Americans Should Know.* Highland City, Fla.: Rainbow.

Ash, Sharon, and John Myhill. 1986. "Linguistic Correlates of Inter-ethnic Contact." In *Diversity and Diachrony*, ed. David Sankoff, 33–44. Amsterdam: Benjamins.

Bahloul, Maher. 1993. "The Copula in Modern Standard Arabic." In *Perspectives on Arabic Linguistics V: Papers from the Fifth Annual Symposium on Arabic Linguistics*, ed. Mushira Eid and Clive Holes, 209–29. Amsterdam: Benjamins.

Bailey, Beryl Loftman. 1965. "Toward a New Perspective in Negro English Dialectology." *American Speech* 40: 171–77.

Bailey, Guy, and Marvin Bassett. 1986. "Invariant *be* in the Lower South." In *Language Variety in the South: Perspectives in Black and White*, ed. Michael B. Montgomery and Guy Bailey, 158–79. University: Univ. of Alabama Press.

Bailey, Guy, and Natalie Maynor. 1987. "Decreolization?" *Language in Society* 16: 449–73.

———. 1989. "The Divergence Controversy." *American Speech* 64: 12–39.

Bakhtin, M. M. 1981. *The Dialogic Imagination: Four Essays.* Ed. Michael Holquist. Trans. Caryl Emerson and Michael Holquist. Austin: Univ. of Texas Press.

Ball, Arnetha F. 2000. "Empowering Pedagogies That Enhance the Learning of Multicultural Students." *Teachers College Record* 102: 1006–34.

Ball, Arnetha F., and H. Samy Alim. 2002. "U.S. and South African Literacy Learners: A Multiple Literacies Perspective." Paper presented at the annual meeting of the American Educational Research Association, New Orleans, Apr. 5–7.

Ball, Arnetha F., and Sarah Warshauer Freedman, eds. Forthcoming. *Bakhtinian Perspectives on Language, Literacy, and Learning.* New York: Cambridge Univ. Press.

Banfield, William C. 2003. "The Rub: Markets, Morals, and the 'Theologizing' of Popular Music." In *Noise and Spirit: The Religious and Spiritual*

Sensibilities of Rap Music, ed. Anthony B. Pinn, 173–83. New York: New York Univ. Press.

Baugh, John. 1979. "Linguistic Style-Shifting in Black English." Ph.D. diss., Univ. of Pennsylvania.

———. 1980. "A Reexamination of the Black English Copula." In *Locating Language in Space and Time,* ed. William Labov, 83–106. New York: Academic.

———. 1983. *Black Street Speech: Its History, Structure, and Survival.* Austin: Univ. of Texas Press.

———. 1992. "Hypocorrection: Mistakes in Production of Vernacular African American English as a Second Dialect." *Language and Communication* 12: 317–26.

———. 1998. "Linguistics, Education, and the Law: Educational Reform for African-American Language Minority Students." In Mufwene et al. 1998, 282–301.

———. 2000a. *Beyond Ebonics: Linguistic Pride and Racial Prejudice.* New York: Oxford Univ. Press.

———. 2000b. "Racial Identification by Speech." *American Speech* 75: 362–64.

———. 2001. "A Dissection of Style-Shifting." In Eckert and Rickford 2001, 109–19.

———. 2003. "Linguistic Profiling." In Makoni et al. 2003, 155–68.

Bauman, Richard. 1977. *Verbal Art as Performance.* Prospect Heights, Ill.: Waveland.

Bell, Allan. 1984. "Language Style as Audience Design." *Language in Society* 13: 145–204.

———. 2001. "Back in Style: Reworking Audience Design." In Eckert and Rickford 2001, 139–69.

Bell, Allan, and Gary Johnson. 1997. "Towards a Sociolinguistics of Style." *University of Pennsylvania Working Papers in Linguistics* 4.1: 1–21.

Bertrand, Marianne, and Sendhil Mullainathan. 2003. "Are Emily and Brendan More Employable Than Lakisha and Jamal? A Field Experiment on Labor Market Discrimination." Unpublished MS.

Brown, H. Rap. 1972. "Street Talk." In *Rappin' and Stylin' Out: Communication in Urban Black America,* ed. Thomas Kochman, 205–7. Urbana: Univ. of Illinois Press.

Bucholtz, Mary. 1996. "Geek the Girl: Language, Femininity, and Female Nerds." In *Gender and Belief Systems: Proceedings of the Fourth Berkeley Women and Language Conference, April 19, 20, and 21, 1996,* ed. Natasha Warner, Jocelyn Ahlers, Leela Bilmes, Monica Oliver, Suzanne

Wertheim, and Melinda Chen, 119–82. Berkeley, Calif.: Berkeley Women and Language Group, Univ. of California.

———. 2003. "Sociolinguistic Nostalgia and the Authentication of Identity." *Journal of Sociolinguistics* 7: 398–416. An earlier version presented during a panel discussion at the 31st annual meeting on New Ways of Analyzing Variation (NWAV 31), Stanford, Calif., Oct. 10–13, 2002.

Butters, Ronald R. 1989. *The Death of Black English: Divergence and Convergence in Black and White Vernaculars.* Bamberger Beiträge zur Englischen Sprachwissenschaft 25. Frankfurt am Main: Lang.

Cedergren, Henrietta J., and David Sankoff. 1974. "Variable Rules: Performance as a Statistical Reflection of Competence." *Language* 50: 333–55.

Chomsky, Noam. 1957. *Syntactic Structures.* The Hague: Mouton.

———. 1965. *Aspects of the Theory of Syntax.* Cambridge, Mass.: MIT Press.

Clark, Eve V. 2003. "Critical Periods, Time, and Practice." *University of Pennsylvania Working Papers in Linguistics* 9.2: 39–48. Originally presented during a panel discussion at the 31st annual meeting on New Ways of Analyzing Variation (NWAV 31), Stanford, Calif., Oct. 10–13, 2002.

Coupland, Nikolas. 1980. "Style-Shifting in a Cardiff Work-Setting." *Language in Society* 9: 1–12.

———. 1984. "Accommodation at Work: Some Phonological Data and Their Implications." *International Journal of the Sociology of Language* 46: 49–70.

———. 2001. "Language, Situation, and the Relational Self: Theorizing Dialect-Style in Sociolinguistics." In Eckert and Rickford 2001, 185–210.

———. 2003. "Sociolinguistic Authenticities." *Journal of Sociolinguistics* 7: 417–31. Originally presented during a panel discussion at the 31st annual meeting on New Ways of Analyzing Variation (NWAV 31), Stanford, Calif., Oct. 10–13, 2002.

Crawford, James, ed. 1992. *Language Loyalties: A Source Book on the Official English Controversy.* Chicago: Univ. of Chicago Press.

Daniel, Jack L., and Geneva Smitherman. 1976. "How I Got Over: Communication Dynamics in the Black Community." *Quarterly Journal of Speech* 62: 26–39.

Dillard, J. L. 1972. *Black English: Its History and Usage in the United States.* New York: Random House.

———. 1977. *Lexicon of Black English.* New York: Seabury.

Dunlap, Howard G. 1977. "Some Methodological Problems in Recent Investigations of the Copula and Invariant *be*." In *Papers in Language Variation: SAMLA-ADS Collection*, ed. David L. Shores and Carole P. Hines, 151–59. University: Univ. of Alabama Press.

Duranti, Alessandro. 1997. *Linguistic Anthropology*. New York: Cambridge Univ. Press.

———, ed. 2001. *Linguistic Anthropology: A Reader*. Malden, Mass.: Blackwell.

———, ed. 2004. *A Companion to Linguistic Anthropology*. Malden, Mass.: Blackwell.

Dyson, Anne Haas. 2003. *The Brothers and Sisters Learn to Write: Popular Literacies in Childhood and School Cultures*. New York: Teachers College Press.

Eades, Diana. 2004. "Intercultural Communities in Legal Contexts." In *Intercultural Discourse and Communication: The Essential Readings*, ed. Scott F. Kiesling and Christina Bratt Paulston, 304–16. Malden, Mass.: Blackwell.

Eckert, Penelope. 2000. *Linguistic Variation as Social Practice: The Linguistic Construction of Identity in Belten High*. Oxford: Blackwell.

———. 2001. "Style and Social Meaning." In Eckert and Rickford 2001, 119–26.

Eckert, Penelope, and Rudy Gaudio. 2002. "Ethnography and Variation." Workshop at the 31st annual meeting on New Ways of Analyzing Variation (NWAV 31), Stanford, Calif., Oct. 10–13.

Eckert, Penelope, and John R. Rickford, eds. 2001. *Style and Sociolinguistic Variation*. Cambridge: Cambridge Univ. Press.

Fairclough, Norman. 1989. *Language and Power*. London: Longman.

———. 1995. *Critical Discourse Analysis: The Critical Study of Language*. London: Longman.

Fasold, Ralph W. 1972. *Tense Marking in Black English: A Linguistic and Social Analysis*, Arlington, Va.: Center for Applied Linguistics.

———. 1978. "Language Variation and Linguistic Competence." In *Linguistic Variation: Models and Methods*, ed. David Sankoff, 85–95. New York: Academic.

Fasold, Ralph W., William Labov, Fay Boyd Vaughn-Cooke, Guy Bailey, Walt Wolfram, Arthur K. Spears, and John Rickford. 1987. "Are Black and White Vernaculars Diverging? Papers from the NWAVE 14 Panel Discussion." *American Speech* 62: 3–80.

Feagin, Crawford. 1979. *Variation and Change in Alabama English: A Sociolinguistic Study of the White Community.* Washington, D.C.: Georgetown Univ. Press.

Fisher, Maisha T. 2003. "Open Mics and Open Minds: Spoken Word Poetry in African Diaspora Participatory Literacy Communities." *Harvard Educational Review* 73: 362–89.

Folb, Edith A. 1980. *Runnin' Down Some Lines: The Language and Culture of Black Teenagers.* Cambridge, Mass.: Harvard Univ. Press.

Foster, Michèle. 2001. "Pay Leon, Pay Leon, Pay Leon, Paleontologist: Using Call-and-Response to Facilitate Language Mastery and Literacy Acquisition among African American Students." In Lanehart 2001, 281–98.

Foucault, Michel. 1984. "The Order of Discourse." In *Language and Politics,* ed. Michael J. Shapiro, 108–38. Oxford: Blackwell.

Frankenberg, Ruth. 1993. *White Women, Race Matters: The Social Construction of Whiteness.* Minneapolis: Univ. of Minnesota Press.

Freire, Paulo. 1970. *Pedagogy of the Oppressed.* Trans. Myra Bergman Ramos. New York: Seabury.

Fries, Charles C. 1963. *Linguistics and Reading.* New York: Holt, Rinehart, and Winston.

Gal, Susan. 1979. *Language Shift: Social Determinants of Linguistic Change in Bilingual Austria.* New York: Academic.

Gal, Susan, and Judith T. Irvine. 1995. "The Boundaries of Languages and Disciplines: How Ideologies Construct Difference." *Social Research* 62: 967–1001.

Gee, James Paul. 1996. *Social Linguistics and Literacies: Ideology in Discourses.* 2nd ed. London: Taylor and Francis.

Giles, Howard. 1973. "Accent Mobility: A Model and Some Data." *Anthropological Linguistics* 15: 87–105.

———, ed. 1984. *The Dynamics of Speech Accommodation.* Special issue of *International Journal of the Sociology of Language* 46.

Giles, Howard, and Peter F. Powesland. 1975. *Speech Style and Social Evaluation.* New York: Academic.

Goffman, Erving. 1967. *Interaction Ritual: Essays on Face-to-Face Behavior.* Garden City, N.Y.: Anchor.

———. 1976. "Replies and Responses." *Language in Society* 5: 257–313.

Goodwin, Marjorie Harness. 1990. *He-Said-She-Said: Talk as Social Organization among Black Children.* Bloomington: Univ. of Indiana Press.

Green, Lisa J. 2000. "Aspectual *be*-type Constructions and Coercion in African American English." *Natural Language Semantics* 8: 1–25.

———. 2002. *African American English: A Linguistic Introduction.* Cambridge: Cambridge Univ. Press.

Gumperz, John J. 1982a. *Discourse Strategies.* Cambridge: Cambridge Univ. Press.

———, ed. 1982b. *Language and Social Identity.* Cambridge: Cambridge Univ. Press.

Gumperz, John J., and Dell H. Hymes, eds. 1964. *The Ethnography of Communication.* Special issue of *American Anthropologist* 66.6.

———, eds. 1972. *Directions in Sociolinguistics: The Ethnography of Communication.* New York: Holt, Rinehart and Winston.

Guy, Gregory. 1988. "Advanced Varbrul Analysis." In *Linguistic Change and Contact: Proceedings of the Sixteenth Annual Conference on New Ways of Analyzing Variation,* ed. Kathleen Ferrara, Becky Brown, Keith Walters, and John Baugh, 124–36. Austin: Dept. of Linguistics, Univ. of Texas in Austin.

Hakuta, Kenji. 2002. "Minority Languages and Education." Paper presented at panel discussion at the 31st annual meeting on New Ways of Analyzing Variation (NWAV 31), Stanford, Calif., Oct. 10–13.

Hannah, Dawn. 1996. "Copula Absence in Samaná English." Ph.D. qualifying paper, Stanford Univ.

Harris-Wright, Kelli. 1999. "Enhancing Bidialectalism in Urban African American Students." In *Making the Connection: Language and Academic Achievement among African American Students,* ed. Carolyn Temple Adger, Donna Christian, and Orlando L. Taylor, 53–59. Washington, D.C.: Center for Applied Linguistics.

Heath, Shirley Brice. 1983. *Ways with Words: Language, Life, and Work in Communities and Classrooms.* Cambridge: Cambridge Univ. Press.

Henrie, Samuel, Jr. 1969. "A Study of Verb Phrases Used by Five-Year-Old Nonstandard Negro English Speaking Children." Ph.D. diss., Univ. of California, Berkeley.

Hill, Jane H. 1998. "Language, Race, and White Public Space." *American Anthropologist* 100: 680–89.

Hindle, Donald Morris. 1979. "The Social and Situational Conditioning of Phonetic Variation." Ph.D. diss., Univ. of Pennsylvania.

Hinton, Leanne. 2003. "How to Teach When the Teacher Isn't Fluent." In *Nurturing Native Languages,* ed. Jon Reyhner, Octaviana V. Trujillo, Roberto Luis Carrasco, and Louise Lockard, 79–92. Flagstaff: Northern Arizona Univ.

Holloway, Joseph E., and Winifred K. Vass. 1997. *The African Heritage of American English.* Bloomington: Univ. of Indiana Press.

Holloway, Karla F. C. 2002. *Passed On: African American Mourning Stories.* Durham, N.C.: Duke Univ. Press.

Holm, John. 1984. "Variability in the Copula in Black English and Its Creole Kin." *American Speech* 59: 291–309.

Hornberger, Nancy. 1989. "Continua of Biliteracy." *Review of Educational Research* 59: 271–96.

Hull, Glynda, and Katherine Schultz, eds. 2002. *School's Out! Bridging Out-of-School Literacies with Classroom Practice.* New York: Teachers College Press.

Hussein, Anwar A. 1995. "The Sociolinguistic Patterns of Native Arabic Speakers: Implications for Teaching Arabic as a Foreign Language." *Applied Language Learning* 6: 65–87.

Hymes, Dell. 1964. "Introduction: Towards Ethnographies of Communication." In Gumperz and Hymes 1964, 1–34.

———. 1972. "Models of Interaction of Language and Social Life." In Gumperz and Hymes 1972, 35–71.

———. 1974. *Foundations in Sociolinguistics: An Ethnographic Approach.* Philadelphia: Univ. of Pennsylvania Press.

———. 1977. "Qualitative/Quantitative Research Methodologies in Education: A Linguistic Perspective." *Anthropology and Education Quarterly* 8: 165–76.

Irvine, Judith T. 1979. "Formality and Informality in Communicative Events." *American Anthropologist* 81: 773–90.

———. 1985. "Status and Style in Language." *Annual Review of Anthropology* 14: 557–81.

———. 2001. "'Style' as Distinctiveness: The Culture and Ideology of Linguistic Differentiation." In Eckert and Rickford 2001, 21–43.

Jahr, E. H. 1979. "Er det sann jeg snakker?" In *Sprak og Samfunn,* ed. J. Kleiven. Oslo: Pax.

Khalidi, Rashid. 1997. *Palestinian Identity: The Construction of Modern National Consciousness.* New York: Columbia Univ. Press.

Keyes, Cheryl. 1984. "Verbal Art Performance in Rap Music: The Conversation of the 80's." *Folklore Forum* 17: 143–52.

Kochman, Thomas. 1969. "'Rapping' in the Black Ghetto." *Trans-Action,* Feb., 26–34.

———. 1981. *Black and White Styles in Conflict.* Chicago: Univ. of Chicago Press.

Krashen, Stephen D. 1996. *Under Attack: The Case against Bilingual Education.* Culver City, Calif.: Language Education Associates.

Kroskrity, Paul V., ed. 2000. *Regimes of Language: Ideologies, Polities, and Identities.* Santa Fe, N.M.: School of American Research Press.

Labov, William. 1966. *The Social Stratification of English in New York City.* Washington, D.C.: Center for Applied Linguistics.

———. 1967. "Some Sources of Reading Problems for Speakers of the Black English Vernacular." In *New Directions in Elementary English: Papers Collected from the 1966 Spring Institutes on the Elementary Language Arts of the National Council of Teachers of English,* ed. Alexander Frazier, 140–67. Champaign, Ill.: National Council of Teachers of English.

———. 1969. "Contraction, Deletion, and Inherent Variability of the English Copula." *Language* 45: 715–62.

———. 1972a. *Language in the Inner City: Studies in the Black English Vernacular.* Philadelphia: Univ. of Pennsylvania Press.

———. 1972b. *Sociolinguistic Patterns.* Philadelphia: Univ. of Pennsylvania Press.

———. 2001. "Applying Our Knowledge of African American English to the Problem of Raising Reading Levels in Inner-City Schools." In Lanehart 2001, 299–317.

Labov, William, and Bettina Baker. 2003. "What Is a Reading Error?" http://www.ling.upenn.edu/~wlabov/Papers/WRE.html.

Labov, William, Paul Cohen, Clarence Robbins, and John Lewis. 1968. *A Study of the Non-Standard English of Negro and Puerto Rican Speakers in New York City.* Cooperative Research Project 3288. 2 vols. New York: Columbia Univ.

Lanehart, Sonja L., ed. 2001. *Sociocultural and Historical Contexts of African American English.* Philadelphia: Benjamins.

———. 2002. *Sista Speak! Black Women Kinfolk Talk about Language and Literacy.* Austin: Univ. of Texas Press.

———. 2004. "If Our Children Are Our Future, Why Are We Stuck in the Past? Beyond the Anglicists and the Creolists." Unpublished MS.

Lee, Carol D. 1993. *Signifying as a Scaffold for Literary Interpretation: The Pedagogical Implications of an African American Discourse Genre.* Urbana, Ill.: National Council of Teachers of English.

Lee, Margaret. 2002. "Rhyming Practices in African American Language." Paper presented at the 31st annual meeting on New Ways of Analyzing Variation (NWAV 31), Stanford, Calif., Oct. 10–13.

LeMoine, Noma. 2002. "Minority Languages and Education." Paper presented at panel discussion at the 31st annual meeting on New Ways of Analyzing Variation (NWAV 31), Stanford, Calif., Oct. 10–13.

LeMoine, Noma, and Sharroky Hollie. 2004. "The Academic English Mastery Program: Inspiration, Dr. Geneva Smitherman." Unpublished MS.

Le Page, R. B., and Andrée Tabouret-Keller. 1985. *Acts of Identity: Creole-Based Approaches to Language and Ethnicity.* Cambridge: Cambridge Univ. Press.

Lippi-Green, Rosina. 1997. *English with an Accent: Language, Ideology, and Discrimination in the United States.* London: Routledge.

Mahiri, Jabari, and Soraya Sablo. 1996. "Writing for Their Lives: The Non-school Literacy of California's Urban African American Youth." *Journal of Negro Education* 65: 164–80.

Major, Clarence. 1970. *Dictionary of Afro-American Slang.* New York: International Publishers. Repr. as *Juba to Jive: A Dictionary of African-American Slang.* New York: Penguin, 1994.

Makoni, Sinfree, Geneva Smitherman, Arnetha Ball, and Arthur K. Spears, eds. 2003. *Black Linguistics: Language, Society, and Politics in Africa and the Americas.* New York: Routledge.

Massey, Douglas S., and Nancy A. Denton. 1993. *American Apartheid: Segregation and the Making of the Underclass.* Cambridge, Mass.: Harvard Univ. Press.

McDermott, Raymond P., and Henry Tylbor. 1995. "On the Necessity of Collusion in Conversation." In *The Dialogic Emergence of Culture,* ed. Dennis Tedlock and Bruce Mannheim, 218–36. Urbana: Univ. of Illinois Press.

MEE Productions. 1993. *Reaching the Hip-Hop Generation.* Final symposium proceedings report to the Robert Wood Johnson Foundation, #18762. Philadelphia: MEE Productions.

Mitchell[-Kernan], Claudia. 1971. *Language Behavior in a Black Urban Community.* Berkeley: Language Behavior Research Laboratory, Univ. of California.

Mitchell-Kernan, Claudia. 1972. "Signifying and Marking: Two Afro-American Speech Acts." In Gumperz and Hymes 1972, 161–79.

Morgan, Marcyliena H. 1994. "The African American Speech Community: Reality and Sociolinguistics." In *Language and the Social Construction of Identity in Creole Situations,* ed. Marcyliena H. Morgan, 121–48. Los Angeles: Center for Afro-American Studies, Univ. of California, Los Angeles.

———. 1996. "Conversational Signifying: Grammar and Indirectness among African American Women." In *Interaction and Grammar,* ed. Elinor Ochs, Emanuel A. Schegloff, and Sandra A. Thompson, 405–34. Cambridge: Cambridge Univ. Press.

———. 1998. "More Than a Mood or an Attitude: Discourse and Verbal Genres in African-American Culture." In Mufwene et al. 1998, 251–81.

———. 1999. "Community." In *Language Matters in Anthropology: A Lexicon for the New Millennium*, ed. Alessandro Duranti, 36–38. Special issue of the *Journal of Linguistic Anthropology* 9.1–2. Repr. in *Key Terms in Language and Culture*, ed. Alessandro Duranti, 31–33. Malden, Mass.: Blackwell, 2001.

———. 2002. *Language, Discourse, and Power in African American Culture.* Cambridge: Cambridge Univ. Press.

Morrison, Toni. 1981. Interviewed by Thomas LeClair. *New Republic*, Mar. 21, 1981, 25–29. Cited in Rickford and Rickford 2000, 4–5.

Mufwene, Salikoko S., John R. Rickford, Guy Bailey, and John Baugh, eds. 1998. *African-American English: Structure, History, and Use.* London: Routledge.

National Council of Teachers of English and International Reading Association. 1996. *Standards for the English Language Arts.* Newark, Del.: International Reading Association and National Council of Teachers of English.

Newman, Michael. 2001. "'Not Dogmatically / It's All about Me': Ideological Conflict in a High School Rap Crew." *Taboo: A Journal of Culture and Education* 5.2: 52–68.

Norfleet, Dawn Michaelle. 1997. "Hip-Hop Culture in New York City: The Role of Verbal Musical Performance in Defining a Community (Rap Music)." Ph.D. diss., Columbia Univ.

Page, Helan E., and Brooke Thomas. 1994. "White Public Space and the Construction of White Privilege in U.S. Health Care: Fresh Concepts and a New Model of Analysis." *Medical Anthropology Quarterly* 8: 109–16.

Parker, Henry H., and Marilyn I. Crist. 1995. *Teaching Minorities to Play the Corporate Language Game.* Columbia, S.C.: National Resource Center for the Freshman Year Experience, Univ. of South Carolina.

Piestrup, Ann McCormick. 1973. *Black Dialect Interference and Accommodation of Reading Instruction in First Grade.* Berkeley: Language-Behavior Research Laboratory, Univ. of California.

Poplack, Shana, and David Sankoff. 1987. "The Philadelphia Story in the Spanish Caribbean." *American Speech* 62: 291–314.

Poplack, Shana, and Sali Tagliamonte. 1989. "There's No Tense Like the Present: Verbal *-s* Inflection in Early Black English." *Language Variation and Change* 1: 47–84.

———. 1991. "African American English in the Diaspora: Evidence from Old-Line Nova Scotians." *Language Variation and Change* 3: 301–39.

———. 2001. *African American English in the Diaspora.* Malden, Mass.: Blackwell.

Purnell, Thomas, William Idsardi, and John Baugh. 1999. "Perceptual and Phonetic Experiments on American English Dialect Identification." *Journal of Language and Social Psychology* 18: 10–30.

Rahman, Jacquelyn. 2002. "Black Standard English." Paper presented at the 31st annual meeting on New Ways of Analyzing Variation (NWAV 31), Stanford, Calif., Oct. 10–13.

Ramsey, Claire. 2002. "Minority Languages and Education." Paper presented at panel discussion at the 31st annual meeting on New Ways of Analyzing Variation (NWAV 31), Stanford, Calif., Oct. 10–13.

Rand, David, and David Sankoff. 1990. *GoldVarb: A Variable Rule Application for Macintosh.* http://www.crm.umontreal.ca/~sankoff/GoldVarb_Eng.html.

Richardson, Elaine. 2003. *African American Literacies.* London: Routledge.

Rickford, Angela Marshall. 1999. *I Can Fly: Teaching Narratives and Reading Comprehension to African American and Other Ethnic Minority Students.* Lanham, Md.: Univ. Press of America.

Rickford, John R. 1974. "The Insights of the Mesolect." In *Pidgins and Creoles: Current Trends and Prospects,* ed. David De Camp and Ian F. Hancock, 92–117. Washington, D.C.: Georgetown Univ. Press.

———. 1979. "Variation in a Creole Continuum: Quantitative and Implicational Approaches." Ph.D. diss., Univ. of Pennsylvania.

———. 1987. *Dimensions of a Creole Continuum: History, Texts, and Linguistic Analysis of Guyanese Creole.* Stanford: Stanford Univ. Press.

———. 1992. "Grammatical Variation and Divergence in Vernacular Black English." In *Internal and External Factors in Syntactic Change,* ed. Marinel Gerritsen and Dieter Stein, 175–200. Berlin: de Gruyter. Repr. in Rickford 1999, 261–80.

———. 1996. "Copula Variability in Jamaican Creole and African American Vernacular English: A Reanalysis of DeCamp's Texts." In *Towards a Social Science of Language: Papers in Honor of William Labov,* ed. Gregory R. Guy, Crawford Feagin, Deborah Schiffrin, and John Baugh, 357–72. Amsterdam: Benjamins. Repr. in Rickford 1999, 219–32.

———. 1997. "Prior Creolization in AAVE? Sociohistorical and Textual Evidence from the Seventeenth and Eighteenth Centuries." *Journal of Sociolinguistics* 1: 315–36. Repr. in Rickford 1999, 233–51.

———. 1998. "The Creole Origins of African American Vernacular English: Evidence from Copula Absence." In Mufwene et al. 1998, 154–200.

———. 1999. *African American Vernacular English: Features, Evolution, Educational Implications.* Oxford: Blackwell.

———. 2000. "Using the Vernacular to Teach the Standard." In *Ebonics in the Urban Education Debate,* ed. J. David Ramirez, Terrence G. Wiley, Gerda de Klerk, and Enid Lee, 23–41. Long Beach, Calif.: Center for Language Minority Education and Research.

———. 2001. "Style and Stylizing from the Perspective of a Non-autonomous Sociolinguistics." In Eckert and Rickford 2001, 220–31.

———. 2003. "Sociolinguistic Approaches to Working with Vernacular Varieties in Schools." Paper presented at the annual meeting of the American Educational Research Association, Chicago, Apr. 21–25.

Rickford, John, Arnetha Ball, Renée Blake, Raina Jackson, and Nomi Martin. 1991. "Rappin on the Copula Coffin: Theoretical and Methodological Issues in the Analysis of Copula Variation in African American Vernacular English." *Language Variation and Change* 3: 103–32. Repr. in Rickford 1999, 61–89.

Rickford, John, and Faye McNair-Knox. 1994. "Addressee- and Topic-Influenced Style Shift: A Quantitative Sociolinguistic Study." In *Sociolinguistic Perspectives on Register,* ed. Douglas Biber and Edward Finegan, 235–76. Oxford: Oxford Univ. Press. Repr. in Rickford 1999, 112–53.

Rickford, John R., and Angela E. Rickford. 1976. "Cut-Eye and Suck-Teeth: African Words and Gestures in New World Guise." *Journal of American Folklore* 89 (353): 194–309. Repr. in Rickford 1999, 157–73.

———. 2002. "Updating Contrastive Analysis: Extending Students' Linguistic Versatility through Literature and Song." Paper presented at the 31st annual meeting on New Ways of Analyzing Variation (NWAV 31), Stanford, Calif., Oct. 10–13.

Rickford, John Russell, and Russell John Rickford. 2000. *Spoken Soul: The Story of Black English.* New York: Wiley.

Robinson, J. S., H. R. Lawrence, and S. A. Tagliamonte. 2001. "GOLDVARB 2001: A Multivariate Analysis Application for Windows." http://www.york.ac.uk/depts/lang/webstuff/goldvarb/.

Rowe, Ryan. 2003. "Dialect, Voice, and Language Ideology in Hip Hop." Paper presented at the 68th biannual Southeastern Conference on Linguistics (SECOL 68), Washington, D.C., Apr 11–13.

Sankoff, David, and William Labov. 1979. "On the Uses of Variable Rules." *Language in Society* 8: 189–222.

Sankoff, Gillian. 2002. "Critical Age." Paper presented during a panel discussion at the 31st annual meeting on New Ways of Analyzing Variation (NWAV 31), Stanford, Calif., Oct. 10–13.

Schegloff, Emanuel A. 1991. "Reflections on Talk and Social Structure." In *Talk and Social Structure: Studies in Ethnomethodology and Conversation Analysis*, ed. Deirdre Boden and Don H. Zimmerman, 44–70. Berkeley: Univ. of California Press.

Schieffelin, Bambi B., Kathryn A. Woolard, and Paul V. Kroskrity, eds. 1998. *Language Ideologies: Practice and Theory*. New York: Oxford Univ. Press.

Sebba, Mark. 1997. *Contact Languages: Pidgins and Creoles*. London: Macmillan.

Sells, Peter, John Rickford, and Thomas Wasow. 1996. "Negative Inversion in African American Vernacular English." *Natural Language and Linguistic Theory* 14: 591–627.

Siegel, Jeff. 2002. "Minority Languages and Education." Paper presented at panel discussion at the 31st annual meeting on New Ways of Analyzing Variation (NWAV 31), Stanford, Calif., Oct. 10–13.

Simpkins, Gary A., and Charlesetta Simpkins. 1981. "Cross Cultural Approach to Curriculum Development." In Smitherman 1981, 221–40.

Singler, John Victor. 1991. "Liberian Settler English and the Ex-slave Recordings: A Comparative Study." In *The Emergence of Black English: Text and Commentary*, ed. Guy Bailey, Natalie Maynor, and Patricia Cukor-Avila, 249–74. Philadelphia: Benjamins.

Smitherman, Geneva. 1973. "The Power of the Rap: The Black Idiom and the New Black Poetry." *Twentieth Century Literature* 19: 259–74.

———. 1977. *Talkin and Testifyin: The Language of Black America*. Boston: Houghton Mifflin. Repr. Detroit, Mich.: Wayne State Univ. Press, 1986.

———, ed. 1981. *Black English and the Education of Black Children and Youth: Proceedings of the National Invitational Symposium on the King Decision*. Detroit, Mich.: Center for Black Studies, Wayne State Univ.

———. 1994. *Black Talk: Words and Phrases from the Hood to the Amen Corner*. Boston: Houghton Mifflin.

———. 2000a. *Black Talk: Words and Phrases from the Hood to the Amen Corner*. Rev. ed. Boston: Houghton Mifflin.

———. 2000b. *Talkin That Talk: Language, Culture, and Education in African America*. New York: Routledge.

Spady, James G., Charles G. Lee, and H. Samy Alim. 1999. *Street Conscious Rap*. Philadelphia: Black History Museum Umum/Loh Pub.

Spears, Arthur K. 1998. "African-American Language Use: Ideology and So-Called Obscenity." In Mufwene et al. 1998, 226–50.

———. 2000. "Stressed *stay*: A New AAVE Aspect Marker." Paper presented at the annual meeting of the American Dialect Society, Chicago, Jan. 6–9.

Stack, Carol B. 1974. *All Our Kin: Strategies for Survival in a Black Community*. New York: Harper and Row.

Stanford Working Group on Federal Education Programs for Limited-English-Proficient (LEP) Students. 1993. *Federal Education Programs for Limited-English-Proficient Students: A Blueprint for the Second Generation*. Exec. director, Diane August. Chair, Kenji Hakuta. Stanford, Calif.: Stanford Working Group.

Stavsky, Lois, I. E. Mozeson, and Dani Reyes Mozeson. 1995. *A2Z: The Book of Rap and Hip-Hop Slang*. New York: Boulevard.

Stewart, William A. 1965. "Urban Negro Speech: Sociolinguistic Factors Affecting English Teaching." In *Social Dialects and Language Learning: Proceedings of the Bloomington, Indiana, Conference, 1964*, ed. Roger W. Shuy, 10–18. Champaign, Ill.: National Council of Teachers of English.

———. 1968. "Continuity and Change in American Negro Dialects." *Florida FL Reporter* 6.2: 14–16, 18, 30. Repr. in *Black-White Speech Relationships*, ed. Walt Wolfram and Nona C. Clarke, 74–89. Washington, D.C.: Center for Applied Linguistics, 1971.

Street, Brian, ed. 1993. *Cross-cultural Approaches to Literacy*. Cambridge: Cambridge Univ. Press.

Taylor, Hanni U. 1989. *Standard English, Black English, and Bidialectalism: A Controversy*. New York: Lang.

Troutman, Denise. 2002. "'We Be Strong Women': A Womanist Analysis of Black Women's Sociolinguistic Behavior." In *Centering Ourselves: African American Feminist and Womanist Studies in Discourse*, ed. Marsha Houston and Olga Idriss Davis, 99–121. Cresskill, N.J.: Hampton.

Trudgill, Peter. 1974. *The Social Differentiation of English in Norwich*. London: Cambridge Univ. Press.

———. 1981. "Linguistic Accommodation: Sociolinguistic Observation on a Sociopsychological Theory." In *Papers from the Parasession on Language and Behavior: Chicago Linguistic Society, May 1–2, 1981*, ed. Carrie S. Masek, Roberta A. Hendrick, and Mary Frances Miller, 218–37. Chicago: Chicago Linguistics Society.

———. 1986. *Dialects in Contact.* Oxford: Blackwell.

———. 1998. "Third Person Singular Zero: African-American English, East Anglican Dialects, and Spanish Persecution in the Low Countries." *Folia Linguistica Historica* 18: 139–48.

Turner, Lorenzo Dow. 1949. *Africanisms in the Gullah Dialect.* Chicago: Univ. of Chicago Press.

Urrieta, Luis, Jr. Forthcoming. "'Playing the Game' Versus 'Selling Out': Chicanas and Chicanos Relationship to Whitestream Schools." In *Performance Theories in Education: Power, Pedagogy, and the Politics of Identity,* ed. Bryant Keith Alexander, Gary L. Anderson, Bernardo Gallegos. Mahwah, N.J.: Erlbaum.

Valdés, Guadalupe. 2001. *Learning and Not Learning English: Latino Students in American Schools.* New York: Teachers College Press.

Villalva, Kerry Enright. 2003. "'Something That People Can Do': The Hidden Literacies of Latino and Anglo Youth around Academic Writing." Ph.D. diss., Stanford Univ.

Walker, James A. 1999. "Rephrasing the Copula: Contraction and Zero in Early African American English." In *The English History of African American English,* ed. Shana Poplack, 35–72. Malden, Mass.: Blackwell.

Wideman, John. 1976. "Frame and Dialect: The Evolution of the Black Voice in American Literature." *American Poetry Review* 5.5: 34–37.

Winford, Donald. 1992. "Another Look at the Copula in Black English and Caribbean Creoles." *American Speech* 67: 21–60.

———. 1998. "On the Origins of African American Vernacular English—A Creolist Perspective." Part 2, "Linguistic Features." *Diachronica* 15: 99–154.

———. 2003. "Ideologies of Language and Socially Realistic Linguistics." In Makoni et al. 2003, 21–39.

Wodak, Ruth. 1995. "Critical Linguistics and Critical Discourse." In *Handbook of Pragmatics: Manual,* ed. Jef Verschueren, Jan-Ola Östman, and Jan Blommaert, 204–10. Philadelphia: Benjamins.

Wolfram, Walt. 1969. *A Sociolinguistic Description of Detroit Negro Speech.* Washington, D.C.: Center for Applied Linguistics.

———. 1974. "The Relationship of White Southern Speech to Vernacular Black English." *Language* 50: 498–527.

———. 1991. "The Linguistic Variable: Fact and Fantasy." *American Speech* 66: 22–32.

———. 1993. "Identifying and Interpreting Variables." In *American Dialect Research,* ed. Dennis R. Preston, 193–221. Philadelphia: Benjamins.

———. 2002. "Reconsidering the Development of African American English: Evidence from Isolated Southern Dialects." Paper presented at the 31st annual meeting on New Ways of Analyzing Variation (NWAV 31), Stanford, Calif., Oct. 10–13.

Wolfram, Walt, Carolyn Temple Adger, and Donna Christian. 1998. *Dialects in Schools and Communities.* Mahwah, N.J.: Erlbaum.

Wolfram, Walt, and Erik R. Thomas. 2002. *The Development of African American English.* Malden, Mass.: Blackwell.

Yancy, George. 2000. "Feminism and the Subtext of Whiteness: Black Women's Experiences as a Site of Identity Formation and Contestation of Whiteness." *Western Journal of Black Studies* 24: 155–65.

Zentella, Ana Celia. 1997. *Growing Up Bilingual: Puerto Rican Children in New York.* Malden, Mass.: Blackwell.